STONEA
AND THE ROMAN FENS

STONEA
AND THE ROMAN FENS

TIM MALIM

TEMPUS

Cover illustration: *Reconstruction of the Roman attack on Stonea Camp by Caroline Malim* ©

First published 2005

Tempus Publishing Limited
The Mill, Brimscombe Port,
Stroud, Gloucestershire, GL5 2QG
www.tempus-publishing.com

© Tim Malim, 2005

The right of Tim Malim to be identified as the Author
of this work has been asserted in accordance with the
Copyrights, Designs and Patents Act 1988.

All rights reserved. No part of this book may be reprinted
or reproduced or utilised in any form or by any electronic,
mechanical or other means, now known or hereafter invented,
including photocopying and recording, or in any information
storage or retrieval system, without the permission in writing
from the Publishers.

British Library Cataloguing in Publication Data.
A catalogue record for this book is available from the British Library.

ISBN 0 7524 2899 3

Typesetting and origination by Tempus Publishing Limited
Printed in Great Britain

CONTENTS

	Acknowledgements	7
Chapter 1	Introduction	9
Chapter 2	The evolution of the Fenland landscape	21
Chapter 3	The Fenland in prehistoric times	29
Chapter 4	Stonea Island: investigations of a landscape in microcosm	43
Chapter 5	Stonea Camp: an Iron Age fort and its political landscape	57
Chapter 6	The Roman town and centre for an imperial estate	97
Chapter 7	Communications, fortifications, towns and drainage	133
Chapter 8	The economic base and rural settlement of the Roman fens	167
Chapter 9	The devolution of the Roman fens	203
Chapter 10	Fenland and the birth of England	225
	Bibliography	246
	Index	251

Tim Malim

ACKNOWLEDGEMENTS

This book is dedicated to Tim Potter who originally suggested the idea of writing a book on Stonea and the Roman fens to Tempus, to present his and The British Museum's Fenland investigations to a wider audience; and I am indebted to Ralph Jackson, Steve Crummy and The British Museum for all their assistance and their permission to use so many drawings and photographs from the Stonea archive and the BM collections. I am grateful for the helpful suggestions Ralph Jackson has made to improve the text on Roman Stonea, and to Martin Welch for his comments on the Anglo-Saxon chapter. Colleagues and friends from the Fenland Survey have been very ready to discuss issues, comment on the text and grant permission for me to use their illustrations, in particular Tom Lane, Martyn Waller, Rog Palmer, David Hall and Rob Silvester. Other friends and colleagues from Cambridgeshire County Council's Archaeological Field Unit have provided invaluable images with permission for me to reproduce them in this volume: in particular Alison Taylor, Mark Hinman, Steve Macaulay, Steve Kemp, Judith Roberts, Carole Fletcher and Jon Cane. I am very lucky to have been allowed to use so many excellent air photographs taken by Ben Robinson from his microlite, and for the additional images he has granted me permission to use from Peterborough Museum. Many other colleagues have helped me with drawings, photographs and information, including Alex Bayliss of English Heritage, Chris Evans and Mark Knight of the Cambridge Archaeological Unit, Mark Leah and Derek Edwards of the Norfolk Archaeological Unit and the Norfolk Museums Service, Ian Meadows of Northamptonshire Archaeology, Ron McKenna of Peterborough Archaeology Group, Don Mackreth and the Nene Valley Archaeological Research Committee, Jason Wood of Heritage Consultancy Services, Elaine Morris of Southampton University, Chris Chippindale and staff of the Cambridge University Museum of Archaeology and Anthropology, Chris Jakes of the Cambridgeshire Collection, Sarah Poppy of

Cambridgeshire's Sites and Monuments Record, Mark Bennet of Lincolnshire's SMR, Ben Robinson and the Peterborough SMR, Rob Davis, William Frend, Jo Richards and Sarah Wroot. Special thanks are due to Michael Green who has brought to my attention many articles and details from his own research which he has generously permitted me to include here. I am grateful to Gifford and Partners for the support they have extended to me in completing this book, and in particular for the help that Gill Reaney and Rochan Jambu have given me. Finally I owe a big thank you to my wife Caroline for the cover illustration and the many coloured maps she has drawn up for this book, in addition to a large amount of other illustration and design work, and for the patience that she, Rufus and Hugo, have had while I spent many weekends and evenings reading, synthesing, writing and checking on Stonea and the Roman Fens.

1
INTRODUCTION

This synthetic study has been possible only through the detailed studies of many different people over very many years. Tim Potter had originally suggested the theme of this book, and he would have been ideally suited to the purpose with his unique blend of international scholarship and local roots, but his sudden death in 2000 deprived us of his powers of synopsis. His Fenland research, starting as a schoolboy around March during the 1950s with his brother, Christopher, and later leading a British Museum excavation programme in extensive investigations at Stonea (*1*) together with his colleague Ralph Jackson, has resulted in a large corpus of material on which I have relied heavily in writing this book. In addition, the previous Roman survey of the region, *The Fenland in Roman Times*, has provided invaluable foundations on which to build with the results of more recent studies; in particular Peter Salway's essays giving the political context and his interpretation of the effect of this on the Fenlands has been most illuminating. *The Fenland in Roman Times* would itself not have been possible without the even earlier studies by the members of the Fenland Research Committee who established much of the basic understanding of the Fenland environment, artifical drainage, and shifting courses of rivers. This Committee was partly reformed in the 1980s and an immensely ambitious project was ingeniously devised by Professor John Coles and funded by English Heritage, called the Fenland Survey and later the Fenland Management Project, which successfully fieldwalked vast areas of the fens, and enabled the production of detailed maps with the distribution of archaeological sites period by period set against their contemporary environmental background. This was a multi-disciplinary study and involved over 200 radiocarbon determinations to provide absolute dates for the various Fenland sequences of peat accumulation and marine sedimentation. A far more complex and geographically diverse pattern of environmental change emerged than had previously been suggested.

STONEA AND THE ROMAN FENS

1 Photograph of Tim Potter recording a well at Stonea. © Jason Wood

The choice of Stonea as a central theme to this book is justified on three accounts. Firstly, Stonea's geographical location makes it a central place within the fens, situated in north Cambridgeshire near the Lincolnshire border, straddling the divide between the peat and silt fens, and equidistant from the western and eastern upland margins (*colour plate 1*). Secondly, Stonea has benefited from a more intensive programme of archaeological investigation and large-scale excavation than any other area in the fens, with the sole exception of the prolific Fengate area of Peterborough. Thirdly, Stonea is one of those archaeologically rich, 'productive' sites that seem to contain significant evidence for almost every period. The importance of the south-western part of Stonea island is characterised by its use in Neolithic times for ceremonial purposes including a cursus monument; for burial practices during the earlier Bronze Age, and settlement in the later Bronze Age; for construction of a high-status fort in the later Iron Age; and for settlement and a temple during the Late Iron Age and Roman times. It continued as a settlement with high-status hall buildings during the early Anglo-Saxon period and became a monastic grange during late Saxon times. It may even have been reused in the seventeenth century as part of Parliamentary defences of the Fenland communication system and an impressive farm house, The Stitches, was built in the late medieval period within the Iron Age fort south of the Grange, which continued as a prominent landmark in the local area until its demolition in the 1970s.

The study of Fenland archaeology and its ancient environment started a very long time ago, and has benefited from the contribution of some well-known

INTRODUCTION

antiquarians, archaeologists, botanists and geologists over the centuries. The famous eighteenth-century antiquarian William Stukeley, who visited many archaeological monuments within the British Isles and recorded them in detail through notes and evocative sketches, was in fact a fenman. He was born at Holbeach in Lincolnshire in 1687 the son of a lawyer, and returned as a doctor in 1710 where upon he helped found the Gentlemen's Society of Spalding; the founding of this institution in time led to the creation of the Society of Antiquaries in London. Stukeley lived at first in Boston and then in Stamford and during these years he collected coins and other curiosities discovered in the fens. He became interested in the roads, sea-banks and canals of the region, and in 1757 formulated the hypothesis that the Car Dyke was part of a long distance system of communications between the fens and Hadrian's Wall (*2*). He also made a clear distinction between the unpleasantness of the peat fens as opposed to the good land of the silt fen.

At the beginning of the nineteenth century Edmund Tyrell Artis, house steward to Earl Fitzwilliam's estate at Milton, just outside Peterborough, began to follow two great passions, geology (or more precisely palaeobotany) and archaeology. He was elected a Fellow of the Geological Society in 1824 and his collection of 1,500 specimens, mainly of carboniferous fossil plants preserved in coalfields, was purchased by The British Museum in 1825. In this year he also

2 The Car Dyke as it might have operated. *Drawn by Denis Cheason*

published the results of these studies in a pioneering book entitled *Antediluvian Phytology*. His interest in archaeology, however, had led to prolific excavations at Durobrivae, Castor (*colour plate 2*) and Helpston from 1821, and he published a volume in 1828 which consisted of his own excellent drawings of excavations, mosaics, walls, kilns, artefacts and other items (*3*). Unfortunately, he never produced a text to accompany these plates, although a number of letters and communications to learned societies provide some essential information. His systematic excavations have inspired later archaeologists because of the quality of the discoveries represented by his graphics and the artefacts he found.

During the nineteenth century, studies into the wastage of fen peat and the origins of Fenland began to be undertaken. In 1848 or 1852 an iron post (allegedly taken from the Crystal Palace) was sunk to its top into the peat at Denton Fen, Holme, on the western fen edge to monitor the loss of peat. This experiment was started at the same time as drainage of nearby Whittlesey Mere was carried out, and within the first 10 years the peat shrank by 1.5m from the top of the post, followed by 1m in the next 10 years. In the subsequent 100 years a further 1.2m of peat disappeared from the post, showing that freshly drained peat fen shrinks by at least 3.7m in 120 years, an average of approximately 3cm a year (*4*).

3 The Remains of Roman Buildings on Mill Hill by E.T. Artis; looking north-west with the town of Durobrivae across the Nene. *From* Durobrivae 1828, *Peterborough Museum & Art Gallery*

INTRODUCTION

4 Two photographs of the Holme Fen post: 1932 and in the 1990s (note the extensive reduction in peat level). *Peterborough Museum & Art Gallery*

Another perspective was attempted by the Cambridge geologist S.B.J. Skertchly, who studied the Fenland deposits through use of data gathered by boreholes and published his findings in 1877 under the title of *The Geology of the Fenland*. He divided the fens into two parts and categorised the organic deposits found in the west as peat fen, and the silts and clays bordering the Wash as silt fen.

In 1923 a pioneering book was published by Sir Cyril Fox, then curator of the Cambridge University Museum of Archaeology and Ethnography, whose doctoral thesis concerned the Archaeology of the Cambridge region. Although this only included the southernmost part of the fens, his approach to mapping the distribution of archaeological finds from each period was to plot them against the major characteristics of the landscape, and so the fens and river systems were shown as a backdrop against which reasoned interpretation for the distribution of different types of site or artefact could be proposed (*colour plate 3*). The essence of his approach was to see the human past as a part of its contemporary landscape, and therefore archaeological remains could only be properly understood in the context of their geological and topographical surroundings. In his introduction to this seminal publication Fox said that the boundaries of his region, which included Stonea some 36 miles north of Cambridge, were determined, not by any particular geographic or political boundary, but because this was the distance he could easily travel by bicycle in order to conduct his research!

In the 1930s a number of people began to study the Fenland in earnest, spurred on by the use of air photography that showed the remarkable Romano-British field systems that survived as earthworks within extensive pasture, and the dendritic pattern of roddons, the ancient watercourses that now stand proud of the peat. Between 1932 and 1940 the Fenland Research Committee of Cambridge University was set up to investigate several leading questions about how Fenland was formed and changed over the past 10,000 years (during the Flandrian period), what successive plant communities spread across it, what was the origin of the 'bog oaks', and how human activity interrelated with Fenland. The Committee adopted a multi-disciplinary approach to this study and involved botanists, geologists, geographers and archaeologists. Their most important site was at Shippea Hill, where an excavation 4.5m deep undertaken by Graham Clark and Sir Harry Godwin revealed Mesolithic occupation on a south-facing sand hill covered by a lower peat, with a Neolithic pottery sherd in a layer above and Bronze Age flints in an upper peat above this (*5*). Another influential member of the Committee, although not an academic but instead the manager of a sugar-beet factory, was Major Gordon Fowler. His studies of the ancient Fenland drainage patterns (*colour plate 5*), the roddons, provided an explanation for their origin and development and also identified the fact that the distribution of Roman sites was heavily influenced by these features: in essence

INTRODUCTION

5 Excavations at Shippea Hill in 1934 with Graham Clark in the top trench; the depth of fenland stratigraphy and alternate layers of deposition are well demonstrated. *Peterborough Museum & Art Gallery*

many of the Roman occupation sites and their salt-making activities were to be found spread along the raised banks of these roddons.

The war years not only saw the cessation of the Fenland Research Committee but also led to the beginnings of the intensive cultivation of the fens, and some of the long preserved Roman earthworks began to be ploughed up, a process which was continued during the following decades. Although no Committee existed, however, Fenland research was slowly picked up in the post-war years by a number of individuals and the floods of 1947 provided clear evidence of the importance for the slight relief within the Fenland landscape, as these were the parts that escaped inundation. From the air it was possible to see in graphic detail the islands and old farms built on roddons surrounded by flood waters and it was apparent to J. Bromwich and others that this largely coincided with the extent of known Roman occupation. This led him to undertake a comprehensive aerial survey between then and 1951. From 1949 to 1952 Sylvia Hallam conducted a

15

detailed survey of the area around Spalding in Lincolnshire, drawing together evidence for the Roman period from all sources, as part of her doctoral thesis at Cambridge University (*6, colour plate 1*). During the late 1950s and early 1960s Peter Salway was studying an area in the southern fens, and excavating sites such as Hockwold on the Suffolk fen edge. The Royal Geographic Society, which had supported Gordon Fowler's study of the ancient waterways and published his work in 1934, had decided after the war that a synopsis of Fenland work was desirable, but unfortunately this was unfinished when Fowler died in 1949. When the Ordnance Survey wanted to publish its third edition of *Roman Britain* it became clear that the Wash coastline was uncertain, and therefore in 1956 the Society agreed to fund a study initially to tackle this question, but in fact one that developed a much wider remit over time, and one that would eventually reach publication in 1970 as a monograph entitled *The Fenland in Roman Times*. This publication drew together the results of these individual researchers, as well as many others, and also systematically reviewed the aerial photographic evidence for Roman activity in Fenland, identifying sites which were then visited and surveyed on the ground, giving vital chronological information, so that a valid comparable collection of data was available with which to evaluate and interpret the Roman development of the fens (*6*).

Roman archaeology within the Fenland region, however, was not exclusive to those involved in the Royal Geographic Society project in the two decades after the war. Graham Clark, for example, excavated the Roman canal known as Car Dyke in 1947 where it intersected with a settlement and drove road at Bullocks Haste, Cottenham, in Cambridgeshire. Charles Green investigated patterns of coastal change since Roman times in East Anglia and excavated sites around the fen edge such as Denver, and Ernest Greenfield studied a number of villas in the region and other Roman sites. In 1949 Michael Green began a 37-year strategy for investigating the Roman town at Godmanchester, as well as undertaking some investigations further afield along the Ouse Valley, at Earith and St Ives for example. In 1956 John Alexander began his campaign of rescue excavation at Cambridge, which carried on until the 1980s.

The most recent campaign of investigation was undertaken from 1976 to 1995 under the title of The Fenland Project and was funded by English Heritage and its predecessors. The concept for this wide-ranging and long-lasting project was designed by Professor John Coles and Dr John Alexander in response to the industrialisation of farming and the conversion of Fenland into pararies of arable cultivation. The erosion of peat and destruction of archaeology during this era of agricultural intensification were self-evident, but the extent to which exceptionally well-preserved remains in the deeper, wet peat, were being rapidly exposed, dried out and ploughed away was unknown. The Fenland Survey

INTRODUCTION

6 Example of a map from *The Fenland in Roman Times 1970* showing occupation on the silt fen at Gedney Hill. *With kind permission of the Royal Geographical Society*

was therefore conceived, at first in Cambridgeshire and then expanded to include Fenland in Lincolnshire, Norfolk and Suffolk, to systematically walk the ploughed fields, recording archaeological evidence and mapping soil change and micro-topography. David Hall was the first field officer, and was joined by Tom Lane and Peter Hayes in Lincolnshire, and Bob Silvester in Norfolk; a total of 249,000ha, 60 per cent of Fenland, was fieldwalked during the survey (*colour plate 1*) and 2,510 new sites were discovered in addition to the 400 already known but re-recorded by the Survey. A palaeoenvironmental dimension was added very soon through Professor Richard West's interest, and a post was created as part of the Survey team for a specialist to record sedimentary and pollen sequences, undertake diatom analysis, and follow through a programme of radiocarbon dating. This study, undertaken by Anne Alderton and Martyn Waller, provided essential environmental and independent chronological frameworks with which the archaeological field survey results could be integrated. Towards the end of the programme of field survey, the Fenland Evaluation Project was set up to assess the significance and archaeological value of a selected number of sites through boreholes and small test-pits, and this in turn led on to the Fenland Management Project which undertook trial trenching and full-scale open area excavation on a number of sites, as well as experimenting with methods for the continued preservation of wet and waterlogged historic landscapes.

In addition to the work of The Fenland Project, other organisations and individuals have contributed research and data to the general knowledge of the fens. The Soil Survey, for instance, conducted a study of peat during the 1980s and the interrelationship between this work and that of the Fenland Survey was of value to both. The British Geological Survey produced maps and memoirs of various parts of Fenland over several decades. Archaeological bodies and Units such as The Nene Valley Research Committee, Cambridgeshire Archaeological Committee, South Lincolnshire Archaeological Unit, Fenland Archaeological Trust, and the County Council archaeology services in Norfolk, Suffolk, Cambridgeshire and Lincolnshire, as well as Peterborough Museum, The British Museum, Durham, Cardiff and Cambridge Universities, plus many voluntary groups and amateur archaeologists, all undertook a vast range of fieldwork and scientific analysis from the 1970s onwards.

The present synthesis has called upon the reservoir of information produced by these many diverse sources in an attempt to give a broad outline to the origins and development of Roman Fenland, its decline and the subsequent period of Anglo-Saxon transition, as the first real summary of the whole region. Previous overviews have concentrated on certain aspects or geographic areas, such as the Fenland Survey or *The Fenland in Roman Times*, but none has had the wealth of information that is now available to draw upon from so many sources. Central to

INTRODUCTION

7 The author at Stonea Camp conducting a guided tour, and holding a manure sack dated 1964 recovered during excavation of the ditches from beneath the pushed-in banks. *Courtesy of Alison Taylor*

this study has been Stonea, a site of great importance for nearly all periods in the past, a site located approximately at the centre of Fenland and a site that provides a recurrent theme throughout the following chapters. Stonea is also a site at which I personally undertook several seasons of investigation and developed a new approach to its management and public presentation, and so this book provides an opportunity to present some of the results from these studies (*7*).

2
THE EVOLUTION OF THE FENLAND LANDSCAPE

INTRODUCTION:
FENLAND TODAY AND THE EROSION OF THE PEAT FEN

The fens of eastern England form the largest expanse of former coastal wetlands in Britain, an area of 4,000km², at their maximum extent stretching 120km north–south and 50km west–east (*colour plates 1* and *4*). Their appearance today as a flat landscape given over to intensive cultivation has developed from major drainage works during the seventeenth century and later times and the many canalised rivers, barrier banks and drains that divide up the modern landscape bear witness to this great endeavour. The richness of the peat and silt soils of the Fenlands have led to their exploitation as agricultural pararies of arable cultivation, but traditionally their use was for grazing and, during the nineteenth and early twentieth centuries, for arboriculture and horticulture, for fruit, vegetable and flower markets in the big urban centres.

In general the fens can be divided into two parts, a western or inland one which is known as the peat fen, and an eastern or seaward zone which is called the silt fen. These distinct parts relate to the sedimentary history that created them. The present surface of the peat can be as low as 2m below sea level, whereas the silt fen is generally around 3m above sea level. The original height of the peat fen, however, was substantially higher than now, and some estimates place the height of the peat fen at its maximum during the Saxon and medieval period as 3.5m above sea level. Since the seventeenth century a large amount of peat has wasted away, calculated at an annual rate of 1.8cm a year and accumulatively to have been between 3.5-5m in total, initially through compaction and later through wind-blow, as a consequence of the major drainage schemes leading to the drying out and decay of the peat. Over much of the peat fens the level of the land as it is today is approximately the same as it was during the Bronze Age, and virtually all Roman and later organic sediments have been lost.

The flat landscape is deceptive, however, as the fens contain low relief which can be of great importance in the study of the ancient past. These slight undulations in the surface, often described by archaeologists as micro-topography, can lead the trained eye to areas which would have been a little higher than the surrounding wet landscape and therefore would have acted as prime locations for settlement and industry. Some of these undulations are the tops of submerged islands, deposits of marine silt, or levees/banks and inverted river-beds, known locally as roddons. In addition the fen islands, which rise to 36m above sea level at their maximum height on the Isle of Ely, and the uplands of the fen edge provided environments in which to settle which were safe from flooding, and yet within such proximity to the fens that the many resources they contain could be readily exploited and animals could be grazed on them during the drier months of summer.

The fen islands are mostly present in the southern fens, principally Cambridgeshire, and these islands effectively divided this part of Fenland into two main embayments, each of which has its own depositional sequence and discrete history of changing environment (*colour plate 6*). The general sequence of Holocene deposits as recorded by Sir Harry Godwin and colleagues in the 1930s consisted of four layers termed Lower Peat, Fen Clay, Upper Peat, and Upper Silt (*8*). This model was followed by many subsequent researchers, whose own results were placed within this framework, with some minor modification. Although this sequence provides a very useful, simple formula for understanding the development of the fens, it

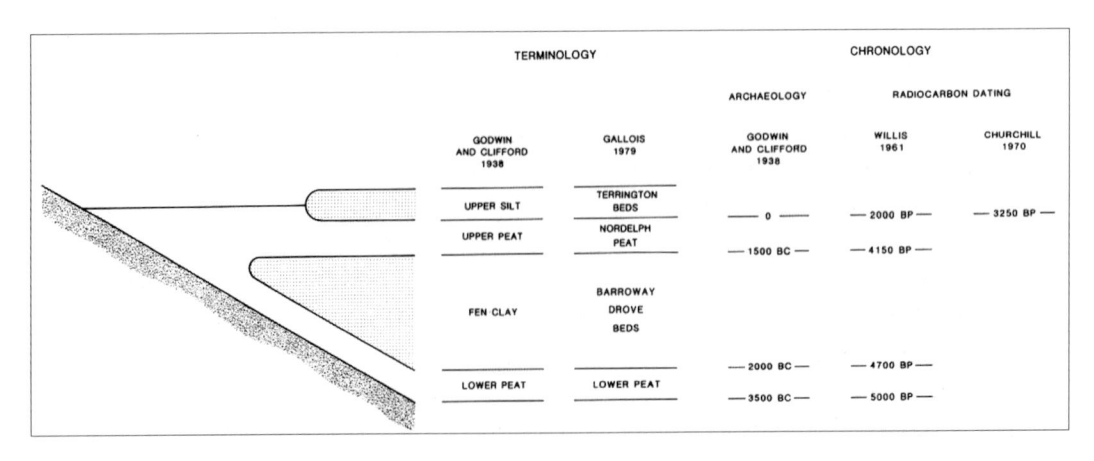

8 Fenland stratigraphy: terminology and chronology pre-1980. With kind permission of Martyn Waller and English Heritage, from East Anglian Archaeology 70

has led to a false equation of chronology with each depositional episode; the assumption was that the Fen Clay, for example, was a Neolithic phenomenon and that a clay deposit in the south-eastern fens is of the same date as a similar deposit on the Lincolnshire fen edge. The radiocarbon dating programme undertaken by the Fenland Survey during the 1980s has demonstrated this assumption to be unfounded, and that similar depositional episodes from different parts of the fens can actually be separated by many hundreds of years.

GEOLOGICAL HISTORY

The North Sea basin, to which the Fenland is geologically linked, was created during the Upper Carboniferous period when the rocks of this era were tilted downwards towards the east. A series of marine environments over the succeeding eras led to the slow infilling of much of this basin. The oldest rocks visible within the Fenland basin are the Jurassic limestones along the western fen edge. Upper Jurassic clays (Oxford, Ampthill and Kimmeridge clays) fill central Fenland, their various depositions determined by different conditions of water depth and sediment source. During the Late Lower Cretaceous, Gault Clay and the Lower Chalk was deposited along the eastern edge of the fens. The North Sea basin established the approximate shape we know today during the Tertiary and one theory is that a large number of eastward flowing rivers formed the Wash by cutting through the cuesta of the Lower Chalk that had been deposited on the eastern side of Fenland. An alternative view suggests a glacial incursion from the North Sea which formed the Fenland basin and was responsible for depositing the Chalky Boulder Clay.

The last two million years, the Quaternary, were characterised by a succession of glacial and interglacial events and, in Fenland, deposits from the last three glaciations (Anglian, Wolstonian, and Devensian) and the three interglacials (Hoxnian, Ipswichian and Flandrian) predominate. Anglian Chalky Boulder Clay (Chalky Till) can be found around Peterborough and on some of the upland, as well as capping some of the fen islands. These deposits are in turn overlain by sands and gravels, as well as marine clays within the Nar Valley. During the Ipswichian, interglacial fluvial sediments were deposited along the major river valleys, together with the remains of the flora and fauna of this warm period; palaeolithic tools have been found distributed in the same areas, and there is every chance that *in situ* deposits within Fenland will one day be found, because the last ice sheet (the Devensian) only reached as far south as the Wash and north-eastern fens, creating a moraine that became Stickney island, and the Hunstanton Till in Norfolk around 18,000BP, whilst gravels were deposited as debris fans around the fen margins.

The periglacial conditions of the Devensian produced a number of local geological features visible in the modern landscape. Large circular depressions over 1km in diameter, thermokasts, can be found at places such as Conington and Farcet on the western fen edge and at Mepal in the central fens. Smaller ones are evident along the eastern fen edge, formed from the melting of ice lenses. Solifluxion deposits and cryoturbation structures are widespread, with the latter visible as polygonal cropmarks on gravels, as evident, for example, during excavation on the edge of Stonea island.

Over the last 10,000 years, during the Holocene period, up to 30m depth of sediments have accumulated in the fens and it is this period which has been of most interest to archaeologists. The sea level has been rising over most of the Holocene and the Fenland basin accumulated large amounts of sediment as a consequence of two factors: marine inundation as the coastline moved inland and peat growth as the rivers backed up during periods when their path to the sea was blocked (*colour plate 1*). The Wash coastline advanced and retreated a number of times during the Holocene and in this zone, alternating between coastal mudflats and peat fen, a series of silt, clay and peat layers can be found bedded against one another, revealing the complex history of environmental change within the fens.

PALAEOENVIRONMENTAL RESEARCH

The nature of environmental change within Fenland has intrigued academics for the last two centuries. The ploughing up of 'bog oaks', the remains of submerged forests, showed clearly that at one time Fenland was a wooded environment, and the Cambridge scientist Skertchly published the first study of Fenland deposits from borehole data in 1877. He suggested that the existing terms for widespread deposits, such as 'buttery clay' and 'lower peat', were misleading as their consistency and spatial cohesion could not be demonstrated. Instead he developed a simple division between peat and silt fen, and accounted for the fens as a direct result of fresh water and saltwater meeting, which could be seen by the distinct deposits they left behind: peats and inorganic sediments.

Although a number of people undertook specific studies in different parts of the fens during the first half of the twentieth century, none looked at evidence from all of Fenland in the way that Skertchly had adopted. This piecemeal approach was to some degree brought together and synchronised by a multi-disciplinary team, the Fenland Research Committee, in 1932 under the direction of the botanist Sir Harry Godwin and archaeologist Graham Clark. Cambridge University provided the base for this group and their study area focused on the central southern fens, especially Shippea Hill. Between 1933 and 1942 more than

14 papers were published, which presented a model for Fenland deposition based on a four-part stratigraphic sequence, and use was made of complementary areas of study, such as pollen, foraminifera and archaeology, to understand the changing environment in terms of its plant communities, water salinity and velocity, and human presence (which also provided a means to date the four stratigraphic units). Godwin pioneered pollen analysis in Britain and used comparative evidence from different samples and boreholes to match sequences and correlate between sites. Foraminifera analysis, for example, demonstrated that the origin of the Fen Clay (or 'Buttery Clay') was estuarine, whilst the Upper Silt was deposited by a higher energy, fully marine phase associated with coastal transgression. The Lower Peat was dated by Mesolithic tools to between 7500 BC along the Ouse to 3500 BC at Shippea Hill, the Fen Clay was assigned to the Neolithic and Early Bronze Age, the Upper Peat was seen as Bronze and Iron Age, and the Upper Silt was Roman.

In the same manner the banks of silt left by ancient watercourses, roddons, were given a Romano-British date, as they seemed to be associated with the Upper Silt and Romano-British sites were often found beside these channels. Gordon Fowler provided a hypothesis for their formation which suggested that the silts carried and deposited by the rivers and creeks were less susceptible to erosion when the Fenland was drained and dessication of the peat led to its shrinkage; this situation was exacerbated when the exposed dry peat was cultivated and became very susceptible to being blown away by the wind, whilst the heavier silts remained in place. This led to recessed channels in the upper peat becoming inverted banks of silt when there was no longer sufficient peat to hold them in.

The introduction of radiocarbon dating in the 1950s provided the opportunity for an independent means to date fen deposits, and as more samples were taken and dated during the second half of the twentieth century so the simple timespans allocated to specific stratigraphic units by the Fenland Research Committee began to become more complex. Archaeological excavations at places such as Hockwold on the fen edge in Suffolk, Maxey in the Soke of Peterborough, or the work undertaken by Tim Potter at Stonea and March islands, demonstrated a distinct epsiode of flooding during the third century AD. In addition, other palaeoenvironmental and soil characterisation studies undertaken by the British Geological Survey and others showed that Lincolnshire had many more identifiable layers of peat than fitted the existing model, and that the description of deposits in Norfolk could be further refined; unfortunately the appliance of these to seemingly similar deposits around Peterborough led to errors in assuming the deposits were of the same period. Detailed soil studies and archaeological fieldwalking by people such as David Hall showed that roddons were complex phenomena, and although the last channels cutting through them may have been Roman in date, nonetheless the banks were already above the level of the surrounding land at this period and therefore attractive locations for Roman occupation; the roddons were therefore shifting watercourses with different sedimentary loads that were deposited throughout prehistoric times. Ian Shennan's studies of coastline change have suggested that there were seven landward expansions of the Wash, and six seaward expansions of Fenland during the Holocene.

In the 1980s the Fenland Survey appointed Martyn Waller to undertake palaeo environmental research alongside its programme of archaeological fieldwalking, and as part of this programme over 200 C14 dates were obtained from peat samples taken from boreholes and exposed sections in dyke sides. Martyn Waller published the results of this work in 1994 and has provided a radical revision of previous interpretations. He abandoned the old terminology and four-part division of the depositional sequence because it equated the stratigraphy based on sediment description with specific periods of time, whereas the lithology alone in fact does not provide any dating evidence as it is merely the result of specific depositional processes. The distribution of C14 dates across Fenland clearly showed that similar sequences had accumulated in separate embayments during widely different periods (*colour plate 5*). Instead Waller proposed that there was a simple division between organic and inorganic sediments, and that the most important areas for study were the transitions between these, the intercalated peat, or 'perimarine area'. It was this that provided the key to understanding the dynamics of interaction between fresh water flooding and saltwater incursion.

Studies of the pollen within the peat layers revealed different formation processes dependent on the prevailing water table at the time of deposition, and a sequence of events as the fen moved from the upland towards the sea (*9*). In essence soils on the fen edge, for much of prehistory, supported woodland communities with lime, oak and hazel predominant. As the sequence moved further out into the fen, the organic deposits were built up by fen woodland (oak, hazel and alder), merging into fen carr (alder and willow), then into sedge fen, reed swamp and finally into the salt marsh and then unvegetated areas adjacent to the sea itself, where the clays and silts accumulated. Through these pollen studies the fluctuating nature of the Fenland environment, changing over time in different ways at different locations, could be reconstructed with reasonable certainty (*10*).

Only ten C14 dates were obtained as part of the Fenland Survey for Roman and later times; nonetheless these dates and studies of diatoms and peat deposits in association with Roman sites at places such as Hockwold, and Willingham on the Upper Delphs, have helped to provide some useful supplementary data for a general understanding of the Roman Fenland. During the Roman period a regional fall in sea level appears to have occurred, and a major fresh water flooding event manifested itself during the third century. Some of the silts in the Lincolnshire fens were found to be post-Roman, and Stonea was identified as

THE EVOLUTION OF THE FENLAND LANDSCAPE

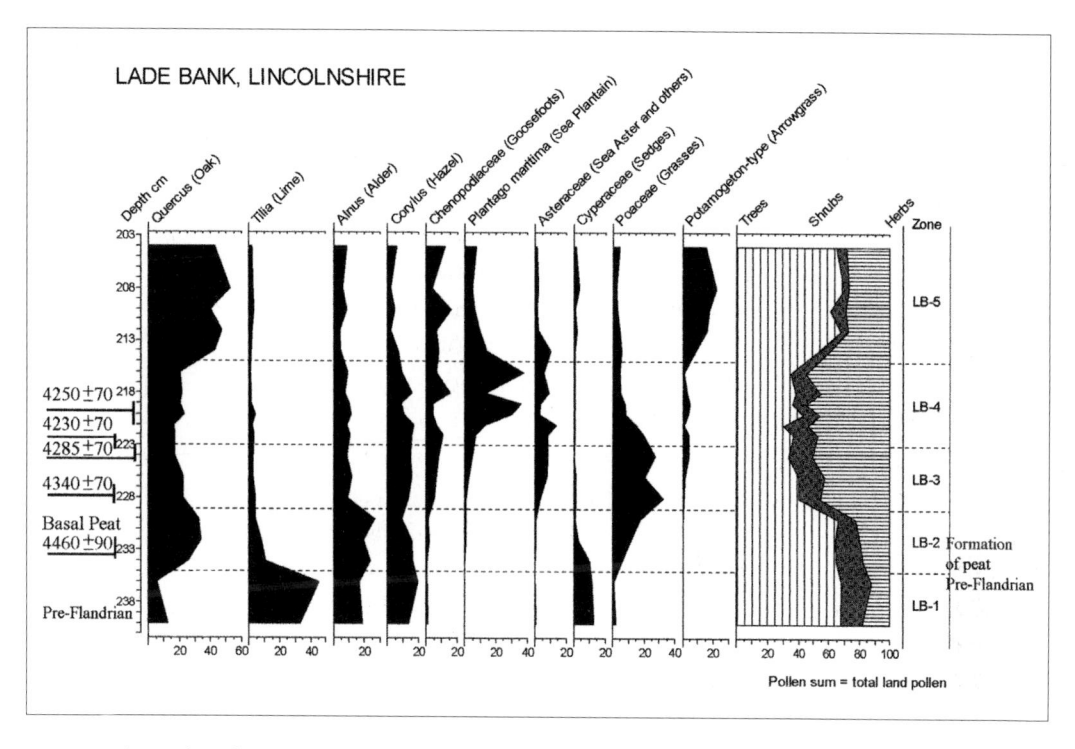

9 Lade Bank pollen diagram showing the onset of fen conditions from the pre-Flandrian lime-dominated woodland (c.4500BP), through a changing environment of alder carr (c.4300BP) as water levels rose and peat formed, and salt-tolerant plants (c.4200BP) as reedswamp and saltmarsh developed nearby. The oak-dominated final phase relates to pollen blown in from the surrounding region. *With kind permission of Martyn Waller*

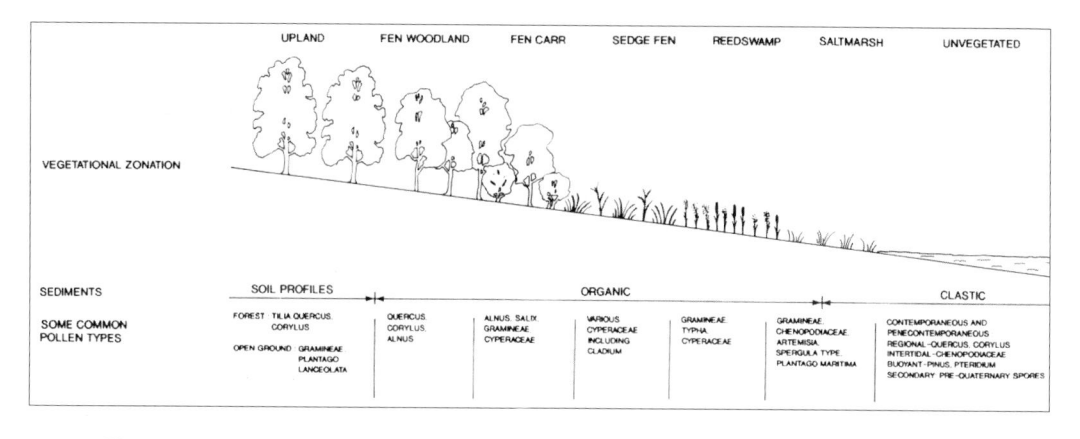

10 Vegetation zones, sediments and pollen types in Fenland. *With kind permission of Martyn Waller and English Heritage, from* East Anglian Archaeology 70

11 Air photograph of Bullocks Haste, Cottenham, Cambridgeshire; a Roman field system partly ploughed out. © Ben Robinson 12/7/90

located on the maximum limit for tidal waters. The fens would therefore have been a reasonably accessible and rich area for settlement during the Roman period, as the environmental conditions would have been benign. The organisation of the empire together with the enterprise of the local population allowed a rapid exploitation of this region, interspersed with at least one period of decline, although the explanation for the third-century flooding is probably more one of political and historical cause than of environmental change. After the Roman period, however, the peat fens became increasingly wetter, reaching their maximum extent during the Saxon and medieval period, and preserving for later study many of the major sites and engineering initiatives of the Roman period. These sites have become vulnerable to rapid destruction only within the last 50 years, due to the increased mechanisation and cultivation of the fens as a consequence of the demands of modern agriculture (*11*). The Fenland Project was just in time to ensure some record of these deposits was made prior to their widespread removal, although on most sites the later Roman layers had already been largely destroyed.

3

THE FENLAND IN PREHISTORIC TIMES

ENVIRONMENT AND HUMAN EXPLOITATION

The prehistoric inhabitants of Fenland lived in what could be considered a relatively inhospitable land of wet fens, winding watercourses and brackish creeks, with pockets of slightly higher land at the fen edge or islands on which settlement was possible (*front cover illustration*). In fact, the fens provided a plentiful land with all sorts of resources to draw upon; fish and fowl, wood and reed, salt and fuel, summer grazing and relative security from outsiders who were not familiar with the terrain.

Around 5,000 years ago, during the Neolithic, much of the Fenland basin was inundated by the sea, so that the effective coastline was coincident with an altitude of approximately -3.5m OD. Inlets ran south-westwards to the Somersham area and south-eastwards to the Hockwold area, around a large block of land which would later become the central ridge of Fenland, and resolve itself into the islands of Ely, Chatteris and March. The northernmost part of Fenland was also covered by salt marsh and coastal reed swamp with an inlet running up the Witham valley, although a large block of land jutted eastwards towards what is now Boston and the present day coastline. Pollen studies have revealed the decline of major trees during this period (*9*) such as lime, oak, elm, ash and hazel, suggesting that not only were rising sea levels affecting the environment, but also that human exploitation was leading to woodland clearances.

A millennium later northern Fenland and all of the eastern part as far south as the Soham area was under the sea, but the western third had seen the growth of a substantial expanse of fresh water fen, in which a number of islands of higher ground provided some dry land in addition to that at the fen edge. This juncture between the marine and fresh water environments occurred at *c*.-2m OD, and the upland edge of the peat fen was at -1m OD. By *c*.3,800 years ago, however, marine flooding and salt marsh had once again covered all land below -1m OD, virtually all of what we now call the fens, encroaching on the Lincolnshire fen edge and extending south-westwards to the area of Ramsey and Willingham, and depositing a clay sediment that became known as the 'Fen Clay' (*colour plate 5a*). Willow and alder carr woodland predominated, gradually giving way to sedge fen as more open water conditions developed. This was a period when increasingly warm climatic conditions began to develop, favourable to farming and colonisation of marginal land over many centuries.

Around the beginning of the Middle Bronze Age *c*.1400 BC, sea levels had risen to much the same level as today, and this had caused considerable backing up of fresh water within the eastern fens. A substantial embayment of peat developed in the south-east, covering much of the Fenland east of the central ridge and south of a line from March to Denver (*colour plate 5b*). The fen edge was at approximately 0.5m OD, and peat formed not only over this extensive tract of Fenland but also along the south and western edge, although 'Fen Clay' (marine clays) continued to be deposited from the sea water covering the rest of the western fens with the exception of some islands such as Whittlesey. Chatteris and March became separated from the Isle of Ely at this time, and Stickney island in the north of the fens was formed.

By about 1000 BC a much larger area of the fens had become covered by peat, which now covered all of the southern half of Fenland, the eastern margins, and areas along the northern and north-western edge, and fresh water meres had developed. This growth of peat encroached on the upland so that the fen edge was at approximately 1m OD, and the Isle of Ely was connected by only a thin isthmus between Willingham and Aldreth (*colour plate 5c*). In the central Fenland the meeting of saltwater and fresh water deposits resulted in beds of peat and clay or silt overlying one another, a phenomenon which led to the terms 'Lower Peat' and 'Upper Peat', with the 'Barroway Drove Beds' in between them given a Bronze Age date. The climate was becoming increasingly wetter.

By the Early Iron Age, around 600 BC, two-thirds of Fenland was covered by peat, a substantial area of the northern fens was still affected by sea water. The interface between peat Fenland and the coastal environments was at *c*.0m OD, and the upland fen edge was at 1m AOD. This seaward expansion of the peat fen led to the maximum extent of fresh water deposits until the climax in the medieval period. Although the peat continued to grow within the southern fens, over the rest of the Iron Age marine inundation recovered some of the eastern peat fen, depositing silts that have been termed 'Upper Silts' or the 'Terrington Beds' and which accumulated to a height of *c*.3m AOD (*colour plate 5d*). During this period,

THE FENLAND IN PREHISTORIC TIMES

intensification in human exploitation of the landscape can be detected as well as gradual colonisation. By Roman times drier conditions began to prevail and much of the northern fens, known as the siltlands, were becoming dry and habitable.

COMMUNICATIONS

An understanding of the ancient landscape, its settlement distribution, farming and industrial practices and ritual and ceremonial monuments, can best be attempted through setting archaeological finds in their contemporary context, as they interrelate closely with the local topography and geology of a region. In the Fenland this is particularly relevant because of the shifting nature of the rivers and changing environment to which human populations had to react over several thousand years. One important aspect in reconstructing past landscapes is to try to establish the major routes of communication within the region and between regions (*12*).

In and around Fenland these communications can be divided into two main types: those by river and those by land, although sea-borne routes were also in operation, connecting Fenland with the east coast northwards and southwards around East Anglia to the Thames estuary and beyond, as well as across the North Sea to the continent. These international connections are demonstrated by finds such as the Isleham Hoard, the largest assemblage of Bronze Age metalwork found in the British Isles and dated to around 1000 BC, which included many items which have been identified as continental imports based upon their metallurgical composition, and in some case by their typological characteristics. It is, however, the more local communication network which interests us in setting a background for the Roman Fenland.

The river routes followed the major drainage channels upstream from the Wash westwards into the heartlands of England, the Midlands, or eastwards into East Anglia (*colour plates 1 and 8*). In the north the Witham provided easy navigation to present-day Lincoln and beyond, making use of a gap in the limestone ridge to connect with the Trent valley. Further south, the Welland and the Nene provided important thoroughfares to what is now Northamptonshire and south Leicestershire. The Great Ouse linked the Wash with the southern fens and what is now Huntingdonshire, Bedfordshire and Buckinghamshire. The Cam, the Little Ouse, the Lark and similar rivers allowed access between the fens and south-eastern uplands of Cambridgeshire and Suffolk, and the Wissey and Nar valleys connected the fens with the central Norfolk hills.

Terrestial communications utilised either the fen edge or, across Fenland via peninsulas and islands, and exploiting banks along watercourses, the silt fen, or ferries in order to cross the wettest parts. In Lincolnshire one of these

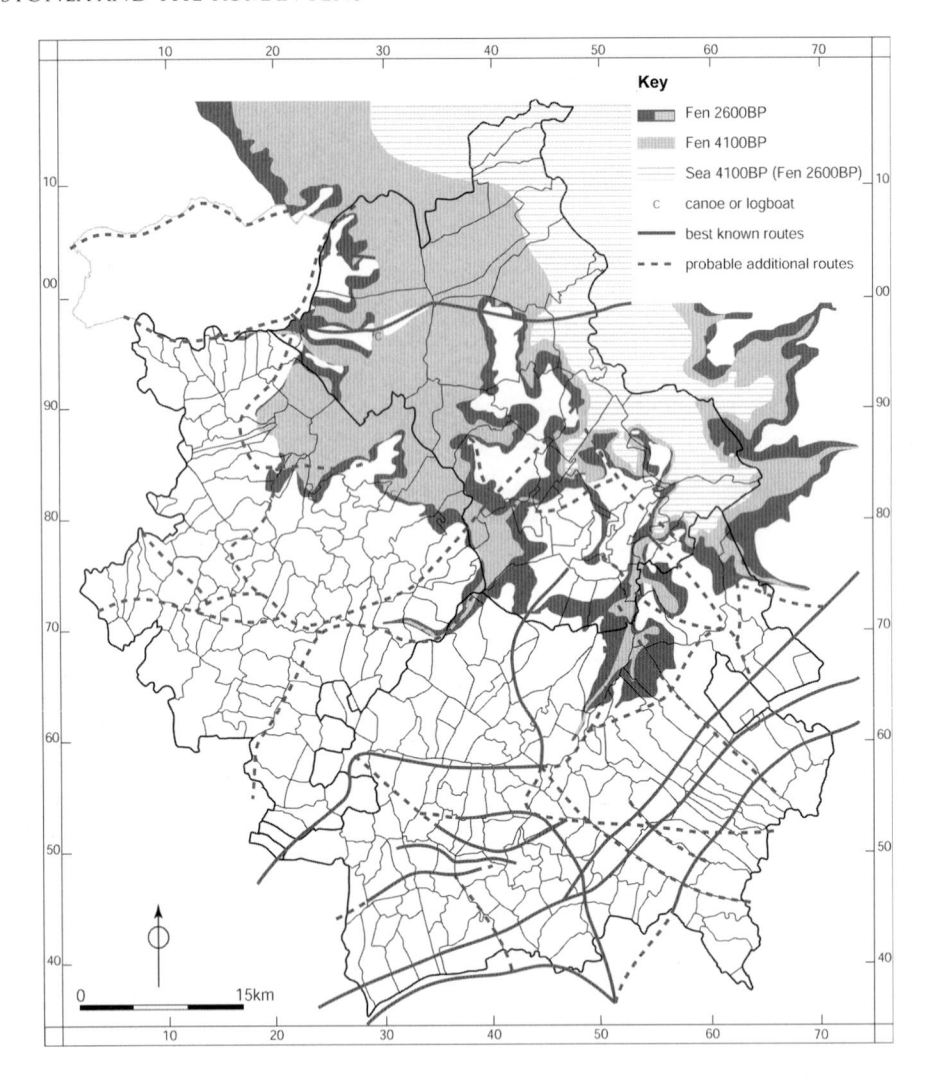

12 Prehistoric routeways in Cambridgeshire and the southern fens. Drawn by Sarah Wroot

routes is known as Salters Way, which runs from the River Soar near Leicester through Salterford to the fen edge at Threekingham, crossing Mareham Lane (a north–south fen-edge route) on its way, and then extending into Fenland across Horbling Fen to Donington.

Further south the Fen Causeway originates from the Bronze Age droveways at Fengate on the eastern edge of Peterborough via a series of islands to the fen edge at Denver in Norfolk. It travels through Flag Fen to Northey (*13*), where the deliberate deposition of Bronze metalwork found in association with settlement helps date the route, and through the two islands of Whittlesey where hoards of

THE FENLAND IN PREHISTORIC TIMES

bronze axes have been found at Whittlesey and Eldernell (at the point at which the Fen Causeway heads off across the wet fen to March island); a log-boat was found at the junction between the two islands, suggesting a ferry crossing. The route from Eldernell then had some 7km of peat Fenland to cross, but gravel digging in the early twentieth century exposed sections of the Fen Causeway with brushwood foundations, strongly suggestive of prehistoric, probably Bronze Age, engineering, similar to the Bronze Age causeway at Fordey–Little Thetford on the Isle of Ely. The route then crossed Westrey, the north part of March island, through Estover to Flaggrass before crossing more fen *en route* for the Norfolk upland at Denver.

Stray finds of axes and the arrangement of some Bronze Age barrows suggest that a possible route ran from the Ouse at the Godmanchester–Huntingdon river crossing through Wyton, Houghton, Woodhurst and Somersham, to cross the fen and West Water of the Ouse in order to reach Chatteris and the other main fen

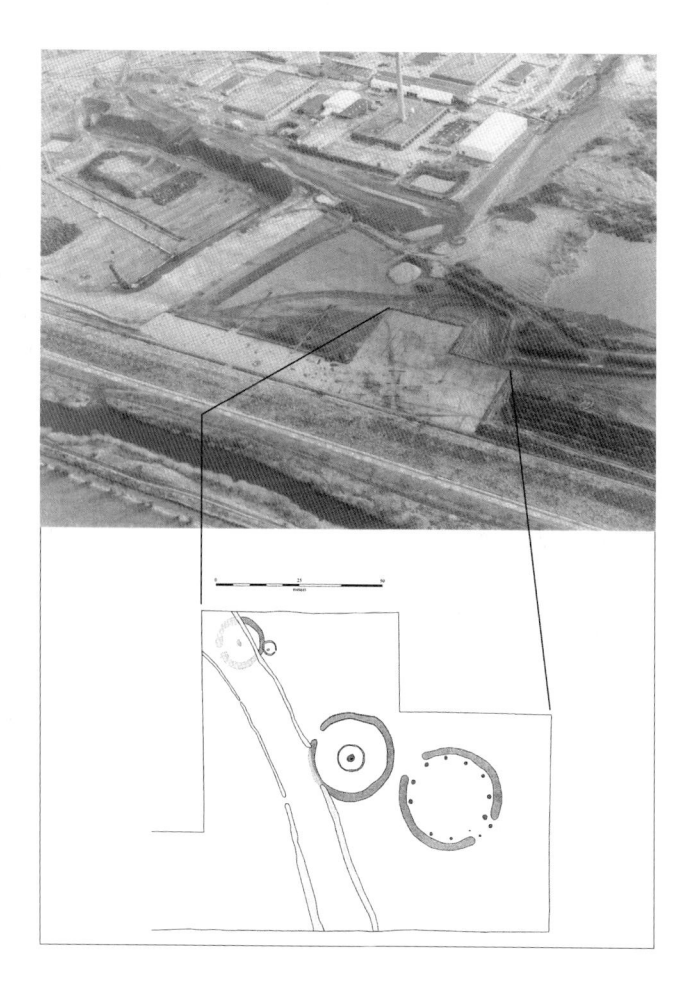

13 The Fen Causeway, Bronze Age burial monuments and a henge at Funthams Lane, Whittlesey Brick Pits 1999. *Air photograph © Ben Robinson 18/12/99; plan of excavated features by Mark Knight and Cambridge Archaeological Unit*

islands. The location of two log-boats, one found on the fen edge at Warboys and the other more or less opposite it on Chatteris island, could suggest that another route, which ran in from the west to the Ramsey area via a brushwood truck in Wood Walton fen, might perhaps originally have carried on by water transport to the fen islands.

Aldreth Causeway connects the fen edge at Willingham with the Isle of Ely at Aldreth, Haddenham. Bronze Age weapons and timbers have been found beside the crossing of the river, originally a tributary but now the course of the Great Ouse itself, and a circular fort of probable Iron Age date controlled access along it. Further causeways to the Isle of Ely are known to have existed from lines of timber piles accompanied by brushwood and Bronze Age artefacts connecting Little Thetford with the mainland at Fordey, and to the north of this from Ely to Stuntney and to Quanea. These routes all gave access from the south-east, from the chalk uplands and the Icknield Way.

THE PREHISTORY OF THE RIVER VALLEYS

The Witham valley is famous for some of the outstanding artefacts and other archaeological finds that have been discovered in its bed or along its banks. Amongst these are the timber piles found in the 1980s at Fiskerton, which have been dated to the Late Bronze Age and Early Iron Age and which have been interpreted either as a bridge or a platform, possibly for the ritual purpose of making votive offerings to the River deity. A spectacular Iron Age shield recovered from the river may well have been one such deposit. Examples of early field systems are, however, absent.

For much of its length the Welland valley is a boundary between modern counties, but it also appears to have been a major political boundary going a long way back into prehistory. It was the limit between the *civitates* of the Catuvellauni and of the Corieltauvi and therefore it was also a very likely boundary between the old tribal entities before the Roman Conquest. Further back in time, the remarkable concentration of major Neolithic monuments, of causewayed enclosures at Barholm, Northborough, Newborough, and a pair at Etton/Maxey, as well as a further pair of enclosures at Upton (*14*) on the north side of the Nene, is quite unlike that around other major rivers of the region, and strongly suggests its major political, as well as sacred, significance.

Lines of settlements and field systems can be detected as having been laid out during the Bronze Age, and the area seems to have been well ordered and populated. Major ditched 'ranch' boundaries and droveways appear to have demarcated territories over long periods of time, off which small paddocks, co-axial field systems, were constructed, such as those encountered around West

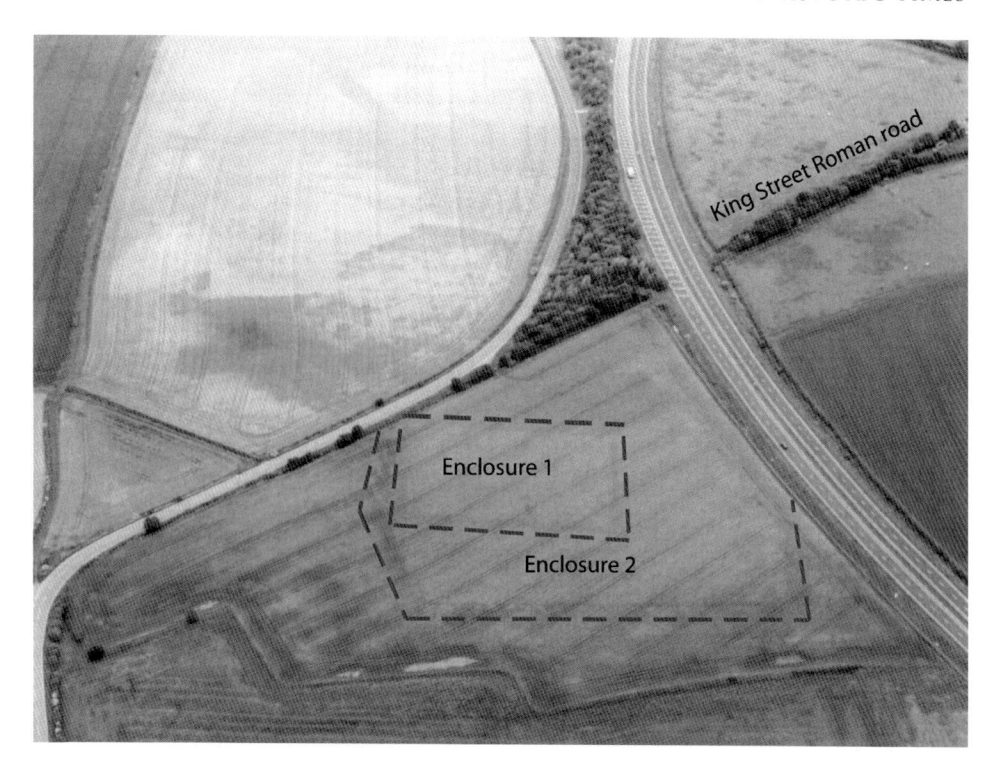

14 The Neolithic enclosures at Upton; their proximity to the Roman road of King Street had led to their interpretation as Roman camps until excavation by Adrian Challands revealed their true date. © Ben Robinson 9/6/03

Deeping and Welland Bank. Bronze Age burials are also found, and one of the earliest was that of a man accompanied by all the trappings of an elite member of society excavated at Barnack in the 1970s; more recently excavation at Deeping St Nicholas revealed three major phases with a child buried beneath the centre of the first mound, two shroud burials later cut into this mound, and then cist graves cut into the second burial mound. The pattern of settlement seems to have been broadly continuous into the Iron Age, and a major circular fort was constructed at Borough Fen (*15, 16, colour plate 8*) around 500 BC, together with a series of multiple ditches, perhaps for added defence from landward attack as it is located on a penisular projecting into the fen.

The Nene valley is famous for its ancient landscapes such as that at Fengate and outstanding sites such as Flag Fen. Some of the earliest planned landscapes in the country include the paddocks and droveways laid out on a regular grid along the fen edge at Fengate and at Eye. Settlement and burial of Neolithic and later date have been found in this area, and the deposition of metal finds in the Flag

15 Borough Fen Iron Age fort; the curvilinear bank can be seen on either side of the road that bisects it. © *Ben Robinson 10/7/94*

Fen basin associated with the route of the Fen Causeway, timber piles, settlement at Northey (Whittlesey), and the possible crannog or platform at Flag Fen itself, all point to the wealth and social cohesion of the prehistoric communities living in this area who controlled sufficient of the hinterland to import large stands of managed timber to construct the causeway and platform at Fengate and Flag Fen. Further west, a log-boat found at Horsey, Stanground could suggest a crossing point of the River Nene as it is located along the line of another probable prehistoric routeway, one that ran north–south along the fen edge.

The valley of the Great Ouse has a series of Neolithic and Bronze Age ceremonial complexes regularly spaced along its length. These begin to impinge on Fenland with the cursus and massive trapezoidal enclosure at Godmanchester, and continue with the Causewayed Camp, Neolithic and Bronze Age barrows, and Iron Age shrine found on the Upper Delphs at Haddenham and Sutton in the Isle. Of the fen islands Chatteris, March and Stonea all contain evidence of Neolithic and Bronze Age monuments, such as the triple ring-ditch complex at Horseley Fen, Chatteris, and the cursuses at Grandford (March) (*colour plate 7*) and Stonea, as well as alignments of Bronze Age barrows along the fen margins on these islands. A rich assemblage of high-quality Bronze Age metalwork has been recovered from Chatteris, including

THE FENLAND IN PREHISTORIC TIMES

a particularly fine example of a shield, and other major metalwork finds, mostly weapons, have come from the Isle of Ely, such as the Wilburton hoard. Large and impressive Iron Age settlements have been found on all the major islands, including an elaborate system of ditches and thorn-topped banks defending a high-status, possible chiefton's estate centre, at Wardy Hill, Coveney. Over 30 round-houses were found during recent excavations just west of Ely, and the Fenland Survey has demonstrated a gradual expansion northwards of Iron Age occupation of Chatteris and March islands during the last part of the first millennium BC, with sites such as Flaggrass and Stonea being of particular importance. Field systems and settlement have been dated to the Bronze and Iron Ages with division of the land on a co-axial pattern revealed, for example, at Huntingdon Racecourse, Meadow Lane, St Ives and Bluntisham. Pit alignments were utilised at the latter sites, with large rectangular houses replacing round ones during the Late Bronze Age. The foundation for these landscapes, however, include evidence of Neolithic origin.

Although the Cam valley has few large earlier monuments, it seems to have formed a political boundary in at least the later Iron Age as a series of forts are found along its length, such as Arbury Camps, War Ditches, Wandlebury and Sawston (*16, colour plate 8*). These probably represent the division between Catuvellaunian and Trinovantian territory in the period before the Roman Conquest, and there are strong suggestions that the symbolic importance of this area extends back into prehistory; recent excavations on the southern fringes of Cambridge at Babraham Road and Trumpington have revealed extensive Bronze and Iron Age landscapes with ritual and burial elements interspersed with settlement. Bronze Age barrow cemeteries are found along the Cam and its tributaries, and a Neolithic causewayed enclosure on a small inlet of the fen is located at Great Wilbraham. Important Iron Age burials are also known from this area, such as that from Lords Bridge, Barton, and cremation cemeteries such as that of the Aylesford-Swarling culture at Hinxton.

Further east along the southern edge of the fens the Little Ouse, Snail and Lark river valleys hosted significant prehistoric populations. A great concentration of continuous settlement from the Neolithic through into Roman times has been mapped on the Soham peninsula and around the south-eastern fen edge. Flint and metalwork scatters and hoards are prolific within this area, places such as Hockwold and Methwold being particularly important, and Bronze Age burial monuments such as the early barrows excavated in the 1930s at Chippenham are found in clusters, whilst an important Iron Age warrior burial was found at Snailwell. Late Bronze Age and Early Iron Age settlement and field systems have been found at places such as Fordham and Dimmocks Cote, Wicken.

From the Norfolk mainland the Wissey and Nar valleys drained westwards into Fenland, and a spread of Iron Age settlement has been found along the

STONEA AND THE ROMAN FENS

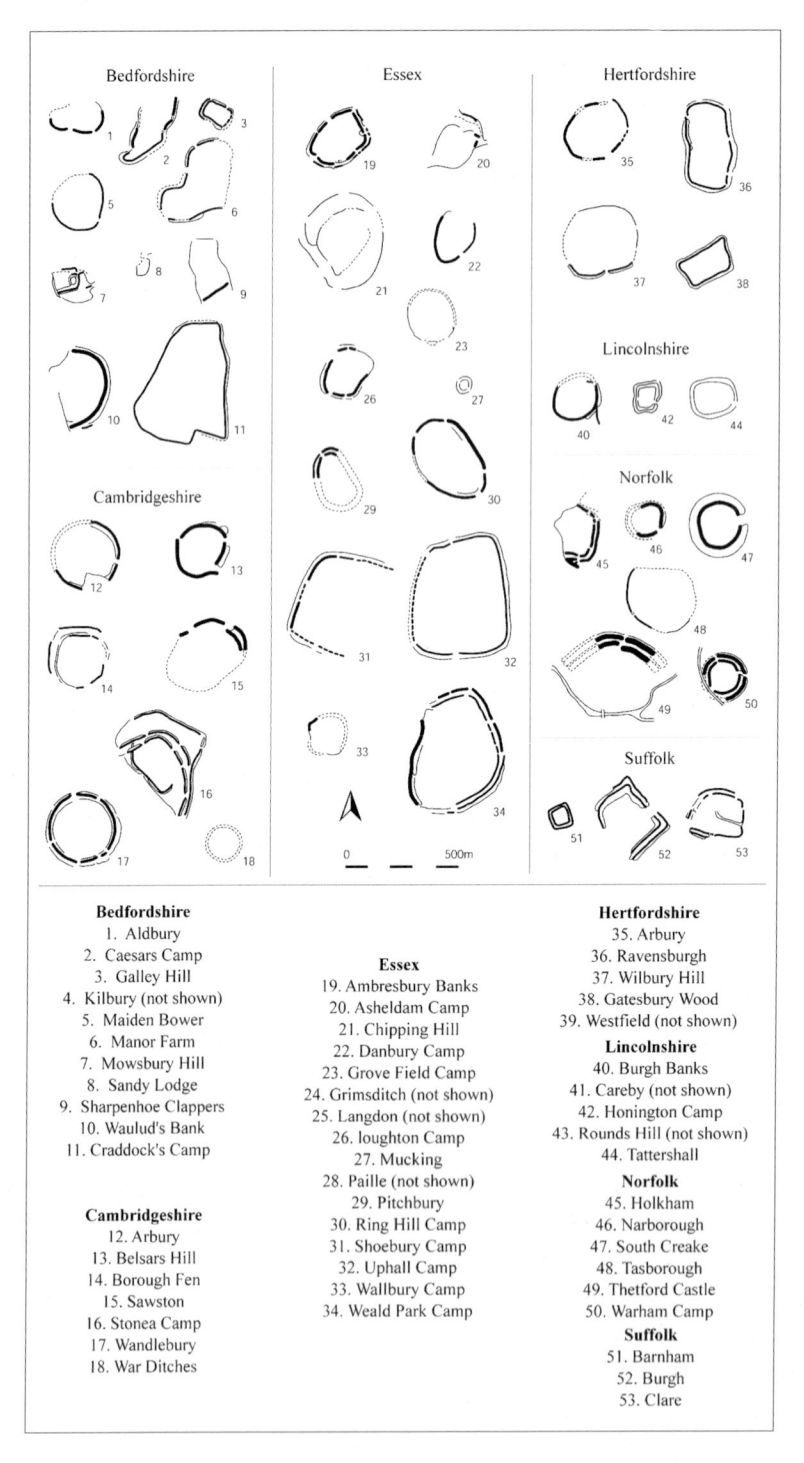

Bedfordshire
1. Aldbury
2. Caesars Camp
3. Galley Hill
4. Kilbury (not shown)
5. Maiden Bower
6. Manor Farm
7. Mowsbury Hill
8. Sandy Lodge
9. Sharpenhoe Clappers
10. Waulud's Bank
11. Craddock's Camp

Cambridgeshire
12. Arbury
13. Belsars Hill
14. Borough Fen
15. Sawston
16. Stonea Camp
17. Wandlebury
18. War Ditches

Essex
19. Ambresbury Banks
20. Asheldam Camp
21. Chipping Hill
22. Danbury Camp
23. Grove Field Camp
24. Grimsditch (not shown)
25. Langdon (not shown)
26. loughton Camp
27. Mucking
28. Paille (not shown)
29. Pitchbury
30. Ring Hill Camp
31. Shoebury Camp
32. Uphall Camp
33. Wallbury Camp
34. Weald Park Camp

Hertfordshire
35. Arbury
36. Ravensburgh
37. Wilbury Hill
38. Gatesbury Wood
39. Westfield (not shown)

Lincolnshire
40. Burgh Banks
41. Careby (not shown)
42. Honington Camp
43. Rounds Hill (not shown)
44. Tattershall

Norfolk
45. Holkham
46. Narborough
47. South Creake
48. Tasborough
49. Thetford Castle
50. Warham Camp

Suffolk
51. Barnham
52. Burgh
53. Clare

16 Comparative plans of Iron Age forts within, and surrounding, the fens (for fort locations see map at colour plate 8). © Caroline Malim

THE FENLAND IN PREHISTORIC TIMES

skirtland at the edge of the fen and on the islands close to the upland. Human burials of Bronze Age date have also been found distributed along this zone, often on low natural mounds if not beneath manmade barrows. A study of metalwork and flint scatters within Cambridgeshire, Suffolk and Norfolk has demonstrated the very close coincidence of these two types of evidence, with a conclusion that generally both sets of finds come from dry land contexts and that the fen edge was a particularly attractive zone for settlement because it allowed easy exploitation of a variety of resources on the upland and in the fens. No earlier monuments are known from the fen edge or eastern river valleys, unlike those on the western side of Fenland, and the distribution of causewayed enclosures, long barrows and henges has been found to lie over the watershed in central and eastern Norfolk. There is also close correlation between the distribution of Iron Age hoards and coins with the late Roman distribution in Norfolk, mostly away from the fen edge, along river valleys and clustered around particularly significant locations such as Thetford.

SOCIAL, POLITICAL AND ECONOMIC FOUNDATIONS OF FENLAND

The socio-political make-up of the region can best be reconstructed for the period immediately preceding the Roman Conquest by use of archaeological evidence supported and illuminated by the texts of classical writers (*colour plate 7*). This pattern can be extrapolated further back in time by a study of the archaeological data for earlier periods. During the later Iron Age we can be reasonably certain that much of eastern and central Fenland came under the control of a tribal group based in Norfolk, the Iceni, whose royal household seems to have been located around Caistor St Edmund. There are six forts in Norfolk and three in Suffolk, in addition to the major Fenland fort at Stonea Camp (*16*). Distribution of Icenian coinage is one way in which the extent of their territory has been mapped, but the tribe is also visible through the fact that the Iceni did not engage in the kind of trade with the continent that their southerly neighbours followed, evident in the fact that luxury imports of wine *amphorae* and the adoption of wheel-turned pottery are largely absent from Norfolk, Suffolk and Fenland. The material culture between the Iceni and the more Romanised southerners is therefore apparent within the archaeological record. This tribe, remembered for Boudica's revolt in AD 60-61, is described by Tacitus as having three loose sub-groups or *pagi*, and it appears that it was the westernmost *pagus*, the Fenland area and Stonea, which rebelled first in AD 47.

On the south-eastern flank of the fens the Trinovantes were located, with the centre of their power at the large, dyke-surrounded *oppidum* of Colchester, and princely burials within this zone at Stanway, but they were absorbed by the powerful king of the Catuvellauni, Cunobelin, in around AD 10. Cunobelin then adopted Colchester as the capital for all his kingdom. A line of forts exists running north–south along the Lea, Stort and Cam valleys, creating an effective frontier between these two tribes from the Thames to the fens.

The south-western fen margins, Huntingdonshire and west Cambridgeshire, were controlled by the Catuvellauni with their centre at St Albans, another *oppida* defined by dykes. To the north their territorial limits with the Corieltauvi, a tribe whose centre was at Leicester, lay within a zone around the Welland and Nene valleys. The Lincolnshire fens, therefore, fell within the Corieltauvi sphere of influence. There is a general absence of forts along the Catuvellaunian fen edge, but a series of small defended enclosures occurs on the edge of the upland in Corieltauvi territory, the southern bastion of which would seem to be the much more impressive circular fort at Borough Fen. The distinctive pottery of this area, scored ware, is found as far south as the Ouse, but seldom beyond it, showing another distinction in material culture between the Fenland population and the wealthier Catuvellaunian heartlands. Differences can also be seen in aspects such as burial rites, not only with the princely burials known from places such as Colchester, Baldock, Welwyn and St Albans and similarly wealthy ones along the Cam valley and southern fen edge, but also with the use of cremation in these southern lands, a rite not witnessed archaeologically north of the Ouse. Some of these cremations were accompanied by caskets and other grave goods, and the use of square ditches around them, or of barrow mounds to cover the graves, was a particular trait of the area; the barrow burials continued into the early Roman period and included some very wealthy ones such as those at Bartlow, the Stukeleys (*17*), and one excavated in 1995 at Butt Lane, Milton (*18*).

The economic basis of this society was primarily from agricultural produce, in particular cattle and sheep, but the growing of cereals was also a significant and important activity. Celtic beer was highly valued in the Roman world, and there can be no doubt that the good arable lands of East Anglia would have been producing grain not only for bread but also for making beer. Granaries and storage pits are prolific features on Iron Age settlement sites, as are droves and enclosures for marshalling stock. Within the Lincolnshire fens salt extraction developed into a significant industry by the Late Iron Age, and iron-working has been traced to a number of sites around the margins of the fens. We also know that items other than Celtic beer were traded with the Roman world, such as hunting dogs, woollen garments, and slaves and that both the Trinovantes and Catuvellauni imported and copied wheel-thrown pottery and received wine and olive oil and many other luxurious commodities in exchange. The *oppida* of southern Britain seem to have been the focus for such activities, and some of these developed aspects of

THE FENLAND IN PREHISTORIC TIMES

17 A reconstruction drawing of the Stukeley barrows. © Caroline Malim

18 Roman pots and cremation urns from beneath the barrow at Milton. Courtesy of Alison Taylor

41

proto-towns with elements such as metalled streets, craft and industrial production, evidence for long-distance trade, and for their role as administrative and religious centres as well as residences for the social elite. The evidence from the settlement and fort at Stonea could well be used to suggest that Stonea was an *oppidum*.

Iron Age settlements can be divided into two types: single, enclosed farmsteads and loose spreads of unenclosed groups of houses and other structures within extensive ditched field systems. The latter are generally to be found in the easily tilled valleys and fen islands, and during the later Iron Age Fenland began to be more extensively developed. The imposition of territorial boundaries, from tribal borders down to others at estate and farm level, can be traced in several ways: the former by linear distributions of major forts or the distribution of coinage to distinguish different tribal areas, and through some of the large ditches along the Icknield Way zone (such as the Mile Ditches at Royston, Black Ditches at Icklingham, or the Foss and Bircham ditches in west Norfolk [colour plate *8*]); the latter through the long linear 'ranch' boundaries within the Nene and Welland valleys to form a well-organised division of the land into large agricultural units. Through careful study of natural features and surviving field patterns which, for example, have been cut or defined by Roman roads, it is possible to map out possible Iron Age estates. There are many other pieces of evidence that need to be brought in to make a convincing argument for this, but later Roman and Anglo-Saxon estates occasionally can be mapped and sometimes identified as the probable successors to Iron Age precursors.

THE SETTING FOR ROMAN EXPLOITATION

The above summary of Fenland in prehistoric times demonstrates that the Roman colonisation of the second century AD was not one of breaking virgin ground but rather a re-exploitation and development of a landscape already well ordered and utilised in past millennia. The aftermath of the Boudican rebellion resulted in severe oppression of the Iceni by the Roman authorities which would have left the fens seriously depressed, with a population decimated if not entirely removed, a landscape of ravaged settlements and crops and famine prevalent for those who survived in the area. In the light of this situation the Roman colonisation would have found a landscape that had been largely neglected for two to three generations and thus they had a largely empty country with which to create a fresh landscape and implant new communities. This new vision included major engineering works such as drainage and communications as part of a planned infrastructure for the new territory, and was in this respect very different from the more organic development that had ocurred during the prehistoric period.

4
STONEA ISLAND: INVESTIGATIONS OF A LANDSCAPE IN MICROCOSM

GEOLOGY AND TOPOGRAPHY

Stonea is an island that rises from 2m above sea level to over 5m at its highest point and was formed on Jurassic Clay from chalky-glacial till (boulder clay) overlain by outwash sands and gravels; sandy clays are evident in parts where mixing of the underlying clay with lenses of sand have occurred, leading to an occasionally hydraulically leaky sub-strata. Solifluction activity is particularly evident in the form of irregular polygons with chunks of boulder clay surrounded by seams of sand, and this has allowed easy drainage and a fluctuating water table. The geology is covered by a soil no more than 0.5m deep. Silt and silty-clay deposits are evident in the southern part of Stonea Camp and were also found during excavations of the Roman town at Stonea Grange; these seem to derive from relatively recent flooding episodes (over the past 5,000 years). A survey by ADAS in 1992 estimated that the present water table is probably 2m lower than at the time when the ditches of Stonea Camp were constructed.

Stonea forms part of the north–south ridge through the southern fens that is physically visible as the islands of March, Chatteris and Ely. This ridge effectively divided the southern Fenland into south-western and south-eastern embayments. The old Ouse flowed to the west around this ridge and, having been joined by the old course of the Nene, the combined river then ran eastwards around the northern tip of March island and to the north of Stonea, towards its outfall in the Wash near Wisbech (*colour plate 15*). A subsidiary channel separated Stonea from the main island, flowing northwards from the edge of Wimblington on March island and Honey Hill on Chatteris island, past the western side of Stonea. A second roddon is visible as a rise in the fields running eastwards from Stonea Camp at the southern tip of the island (*colour plate 10*).

CHANGING ENVIRONMENT

The shape and extent of the island at Stonea were constantly changing during the Flandrian, but in essence it stood at the junction of peat and silt fens, at the border between fresh water and saltwater deposition. During the Neolithic and Bronze Age Stonea was joined with the island of Manea and was surrounded by peat fen (see *12*). A major watercourse drained northwards along the western edge of the island, and tidal surges up this creek brought episodic floods of brackish water. During the Iron Age a more extensive period of marine inundation is recorded by the amount of silt that has been found deposited around the edges of most of the island. Three major drainage channels developed during this period, two flowing north to join and run along the western edge of the island, and a third drained east along the island's southern edge. This pattern continued during later periods, but increasing human control of Fenland drainage, through canalised rivers, canals and dykes, gradually usurped and replaced the natural drainage system.

The peat fen survives to almost 1m in depth and laps up to the south-western side of Stonea. A single radiocarbon sample was taken by the Fenland Survey at Manea from this peat sealed beneath marine silts and a date of between cal BC 825-550 was obtained. Two radiocarbon dates from Stonea Camp in 1993, however, gave dates of cal BC 2200-1830 for the base of the peat as it ran up on to the island, and cal BC 1889-1520 for the surviving top of it, placing the formation of the peat well into the Bronze Age (see specialist feature on radiocarbon dating in Chapter 5). This peat deposit was 0.5m thick and situated *c.*50m to the south-west of the Camp. The pollen evidence replicated the results obtained from the primary infill of the later ditches of the Camp, a partly wooded island of oak and birch, with fen carr and reed fen in close proximity, suggesting a general continuity in local environment from the Middle Bronze Age into the Middle Iron Age. The peat sequence was sealed by clays, silts and sands, demonstrating increased water movement over the subsequent millennium. Marine incursions dated to the Iron Age can be seen to have occurred as silt deposits found on the north and east sides, at one point virtually encircling the island. Some of this silt was found during excavations of the Roman town at Stonea Grange, confirming Late Bronze Age occupation and with features of Roman date cut into it. A Roman road overlay silt which was sampled for diatoms and the results from this analysis showed that Stonea lay at the edge of direct tidal influence. Infill in the outer defences at Stonea Camp also contained a brackish silt deposit interpreted as flooding, but perhaps of a later date than the other silts, even possibly within the Roman period itself (see *30*).

Pollen evidence and excavated timbers show that the local Iron Age environment was one of mixed flora, with managed oak, birch and alder woodland on the island, changing to grazed pastureland by the Roman period. Fen carr woodland was also present in the locality, running down from the fen edge into the fen itself. The changes in the local environment during this period reflect the intervention of man rather than change through natural causes, and the predominantly pastoral use that prevailed from Roman times probably continued uninterrupted until the late twentieth century. During the Neolithic and Bronze Age the level of the fen rose from approximately 1m below sea level to about mean sea level as we know it now, but climatic conditions worsened during the Iron Age to take it to *c*.2.5m above sea level. There was shrinkage of the peat during Roman times when the fen fell to around 2m above sea level, but during the late Anglo-Saxon and medieval periods the climate became wetter again, leading to growth of the peat fen, which rose to its maximum extent during the high medieval period of *c*.3.5m above sea level.

A FOCUS FOR INVESTIGATION

The known productivity of Stonea has acted as a magnet for both archaeologists and metal-detectorists. The earthworks of Stonea Camp have been the most tangible form of Stonea's ancient past, and have been mapped by the Ordnance Survey, together with some other features described as 'earthen rings', although coin hoards were reported from Stonea as early as the nineteenth century. The introduction of air photography revealed more of its buried landscape, with barrows, ditches, field systems and enclosures becoming visible (*19* and *20*). The first archaeological excavations were conducted at the Camp by Tim and Christopher Potter in 1959, and this was followed during the early 1960s by excavation of a Bronze Age barrow just to the east (which also revealed a Neolithic occupation site preserved beneath the mound) and of a Roman site at the Golden Lion Inn next to Stonea Halt. Metal detectors began to be used during the 1970s and their use became a major menace during the 1980s when Stonea Camp and Grange were systematically looted by unscrupulous and illegal detectorists. In 1980 The British Museum began excavations at Stonea Camp, but then switched their focus of attention to the Grange to examine a Roman building discovered by David Hall during the Fenland Survey. This sustained

STONEA AND THE ROMAN FENS

campaign of investigation lasted several seasons from 1981-85, although every year the site was raided at least once by gangs of metal-detectorists, robbing the site of important artefacts and damaging their stratigraphic context. Geophysical and phosphate surveys were undertaken at Stonea Camp during the 1980s, and a fresh initiative of investigation and reinstatement was undertaken by the author and Cambridgeshire County Council's Archaeology Section from 1990-92 (*26, colour plate 9*).

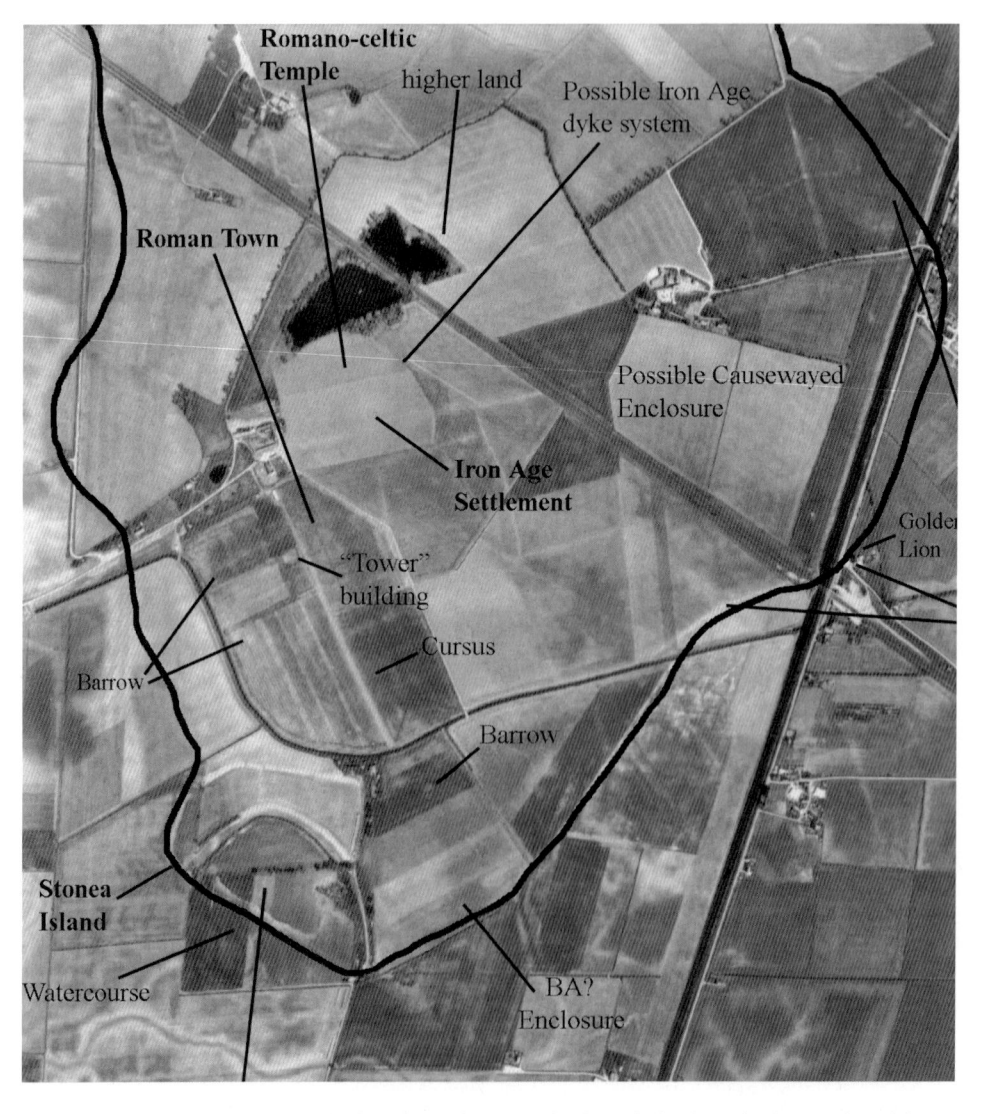

19 The Stonea area with major archaeological sites and edge of island marked up. *Adapted from photograph. Copyright reserved Cambridge University Collection of Air Photographs*

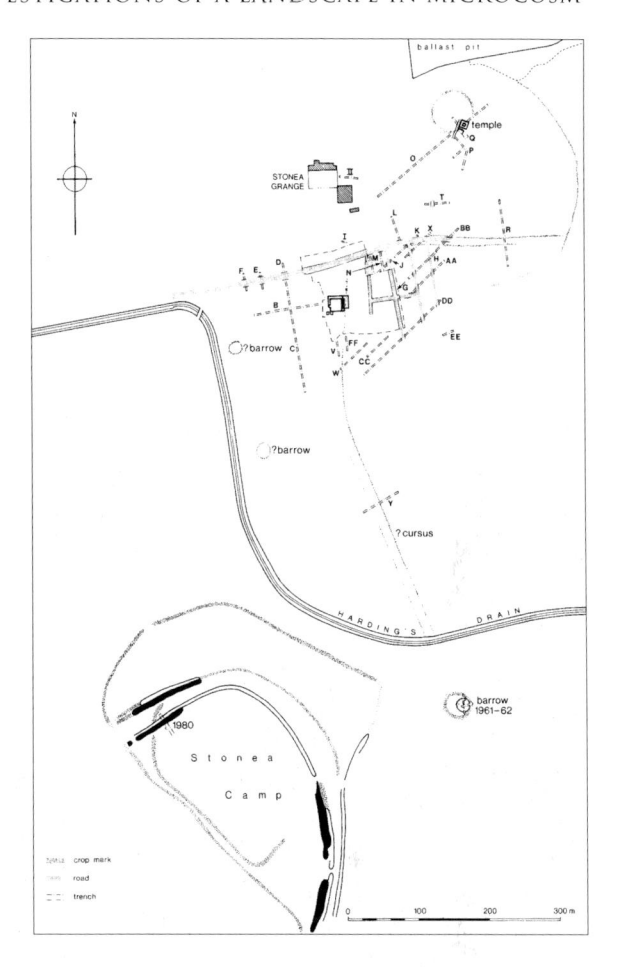

STONEA ISLAND: INVESTIGATIONS OF A LANDSCAPE IN MICROCOSM

20 Plan of Stonea island showing the concentration of prehistoric and Roman monuments in the south-western peninsula. © British Museum

A RICH AND PRODUCTIVE SITE

Stonea is one of those sites that archaeologists refer to as 'productive'; in other words it is a site that continues to produce a surprisingly rich assemblage for a number of different periods. For nearly every period since the introduction of farming Stonea has provided evidence for occupation or use, and it continues to be a place that rewards archaeological study. As an island it contains a variety of sites and therefore provides comparative information between different types of site of the same period, and allows an examination of the potential for direct continuity between one period and the next. While Stonea's principal fame is, however, for the high status of its remains most clearly seen in the Roman town and the Iron Age fort of Stonea Camp, its significance in other periods is also important and therefore these periods are discussed briefly below.

PREHISTORIC ORIGINS

The underlying gravels of the area are associated with evidence for ancient man; for example two palaeolithic hand-axes have been found at Stonea. A flint assemblage from Stonea Camp collected during excavations in 1992 has been dated in part to the Mesolithic, and axes of this period have also been recovered by chance from the surrounding peat fen.

Tangible evidence for occupation and ritual use at Stonea starts during the later Neolithic, c.3000 BC. Pits, post-holes, pottery and domestic debris were found by Tim Potter in 1961-2 whilst excavating a Bronze Age barrow immediately to the east of Stonea Camp. He interpreted this as an old ground surface dating from the Neolithic and only preserved because of the burial mound that had been placed above it. We could therefore infer from this that the island once contained evidence for further Neolithic settlement, but that modern farming and the fragile nature of Neolithic pottery has led generally to their destruction except for ephemeral traces. Flint tools, including arrowheads, have been found at both the Camp and Roman town, and excavations at the latter found some Ebbsfleet pottery (c.4000-3000 BC) and a gully from this period. Two sherds of Neolithic pottery were also found preserved within disturbed bank material behind the inner D-shaped ditch at the Camp (Trench F) (see *31*); this evidence and flint arrowheads found at the Camp, in association with infilled ditches that predated the later Iron Age defences, offers a tantalising possibility that a Neolithic enclosure might have existed in the same location as the later Camp. The majority of the small flint assemblage that was found during the 1992 season came from the open-area excavation within and around a ring-ditch (Trench XVIII) (*21*); this assemblage was examined by Twigs Way, who saw it as residual material of late Mesolithic and Neolithic date. It was characterised predominantly by a blade industry together with a scarcity of scrapers (results which contrasted with the earlier fieldwalking in 1990) and tools were manufactured from local cobbles. The assemblage demonstrates that this part of the island was clearly an attractive area for occupation during the Neolithic, and possibly also from an earlier period.

These rather meagre assemblages of flint and (especially) pottery are largely consistent with the pattern in many other places, and it is more usual to find evidence for Neolithic activity through their great monuments rather than through their settlements. It seems that Stonea has traces of such monuments including features that may well represent the remains of a cursus, and possibly of a large ditched enclosure to which the cursus was leading. This enclosure is on the southern edge of the island, and was reused during the Bronze Age for location of a barrow. Both the cursus and enclosure have been tentatively identified from air photographs, the cursus consisting of a pair of ditches 20m

STONEA ISLAND: INVESTIGATIONS OF A LANDSCAPE IN MICROCOSM

21 Ring-ditch under excavation (from west) in Trench XVIII. Author's collection

apart, one of which has been excavated and shown to be U-shaped, 3.7m wide and 1m deep. It runs north-west/south-east for approximately 400m, with a single turn to the north near its northern end. On another air photograph showing the area between Stonea Farm and Stonea Halt there is a vague hint that a further Neolithic monument may exist. A series of dark features can be seen that might represent the circuit of a series of interrupted ditches from a causewayed enclosure. Although this has never been previously suggested and would need to be established by excavation, nonetheless the presence of such monuments on other Fenland islands such as the Upper Delphs at Haddenham and Etton/Maxey, helps to support the potential hypothesis that Stonea not only acted as a focus for Neolithic ceremony through its cursus and associated enclosure, but also might have had an earlier major monument in the form of a causewayed enclosure.

Evidence for a Bronze Age presence is more substantiated, but spread over *c.*1,500 years. There are possibly as many as five burial monuments, barrows and ring-ditches, running from the north-west/south-east, inside and just outside the Camp, thereby seemingly dividing the peninsula, which later held the Iron Age fort from the rest of the island. This alignment appears to respect the one previously set by the Neolithic cursus, and there are possible outliers to this cemetery on Honey

Hill, Chatteris, 1km to the south. A further three barrows are located in the north-eastern part of the island and may form a separate small group.

The barrow excavated in 1961 was 19.5m in diameter and produced a primary burial pit containing the cremation of a woman between 30-40 years in age and accompanied by 17 jet and 11 amber beads, dated to the Early Bronze Age. A secondary cremation of a man in his twenties was found in an urn close by. Further north a single unurned cremation of an adult dating to *c.*1100 BC was also found during excavation at Stonea Grange, in an area subsequently used for Late Bronze Age settlement.

One of the ring-ditches, shown on the 1926 OS map as an 'earthen ring', was excavated by the author in 1992 and revealed a 10m diameter annular ditch 1m wide and 0.4m deep, filled with stone and earth packing around small post-holes; no break in the circuit was found to indicate an entrance (*21*). No real evidence for domestic occupation was found, although Mesolithic and Neolithic flints were recovered from the overburden and from the small samples of ditch fill that were excavated. On such evidence it seemed unlikely to have been a round-house and therefore is interpreted as a ritual monument, perhaps some form of palisaded barrow.

During The British Museum's excavations at Stonea Grange, flints and a single sherd of Beaker pottery were recovered as residual material from the beginning of the period, and also a Late Bronze Age occupation deposit well-preserved beneath the silts of an Iron Age flooding episode. Survival of this evidence had been badly affected by later, mostly Roman, activity, but there was sufficient preservation beneath the main east–west road of the Roman town to allow a stratigraphic sequence to be reconstructed. A large collection of Post Deverel-Rimbury pottery dating to between the ninth and sixth centuries BC, bronzework, flints and stone artefacts were found in association with a well, post-holes and a 13m diameter penannular gully (1m wide and 0.45m maximum depth) with entrance to the east, evidence for a probable round-house.

Five socketed bronze axes and three ingots were found prior to 1935 from the north of Stonea Grange. A selection of other metalwork including fragments of swords, a razor and socketed chisels and axes were found in addition to crucible and mould fragments from surface metal-detecting and during the excavations at Stonea Grange itself in the 1980s. This material is all of Late Bronze Age date. A gold hair-ring of this same period, and a looped spearhead of the Middle Bronze Age have been reported as further metal-detected finds. Such a concentration of important metalwork and evidence for metalworking, in association with settlement and burial evidence, demonstrates that Stonea was an important centre of activity during the Bronze Age.

STONEA ISLAND: INVESTIGATIONS OF A LANDSCAPE IN MICROCOSM

IRON AGE, ROMAN AND DARK AGE SETTLEMENT

In the following chapters the evidence for the Iron Age fort and settlement, Roman town and Anglo-Saxon estate centre are described in detail. In brief, Stonea island contained a series of sites of both Iron Age and Roman date, of both high and low status. Stonea Camp appears to have been started during the Middle Iron Age, around the third or second centuries BC, and continued in use with additions and rebuildings until the first century AD. To the north of this an extensive area of settlement has been detected, perhaps defined by existing curving field boundaries which seem to replicate the pattern of the Stonea Camp earthworks (*19* and *20*). This settlement included a temple and a large assemblage of coinage suggesting extensive contact with neighbouring tribes. Tim Potter has even suggested that Stonea might have been an *oppidum* of the Iceni, a trading centre and proto-town, and the curving field boundaries around it might represent fossilised dyke systems which would have defined the *oppidum* in the manner of those near Colchester or St Albans. Tacitus may have been describing Stonea

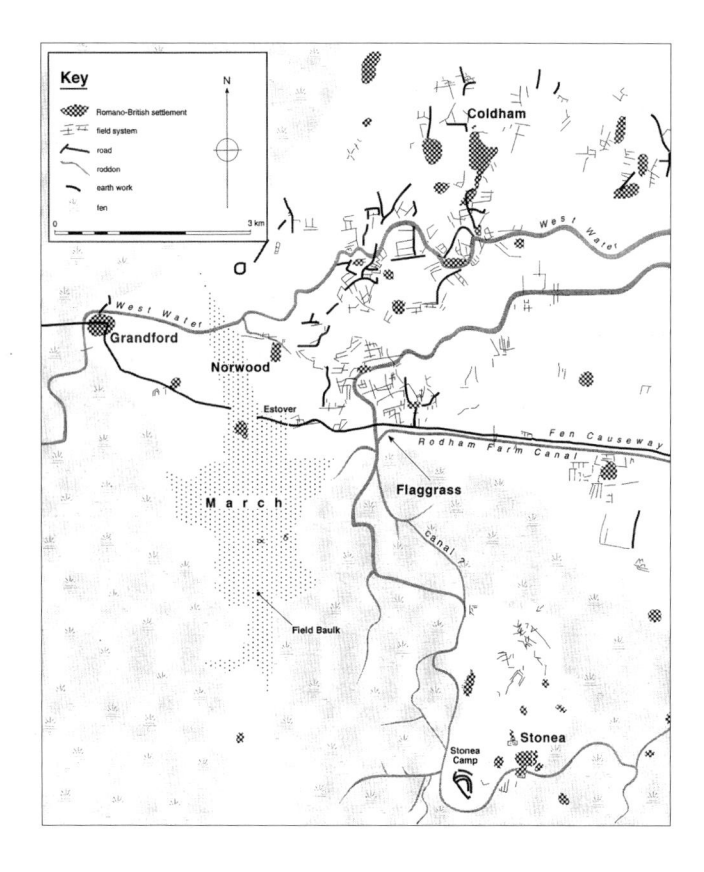

22 Map of the Roman fens around Stonea and March. © *British Museum*

when he details a battle between the Romans and Britons who had retreated into a rustic earthwork which was stormed and the defenders overwhelmed (see *cover illustration*); skeletons have been found at the Camp, one even with a probable sword cut, and radiocarbon dating has placed at least one skeleton within this general period. A Roman military presence has been identified at the Camp and dated to the period AD 40-60, and a town was built to the north of it during the second century. This town declined during the third century but continued to be occupied into approximately the sixth century with the latest houses built in the style of Anglo-Saxon halls and their ancillary buildings.

Elsewhere on the island a number of other sites provide evidence for simpler rural and industrial settlements of the Iron Age and Roman periods, including salt-making. Four other Iron Age sites (some of Early Iron Age date) and 13 Roman have been recorded by the Fenland Survey in addition to Stonea Camp and the Stonea Grange complex, as well as extensive cropmark field systems generally assigned a Roman date (*22*).

ANGLO-SAXON, DANISH AND MEDIEVAL ACTIVITY

The Camp has been attributed a Viking origin by some authors, primarily based on the D-shape of the defences, which is seen as characteristic of Danish defended encampments. From excavated evidence we can trace Stonea Camp's origins to at least the Late Iron Age, and they are probably of Middle Iron Age date, but the double D-shaped defences are the latest phase of construction, and could conceivably be of a much later date. They seem to have replaced an earlier inner-defensive circuit, the ditch for which was found during investigations in 1992 (see *28*), but the surviving causeways reveal staggered entrances which are similar in concept to many known from Iron Age forts. At Thetford in Norfolk a similar double D-shaped arrangement was used to create a fort which backed on to the river, and this has been shown to have an Iron Age date as well. Thus, although a Danish date cannot be discounted at Stonea, there seems at present to be no evidence that really supports such a supposition.

Stonea and Stitches Farm are, in origin, Anglo-Saxon names meaning gravelly marshland, literally 'stoney island'. The earliest documentary reference to Stitches Farm is from 1251 when it is referred to as '*stichebeche*' or 'pieces of land', but much earlier Anglo-Saxon charters mention Stonea in connection with a grant of land to Wulstan of Dalham from a widow, Aescwen of Stonea. In 955 Wulstan gave the land to the monastery at Ely, and Domesday records that a grange for Doddington Manor, which was held by the Abbot of Ely, was situated at Stonea. The British Museum excavations at Stonea Grange uncovered traces of a large timber building and a pin and strap-end dated between the ninth and tenth centuries. In addition, a radiocarbon date from timbers within one of the post-holes gave a date of AD 955-1045, providing direct archaeological evidence for the documentary sources. Important fisheries and a special cattle farm (a 'vaccary') are also recorded at Stonea from the eleventh and twelfth centuries. It seems possible that a Saxon minster was located at Doddington on the southern part of the island of March, and that Stonea, together with the major settlements on March island (Benwick, Wimblington and March itself), were hamlets subordinate to Doddington. By the Middle Ages, however, Stonea had become part of the parish of Wimblington.

The monastic grange at Stonea initially prospered and became part of the Bishop of Ely's estates when Ely became a bishopric in 1191. The monasteries were responsible for some of the early Fenland drainage, making more land available for arable cultivation and all-year-round pasture, and thus increasing the productivity of the estates. On Stonea it is very likely that Hardings Drain, a major dyke that curves through the island separating the Camp from the site of the Roman town and medieval Grange, was constructed at this time. At its height the Grange was walled and included two windmills, an oxhouse and a 'grindery', but went into decline in common with other Fenland granges during the fourteenth century due to the Black Death and rising water levels. There were three main centres on the island by the end of the Middle Ages: Stonea Grange, which was closely coincident with the Roman town, Stonea Farm which is located close to the railway 'station' and Golden Lion public house, and Stitches Farm, located at Stonea Camp.

POST-MEDIEVAL OCCUPATION AND THE CIVIL WAR

During trial trenching of the Camp defences in 1990 a highly unexpected find was that of a cannonball from the infill of the outer north-western ditch (see 29). The size of this iron ball at 50mm diameter was consistent with some of the ordnance used during the Civil War, and it is known that older defences were often reused and refurbished during this period. Stonea appears superficially to be far removed from any possible zone of conflict and need for a defence, but a wider understanding of the political and military environment during the 1640s can actually suggest a reason for reuse of the earthworks at Stonea Camp.

The southern fens were Parliamentarian country, but Royalist garrisons and attacks are recorded at Kings Lynn and around Crowland, eventually leading to the sacking of Huntingdon. The fens, in common with their ancient past, provided a barrier to easy movement of a foreign force, but there were major routes through them which were well known, such as the Fen Causeway to travel west–east, and island-hopping to travel north–south. This latter route was created into a more substantial road by Ireton, Cromwell's son-in-law, connecting the Isle of Ely, Chatteris and March by a route along the ridge of these islands. To protect this route Ireton may well have constructed a number of small defences, and the remains of some Civil War sconces are known in a line north from Chesterton (Cambridge), via Denny Abbey, Braham Farm, Stretham, to Cavalry Barn, Battery Hills March. From the Westwater of the Great Ouse, in a line between Chatteris and March, a medieval canal had been built, Doddington Leam, to make a shortcut connecting with the channel of the Ouse and Nene east of March, thus allowing a more direct route north to its outfall at Wisbech. This canal passed about midway between the sconce at March and Stonea Camp and if batteries were positioned in both locations they could effectively have controlled any movement along it.

A substantial farmhouse called The Stitches was built in the north-eastern corner of the Camp at some point in the late medieval period, or possibly in the sixteenth century (*23* and *24*). This was built close to Hardings Drain and had deep, dry cellars (according to Mr G.W. Cross, who was born and lived in the house). Two towers, one on either side, contained staircases that led down to the cellar and up to the attic. The house was brick facaded, but its structural foundation was timber-frame. It was demolished in 1973, about a decade after a similar fate had befallen Stonea Grange. The substantial farm of Stitches is depicted on a seventeenth-century map (*24*) and some of the modern entrances through the banks and ditches of the Camp were probably created at this time for access to fields. It is also quite likely that the pond at the west end of the Camp was excavated for stock at this time. A well existed on the eastern side of the Camp for domestic use, a little removed from the house itself, which was probably located on the driest part of the southern end of the island.

The drainage of the fens had been started in earnest just before the Civil War by the Duke of Bedford and his financial backers, the Adventurers. This drainage was attempted by cutting wide, deep and long rivers through the peat and, once initial drainage had shrunk the peat, using windmills to raise the water from the fields into the new channels. In 1651 the 20ft river was cut, which runs about a kilometre to the east of Stonea Camp and skirts the eastern tip of the island. This, and its service dykes, must have made a profound difference to the available farm land around Stonea and would have ensured a relatively increased value to the three principal farms on the island. By Victorian times a second large farmhouse stood on a roddon south of Stitches and the Camp, clearly demonstrating the wealth that this farm had generated. During this period the March–Ely railway was built across the island with a halt provided at the Golden Lion and large

STONEA ISLAND: INVESTIGATIONS OF A LANDSCAPE IN MICROCOSM

23 Photograph of Stitches Farmhouse shortly before it demolition in the 1970s; note the stair tower giving access to the upper storey. A similar tower on the other side gave access to the cellar. *Photograph by G.W. Cross*

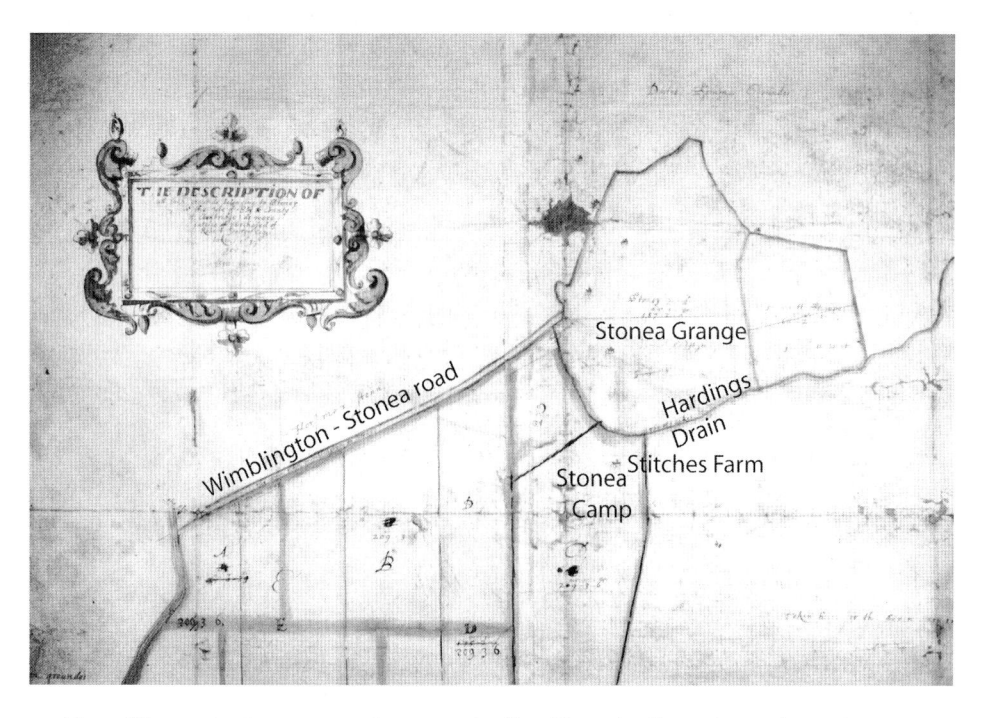

24 Map of Stonea in the seventeenth century by Ben Hare; the Camp is not shown but Hardings Drain (The Old Lake), Stitches Farmhouse, and Stonea Grange are all evident

ballast quarries on the highest part of the island immediately north of Stonea Grange were dug for gravel to construct embankments.

During the twentieth century Stonea Camp continued as pasture until living memory, with its earthwork banks covered in blackberries and dog-roses, and scrub growth on these and in its ditches. The land was acquired by the local authorities and rented out to tenant farmers. This was the kernel of the Cambridgeshire County Farms Estate, begun after the First World War to allow young men a chance to make their living as smallholders. When Cyril Fox visited in the 1920s he foresaw no problem in the continued preservation of the site, but unfortunately agricultural policies during the 1960s concentrated solely on increased productivity and, to achieve this aim, grants were given to farmers to infill dykes and remove obstacles to ploughing such as hedges and earthworks. In 1963-4 much of Stonea Camp was turned over to arable, with most of the banks being bulldozed into the ditches (*7*) leaving visible just two inner banks and a ditch remaining on the western side (*colour plate 9*) and an inner bank and ditch on the eastern side. Its status as a scheduled monument did nothing to protect it and it began to be ploughed; the plough eroded the undisturbed archaeology within the Camp and also cut into the remaining banks. In 1973 the old farmhouse of Stitches needed to be re-roofed, but instead it was demolished as it was cheaper to build a new bungalow. English Heritage's predecessor bodies, the Ministry for Public Buildings and Works and the Department of the Environment, tried to preserve what remained by placing a series of concrete posts around the surviving sections of bank; these were gradually knocked down and removed over the years, and it was not until a review of the archaeology on the Estate undertaken by the author, and a sympathetic regime of farm managers, that reversal of this situation was possible in 1990. Investigations were undertaken over three seasons between then and 1992 so that sufficient information was learned about the site to enable its reinstatement as it was prior to 1960. This reinstatement included attempts to reverse the drainage of the previous generation and to give the site back its Fenland feel. Ancient footpaths to the site allowed the public to visit a place that once again was worth seeing, and one that now had a series of interpretation boards and activity days so that its history could be fully appreciated (see *25*).

5

STONEA CAMP: AN IRON AGE FORT AND ITS POLITICAL LANDSCAPE

Stonea Camp lies on the south-western edge of Stonea Island, now situated in a drained Fenland landscape of intense cultivation which has largely divorced the Camp from its original concept and environment (*19*). As a landscape feature, however, the monument still stands out from the gridlike regularity of the Fenland fields dominated by drainage dykes because of the curving patterns that its banks and ditches form. It was scheduled as an ancient monument in the 1920s by Sir Cyril Fox, who wrote at the time, 'It is almost wholly ancient pasture and no difficulty should arise in respect of preservation. There are so few large earthworks in the Fenlands; and so little is known of the condition of life in early times that the preservation of this camp, for future careful exploration, is much to be desired'.

Stonea Camp owed its survival to the fact that to level its massive earthworks would have required an amount of labour that was uneconomic within the farming regimes of the past 2,000 years. Its historic importance also made it the location for Stitches Farmhouse, a brick-built structure with external towers incorporating stairs leading to a cellar and the upper storeys (*23*). It was of at least sixteenth-century date but might well have originated in medieval times. The area of the Camp, therefore, had become the inner fields of the farm, and had been used primarily for pasture. The banks survived with much growth of scrub on them, and the number of trees proliferated, including a nineteenth-century field division which bisected the innermost part of the Camp. This then was the scene that had greeted Cyril Fox on his visit, but his belief in the ease of continued preservation was sadly misplaced. Pressures of modern agriculture to intensify arable production included ever more powerful tractors which needed much larger fields to cultivate in a cost-effective manner, and government grants were made available to rip up hedges and fill in ditches in order to create bigger agricultural units. In the 1960s Stonea Camp suffered badly from this new farming regime; the outer circuit of defences was completely obliterated and only one curving ditch and two discontinuous lengths of bank were preserved within several newly created arable fields (*28, colour plate 9*). Ploughing over the following 25 years continued to erode what was left of the monument, severe damage was caused by illicit metal-detecting of the cultivated fields and in the 1970s the ancient house was pulled down as it was more economic to build a bungalow on another part of the farm than to repair the roof of Stitches Farmhouse. Such was the level of institutional vandalism of a previous generation!

Stonea Camp is one of the oldest upstanding monuments within the Fenlands and Tim Potter has even suggested that it might be the first historically recorded site in England. Its characteristics fit well with the description provided by Tacitus in his *Annals* when he describes a battle between the Iceni and the Romans in a rustic earthwork which was stormed by the army and much slaughter ensued:

> The surrounding tribes followed their lead and chose a site for a battle enclosed by a rough earthwork and with an entrance narrow enough to prevent the cavalry getting in. The Roman general set himself to break through these defences even though he was commanding allied troops without legionary strength ... his soldiers stormed the earthwork and threw the enemy into disorder, for they were obstructed by their own defences. Aware that they were rebels and with their escape routes blocked, they fought with prodigious bravery ... [see *cover illustration*].

The site can now be visited by the public (*25*) and some of the feel for its topographic location and atmosphere can be recaptured, especially on cold, wet and windswept Fenland winter days. Three campaigns of investigation have taken place since the 1950s and the last one of these involved the reinstatement of the Camp (*26*) as it was before its partial destruction in the 1960s. The first investigation was by Tim Potter and his brother in 1959 when a single test-pit was dug into the inner D-shaped ditch and a barrow adjacent to the Camp was excavated. A more substantial excavation was undertaken by The British Museum in 1980-81 with a trench laid across the internal banks and ditch (*27* and *31*), and this was supported by a programme of phosphate and magnetometer survey of the interior of the Camp. The final investigations were conducted over three seasons from 1991-92 by Cambridgeshire County Council's Archaeological Field Unit under my own direction when a total of 30 trenches were cut across strategic areas of the site to

STONEA CAMP: AN IRON AGE FORT AND ITS POLITICAL LANDSCAPE

25 Interpretation board and visitors following reinstatement of the Camp, 1992. *Author's collection*

26 Air photograph of Stonea Camp following investigations and reinstatement, 1990-92 (note: compare to *colour plate 8* and *fig 26*). © *Ben Robinson 28/6/03*

27 Photograph of excavations by the British Museum through the surviving bank and ditch of the inner D-shaped defence; the figure in the distance is standing in the outer D-shaped ditch. © Ralph Jackson

provide essential information prior to reclaiming the site as a monument in its own right, and to answer a number of research questions (*28*).

Stonea Camp is a 24 acre (9.6ha) area originally enclosed by multiple earthen banks and deep-cut ditches which formed complete outer and inner circuits constructed in a series of phases. It is located at 2m above sea level on the very edge of Stonea Island, and would have had wet Fenland to the south and west, rising to 3m OD in the east and north (*19*). The major defences were therefore built on the northern and eastern flanks, facing on to the drier and higher land of the island itself. Such a construction and location gives the Camp strong parallels to Iron Age promontory forts, which were built to take strategic advantage of the natural topography and thereby maximise their defensive qualities. The ditches varied considerably in shape and size, which might have been due to the different ground conditions that they were cut into. On the south side the ditches cut peat deposits, but to the north they went through heavy clay and on the west sand and silts (*23-32, colour plates 11-13*). The edge of the island is of very mixed geology, with solifluction activity evident as lumps of boulder clay brought close to the surface, and seams of sand forming irregular polygons extending to about 1m in

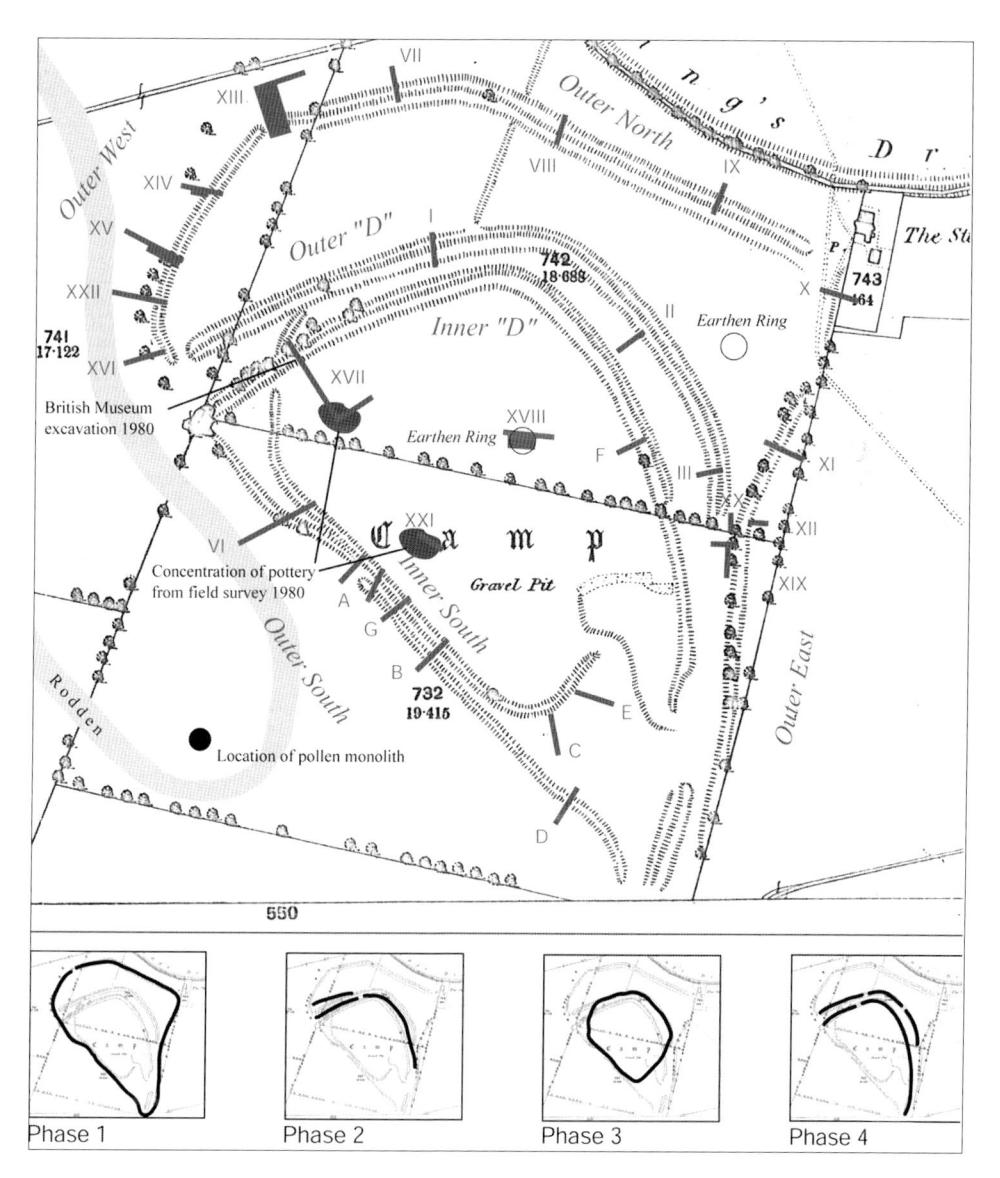

STONEA CAMP: AN IRON AGE FORT AND ITS POLITICAL LANDSCAPE

28 Plan of Stonea Camp based on the 1926 Ordnance Survey map, showing excavated trenches and probable main phases of construction. © *Caroline Malim*

depth. The diversity in the design of the ditches, however, is more probably due to different phases of construction.

The largest ditch was the outer circuit which, on the northern, western and eastern sides, had been cut with a steep-sided, flat-based profile to a depth of approximately 1.5m, was 2m wide at the base and survives today to a width of 4.5-5m at the field surface (*29* and *30, colour plates 12* and *13*). The bank behind would have been formed with the upcast from the ditch and, even allowing for slumping, the height of the combined bank and ditch must have been in excess of 3m. If a timber structure had been used to give a framework for the bank or to revet it, then these defences would have been impressive, and were perhaps topped by a timber rampart. Some evidence for this was found during the excavations in the form of pointed timber stakes or posts, and of a post-hole behind one of the inner banks in a possible palisade trench (Trench F).

Within the Camp a second circuit was formed by two D-shaped ditches (*28*). These might represent two different phases, but were probably part of the same building programme as there are two original causeways through them, one of which was designed to form a dog-leg to aid in defence, a known design feature of Iron Age forts elsewhere in Britain. The D-shaped ditches also overlie an earlier ditch, following much the same alignment, which had been back-filled prior to their construction. In 1981 The British Museum excavated a trench through a part of the surviving bank and ditch of the inner D and revealed a U-shaped profile for the ditch and a 7m wide bank surviving to 1m in height built of clay and silts laid on top of the old ground surface (*27* and *31*). The ditch was 2m in depth and 5m wide at the surface. At the base of the ditch dark, peaty turves were found, which were interpreted as part of the rampart which had been slighted and pushed into the ditch. No other archaeological trenches have been cut across this inner defence; elsewhere along its length the ditch only survives today as a modern drain, but an investigation in 1992 of where the plough-damaged bank used to stand (Trench F) revealed a remnant core surviving, and on the inside of this remnant bank a further, previously unsuspected ditch was discovered. It was 1m in depth and 1m in width at its base, with a post-pipe clearly evident in the centre of the fills (*31*). This suggests that the ditch might have acted as a trench for a palisade, perhaps indicating that the earthen ramparts would have had a timber revetment or lace framework to consolidate them.

Sections that were cut through the outer D-shaped ditch in 1992 (Trenches I-III) showed this was of a similar design to the inner D, with a 5m wide ditch at the surface, 1.75m in depth but with a slightly better defined profile than was evident within the inner D-shaped ditch. At least one section showed the same design as the main outer defensive ditch, with steeply cut sides and a flat base (Trench I) (*31*). Turves were detected, however, within the bottom of a more

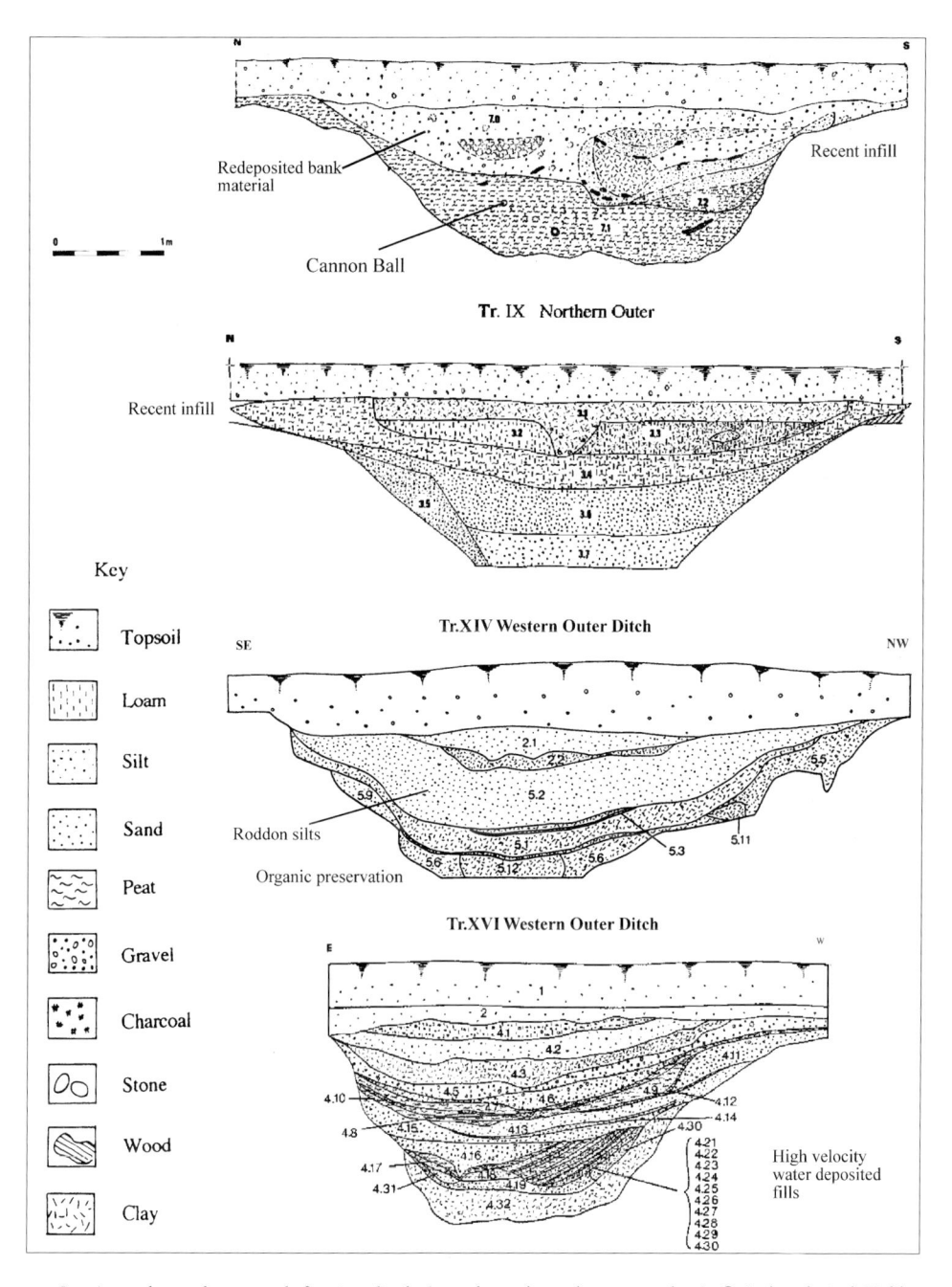

STONEA CAMP: AN IRON AGE FORT AND ITS POLITICAL LANDSCAPE

29 Sections through outer defensive ditch (see also colour plates 12 and 13). ©Archaeological Field Unit Cambridgeshire County Council

STONEA AND THE ROMAN FENS

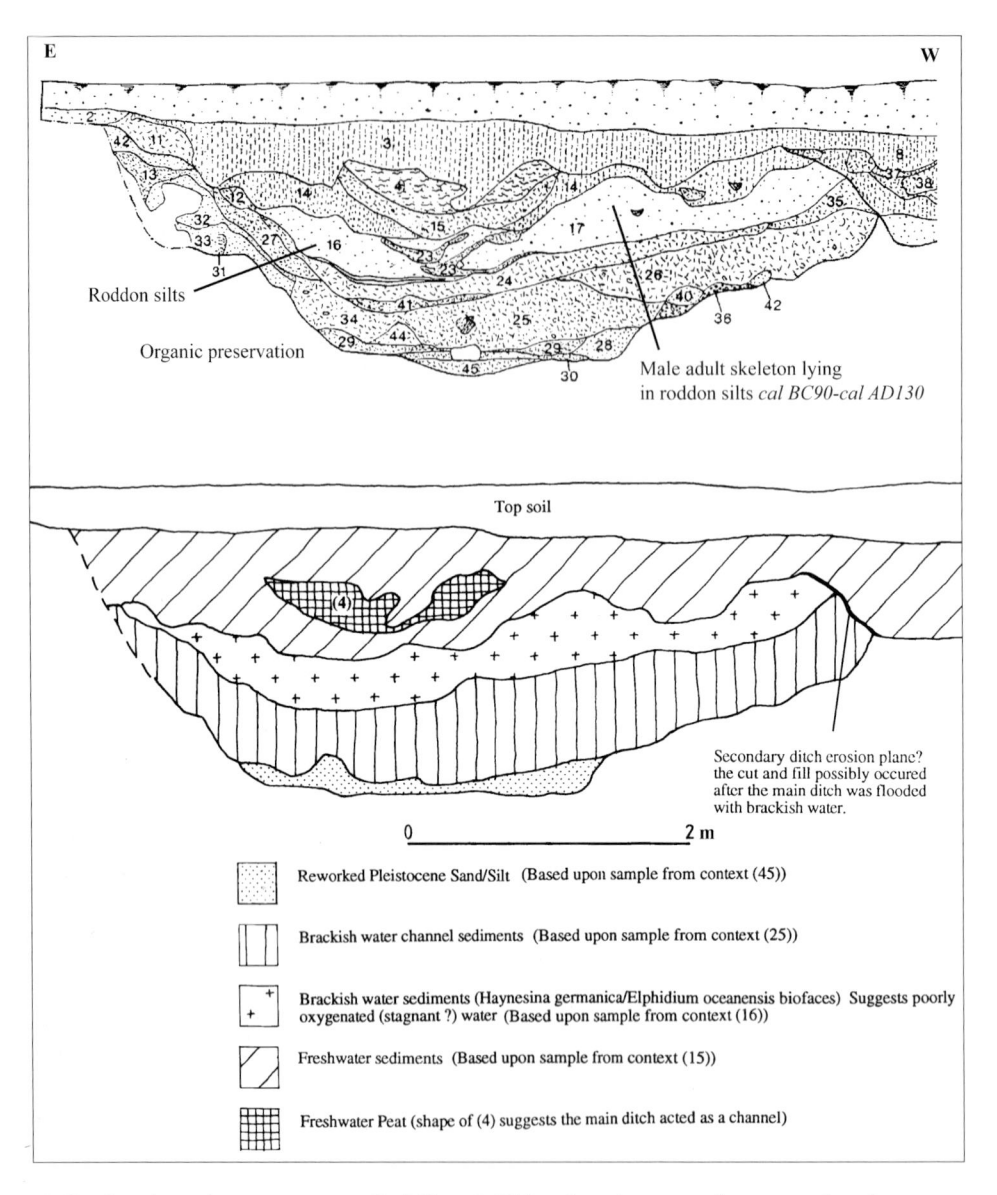

30 Section through western outer ditch Trench XV and environmental sequence based on the evidence of foraminifera. ©*Archaeological Field Unit Cambridgeshire County Council and Mike Godwin*

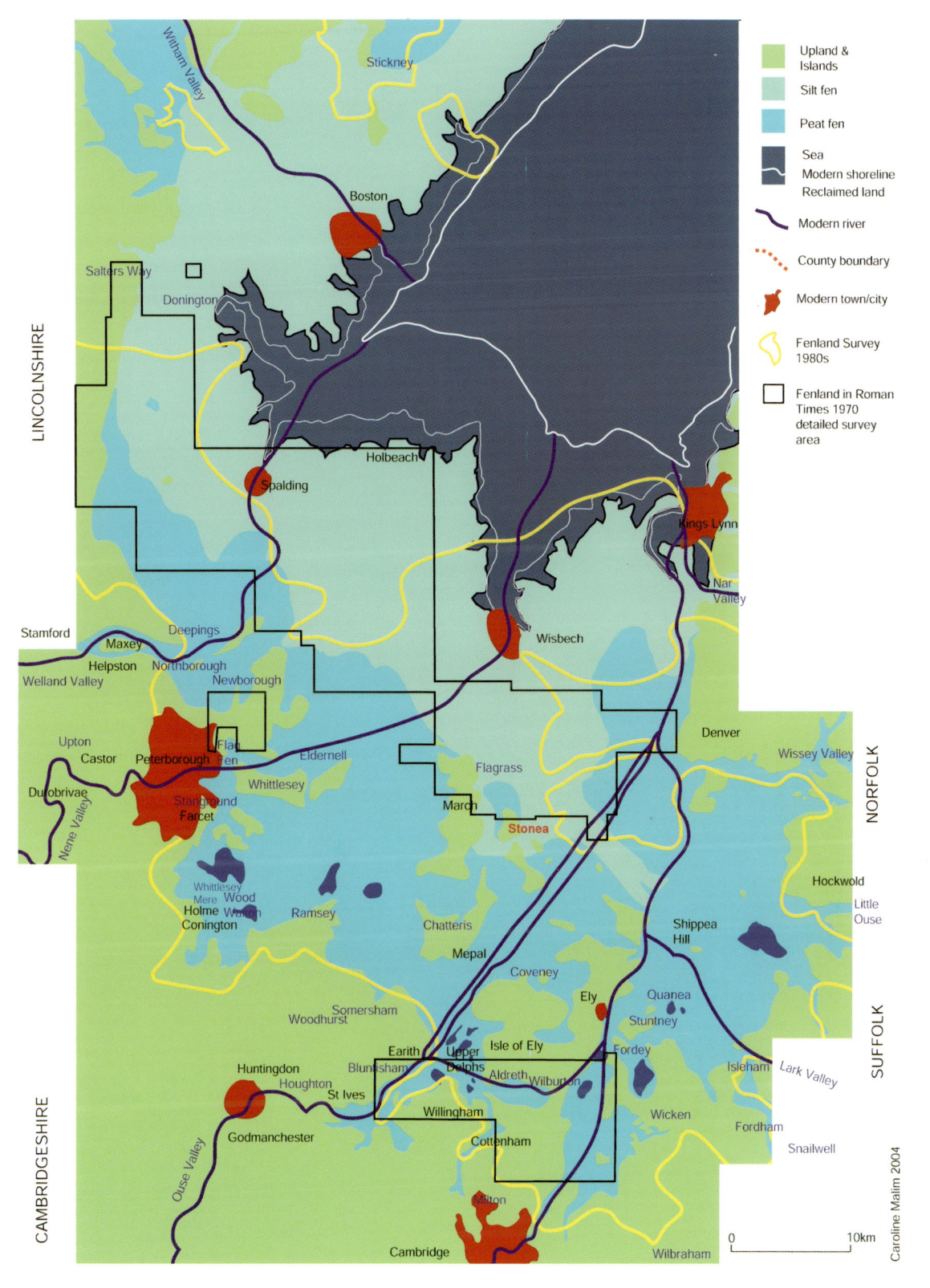

1 A map of the Fenland area with modern rivers and towns, place names mentioned in Chapters 1 and 2. Place names for Chapter 3 are shown in blue. The areas subject to detailed survey by The Fenland in Roman Times, and the areas covered by the later Fenland Survey, are shown. © Caroline Malim

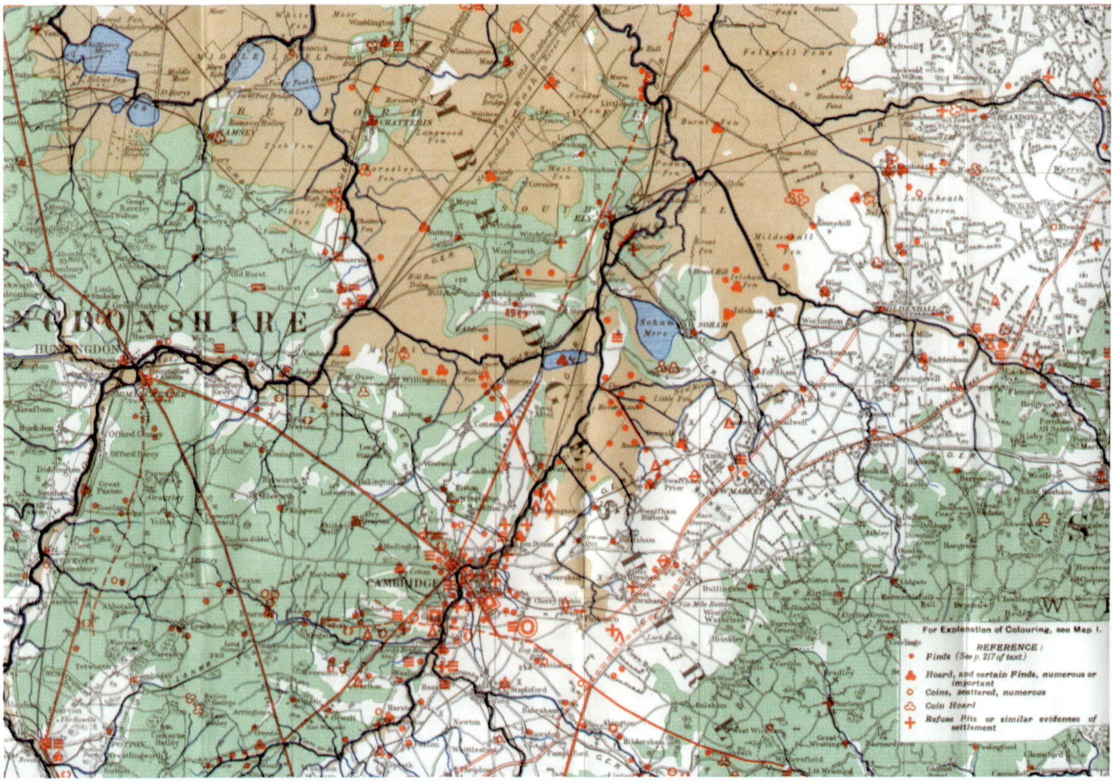

HUNTINGDON
CAMBRIDGE
NEWMARKET
SOHAM
Soham Mere
For Explanation of Colouring, see Map I.
REFERENCE:
Finds (See p. 217 of text.)
Hoard, and certain Finds, numerous or important
Coins, scattered, numerous
Coin Hoard
Refuse Pits or similar evidences of settlement

Opposite page:

2 Above Air photograph of Castor showing hill behind St Kyneburgha's church on which the Roman palace would have stood.
© Ben Robinson 29/6/02

3 Below The Archaeology of the Cambridge region: Roman period. *Map by Cyril Fox 1923*

4 Above Regiones Inundatae: J. Blaeu's map of the fens 1648 showing the fens prior to their drainage (note: north is to the right of the map). *Courtesy of the Cambridgeshire Collection, Cambridgeshire Libraries*

5 Right Fenland waterways. *Gordon Fowler 1946*

Map 6

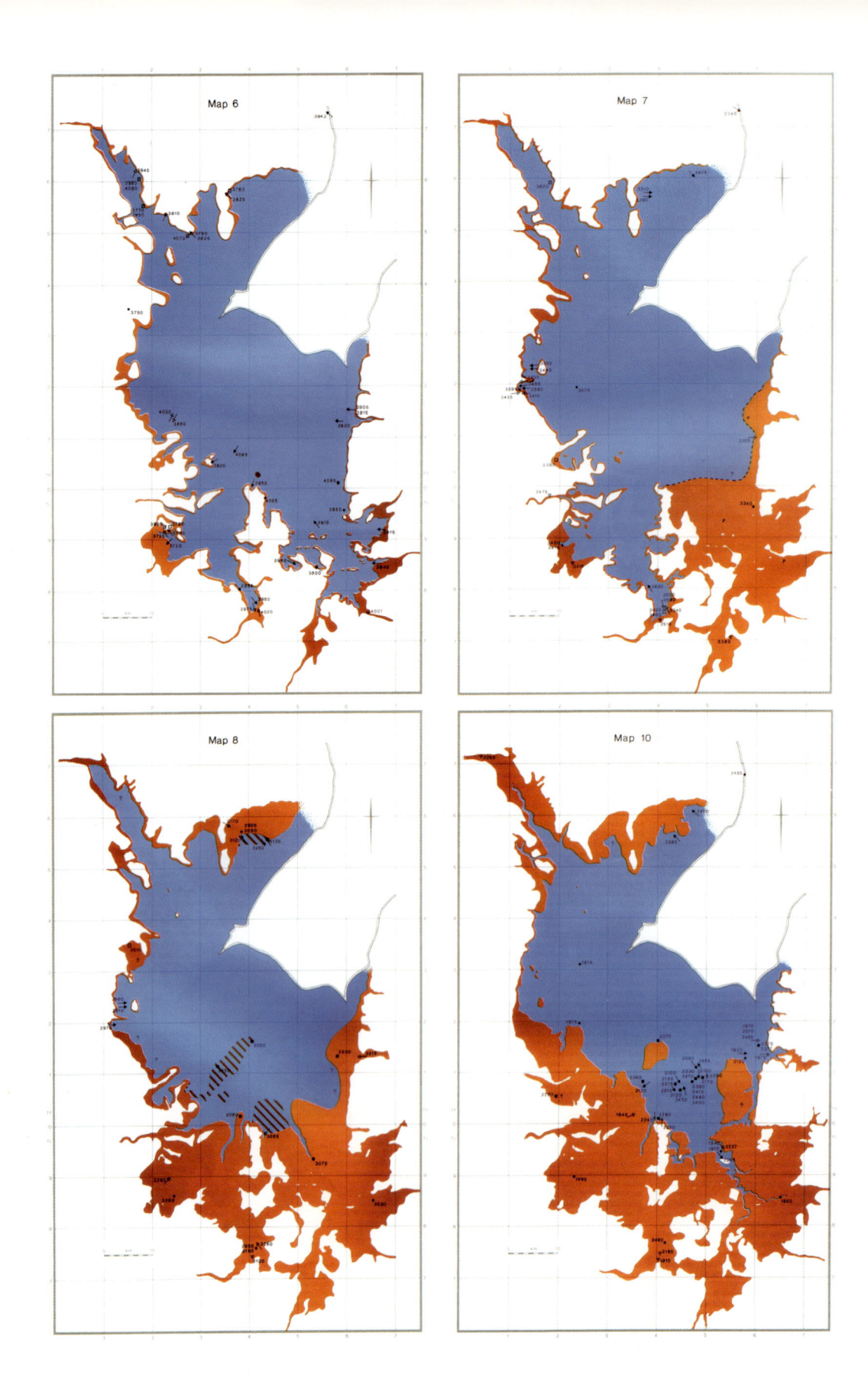

Map 7

Map 8

Map 10

6 Opposite The changing Fenland: four maps showing the growth of peat and marine incursions during the Late Neolithic/Early Bronze Age, Middle Bronze Age, Late Bronze Age and Early Roman period. *With kind permission of Martin Waller and English Heritage, from* East Anglian Archaeology 70

7 Above An aerial view of Grandford, March, with cropmarks showing a possible cursus, two Roman forts and the Fen Causeway bisecting them. © *Ben Robinson 18/7/99*

8 Right The political geography of the later Iron Age in the Fenland region (note: fort numbers relate to figure 16). © *Caroline Malim*

9 Above Aerial view of Stonea Camp in 1990 showing levelled defences as soilmarks, trial trenches and ring-ditch of barrow excavated in 1961 (top of picture). © *Ben Robinson*

10 Right A map of the Stonea area during the Roman period reconstructed from aerial photographs and Fenland Survey data. *With kind permission of Rog Palmer and English Heritage, from* East Anglian Archaeology 79

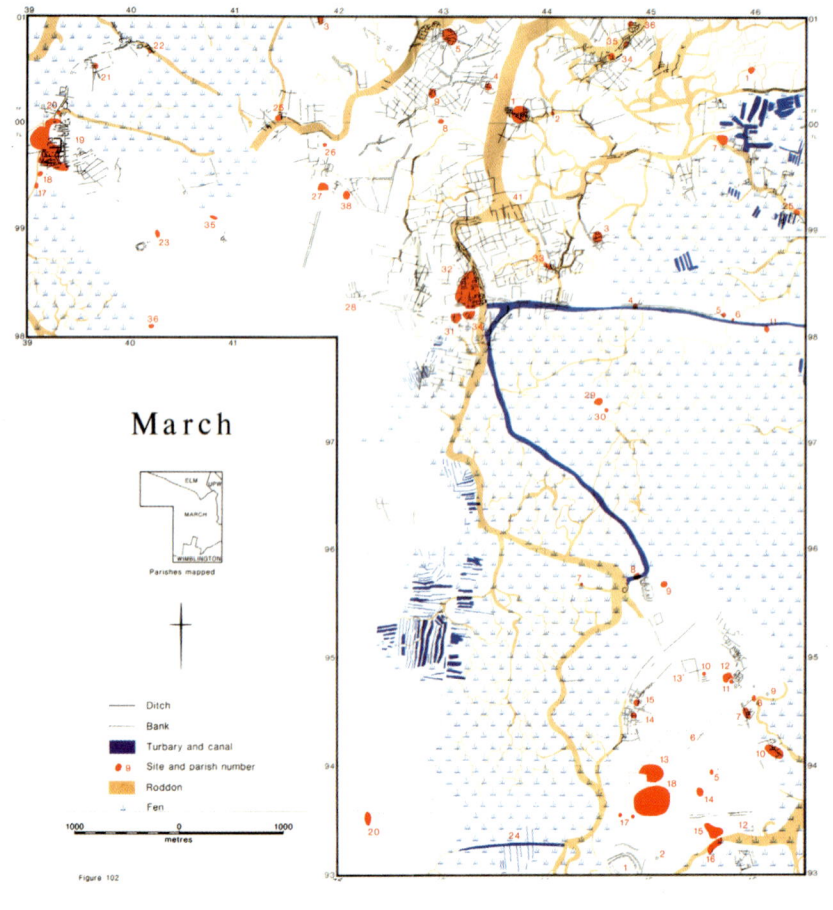

11 East-facing section through southern inner Camp ditch showing the sequence of fills in Trench A; the human bones and child's skull were found in the dark organic layers near the base. Author's collection

12 South-facing section through the western outer Camp ditch Trench XV; the human skeleton was found in the top of the yellow silts. Author's collection

13 North-facing section through western outer Camp ditch Trench XVI; note the many thin layers deposited by high-velocity water. *Author's collection*

14 Gold plaque from Stonea Temple. © *Ralph Jackson and The Trustees of the British Museum*

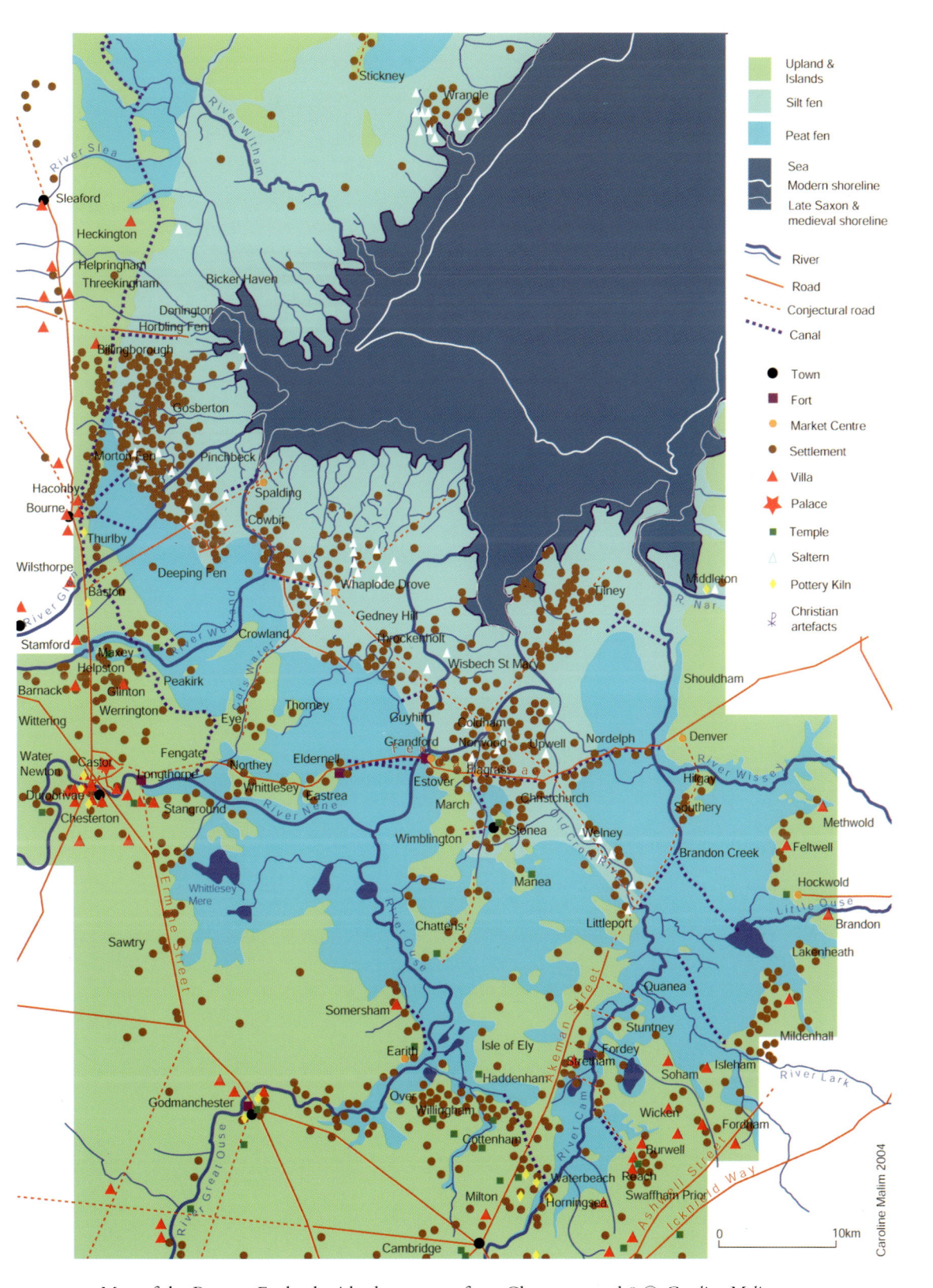

15 Map of the Roman Fenland with place names from Chapters 7 and 8. © *Caroline Malim*

16 A section through the Fen Causeway at Fengate, 1989. *Author's collection*

17 A section through the Fen Causeway at Downham West, 1993. *With kind permission of Mark Leah and Norfolk Archaeological Unit*

18 Above Remains of a Roman grain warehouse at Car Dyke, Waterbeach, 1997. © *Archaeological Field Unit Cambridgeshire County Council*

19 Right Reconstruction of the landscape and pottery kiln at Haddon during the first century AD. © *Jon Cane, with permission of Mark Hinman, from BAR 358*

20 Left A reconstruction of the landscape at Haddon during the second century AD. © *Jon Cane, with permission of Mark Hinman, from* BAR 358

21 Below A reconstruction of the landscape at Haddon during the third to fourth centuries AD. © *Jon Cane, with permission of Mark Hinman, from* BAR 358

22 Above Roman tile kiln during excavation at Wittering 1993. © *Ron Mckenna*

23 Right Mosaic from the Durobrivae workshop *c.*fourth century. *Drawn by E.T. Artis, from Durobrivae 1828; Peterborough Museum and Art Gallery*

24 Above Reach port, Roman canal, Devils Dyke and surrounding landscape (looking south towards Swaffham Prior Temple). © *Ben Robinson 22/8/95*

25 Left An aerial view of excavations at the Romano-Celtic temple at Swaffham Prior, 1993 (looking north; see also Figure *92*). © *Ben Robinson*

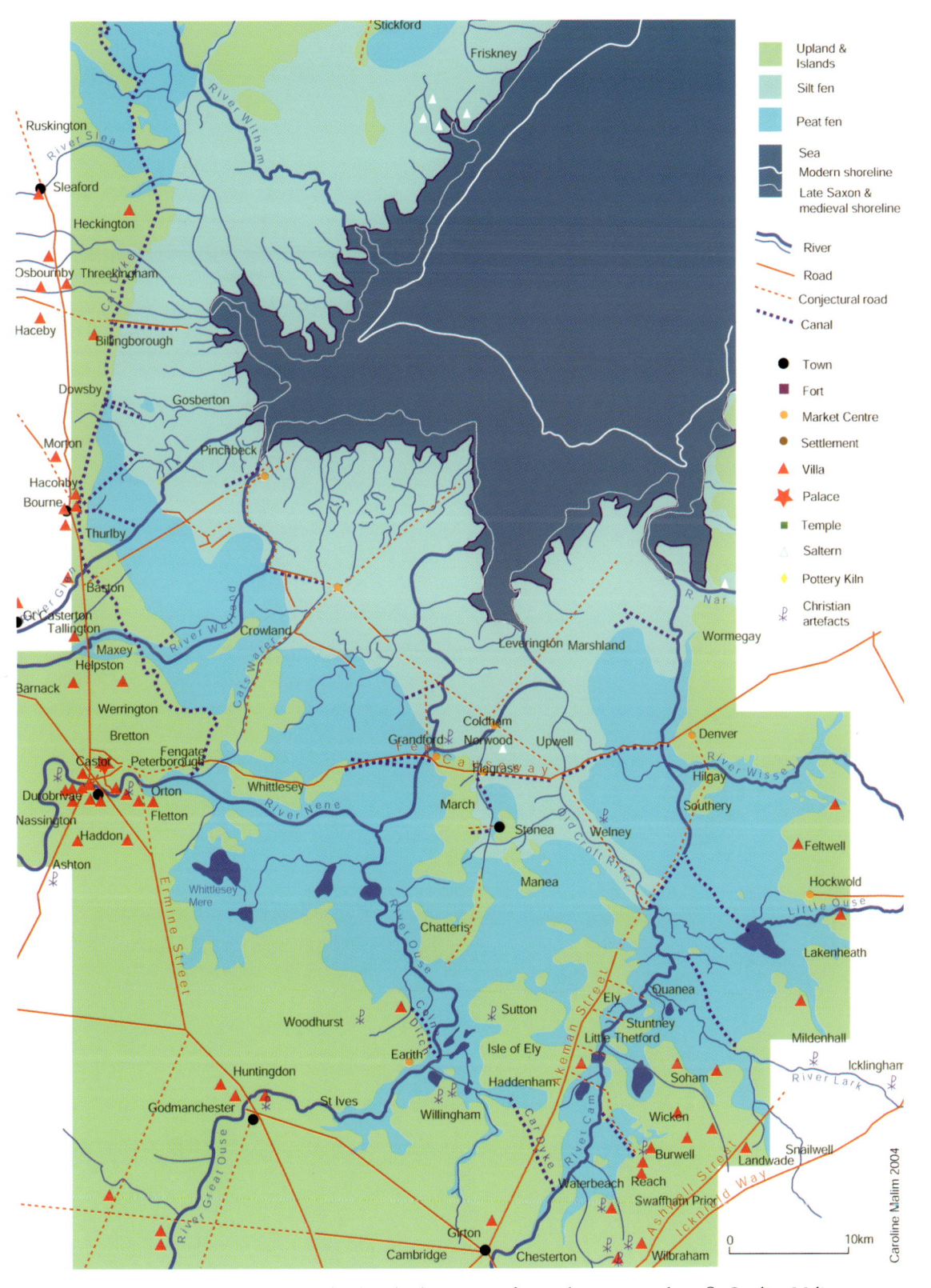

26 Map of the later Roman Fenland with place names from Chapters 9 and 10. © *Caroline Malim*

27 The Water Newton Christian altar set. © *The Trustees of the British Museum*

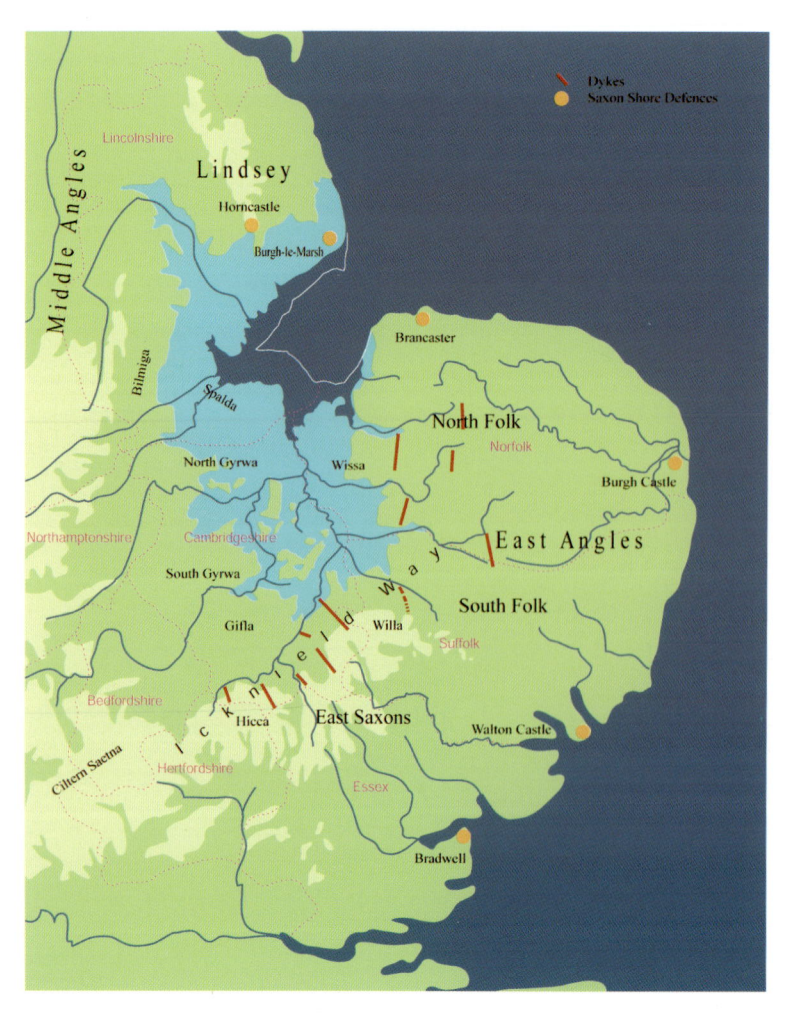

28 The political geography of the Early to Middle Anglo-Saxon period in the region, with Saxon Shore defences and the East Anglian dykes. *Drawn by Caroline Malim and Gill Reaney*

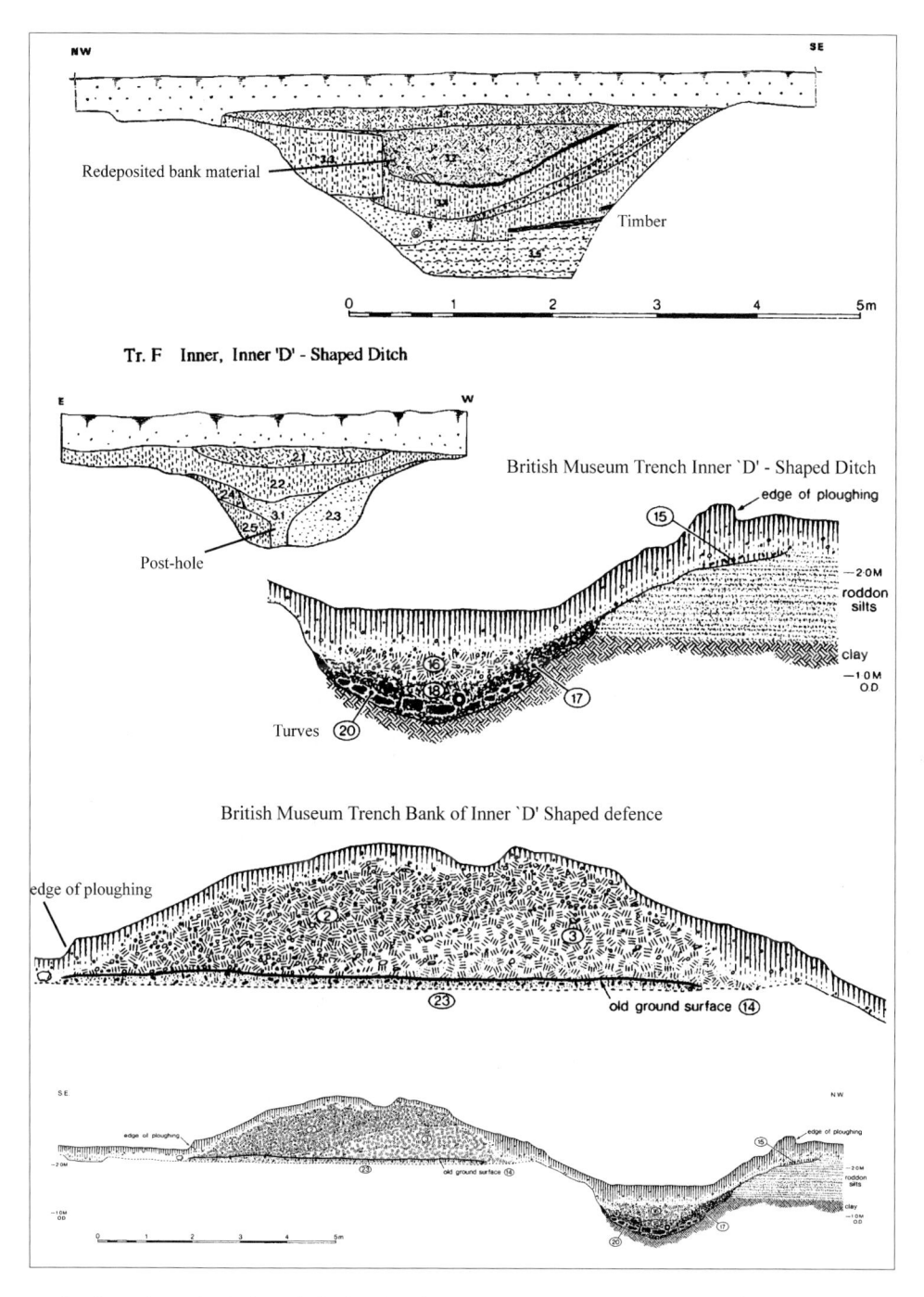

STONEA CAMP: AN IRON AGE FORT AND ITS POLITICAL LANDSCAPE

31 Sections through D-shaped ditches (see key to coneventions on *Figure 29*). ©*Archaeological Field Unit Cambridgeshire County Council and The Trustees of The British Museum*

65

STONEA AND THE ROMAN FENS

U-shaped profile section (Trench III), strongly resembling the results obtained by The British Museum.

The southern ditches were more complex and pose more problems with interpretation, partly because of their poor preservation. Due to having been cut through peat, significant erosion and slumping has occurred, with the loss of what original profile they would have had, and their profiles therefore were less regular (*32*). Enough evidence remains, however, to indicate that they probably conformed with the steeply sided, flat-based profiles revealed elsewhere in the outer ditch of the Camp. These ditches ran around the south-western flank and seem to have consisted of two discrete phases. At times they were found to intersect and form one elongated ditch (Trench G), but in other parts they form two distinct ditches separated by a bank (e.g. Trenches A, B and VI). The outer of

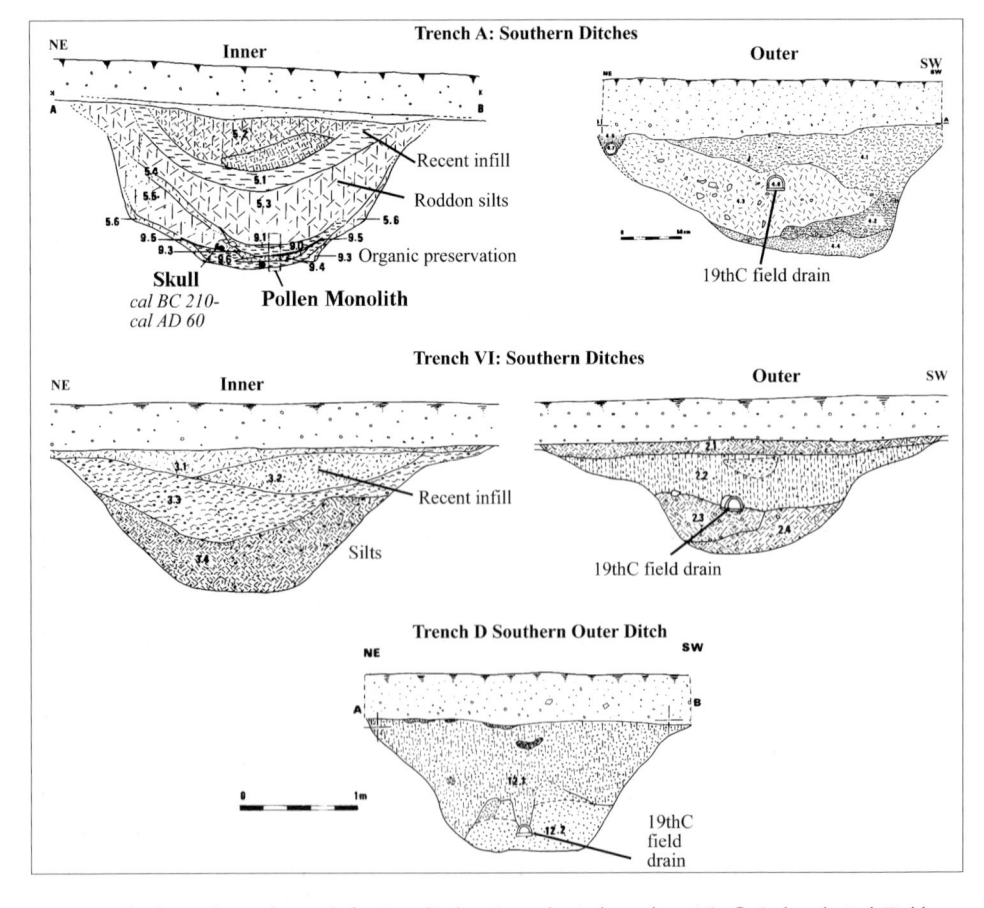

32 Sections through southern defensive ditches (see also *colour plate 11*). ©*Archaeological Field Unit Cambridgeshire County Council*

these two ditches (Trench D) (*32*) formed part of a continuous circuit with the Camp's outer ditch, whilst the other ditch (Trenches C and E) formed an inner enclosure which predated the double D-shaped defences that abut the outer ditch (Trench XX) (*28*). These ditches would always have been waterlogged and indeed most of the other ditches periodically also held water. The ditches survive to about 1.2m deep but their original depth would have been greater prior to the dessication and shrinkage of the fen peat. Generally the base of the ditches was around 1m wide, and the width at the present surface is approximately 3m.

Only one entranceway was known prior to the 1990-92 seasons of investigation. This was on the north-western edge of the Camp and had been identified originally as a gap in the earthworks, and as a gap in the cropmarks after the earthworks along this section had been levelled. Other gaps or depressions in the earthworks also existed but had been attributed to post-medieval usage of the site. In 1992 the eastern half of the north-western entranceway was excavated and we expected to find evidence for a complex timber structure and highly defended gateway (Trench XIII). In the event, although there was plenty of geological activity in the form of solifluxion features, almost nothing was found that could safely be assigned of archaeological interest. In my imagination we could perhaps trace the incomplete line of a bank at one point, but there was little to substantiate this wishful thinking!

The excavations revealed, however, that other entrances formed by causeways between sections of the ditches on the inner D-shaped circuit originally existed (near Trenches I and II). Previously these features had been thought of as nothing more than farm tracks which had involved infilling of the ditch at their crossing point.

EVIDENCE FROM THE EXCAVATIONS

Important though their design is, it is the deposits that filled the ditches and what they had, or had not, enclosed, that tells the real history at Stonea. The infill of the ditches has developed over two millennia and, although the latest episode for many had been the bulldozing of the banks into the ditches (*33*), beneath this plug lay a rich sequence of soil deposition which extended back from post-medieval to pre-Roman times. Many of the infill deposits were composed of dark, organic-rich peaty soils, with silty-clay layers, and waterlogging in the base of the southern and western ditches (*30, colour plates 11-13*). These contained a wealth of evidence on the changing environment over the centuries as the anaerobic, waterlogged conditions in the basal ditch fills, sealed by highly compacted silty-clay layers above, had prevented the normal agents of decay from destroying the organic remains. The preservation of insects, pollen, seeds, twigs and leaves

33 Excavation through defensive ditch showing Iron Age deposits at base, gradual accumulation above, and inverted dome of clay and gravel from the bulldozed bank which was pushed in to fill the ditch c.1964. Author's collection © Archaeological Field Unit Cambridgeshire County Council

was very good, and even some timbers had survived in places. Molluscs and bone had also survived well, and this variety of material allowed us to submit a number of samples from critical contexts for radiocarbon determination which, in combination with the stratigraphic analysis of the ditch fill sequences, has established a series of dates that would otherwise have been impossible given the paucity of artefactual recovery during the excavations.

In contrast to the relatively slow-moving water-filled southern ditches, on the western side high-velocity water flow through the ditch was detected where a complex of sandy layers had been deposited at the south-western curve of the defences (Trench XVI: *29, colour plate 13*). Further north along this same ditch the outer side had collapsed and a large influx of roddon silts was evident in the section cut across the ditch (Trench XV: *30, colour plate 11*). These derived from the adjacent contemporary watercourse running down the western side of the island, and foraminifera show that this water was brackish. Although it is possible that this flooding had been caused deliberately to slight the defences, there are easier ways than this to reduce the height of the bank and ditch; for example by shovelling part of the rampart into the ditch. It is more likely, therefore, that the unstable nature of the geology at the edge of the island had contributed to a natural fault, such as the effect that the edge of a solifluxion polygon would have had if the ditch had been excavated through it, and that the side of the ditch had given way of its own accord, swamping the ditch with brackish floodwater from the roddon. Whatever the cause of this large-scale and probably rapid deposition, in the top of this layer a skeleton was found.

HUMAN REMAINS

This find was a complete surprise and by good fortune the whole body was found within the space of the trench that we excavated across the ditch (*34*). The skeleton was of a man, aged about 25-35, who displayed no signs of having had a violent death. No sign of a grave-cut could be seen within the roddon silts, and

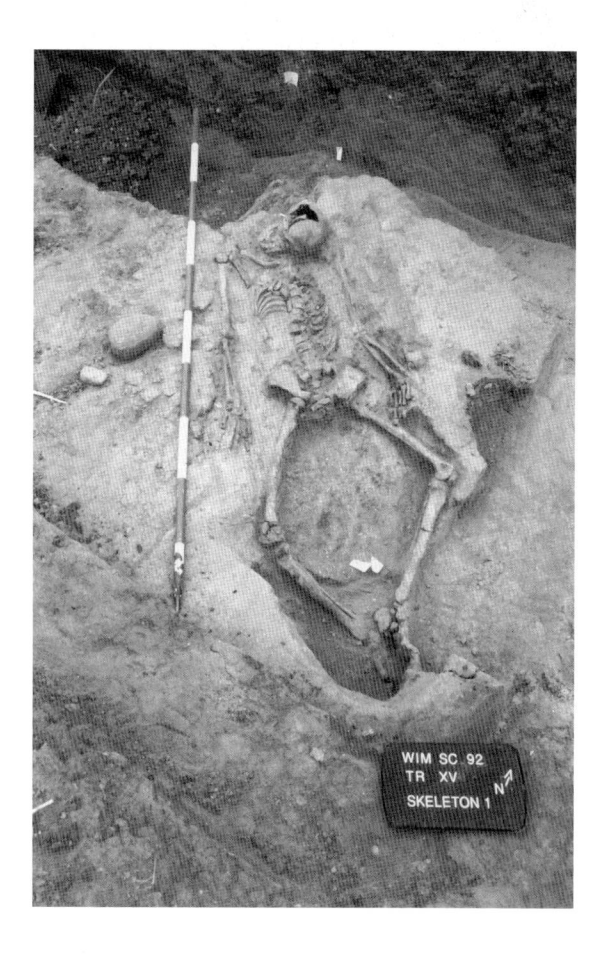

34 Skeleton of a man found in silts that form a distinct infill episode in the outer ditch ©*Archaeological Field Unit Cambridgeshire County Council*

the way in which he had been lying coupled with the apparent contemporanity of his burial with the wet silt deposits, strongly suggests that he was dumped into the wet ditch as a simple and effective way of disposing of the body (*30*). Such burials of later Roman date have been found in flood deposits elsewhere in the fens, for example at Grandford and Hockwold. There is little his bones have been able to tell us about how he came to die or be buried in the ditch, but from studying his skeleton it is possible to say he was around 5ft 10in (1.78m) tall and that he had strongly developed muscular markings on the forearm. In childhood he underwent a period of severe malnutrition or severe fever, as his teeth revealed a condition known as hypoplasia. Samples from this skeleton were sent for radiocarbon dating and they provide a broad period over two centuries when the man might have lived, ranging from the first century BC through the first century AD (cal BC 97–cal AD 133).

Other human remains were also found in one of the southern ditches (Trench A inner ditch: *35*). In this case we retrieved parts of three bodies but no complete skeleton. Unlike the man from the western ditch, these other bones all came from the base of the ditch, below the level of any brackish water flooding (*32*, *colour plate 11*). They were found in a matrix of rich organic mud which included

35 Human bones found in basal deposits of southern inner ditch. ©*Archaeological Field Unit Cambridgeshire County Council*

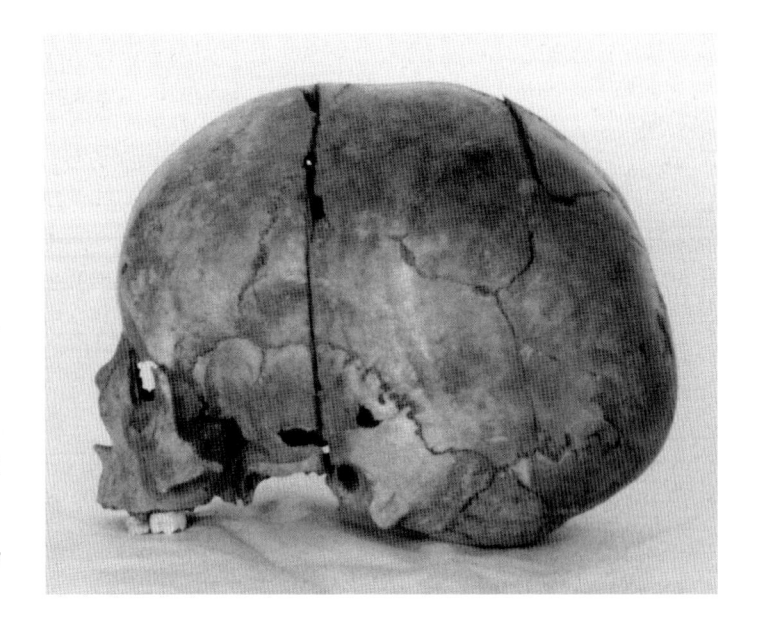

36 Skull of young child with two sword cuts. ©*Archaeological Field Unit Cambridgeshire County Council*

twigs and leaves and therefore a series of radiocarbon dates could be taken, one from the bone itself and two from associated leaves which can provide far finer samples than that achieved by bone, especially disarticulated bone. The dates were fairly broad but consistent, ranging from the fourth century BC to the first century AD (*38* and special feature on radiocarbon dating). Bones from three people were found, represented by ribs and parts of the left arm of an adult and two children of three and four years of age, the younger one with only arm bones and a fragment of shoulder blade being found. It was the skeleton of the four-year-old, however, that was the most significant. Bones from the right and left arms, upper back and neck, and parts of the upper left leg and pelvis were found, together with the skull. This was well preserved, although lacking the mandible, and the condition of the teeth and fusing of the skull bones allowed a close estimate of age. Into the top of the skull two cuts were visible which, under examination by a scanning electron microscope, showed clear evidence for them to have come from blows delivered by a sharp-edged weapon such as a sword (*36* and *37*), which would undoubtedly have killed this child if it had been alive when the wounds were made.

In contrast to these finds of human remains within the ditch fills, animal bone, which is normally found as abundant waste around settlements, was very sparse (see *Table 1*). Such an imbalance between the amounts of human and animal bone is of considerable significance in the interpretation placed upon Stonea Camp and the events that occurred there.

STONEA AND THE ROMAN FENS

TRENCH	CONTEXT	DITCH	PHASE	SPECIES	BONE ELEMENT
A	5.1	S Inner	3	Sheep/Goat	Mandible
				Sheep/Goat	Molar (x3)
A	5.5	S Inner	3	Human	Child of 4 years; Skull *without mandible, Almost complete right* arm, Left humerus, *portions of the upper* neck, Shoulder girdle, *left femur and associated portions of* innominate bone, a few hand bones.
				Human	Adult; Portions of left ulna, Ribs (3), *Few* hand bones.
				Human	Young Child (under 4); Left radius, Right radius, Ulna, Hand bone (1), Fragment of Clavicle
C	3.2	S Inner	3	Cattle	Radius
				Cattle sized	Tibia
D	12.1	S Outer	1	Cattle	Molar (worn)
I	?	N Outer	1	Cattle sized	Femur
II	2.3	N Outer	1	Unid. Bird	Radius
X	?	E Outer	1	Crow	Tib.-tarsal
X	?	E Outer	1	Dog	Tibia
X	4.3	E Outer	1	Cattle sized	Long Bone frag.
				Sheep/Goat	Vert. Frag.
X	4.2	E Outer	1	Sheep/Goat	Premolar (x2)
XIII	2.1	N Outer	1	Domestic fowl	Coracoid (2), Scapular (2), Humerus (2), Ulna (2), Radius (3), Carpo-Metac. (2), Femur (2), Tib.-tarsus (5), Tarso-metat. (5), Skull, Synacrum/pelvis, Sternum (2), Wishbone, Vert. (9), Pygostyle, Phalanx
XIII	2.2	W Outer	1	Cattle	Scapular
				Sheep/Goat	Pelvis, Mandible
XIII	2.3	W Outer	1	Cattle sized	Vertebra
				Cattle	Metapodial, Mandible, Metac.
XV	4	W Outer	1	Cattle	Phal.prima, Pre-molar
				S/G sized	Femur
XV	25	W Outer	1	S/G sized	Long Bone frag.
XV	3	W Outer	1	S/G sized	Vertebra
XV	17	W Outer	1		
XV	8	W Outer	1	Human	Male Adult of 25-35 years; Skeleton (95% complete)
				Sheep/Goat	Humerus
XV	4	W Outer	1	Cattle	Molar
XV	15	S Outer	1	Cattle	Metapodial
XVI	4.13	W Outer	1	Pig	Canine
XVI	4.2	W Outer	1	Cattle sized	Long Bone frag.
				Human	?Ulna frag.
XVI	3.2	W Outer	1	S/G sized	Long Bone frag.
XVI	2/19	W Outer	1	Small mammal	Long Bone frag.
XVII	1	N/A	N/A	Cattle	Molar
XXII	2	W Outer	1	Domestic fowl	Tarso-metat
XXII	3/3.1	W Outer	1	Cattle sized	Long Bone frag.

Table 1: Human and animal bone recovered from excavation 1990-92 (rabbit bone has been exclueded as intrusive)

ENVIRONMENT AND SURVIVING TIMBER ARTEFACTS

From the southern and western ditches rich organic deposits and waterlogging had resulted in good preservative conditions not only for molluscs and insects but also for pollen, seeds and other remains of ancient vegetation. From this evidence a picture of the changing environment contemporary with the lifespan of the Camp has been made possible.

The earliest deposits that survive are those within the basal fills and these show that the landscape into which Stonea Camp was built was one of dense woodland dominated by oak, but also containing birch, hazel, sloe, thorn and alder, and that the southern ditch was a water-filled feature (*32, colour plate 11*). Other species represented included bramble, fat hen, thistle, gypsywort, dock and woody nightshade, as well as some sedge, beetles and waterfleas.

As time progressed the surrounding conditions became more open, revealed by pollen of weeds and grass, although oak still dominated the tree pollen record. The finding of ivy pollen, which needs tall stands (such as oak trees) and unshaded conditions to flower, adds to the picture of open woodland. Aquatic species such as sedges, duckweed, pondweed, hemp and meadowsweet were found to be more common, however, perhaps indicating an increasingly wet environment, and a particular type of snail (*Anisus leucostoma*) which is normally found in muddy fresh water was also evident. Evidence showed that the ditch must have had sufficient depth of water to support small fish such as stickleback,

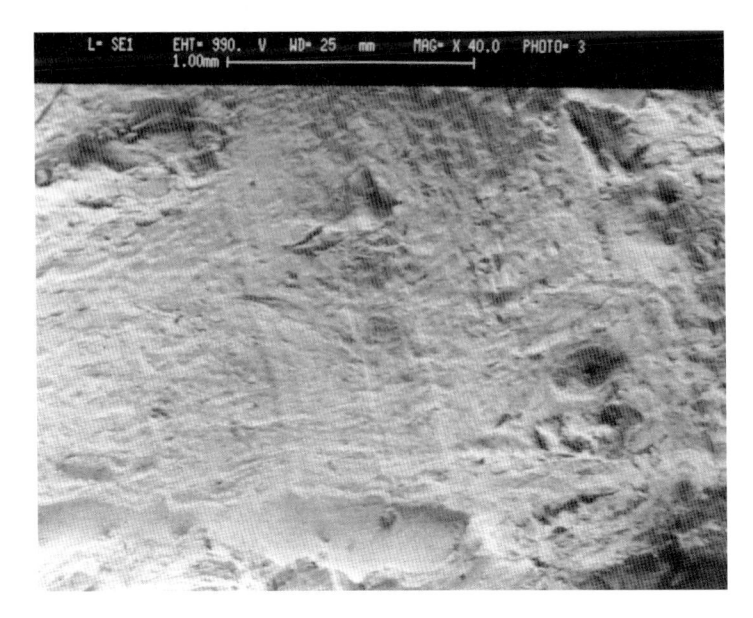

37 Scanning-electron micro-photograph of cranium showing striations caused by sword cut. ©Archaeological Field Unit Cambridgeshire County Council

and it was into these waterlogged deposits that human bodies (or disarticulated skeletons) had been dumped, including the child's skull with the sword-cuts.

Above these layers brackish-water flooding is represented by saltwater foraminfera and halophytic plants found within the kind of finely laminated silty-clay sedimentation indicative of tidal creek activity (probably roddon-derived material (*30* and *32*)). At the south-western corner of the Camp a series of interleaved layers (Trench XVI: *29, colour plate 13*) showed high-velocity water movement depositing sands, separated by lenses of silty-clay. The species recovered from these layers show alternating fresh and brackish water conditions, and the mollusc assemblage was dominated by the gastropod *Hydrobia ventrosa* which is found in estuarine conditions.

The layers sealing the brackish flooding episodes consisted of a clayey loam with well-preserved pollen including species representative of weedy, possibly grazed, grassland, with mixed woodland and scrub. Increased salinity from the previous period might have contributed to less tree growth within the lower-lying wetter parts of the site, rather than deliberate tree clearance but, whatever the reason, these later Iron Age and Roman deposits show a more open landscape. Evidence for animal trampling and cessy deposits was found but, as with earlier deposits, no cereals were present.

This sequence is unusual for the period, which is usually one that shows a largely tree-cleared landscape with mixed farming at other sites in East Anglia.

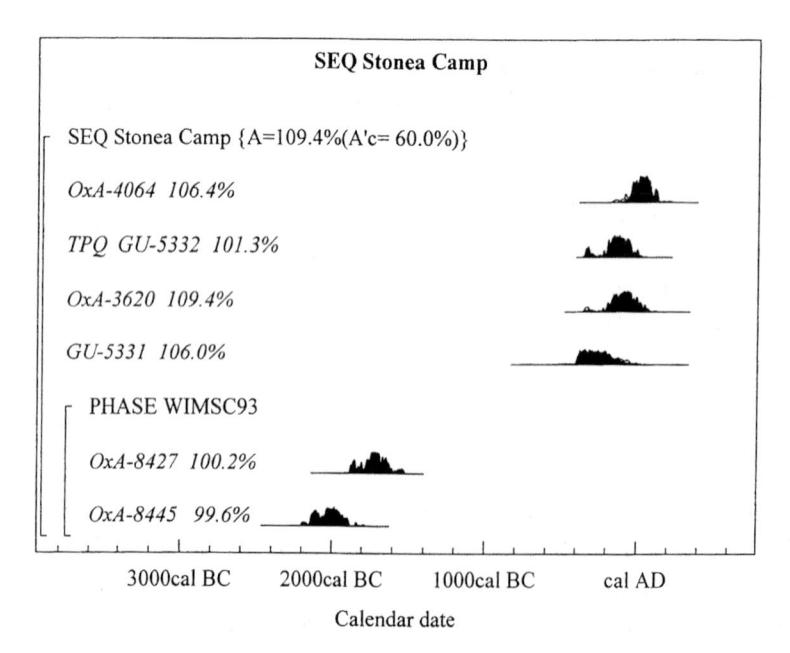

38 Chart of C14 dates showing period of activity associated with human remains, and earlier peat growth. With kind permission of Alex Bayliss and English Heritage

At Stonea, woodland, especially oak, predominated and there is no evidence at all for cereal cultivation. Only in its later history do we see some environmental evidence for animal husbandry associated with the site in the form of grazed grassland, but small particles of charcoal found throughout the sequence, and the deposition of human remains within the basal fills, clearly demonstrate considerable human activity other than that of farming.

Timber fragments also survived and have been examined, although none has managed to provide absolute dates by means of dendrochronology. Two samples had over 50 rings and were submitted for measurement and analysis; unfortunately the paucity of comparative samples in the tree-ring sequence for this period of prehistory meant that no matches could be found.

The tree species identified from the timber fragments included oak, ash and hazel, which provided conflicting evidence as to whether they derived from managed or unmanaged woodland. Recent dessication had meant that there had been shrinkage and loss of surfaces, but amongst the larger oak timbers some evidence for woodworking had survived. These timbers were found in the basal fills of the outer western ditch (Trench XIII) and were radially cleft pieces of straight-grained oak from trunks that had been split into eighths. Their growth rings were 2-3mm – indicative of fast growth – and this evidence, together with the fact that they came from trees that were less than 70 years old at felling, strongly suggests that they were products of managed woodland. They were approximately 200mm wide, pointed by means of a single facet on one side, and the survival of sapwood suggests that these timbers were found in, or very close to, their original locations. They were good-quality, valuable pieces of timber and in all likelihood represent piles or stakes for a revetment.

A hazel rod that was found in the base of the western outer ditch (Trench XVI) had had three facets removed by a single tool to form a pointed stake. The rod appears to have come from a coppiced tree but other bits of roundwood found in the outer ditch were identified as ash, with narrow growth rings less than 1mm, indicating the possibility of dense, unmanaged woodland – a situation similarly seen in another (unworked) piece of slow-growing oak found from the base of the ditch (Trenches XIII and XV).

POTTERY

Pottery was collected from unstratified contexts during fieldwalking from 1959-61 and in connection with the 1980 and 1990 excavations, and also secondly from *in situ* deposits revealed through trial trenching from 1990-92. The former method of recovery led to the discovery before 1980 of two general concentrations within the inner circuit of the Camp (see *28*) which in broad terms could be interpreted as representing an episode of occupation. Subsequent excavation of these areas (Trenches XVII and XXI), however, showed no features (such as post-holes for timber buildings) cut into the subsurface. The pottery retrieved from the other excavation trenches probably derived from the same source as that found in fieldwalking, but the importance of this assemblage is in the fact that it all dates to the Conquest period. The pottery found in the Iron Age and early Roman fills was clearly the same as that found in the topsoil from fieldwalking, reasonably closely dated to the period AD 40-60. Pottery is, however, noticeably absent from the location of a circular structure (probably of stake and wattle construction) which was excavated in 1992 to assess whether there was evidence for settlement within the Camp, and this has therefore been interpreted instead as an earlier monument. The only earlier ceramics were two sherds of Neolithic pottery (Ebbsfleet and Mortlake wares) which were found in a deposit of disturbed bank material within Trench F, 60m to the east of this circular structure.

In general the pottery was a quartz-gritted, brownish ware with a dark grey core and consisted primarily of jars for storage and cooking, but also included a dish that was an imitation of a Gallo-Roman platter. The assemblages were examined by Fiona Cameron (1980s) and Lindsay Rollo (1990s). In addition, some grog-tempered ware was also found, which might suggest a slightly earlier period. Small quantities of pot were recovered during site visits between 1959 and 1961 including five pre-Flavian Samian sherds, but they were only located within the area of the inner defences, and seemed to concentrate at the south-western side of the Camp. Only 15 coarseware sherds were found in fieldwalking in 1980, and one in excavation, but during the 1990-92 seasons a further 68 sherds in total were recovered, the majority of which again came from the ploughsoil found during fieldwalking, but with five from stratified contexts. This unexceptional assemblage would be in keeping with the vessels required for storage and cooking of a small military detachment stationed at the Camp in the immediate post-Conquest period.

These finds strongly suggest that Stonea Camp had no permanent settlement during the Iron Age, but that a short-lived spell of occupation occurred during the middle of the first century AD, as is also illustrated by the metal finds. The form and quality of the pottery in general suggest local manufacture for mundane activity connected with the storage and preparation of food. There is a hint, however, that this period of occupation also included fine tablewares, because, in addition to the copy of a Gallo-Roman platter, two sherds of early Samian were found, and a further five had been found previously during the Potter brothers' 1959 trial pit, located within the infill of the inner D-shaped ditch.

STONEA CAMP: AN IRON AGE FORT AND ITS POLITICAL LANDSCAPE

39 Air photograph of Stonea Camp before restoration; note that the ploughed-out bank shows as a white line along the southern side (i.e. the bottom of the photograph) and proves that the inner circuit post-dates the outer defensive circuit (see phasing). © Derek Edwards and Norfolk Museums Service

METALWORK

Although a small assemblage of metal artefacts and coins has been more or less securely associated with Stonea Camp, a great many more are suspected of having been found there through illicit metal-detecting over the years. The known artefacts are all of copper-alloy and include part of a bracelet, a tankard handle (see *58*) and 13 brooches (*40*). The dates assigned to all of these fit comfortably within the first century AD, and the brooches refine the date to a tight range from approximately AD 43-60.

A number of coin finds have been identified also as coming from the Camp, and very many more, including three hoards, have been attributed to it. Almost all of these came from illegal metal-detecting and it is difficult to piece together any real meaning from these given the unreliability of their general provenance,

STONEA AND THE ROMAN FENS

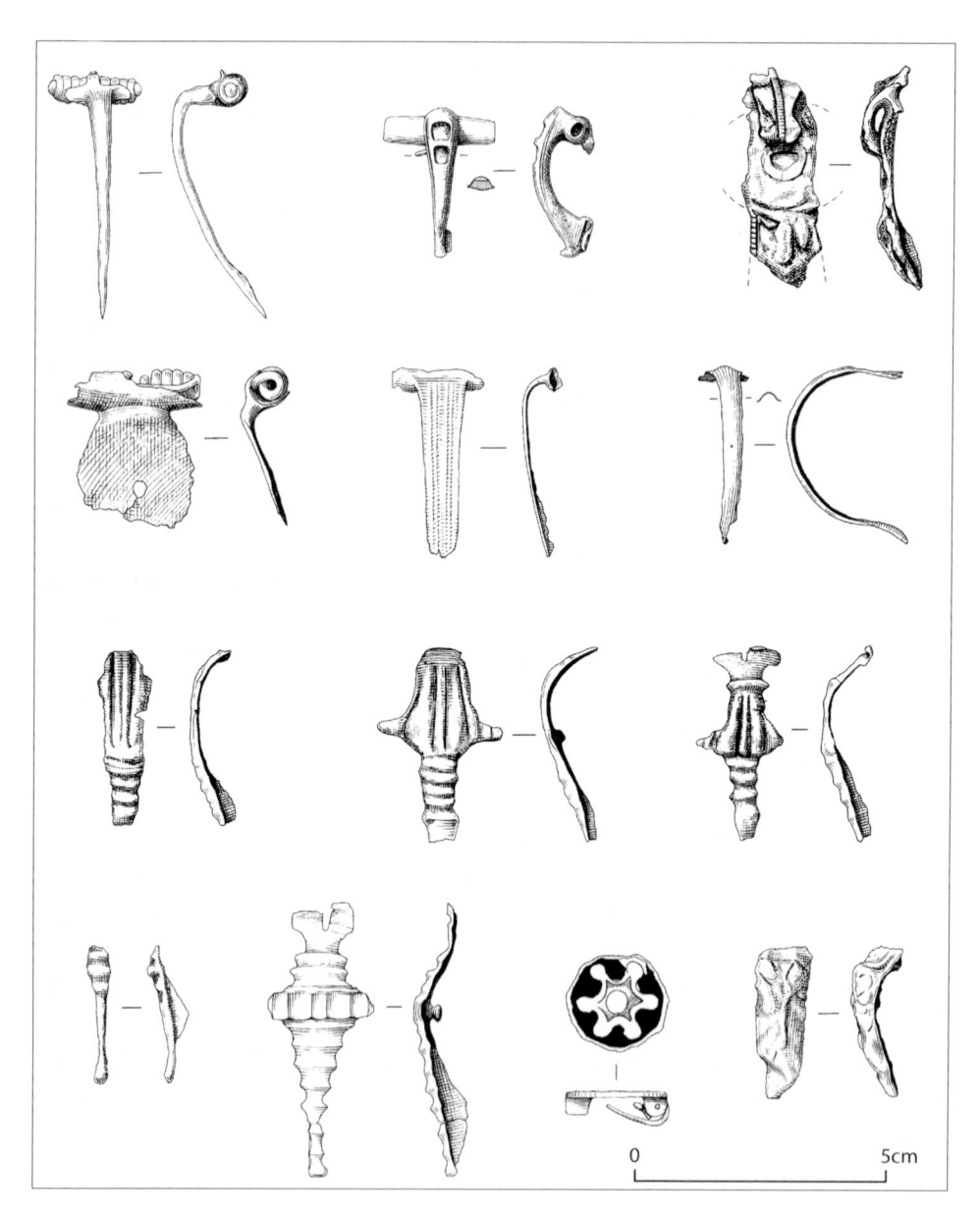

40 Brooches from Stonea Camp, mid-first century AD; Colchester, Aucissa and Hod Hill types, probably of military origin (note: the round plate brooch is an exception dating to the second to third centuries AD). © *Trustees of the British Museum*

let alone specific context. An assemblage of Iron Age coins was also recovered from the Grange and the nature of these (fragmentary, forgeries and plated issues, covering a variety of dates and including coins from other tribes) reflect their loss from settlement activity rather than deposition as a hoard.

The coins that can be ascribed to the Camp with reasonable certainty were ones recovered by the farmer, Mr G.W. Cross, from a man he caught stealing from the site. There were 21 coins, of which three date to the Conquest and its immediate aftermath (issues of Gaius and Claudius). Within this collection there is then a period which is not represented until Hadrianic times when coins from AD 118 occur. The majority of the coins, however, are late Roman issues and date to the later third century (10 coins between AD 259-275 and one for the following two decades), with a small group occurring again in the fourth century between AD 330-378. This pattern of loss conforms to that from the area of the Roman town.

Three hoards and many individual coins possibly also originated from the Camp. These include a hoard of gold Cunobelin staters, and hoards of silver coins from both Corieltauvi and Iceni issues. Base coins such as *potins* and *denarii* have also been attributed to the Camp, as well as a further hoard of 25 third-century coins (AD 259-268) currently in Wisbech Museum. A hoard from the nineteenth century, however, which is reported as having come from Stonea Camp, has been discounted by recent research. It was reputed to have been found in the dyke on the southern edge of the modern fields which subdivided the Camp.

If any of these hoards really derive from the Camp or surrounding area they demonstrate two important points: firstly, a date range of activity which includes the early first century AD, and, secondly, that the nature of this activity was markedly different from the majority of coin hoards (and individual loss) from this early period found elsewhere in the area. The Camp would appear to have acted as some kind of special focus which, unusually within Icenian territory, attracted deposition of coins from diverse tribal groups. Later hoards can often be attributed to political events surrounding the Icenian revolt of AD 60-61. These earlier hoards are unlikely to have occurred in tandem with domestic occupation at the Camp and we must, therefore, look for other significance in the practice of their deposition.

DATING AND PHASING

Four samples from the basal fills of the southern and western ditches were submitted for radiocarbon dating. These samples included two from human bone (one from the adult buried near the top of the sequence and the other from the bones near the base of the ditch) and two samples from oak leaves and twigs from the same layer as the lower human bones were found. The range of dates provided by analysis of these samples reveals a far longer and more complicated pattern than had been previously believed, stretching over perhaps as long as 500 years (see special feature 'Radiocarbon Dating'). The precision of radiocarbon dating during the Iron Age is not very accurate as the calibration methods used to help convert the results to actual dates BC or AD rely on dendrochronology and – as we have already seen above with the timber samples submitted for tree-ring dating – the master curve of comparative samples is poor during this period. The dates themselves, therefore, give wide bands, but by use of stratigraphic data and mathematical modelling it is possible to refine individual dates when they form part of a sequence, as is the case at Stonea. The two human burials that were sampled have been given date ranges of cal 210 BC to cal AD 60 and cal 90 BC to cal AD 130. Although the overlap between these ranges could suggest that the bones were broadly contemporary, the ranges also reflect the stratigraphic evidence which shows a period of time elapsed between deposition of these human remains. The first sample came from disarticulated bones found in the basal fills of the southern ditch and was associated with the child's skull with sword cuts to it. We know that these burials were sealed by a deposit of brackish water and silty clays and that the other burial that we dated (the articulated adult male) came from the top of this deposit; therefore it was later. It seems very likely that all the burials come from the Late Iron Age, or earliest Roman times, and that there might be about a century between the time when these burials occurred; equally they could be much closer in time than that. The lower burial has some corroborative dating evidence provided by the oak detritus (leaves and twigs) from the surrounding matrix. Two samples were sent and these were given date ranges of cal 410-50 BC and cal 230 BC to cal AD 10. There is some 200 years' overlap between them and the logic of their mutual origin from the same muds that surrounded the human bone, and the fact that the samples came from leaves and twigs so would not have the breadth of age and associated error that a sample from timber would have, helps refine our estimation of the date to the second or first centuries BC – around 100 BC. This is in accordance with the dates from the bone itself, whereas the later burial is more likely to fall around the end of the first century BC or early first century AD (see 38).

How does this help us with understanding the complex phasing of the Camp? All four of the absolute dates come from what would appear to be the outer ditch circuit, and these dates give a sequence of at least two centuries during which the Camp was first constructed and then slowly accumulated deposits within its ditches. A sudden event involved the introduction of an extensive layer of sedimentation from brackish water, after which the landscape of the Camp was changed to one of grazed pastureland. Pre-dating this deposit, human bones were found to have been put into the ditch, and post-dating it a body was buried in the top of this sudden flooding episode, perhaps suggesting a burial tradition over a long period of time.

From the 1990-92 programme of investigations the latest phase in construction was shown to be the outer D-shaped enclosure which had ditches and banks that terminated a few metres short of the outer defensive ditch; exactly what would be expected if a bank had stood behind the outer ditch and the D-shaped ditch had been built to butt up against it. This D-shaped ditch and its inner twin cut across earlier ditches, one of which had been infilled in antiquity but shows on the surface as a depression and colour difference in the grass. A second bank and ditch physically cut by the inner D-shaped ditch survived as an earthwork until the 1960s, but this in turn had cut across the earlier infilled ditch. We therefore have at least three phases directly linked by stratigraphic means, plus the main outer defensive circuit which I would interpret as representing the first phase of the Camp. To complicate matters further, however, the southern ditches run together, possibly intersecting or crossing over along the middle part of their length. The Ordnance Survey plans of the earthworks in the 1920s (*28*), and the air photographs taken before they were levelled in the 1960s, show the outer southern ditch turning in to join with the inner one. This might suggest that there was an entranceway on this side. The best clue to phasing these two ditches, however, comes from a study of the air photographs after they had been levelled and ploughed. These show a continuous bank (seen as a white band in *39*) following the inner ditch and this evidence must demonstrate that the inner defence cut into, and was superimposed over, the outer bank, thus proving that it post-dated the outer defence. A comparison of the infill episodes between the inner and outer southern ditches (*32*) also helps corroborate this interpretation. Although the inner ditch conforms to the general pattern of the other Camp ditches, the outer southern ditch is different in that it does not reveal a pattern of gradual primary deposition sealed by inverted domes of more recent infill, but instead contains horizontal layers which suggest deliberate back-filling and levelling as part of a re-modelling of the defences during the Iron Age.

WAR WOUNDS OR SACRIFICE?

The finding of so many human bones in the small sample of the Camp that has so far been subject to excavation is highly significant and stands out in contrast to the paucity of animal bones (*Table 1*). The fact that amongst these bones we found evidence for death by physical violence, probably from two blows by a sword (*36* and *37*), to a four-year-old child immediately suggests two possible interpretations. The first is conflict and that these bones represent the victims of warfare when the Camp was attacked. The second hypothesis would suggest that these human remains represent the results of ritual activity such as burial (possibly through excarnation and dismemberment, with deposition of the bones in the wet ditches rather than burial in the ground) or possibly through human sacrifice.

There are plenty of examples for both kinds of interpretation from skeletons found at other Iron Age forts. At places such as South Cadbury or Maiden Castle death during battle has clearly been demonstrated. The practice of burying parts of human bodies in ditches of large enclosed areas, however, is a well-known facet of prehistoric life from Neolithic times through to the Iron Age. The association of sacrifice and wet places has been seen in the finds of bog bodies such as Lindow Man in Cheshire, and within the fens there have been reports of similar finds, although none known from recent times or investigated by modern methods. At Wandlebury, immediately to the south of Cambridge, numerous bodies have been found in pits outside and within the circular rampart of the Iron Age fort, and adjacent to Wandlebury the *fosse* at the ringwork of War Ditches contained burials presumed by the excavators to have been of Iron Age date. Many of these burials were found to contain parts of bodies, mostly articulated but often also contorted and dismembered.

There could, in fact, be a difference in interpretation between the skeletal remains discovered at the Camp. The later burial is of a fully articulated adult male, seemingly dropped into a soft, wet mud. This could well represent a rapid and easy burial for a reason such as disposing of battle victims. The bones found in the basal deposits which include the child's skull with its sword cuts are different, however, in the nature of their incompleteness. There are some related bones suggesting that parts of three bodies were placed in the ditch, but there seems little reason as to why more of the bones were not present in the excavations if the bodies had been intact when they were originally buried there. It seems likely, therefore, that in contrast to the later burial from the roddon silts, these earlier ones were deliberate burials of selected parts of a body only.

The presence of oak and birch woodland in close proximity would be tactically inadvisable for a defended fort as such trees would provide cover for enemies. Sacred groves, however, are well attested in connection with Iron Age shrines and ritual sites, and this could lend credence to the suggestion that Stonea Camp had more than the single function of defence, but instead could have been used for other purposes as well, including religious ceremonies and exposure burial.

STONEA CAMP: AN IRON AGE FORT AND ITS POLITICAL LANDSCAPE

A SIGNIFICANT LACK OF SETTLEMENT EVIDENCE

In spite of several episodes of investigation at Stonea Camp since 1959 no indication of domestic use has been found, except possibly for a brief period of military occupation around AD 40-60. The evidence for this came from 13 brooches of Aucissa/Hod Hill types, as well as a copper-alloy tankard handle and a bracelet, both dated to the second half of the first century AD (*40*) and all found by illegal metal-detecting but attributed to the Camp. Some coarse pottery that was found in two small areas during fieldwalking in 1980 was similarly dated to this period by the parallel between the types of pottery found at the Camp and at three early military sites elsewhere in East Anglia (Longthorpe, Peterborough; War Ditches, Cambridge; and Needham, Suffolk). The interior of the Camp has had extensive geophysical surveys conducted (resistivity in 1981 and magnetometer in 1983) which were not successful at finding archaeological features, probably due to the very mixed nature of the geological background; this was confirmed by a further attempt in 1991 when a resistivity transect was located across the line of the infilled outer defensive ditch, but failed to identify it. A phosphate survey in 1981 of the southern part of the Camp revealed some concentration on the exterior to the south-west, and a little within the defences in this same general area, but the levels of phosphate recorded were not sufficient to interpret as evidence for settlement. Phosphates build up in locations where there has been intense human domestic activity or from corralled or concentrated animals, from dung and urine.

The normal evidence for habitation is provided by domestic rubbish that has survived the course of time, such as broken pots or butchered animal bone. Very little of such evidence has been found, either in the ditch fills (a location where rubbish is often found to have accumulated) or in pits in the interior of the Camp. In spite of two trenches in 1992 having been deliberately placed over the areas where pottery had been found in fieldwalking in 1980, no subsurface features such as pits, post-holes, beam slots, gullies or further finds of pottery were found, although deep plough marks were found cutting into the sub-soil on a regular grid. A series of test-pits were also dug through the topsoil to see if the evidence for settlement had been ploughed away and only remained in the ploughsoil, but this exercise again came up with virtually no finds.

There was one other possible clue to settlement at Stonea Camp that showed on the 1926 OS map. This consisted of a couple of circles labelled 'Earthen Ring', and so in 1992 we decided to try to locate one of these by trenching (*28* and *21*). A 10m diameter circular ditch, 1m wide and 0.4m deep, was found with a series of post-holes and stone packing in it. No internal features were seen, however, and the only dating evidence came from worked flints. It seems unlikely that this ring-ditch represents Iron Age settlement, and is easier to understand in the context of a series of further ring-ditches running along the north-eastern flank of the Camp, culminating in a Bronze Age barrow excavated by Tim Potter in 1959-61. Thus, the ring-ditch constituted part of the earlier prehistoric landscape and when the Camp was built it incorporated two of these structures within its enclosure.

In contrast to the dearth of settlement evidence we have two trenches that produced human skeletal remains, altogether representing four individuals, one of whom had been cut twice on the head by a sword. Anecdotal evidence records that a farmer ploughed up other bones on the site during the later twentieth century, but it has not been possible to verify this. It would seem to be beyond the bounds of chance that of the very small areas of the ditches that were actually excavated we could have located two of our trenches over the only human remains on the site. It seems likely that many more deposits of human bone, possibly of burials, possibly of disarticulated and dismembered or wounded bodies, remain to be discovered.

Stonea Camp was not a fortified settlement, nor a meeting place for events including feasting and shows little evidence of any use beyond the disposal of the dead, and possibly deposition of valuable coins. It has been suggested that some of the big Iron Age enclosures might have served as seasonal points to bring together the cattle of the tribe, to corral them for a period perhaps at *Samhain* before a culling of the weaker and older animals and smoking of the meat to preserve it for the winter to come. The phosphate survey undertaken at Stonea and the lack of animal bones (apart from a few intrusive rabbit and other small species) would suggest that such an interpretation would not be applicable to the Camp. We must conclude that although its use was perhaps one of occasional defence, its main function was perhaps more akin to the much earlier Neolithic monuments that are found sprinkled across the British landscape, enclosures that were built to delimit space and to act as a location for ceremonial and burial practices.

AN ORGANISED LANDSCAPE: SETTLEMENT, INDUSTRY, FARMING AND SACRED LANDSCAPES

To the north of the Camp the land rises to 5m above sea level, to Stonea Grange and the highest point of the island. In this area it is possible to see an existing field boundary ditch which parallels the curving pattern of the Camp some 600m away. During the 1980s The British Museum excavated at Stonea Grange, and they put some of their trenches to the north-east of the main excavation area, towards the curving field ditch (*20*). A mass of features were found consisting of gullies, pits, ditches, post-holes, and a Romano-Celtic temple (see *51*). A 1m thick layer of silt had been deposited over this area in the Saxon period, preserving

STONEA CAMP: AN IRON AGE FORT AND ITS POLITICAL LANDSCAPE

the archaeology. Surface collections, mostly by metal-detecting, revealed a range of high-status Iron Age artefacts (*41*) and the features themselves produced large amounts of Iron Age pottery. In short, it would seem that this was the area of the Iron Age occupation, close to, but distinct from, the Camp.

The evidence shows activity spanning a long period of time, quite possibly continuous from the Late Bronze Age onwards. A round-house and pits, with an assemblage of pottery dating between the ninth and sixth centuries BC, were found on the area of the main excavation at Stonea Grange, but pottery dating from the sixth to second centuries BC was found in the features near to the temple complex. Bronze objects included an attachment finely fashioned in the shape of a duck, whose design and mode of manufacture has been dated from the early third century BC, and an ornate strap-union and two terrets; the former dating from *c*.200 BC and the latter from around the first century BC (*41*). These are prestige items and not what one would expect to find if the site had been a simple Iron Age farming settlement. The strap-union and terrets came from horse harnesses, and parallels for the former can be drawn with 'chariot' burials at Kirkburn and Garton Station. Fifty-nine Iron Age coins were found from surface collection and metal-detecting, and two more from

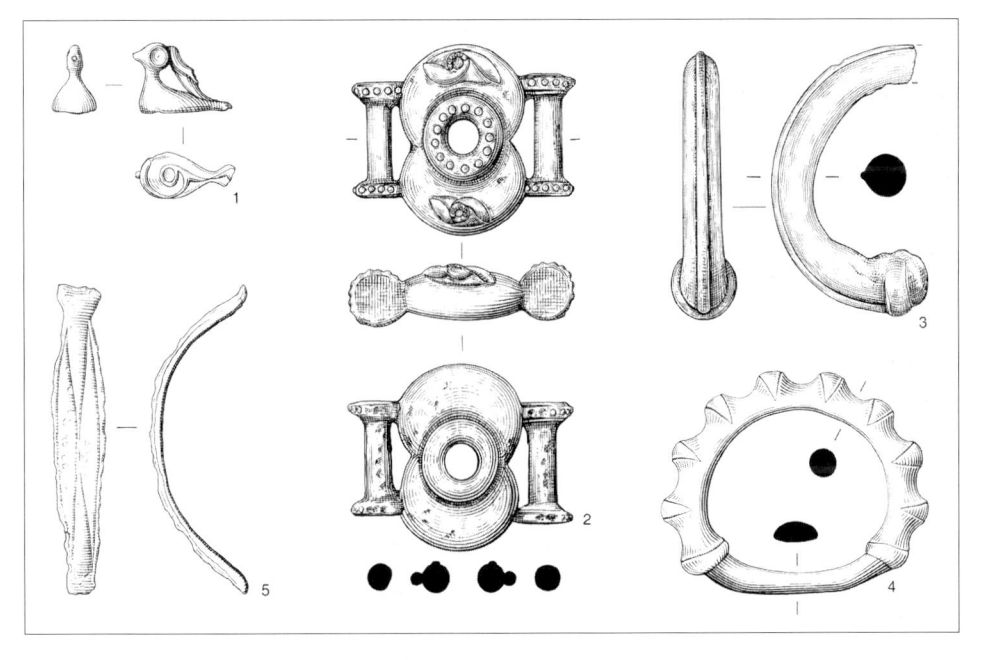

41 A selection of prestigious Middle to Late Iron Age metal artefacts from the Stonea area (note: first century AD tankard handle found at the Camp is also shown in *Figure 58* together with an example of a stave-built tankard). © *The Trustees of the British Museum*

excavated contexts, including 26 Icenian issues. This assemblage appears to be relatively early in date, with Gallo-Belgic and Potin coins making up 24 per cent, suggesting a date of mid-first century BC to mid-first century AD. The nature of the coins themselves, in a generally poor and fragmented state, and with 15 per cent composed of contemporary forgeries, is highly suggestive of loss from an important settlement site rather than a ploughed-out hoard.

Although excavation has been very limited, the evidence that has been gathered indicates that this general area on the south-west side of Stonea Island was clearly an important site for occupation over several hundred years. It would make good sense if the settlement focus for the builders of Stonea Camp was in fact on higher (and therefore drier) land rather than on the fen edge, where the Camp itself is situated for very sensible strategic reasons. The environmental indicators found preserved in the ditches of the Camp show that it was built into a wooded landscape, with no cereal cultivation in the immediate vicinity, and that it was only after inundation from the roddon during the Roman period that a change of landscape came about with a move to grazed pastureland. We can imagine a settlement on the highest part of the island, perhaps with farmland around it, separated from one part of the island in the south-west which had been set aside as a special zone for other uses and left as a predominantly wooded area, continuing a tradition of burial visible to them in the barrows and other earlier prehistoric monuments. Trees and glades were often identified as sacred in Celtic religion and the fact that the environmental evidence shows a wooded landscape for Stonea Camp, which might be less than satisfactory in a strategic context, helps to emphasise the special significance that the Camp might have been imbued with. The presence of an adjacent temple within the zone of occupation to the north helps to support a hypothesis for a sacred area, and Miranda Green has discussed the importance of the war-goddess Andraste to the Iceni, referring to feasts and sacrifices undertaken in her sacred grove as recorded by both Tacitus and Dio Cassius. At the temple excavated in Fisons Way, Thetford, Tony Gregory interpreted three square lines of post-holes set within the temple compound as representing such a sacred grove. Perhaps at Stonea the temple, grove and Camp were discrete elements of a single ritual complex.

Three further potential settlement sites have been located on Stonea Island through fieldwalking. These are all close to the fen edge and are evenly spaced, effectively dividing the island up into blocks of land with farms at their core. The pottery has been attributed to the Early Iron Age, contemporary with some of the activity at Stonea Grange, and it would not be unusual to find long periods of occupation at each of these other sites if excavation was ever to be undertaken. Apart from dark earth from organic debris and animal bone, these sites have also produced some briquetage connected with salt-making, and a loom-weight. The sites were not only located close to the contemporary edge of the fen, but

STONEA CAMP: AN IRON AGE FORT AND ITS POLITICAL LANDSCAPE

also near to contemporary watercourses which would have been brackish at the time, thus providing a source for this local saltern industry and providing easy communication by boat to other islands and the Wash.

West of Stonea on the north part of March Island two Early Iron Age sites have been found at Grandford and Flaggrass (see *61*), and early salt-making has recently been found in this northern part of the island. Flaggrass continued into the Late Iron Age, and an adjacent site is also of this date. These were located beside a contemporary watercourse which would have allowed direct contact with the community on Stonea. Elsewhere on March island, which stretches south to include Wimblington, Benwick and Doddington, only two further sites have been identified, 1km to the west of the Camp and Stonea Grange, across wet Fenland (*61*). Given the extensively built-up area of March Town, it is perhaps not surprising that comparatively few Iron Age sites have been identified on this large and relatively high fen island, but those that have been identified signify that it was indeed being exploited during this period. There is one further find of very great importance which came from an area housed over in 1983: the Field Baulk coin hoard (*20* and *42*). This consisted of a pottery vessel which had been deposited in a ditch, possibly part of a round-house, and that contained

42 The Field Baulk Hoard of Icenian coins from March, spilling out of the pot that contained them; found and excavated in 1982. © *The Trustees of the British Museum*

872 silver Icenian coins. The dating of the beaker in which the coins were found was between AD 60-70 and the coins themselves do not include early issues; it is therefore extremely likely that the deposition of this hoard can be put into historical context as having occurred at the time of the Boudican rebellion.

Further south on the islands of Manea and Chatteris a total of 10 further occupation sites have been found from field survey, clustered in two groups in the east of Chatteris, and on the Isle of Ely 11 more sites have been found, including an interesting double-ditched enclosure containing round-houses and high-status artefacts such as tankard staves. The banks had been protected by thorn bushes and the location of this, at Wardy Hill, Coveney, was ideally situated for controlling access along a fen inlet to the island. The distribution of these sites are all on the northern edge of the island, with several occupying promontories. In addition to these sites a settlement of around 30 round-houses has been recently excavated 1km west of Ely at West Fen, and this constitutes the largest single excavation of Iron Age round-houses from the fens.

THE POLITICAL LANDSCAPE

In broad terms the Late Iron Age tribal groupings are well known and geographically distinct (*colour plate 8*). Norfolk and Suffolk were occupied by the Iceni, a tribe made up of three regional groups or *pagi* who had a pact with Rome as a client kingdom during the early years of the Conquest. To the south the land was Trinovantian with its tribal capital at Colchester, until this area was conquered by their powerful Catuvellauni neighbours based at St Albans in *c.*AD 10. Cunobelin, king of the Catuvellauni, made his centre at Colchester, which became an *oppidum* known as Camulodunum covering a large area defined by dykes, as was his original capital at St Albans. Catuvellaunian influence extended up to the River Nene, and the area between this and the Welland was a frontier zone with the land of the Corieltauvi. Thus the northern fens were in the Corieltauvi sphere of influence, the central fens seem to have belonged to the Iceni, but the southern fens, and south and east Cambridgeshire, were an area of uncertain political hegemony.

To accentuate this point a chain of forts can be seen to run north–south from the fens to the Thames following the line of the Cam, Stort and Lee rivers (*colour plate 8*). This has been interpreted as marking the border between the Trinovantes and the Catuvellauni in approximately the first century BC. At the northern end of this line of defence several circular forts are found (*15*) at Wandlebury, War Ditches and Arbury. Such ringworks are also found in Norfolk at Narborough, South Creake and Warham Camp, and around the western edge of the fens at Willingham and Borough Fen.

Stonea Camp, however, is different in form from these circular forts; its plan is one that has been derived largely from the strategic use of local topography. The fort is located on the peninsula of a fen island so that the roddons and marsh on the west and south helped with its security. The largest bank and ditch defences were positioned facing into the dry and slightly higher land of the island north and east, and were given defence in depth by provision of the internal double D-shaped ramparts. Similar arrangements are discernible at Holkham and Thetford Castle, both Icenian forts which back unto river loops.

Not all the Iron Age forts in the region have been excavated, but of those that have been investigated very different histories can be told for each. Borough Fen, a bivallate fort near to Peterborough on the western edge of the fens, has clear evidence of occupation radiocarbon dated to 2090 ± 70 BP, and has hand-made (middle) Iron Age pottery including scored wares. Excavations by Ron Mckenna and the author in 1992 revealed a ditch 2.3m deep and 10m wide, with an inner bank 7.5m wide that had been revetted. Apart from identifying a buried soil and dark occupation horizon inside the monument, 183 sherds of pottery were collected and a defleshed horse skull with pot-sherd 'placed' on its nose was recovered from the base of the ditch. After its primary use, environmental evidence points to the fort becoming grazed pastureland (very similar to what also happened at Stonea) before it became flooded some time in the Roman period. Borough Fen appears to be a southerly bastion of a group of forts protecting the Corieltauvi from the Catevallauni, the others being also sub-circular in design and found inland at Careby, Rounds Hill and Burgh Banks in Lincolnshire.

Arbury Camp on the northern edge of modern Cambridge is a near circular single ditched fort which has revealed no evidence of occupation in spite of intensive investigation by Chris Evans, although a remarkable discovery of leather offcuts dating to 380-40 cal BC has been found in the northern ditch terminal. The ditch and bank would have been built earlier than this deposit, in which a human scapula was radiocarbon dated to 410-160 cal BC. The ditch was c.7m wide and 1.25m deep, and the bank ranged from 5-8m wide. A massive timber gateway on the eastern side of the enclosure was found, which seems at odds with the apparent lack of evidence for internal settlement: what was it defending?

A circular fort of almost identical size to Arbury is found at Wandlebury on the Gog Magog hills immediately south of Cambridge, and the two enclosures have often been regarded as twinning one another, one on the upland and one in the lowland. Wandlebury is in fact a bivallate construction and it contains settlement evidence dating to the Early and Middle Iron Age, perhaps from the fifth century BC. Some of this settlement evidence, such as pits with pottery and animal bones, as well as several human burials, has been found outside of the inner circuit, and it seems likely that a second phase to Wandlebury perhaps led to enclosure of a previously undefended settlement. The bank was revetted and the ditch counter-scarped, and the largest ditch was 11.5m wide and 5m deep. The human burials included partially articulated bodies, some perhaps dismembered, and others perhaps killed and buried in pits both inside and outside the defences.

Close to Wandlebury, within 2km to the north, another circular fort, War Ditches, was located on a hill top above Cherry Hinton. This was a single-ditched, circular fort with large, V-shaped ditch in which a number of skeletons were found when this was excavated at the beginning of the twentieth century. A further fort at Sawston has recently been identified and partially investigated and this had a similar large, V-shaped ditch with apparently similar infill history (*43*) and geophysical survey has indicated settlement activity within the defences. The fort was irregular, appears in places to be double ditched and, rather like Stonea, its defences arched round to meet with wetlands (a river) at its rear. To date no burials have been found at Sawston.

43 Photograph of the ditch at Borough Hill, Sawston, during excavation by John Samuels in 2001 which is of similar design and dimensions to the comparative profiles shown in *Figure 42*. *Author's collection*

STONEA CAMP: AN IRON AGE FORT AND ITS POLITICAL LANDSCAPE

Stonea
- Southern Outer Phase 1
- Southern Inner Phase 3
- Western Outer Phase 1
- Northern Outer Phase 1
- Eastern Outer Phase 1
- Outer 'D' Shaped Phase 4
- Western Outer Phase 1

Arbury

Borough Fen

War Ditches — Phase 1

Wandlebury — Phase 1, Phase 2

Wandlebury

Wandlebury
War Ditches
Stonea

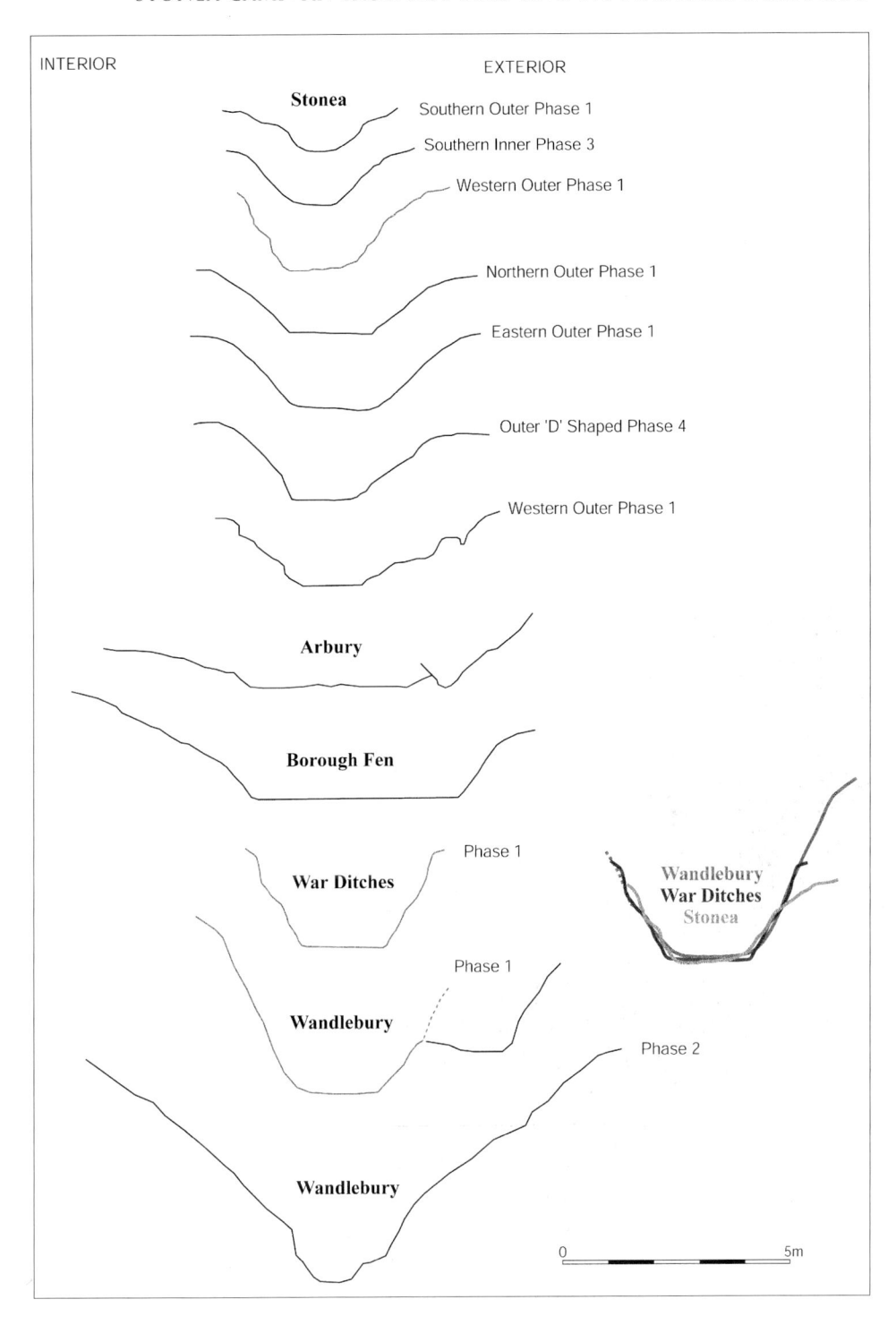

0   5m

44 Comparative profiles of Iron Age fort defensive ditches from Cambridgeshire showing the similarity in design of the earlier (Middle Iron Age) phases. © *Caroline Malim*

Fort name	Enclosed area	Interior ditch top width	depth	Exterior ditch top width	depth	Rampart width	height	Dating/Phases
Arbury Camp Hinton	5ha	6.1-10.5m	1-1.5m			4.6-8m	0.3-0.5m	4th-2ndC BC 410-160 cal BC 380-40 cal BC
Belsars Hill Willingham	2.57ha	6-12m					2m	
Borough Fen	3.8ha	10.5m	2.3m			7.5m		3rd-2ndC BC 2090 ± 70 bp
Borough Hill Sawston	8ha	5m		5m		6.4 - 11.1m	1.1-1.4m	
Stonea Camp Wimblington	4.05ha Inner D 6.07ha Outer D 9.61ha Outer	2.2-5m	1-1.75m	2.6-5.5m	1-2m	7m	1m	3-4 phases 3rd BC – 1st AD
Tattershall Thorpe	1.8ha	5.75m	0.9m	5m	1.45m	None (but hedges existed)		400 ± 90 bc
Wandlebury Stapleford	3.73ha inner 5.64ha outer	11.5m	5.2m	5.5m	4.57	10m (inner) 3.9 (outer)	4.9m (inner) 4.6m (outer)	Two phases 5 th - 1stC BC
War Ditches Cherry Hinton	1.82ha	5.5m	4m					

Table 2: Dimensions of Iron Age fort defences in Cambridgeshire

The construction of all of these forts attest a significant investment by the Iron Age peoples of the region, and a comparison of their respective ditch profiles (*Table 2* and *44*) suggests that a reasonably consistent design or template is discernible for the earliest phases of ditch defence. The forts are not alone as physical monuments reflecting the political posturing of the period because large linear earthworks – dykes – also exist. Those in Cambridgeshire controlling the Icknield Way zone have been shown in their present massive form to be Anglo-Saxon in date but they in all probability had earlier precursors. In Norfolk and Suffolk, however, a series of dykes exist which would seem to date in origin to the Iron Age. These include the Black Ditches at Icklingham, Laun Ditch and possibly Panworth and Gaboldsham Ditches, and they generally appear to cut off promontories, terminating in rivers at either end (*colour plate 8*).

The dates of many of the forts would seem too early to relate directly to the Roman invasion and later exploitation of the fens, but nonetheless they are important in setting the scene, in trying to establish the political environment immediately preceding the Claudian invasion and therefore in understanding the local tensions and differences between the various communities in East Anglia and the east Midlands. We know, for example, that the Trinovantes had treaties with Rome and had been conquered by the Catavellauni. Roman imports of wine and exotic goods, and wheel-made pottery, can be witnessed from Colchester and other parts of the south-east, whereas within Icenian territory there appears to have been much less contact between the two worlds, and the type of pottery remained hand-made and similar to the technology of the Middle Iron Age. At the Conquest the Iceni became a client kingdom, but there were clearly tensions, which erupted in 47 AD when some of the Iceni rebelled and were crushed by the Roman army. The king of the Iceni at this time was Prasutagus, husband of Boudica, but the fact that he carried on ruling his people and minting coins shows he maintained an independence until his death in AD 60, which then precipitated Roman attempts at acquisition of the land of the Iceni, with rebellion its disastrous aftermath.

Stonea Camp needs to be seen in this context. It was built at a time when several powerful tribes vied with each other for supremacy. They competed not only through raiding cattle and warfare, but also through construction of elaborate earthworks, and displayed their wealth in different ways; some through imported goods from the Mediterranean world, and others through traditional means such as golden torcs. Minting of coins in imitation of those from the Roman world was important to all the tribes, but Icenian issues were generally of a lower silver content than their contemporaries. Large centres grew up which acted as trading entrepots, focuses for industry and manufacturing and settlements for elite families with attendant religious and burial complexes. These were the *oppida* such as Camuldonum and Verulamium, but possibly also Stonea. The fens appear to have been a border land, with Stonea and perhaps March islands as western outliers of Icenian power. The revolt of AD 47 resulted in the Roman army taking control of the Camp, and the events of AD 61 can be witnessed by the Field Baulk hoard of coins found at March. The Iceni were conquered after Boudica's rebellion and a period of repression and probably famine descended on the lands of the Iceni. Eventually, Stonea was to rise again from this great period of turmoil to continue the position of importance in the central Fenlands that it had held for several hundred years; it was chosen to become the site of a Roman town.

RADIOCARBON DATING

Alex Bayliss

Six samples were submitted from the Camp for radiocarbon dating. Two were processed by the Scottish Universities Research and Reactor Centre in 1993 and four by the Oxford Radiocarbon Accelerator Unit, two in 1992-3 and two in 1999. Two samples were of human bone, the rest of plant detritus. Samples processed in Oxford were measured using Accelerator Mass spectrometry[1] and samples processed in Glasgow were measured using liquid scintillation counting.[2]

The calibration of these results, which relate the radiocarbon measurements directly to the calendrical time scale, are given in Table 3 (quoted in accordance with the international standard known as the Trondheim convention)[3] and in outline in *Figure 38*. They have been calculated using the maximum intercept method,[4] the computer program OxCal (v2.18).[5] The date ranges cited in the text are those for 95 per cent confidence.[6]

Although the simple calibrated date ranges of the radiocarbon measurements are accurate estimates of the dates of the samples, this is usually not what we really wish to know as archaeologists. It is the dates of the archaeological events that are represented by those samples which are of interest. Fortunately, explicit methodology is now available which allows us to combine the results of the radiocarbon analyses with other information which we may have, such as stratigraphy, to produce realistic estimates of these dates of archaeological interest. It should be emphasised that these distributions and ranges are not absolute, they are interpretative *estimates*, which can and will change as further data becomes available and as other researchers choose to model the existing data from different perspectives.

The technique we have used is known as 'Gibbs' sampling'[7] and has been applied using the program OxCal v2.18.[8] The algorithms used in the model described below can be derived from the structure shown in *Figure 38*.

Stratigraphic evidence and the fen-edge gradient of Stonea island demonstrates that the peat recovered from the monolith at WIMSC93 is earlier than the defensive ditch. GU-5331 consisted of waterlogged leaves and twigs which had accumulated in the basal fill of this ditch; OxA-3620 was a sample of human bone from immediately above this fill and was associated with a sword-marked

Lab No	Sample Number	Sample type	Radiocarbon Age (BP)	ä¹³C (‰)	Calibrated date range (95% confidence)	*Estimated date range (95% probability)*
OxA-4064	WIMSC92/1	Human bone from basal fill of outer ditch	1985±55	-19.2	cal BC 120–cal AD 130	*cal BC 90–cal AD 130*
GU-5332	WIMSC92 2.5/34	Oak leaves & twigs from basal fill of outer ditch	2110±50	-26.0	cal BC 360–cal AD 1	*cal BC 230–cal AD 10 (85% confidence)*
OxA-3620	WIMSC91 SK2	Human bone from flood silts in outer ditch	2070±65	-19.5	cal BC 350–cal AD 80	*cal BC 210–cal AD 60*
GU-5331	WIMSC91 9.6	Oak leaves & twigs from basal fill of outer ditch	2210±90	-26.2	cal BC 410–1	*cal BC 410–50*
OxA-8427	WIMSC93/1:20 (34)	Peat deposit	3415±55	-29.0	cal BC 1880–1520	*cal BC 1880–1600 (91% confidence)*
OxA-8445	WIMSC93/1:20 (16)	Peat deposit	3645±55	-28.6	cal BC 2200–1830	*cal BC 2150–1880 (93% confidence)*

Table 3: Radiocarbon Age Determinations

child skull. Although the material dated was not articulated, the defensive nature of the ditch suggests that the dated bone was functionally related to the deposit and was not residual. This hypothesis about the taphonomy of the dated material is supported by the good agreement between the radiocarbon results and the stratigraphic sequence (*38*; A=106.3 per cent and 109.9 per cent).

GU-5332 also consisted of waterlogged leaves and twigs from the basal fill of the ditch, although from a different part of the ditch. Consequently this sample must also be later than those from the peat, but is not securely related stratigraphically to OxA-3620. However, all these samples from the primary fills of the ditch must be earlier than the articulated burial that was found in roddon silts much further up the ditch sequence.

The model that combines this relative dating information which is available from archaeological stratigraphy with the radiocarbon results is shown in *Figure 38*. The solid areas in the graph and the estimated date ranges in *Table 3* result from this model.

It should be noted that the two samples from monolith (WIMSC93) are from different levels within the peat profile. However, the lower sample at 34cm (OxA-8427) appears to be significantly younger than the upper one at 16cm

(OxA-8445). It is possible that this anomaly has been caused by the inwash of soil containing older carbon than the accumulating peat itself. For this reason, the apparent relative chronology has not been included in the model. Nevertheless, the results from this peat sequence are sufficiently similar to demonstrate that it dates to the beginning of the second millennium cal BC and, thus, represents a period considerably earlier than the Iron Age monument.

Notes

1 Prepared using the methods outlined in Hedges et al. (1989, 102) and Bronk Ramsey and Hedges (1997)
2 Noakes et al. 1965 and processed according to methods outlined in Stenhouse and Baxter (1983)
3 Stuiver and Kra 1986. They are conventional radiocarbon ages (Stuiver and Polach 1977)
4 Stuiver and Reimer (1986)
5 Bronk Ramsey 1995, and the dataset published by Stuiver et al. (1998)
6 They are quoted in the form recommended by Mook (1986), with the end points rounded outwards to 10 years
7 Gelfand and Smith 1990
8 (http://units.ox.ac.uk/departments/rlaha/). Full details of the algorithms employed by this program are available from the on-line manual or in Bronk Ramsey (1995), and fully worked examples are given in the series of papers by Buck et al. (1991; 1992; Buck, Litton et al. 1994; Buck, Christen et al. 1994)

6

STONEA: THE ROMAN TOWN AND CENTRE FOR AN IMPERIAL ESTATE

DEFINITION

Many towns are known from Roman Britain. Most of the larger ones have since become cities, and it is easy to accept that the origin of some of our historic centres lies in the Roman period; London, Canterbury, Colchester, Exeter, Lincoln, Leicester and York to name but a few. The modern sense of a town, however, was not necessarily the same 2,000 years ago, and the relationship between military base (*castra*), associated settlement for camp-followers and traders (*canabae*), official settlement of retired soldiers (*colonia*) and the establishment of a civil administration (*pagus, vicus, urbs, civitas* and *municipium*) can be complex. Some smaller towns today also originated as important Roman centres, places like Cirencester, St Albans, Godmanchester and Caister by Norwich, smaller in size to those listed above, but have not grown into large cities. Then there are some others that have all but disappeared, such as Silchester, Wroxeter, Water Newton and Stonea.

There has been much debate as to what exactly defined a Roman town, but in general the functions that seem to identify a small town include civil administration and baths, street pattern, a market, specialist services and industry, a religious centre and ordered cemeteries and, in later times, defences. This definition, however, is not perfect, and some large villa estate centres could include all of these roles and yet they were not a town; within the general label of a town a hierarchy existed of upper, middle and lower order settlements which had decreasingly definable town characteristics as they reduced in size and importance. In fact, there is much to suggest that the major towns, the *civitas* capitals, although political and administrative centres, were in the long run perhaps not as economically buoyant as smaller towns which served local needs as centres for trade and manufacturing.

Perhaps of more relevance to Stonea are those towns that developed on pre-existing tribal centres. Colchester and Verulamium are examples, as are Wroxeter and Silchester. Stonea town was founded close to the regionally important site of Stonea Camp, in between this tribal centre and its related settlement located on a higher part of the island. It appears, therefore, to have been designed to display authority, taking some of its prestige from the fact that it usurped, or wanted to be seen as the continuance of, the symbolic power of the Iron Age fort. As an administrative centre it may have been relatively short-lived compared to some others, but as a settlement it successfully continued for several centuries, well into the Anglo-Saxon period.

CHRONOLOGICAL DEVELOPMENT

Dating for the various phases of Roman Stonea has come from artefacts recovered from pits and wells, ditches, and destruction levels, and include coarse pottery, Samian and metalwork. From all this material the origins for the town can be traced back to *c*.AD 125, and its floruit extended through the rest of the second century and into the first 20 years or so of the third century, after which the character of the settlement changed to that of a farming community.

Around 100 years after its foundation the great establishment buildings, the administrative block and the temple (*45*), went out of use. Specific deposits of artefacts placed in pits and ditches seem to indicate a rite of closure and thereafter they were abandoned, eventually to be systematically demolished with all useful building material being recycled.

The settlement itself, however, continued throughout the third and fourth centuries, with fresh buildings and ancillary structures of a character similar to farming units, a pattern that was to continue into the post-Roman period of the fifth and sixth centuries (see *94*). Property boundaries and street pattern were, in general, respected, although the settlement began to resemble a more rural arrangement. Timber-frame houses of Roman and Anglo-Saxon type were built and abandoned over this period, and a shift can be detected during Anglo-Saxon occupation on to the slightly higher areas of the raised roads (see *94* and *107*). Fresh wells and pits for storage and refuse disposal continued to be dug during the third century as the older ones became filled with debris or domestic rubbish and ditches or gullies were cleaned out, recut or added to over the centuries. All

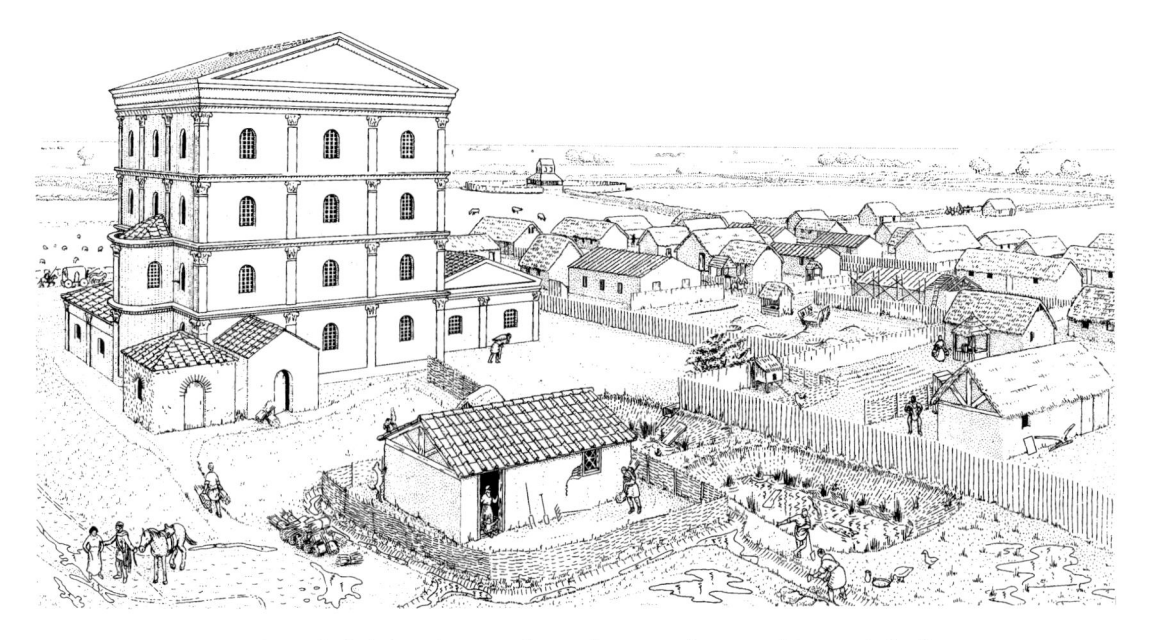

THE ROMAN TOWN AND CENTRE FOR AN IMPERIAL ESTATE

45 Reconstruction of administrative complex and town at Stonea, with temple in distance, from the south. © The Trustees of the British Museum, drawn by Simon Jones

this evidence suggests a dynamic settlement and stable population bridging the transition from Roman into Anglo-Saxon times, with a mainstay of the economy based upon sheep farming. There is some indication, however, that elements of Roman luxury continued into, or were re-established during, the fourth century; evident in items such as window glass, mosaic floors and hypocausts for heating important rooms, within new stone structures reusing the levelled area of the original stone administrative 'tower' building.

STREETS AND *INSULAE*

A regular grid of streets was laid out during the first half of the second century AD on an axis roughly corresponding to the cardinal points (*46A*). The streets were metalled with gravel and partly bordered by drains. Although these ditches were initially incomplete, their extent slowly developed over time as property boundaries were re-emphasised by recutting and addition of ditch sections and gullies.

The streets defined a regular layout of *insulae*, or blocks of properties within which houses, outbuildings, wells, courtyards, ovens, pits and wells were found (*46B*). A general tendency is apparent conforming to blocks of 50 Roman feet

STONEA AND THE ROMAN FENS

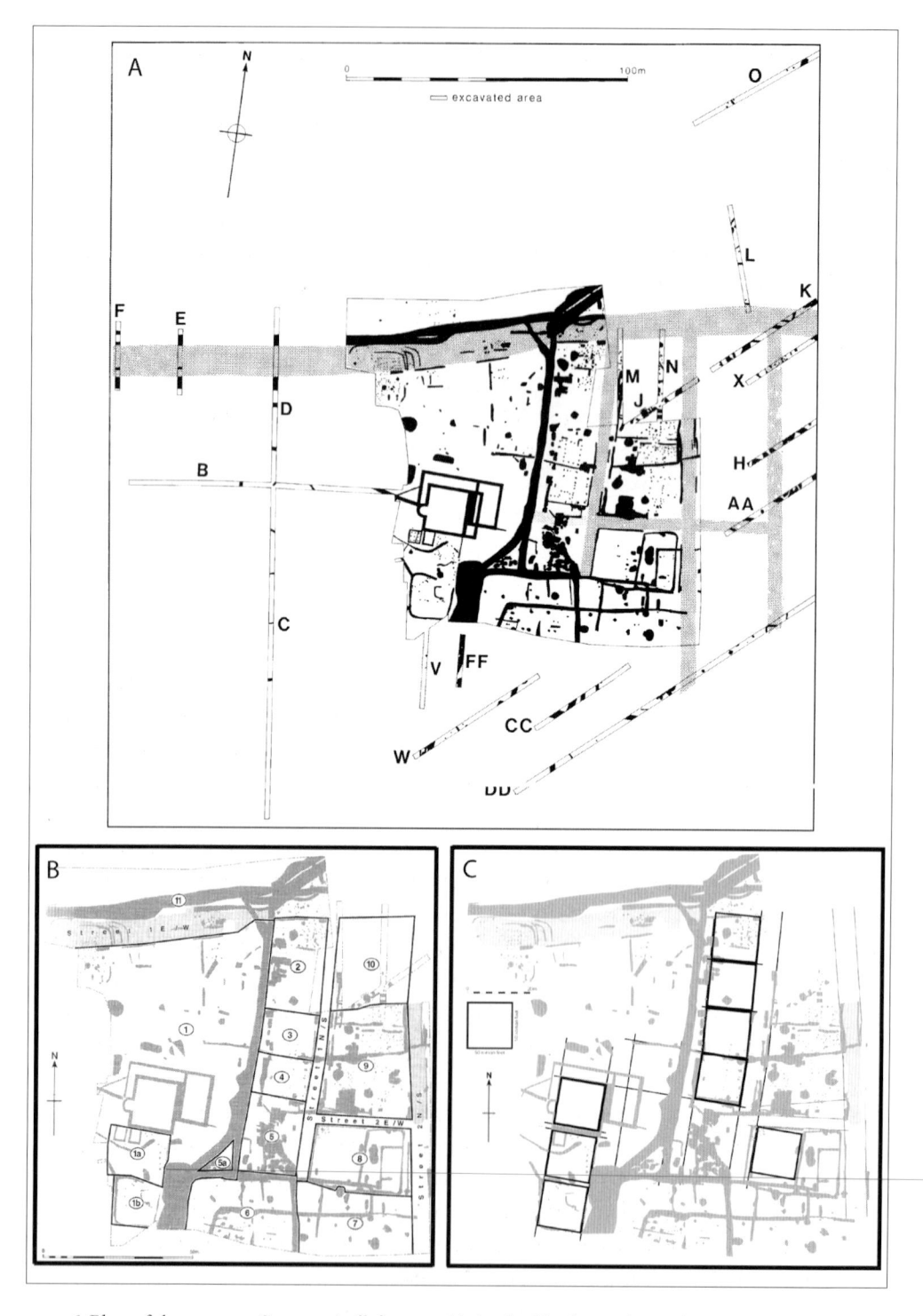

46 Plan of the town at Stonea: a) all features; b) *insulae* block numbers; c) 50 Roman feet squares. © *The Trustees of the British Museum*

(46C), demonstrating a planned layout which created a proto-urban settlement and the streets were 15 Roman feet in width, suggesting central control rather than organic growth. The axis of the earliest blocks and streets were offset from the cardinal points, but a slight change to this orientation in streets further east and south reveal a second grid aligned on true north and suggest a second phase in the development of the town. Some of the southernmost streets, however, seem never to have been developed after they were initially laid out and in later years were encroached upon or blocked. Similarly, some of the property units also appear never to have been built upon or developed, instead becoming used for other purposes such as pits for latrines or rubbish disposal.

The main artery was an east–west oriented street on the northern edge of the town (the *via decumanus?*) that ran for perhaps 500m and probably formed part of a road that would have connected the settlement at Stonea with the bigger island of March to the west. It may also have continued eastwards to link with other Roman settlements on the eastern fringe of Stonea island. This street varied between 7.5-10m in width and had a discontinuous shallow ditch to the south and a continuous, but sinuous, ditch along the north side. Its importance as a boundary was even carried on into post-medieval times. Offset to the south were a series of streets on a north–south axis.

The westernmost one was a major north–south running street which separated the precinct of the administrative building from the rest of the town. This street was *c*.4m wide and ran for 80m. It had streetside gullies and its importance must have continued long after the abandonment of the administrative block because, unlike other streets, it did not have any features cut into it at a later date.

Three further north–south oriented streets were found within the excavation area at 25-30m intervals east of this first street. They were approximately 5m wide and were between 60 and 120m in length. These were cut by a second east–west running street, some 60m south of the main east–west artery that ran along the north of the settlement area. Roadside gullies were found to be discontinuous, but appear to have been rigidly gridded to begin with, becoming increasingly less standardised in their nature the later in the life of the town they were cut. The earliest phase seems to represent small-capacity gullies for local drainage, in some cases preceded by fence lines as property markers and fenced compounds. Over time these divisions became more marked by a group of larger gullies and ditches, implying greater needs for drains to cope with increased water consumption and waste management. The development of such substantial divisions probably helped to maintain the integrity of individual properties throughout the changes that occurred in later Roman and early Anglo-Saxon times.

The blocks or *insulae* that were laid out within this pattern of streets were not entirely regular in size and shape, although a considerable level of consistency can be detected. Eleven blocks have been revealed by excavation, but more await discovery (*46B*). The blocks that have been investigated display a diversity of use and function over time. Block 1, the westernmost part of the town, was entirely given over to the principal building, service complex, yards and gardens of the administrative hub. It measured 90m north–south and 64m west–east.

Blocks 2, 3, 4 and 5 ran parallel to Block 1 but on the eastern side of the main north–south street, separated from it by a major property boundary surviving as a ditch. These blocks all seem to be laid out to the same standard of measurement, the Roman foot (*pes monatalis*), with, for example, Blocks 3 and 4 being 50 Roman feet square each, and a 15 Roman feet separation between each group of blocks; the same measurement was used in the width of the streets (at a conversion of 29.57cm to 1 Roman foot). All the blocks were approximately 18m across east–west, and the northernmost, Block 2, was 29m long (north–south), with Blocks 3 and 4 each being 13.25m long, and Block 5 24m long.

Blocks 6 and 7 are 36m x 22m and 37m x 23m each, perhaps again following a general standard of measurement (36m being twice 18m which is the width of the previous blocks), although the southern limit is unknown as Blocks 6 and 7 extend beyond the limit of excavation. These two blocks formed the southern limit of excavation, with a large north–south ditch defining the boundary between them. The main north–south street terminates against Block 7, and a second east–west street separates Block 7 from its northern neighbour, Block 8. The initial standardisation is lost as the settlement progressed eastwards.

Blocks 8 and 9 are trapezoidal in shape and therefore have measurements that do not conform so well. Block 10 is different again at 29m x 25m, and Block 11 is very different at 94m x 8.5m although this is largely a consequence of its limited exposure within the excavation trench. Blocks 8-10 run parallel to Blocks 2-5, on the eastern side of the main north–south street. Block 11, on the other hand, occupies all the area north of the main east–west street (*via decumanus*) opposite Block 1.

To the east of Blocks 7-10 a second north–south running street was found, and a third lies beyond this, thus defining further blocks which were not investigated. From the evidence of some of the trial trenches which were cut further east during the programme of investigation it is clear that a concentration of features occur (such as pits, gullies and post-holes) and it must imply a continuation of the town in this direction, a town that may have extended to at least 20 blocks according to the results of trial trenching.

The alignments of the street pattern and the blocks between them suggest two slightly different grids were used. The primary one appears to have been NNE–SSW and is best represented by the principal building, the administrative complex, and its eastern perimeter ditch, plus Block 5 and perhaps 8. The second grid is closer to the cardinal points and is shown by Blocks 2-4, 6 and 7, and

Blocks 9-11. The second north–south running street is entirely laid out on this second grid and this accounts for the trapezoidal shape of Blocks 9 and 10.

How do we account for this use of two grids? Why is the town not uniform in its alignment, if it was all planned and surveyed in one go? This divergence in grid would suggest that there was a time lag between the initial foundation and construction of the principal building, and the subsequent expansion of the town in all directions except west. For some reason the second stage of construction involved a change, or possibly a correction to the grid that had been laid out originally. There is no obvious clue from the archaeological evidence as to why this should be so, but it might possibly reflect a change from foundation under military control, which was then withdrawn after the first stage was complete, the nascent town being handed over to a civil administration (and perhaps some element of private enterprise), resulting in a detectable change to the plan and uniformity of the layout.

Such variability in town grids can be seen in other Roman towns such as Silchester, a town which it has been suggested was surveyed using *pes monatalis* approximately equivalent to 2.21m. If this unit of measurement is used in analysing the dimensions of the *insulae* at Stonea it can be seen that a good level of correspondence can be found for the measurement of those blocks sufficiently excavated to be sure of their limits. The width of streets at Silchester was 5-6m and the size of the *insulae* varied between *c.*75m-125m (*c.*250-425 Roman feet).

STRUCTURES

The majority of the structures appear to have been timber-framed houses and ancillary buildings with wattle and daub walls, but there were also some more substantial constructions in timber, *opus signinum* (Roman concrete) and stone. Amongst the latter was the showpiece of the Roman town, the administrative complex, which may have included a tower building rising up from major foundations for perhaps four storeys in height (*47*). In an essentially flat landscape such a structure would have been a significant landmark, similar to that provided by the medieval cathedral at Ely in later times.

The foundations for this possible tower reveal a building of at least two phases, with the original core consisting of a central block 16m x 17m, with an apsidal extension off-centre to the west and an entrance on the east. A platform was prepared 0.5m high from excavation of a box trench for the foundations of the 1.2m wide walls which rested on pitched limestone blocks capped by lime mortar. Above this the foundations consisted of two courses of a mortared rubble core with limestone facing, and the pattern was then repeated by pitched

STONEA AND THE ROMAN FENS

limestone blocks, two courses of mortared core and faced walling and a final layer of pitched limestone, until the main wall was built above this. These were massive foundations (*48*) and must indicate the need to support a building of considerable size and weight; hence its reconstruction as a tower with interior dimensions that would have conformed to a square of 50 Roman feet each side and a height of possibly as much as 17m. The raft foundations were 0.8m thick, with a *hypocaust* 0.7m deep above this, and a *praefurnium* (the fire-house for the heating system) attached on the south side of the building. To the north a large paved area 60 x 40m probably acted as a piazza or market place (*forum*), with access from the main east–west road which had no ditch boundary and was unfenced along the north side of the piazza (*47*).

The second phase of construction involved corridor-like additions to the north (19m x 3m internally) and partly on the west, a larger annex on the east (14m x 7.5m internally), and a small room to the south (*49*). These additions were not built with the same intensity of foundations, as they abutted the existing walls

47 Reconstruction drawing of administrative centre and piazza, with town in background, from the north. © The Trustees of the British Museum, drawn by Steve Crummy

48 Excavation of the foundations to the administrative 'tower' building. © Ralph Jackson

of the main block, and they would probably have been single-storey structures. The northern and eastern annexes were unheated. The entrance was changed from the east to the north, and thus the northern addition would probably have been a classical-style formal entranceway. The small room on the south side that served as the fire-room for the main building had a second structure attached to it of similar dimensions (4.5m x 4m) in which nine limestone *pilae* were found, indicating that this room was also heated. It was on the same orientation as the main building but was built of timber and daub with a tiled roof. A cobbled surface of limestone chips was found on the outside of it, presumably a courtyard for heavy traffic, bringing in supplies such as firewood. To the south lay a well with three steps set in *opus signinum* and wooden decking surrounding it.

In addition to the central heating system the main building also had luxurious finishings. In demolition deposits painted wall plaster with scenes of figures and landscapes, panelling and marbling effects were found, along with 1,300 pieces of window glass (the second largest collection of Roman window glass in Britain after the palace at Fishbourne). The largest surviving fragment was 283 x 241mm and on this basis at least 13 panes are represented in the assemblage. The glass was probably manufactured locally by casting sheets of 2-4.5mm thickness from recycled vessels, predominantly of blue-green and greenish hues; a high proportion

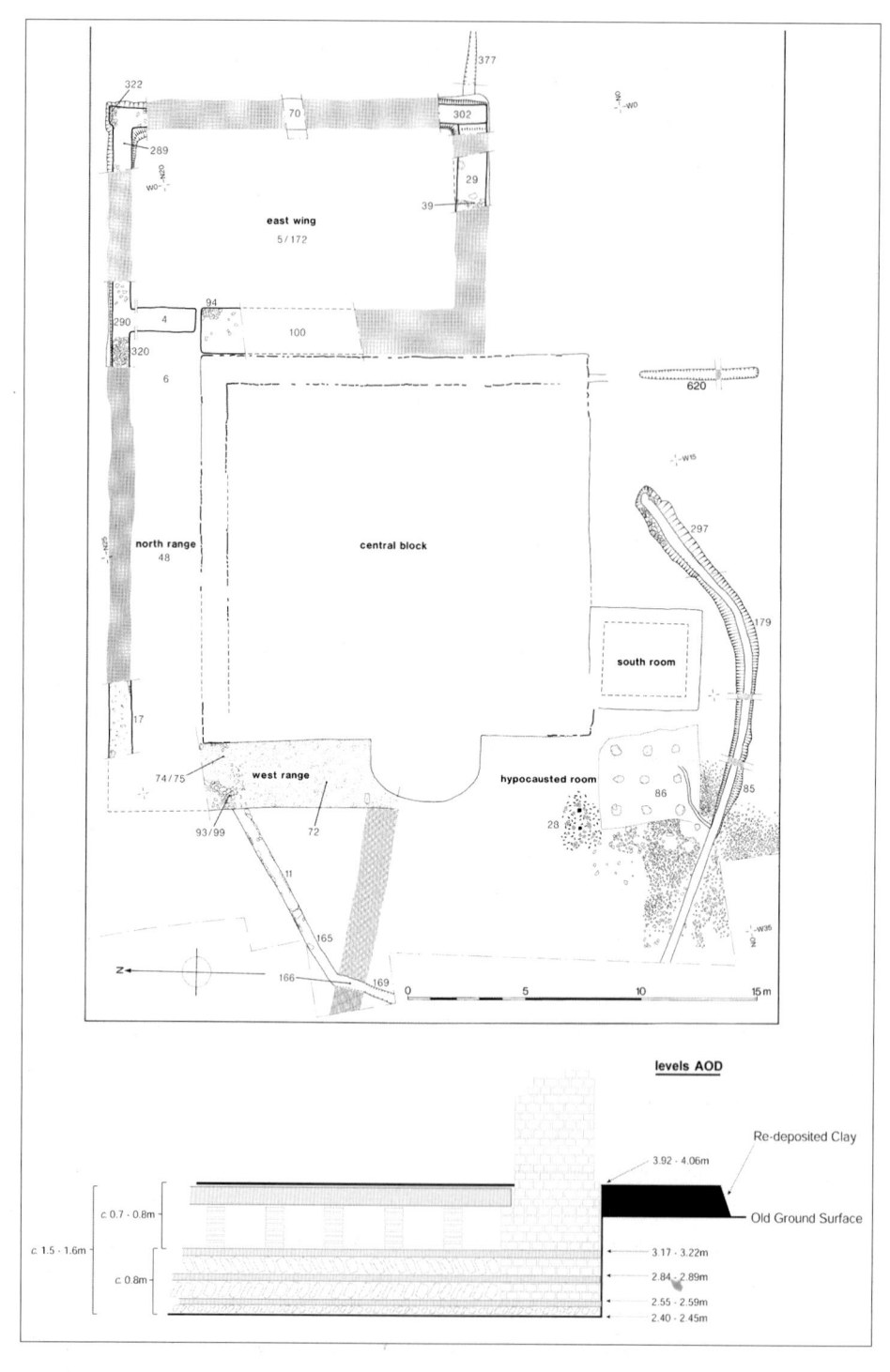

49 Plan and elevation of the foundations to the 'tower' building and photograph of it during excavation. Plan © The Trustees of the British Museum; photograph Ralph Jackson

No.	Insulae	Centuries	Length	Width	rooms	hearth	stone/mortar	earth-fast posts	beam-slots	eaves-drip gullies	rebuilds	wells	ovens	pits	high status finds
R1	1	2nd-3rd	29.5	27.5	6		hypocaust walls & floor								
R2	1	3rd-4th	11.5	9.5	1		hypocaust walls & floor	yes			1				stylus, glass
R3	1	2nd-3rd	5.5(12)	3.5(6)	1(2)			yes							
R4	1	3rd	5	3				yes		2		1	2		metalwork
R5a	2	2nd-4th	6.6	4.7	1	1			yes			4		10	samian
R5b	2	2nd-4th	5	3	1			yes			1		3		
R6	3	2nd-3rd	7(4.5)	5.8(3.5)	2			yes		1		3	1	9	
R7	4	2nd-3rd	10.8	9.2	3	1		yes		1		1		7	
R8	8	2nd-3rd	11	5					yes	6		1	1	16	
R9	8	3rd-4th	?		1			yes							
R10	9	2nd-3rd	4.5	4	1			yes		8		6		33 + latrine	
R11	9	2nd-3rd	5	4	1			yes							
R12	9		8(4)	6(3)	2			yes		4					
R13	9	2nd-3rd	15.5	9.5	1			yes				yes		yes	Egyptian blue pellet
R14	9	2nd-3rd	5.5	3.5	1			yes							
R15	temple	2nd-3rd	5.6	5	1		walls								

Table 4: Dimensions and nature of Roman buildings at Stonea Grange

of colourless panes were also evident. From the main concentrations of glass it can be suggested that the 'tower' would have had glazed windows on the west, north and south walls. Pieces of window glass were, however, recovered from all parts of the excavated site. As window glass was usually recycled it is particularly interesting to find such a large quantity surviving at Stonea. It is unknown how the windows were fitted into the apertures; two pieces of thin slotted wood were found in waterlogged conditions which might have originated as a frame and possibly they could have held glass.

This main structure of the town, a square building heated by a *hypocaust*, constructed upon massive foundations to support several storeys in height and with later additions to three sides, must have been a place of great importance. Tim Potter and Ralph Jackson, who excavated the town, believe this building to have been an administrative centre, designed to impress the local population, hence its size and towering nature. In the fens a high building would be much more effective in displaying power and central control than a building with a larger groundplan, because it would have stood out for miles in the flat landscape. Other Roman towns within the province of Britannia might have had a substantial *forum* and *basilica* at their administrative and commercial centre, formal public spaces and buildings that were often large and impressive by length and facade, but few would have paralleled the Stonea tower with its sheer mass and skyward presence. It is a singular building, which the excavators saw as probably unique outside of Italy, and draws comparison to the standing building of similar proportions at Le Mura di Santo Stefano, near Anguillara, north of Rome.

Possible parallels in its form of construction do, however, exist within the northern empire, and these are generally temples. The example at Autun is approximately the same dimensions as the tower building at Stonea, but at Autun

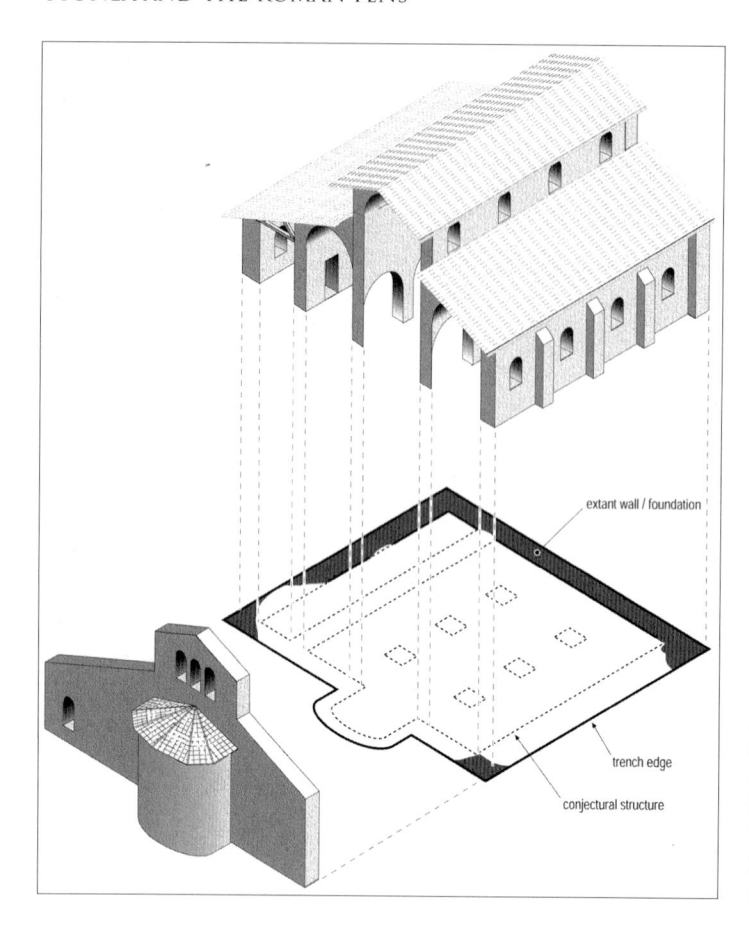

50 Alternative reconstruction of administrative building. © The Trustees of the British Museum, drawn by Steve Crummy

two storeys still survive, with three windows in the upper, and an entrance flanked by two windows in the lower (*63*). Alternative reconstructions from the ground plan recovered at Stonea based on other Roman models suggest less of a tower and more of an aisled building with a central core rising higher than the sides (*50*), much in the way that churches and cathedrals developed. Unlike Stonea, however, Autun is surrounded by a portico, a classic feature of a temple. An ephemeral feature was detected at Stonea which at first was interpreted as a portico, but later dismissed as some unused foundation trench or some feature used as part of the marking out of the central block.

The second most imposing building after the tower complex was the temple discovered some 250m north-east of the administrative core of the town. Although not completely excavated, sufficient of its ground plan was recovered for it to be seen to be a temple of Romano-Celtic design with some hybrid classical pretensions. This building consisted of a 5.6m x 5m *cella* with mortared

THE ROMAN TOWN AND CENTRE FOR AN IMPERIAL ESTATE

limestone walls 0.5m wide and central pit sealed by the grey, stone-free silt floor make-up material. The same silt was found around the exterior of the room to 2.5m in width, where a line of post-holes provided evidence for a colonnade and ambulatory surrounding the central room, giving exterior dimensions of 10.5m x 11m. The orientation was NNE–SSW for the longer side, with a double colonnaded frontage and 2.5m wide entrance unusually set on the south side rather than the east, but through this orientation it was pragmatically sited for easy access and views from the town. Immediately in front of this entrance was a 7m x 8m mortared area, possibly the base for a paved forecourt. Both this area and the building to the north of it had been constructed on a gravel platform 27m x 16m to give it extra elevation (*51*).

The temple was located offset to the north within an area defined by a circular ditch some 50m in diameter, which defined the *temenos* of the temple complex. A cambered 3-4m wide gravelled street curved north-eastwards from the core of the town to give access to the temple. Finds from metal-detecting (*52*) and from one rich deposit within a pit to the south-east demonstrate its use as a temple, most probably for Minerva, and perhaps for Mercury and Epona as well. Metal objects include two model axes, a cockerel finial, animal figurines, votive plaques

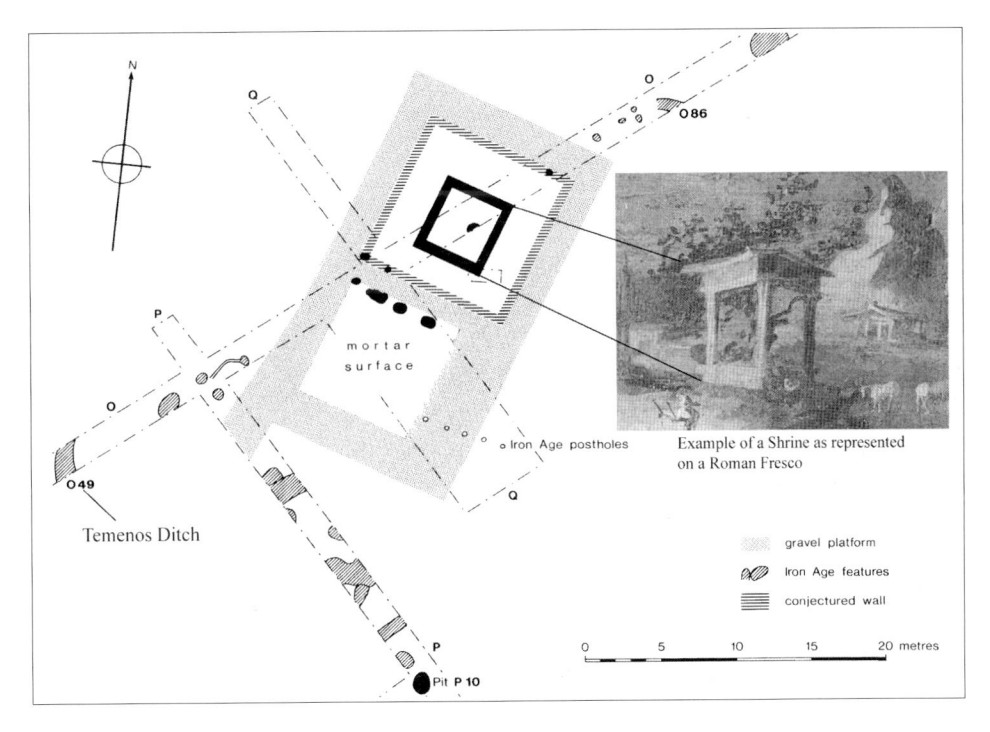

51 Plan of Stonea temple and Roman fresco of a shrine. © *The Trustees of the British Museum*

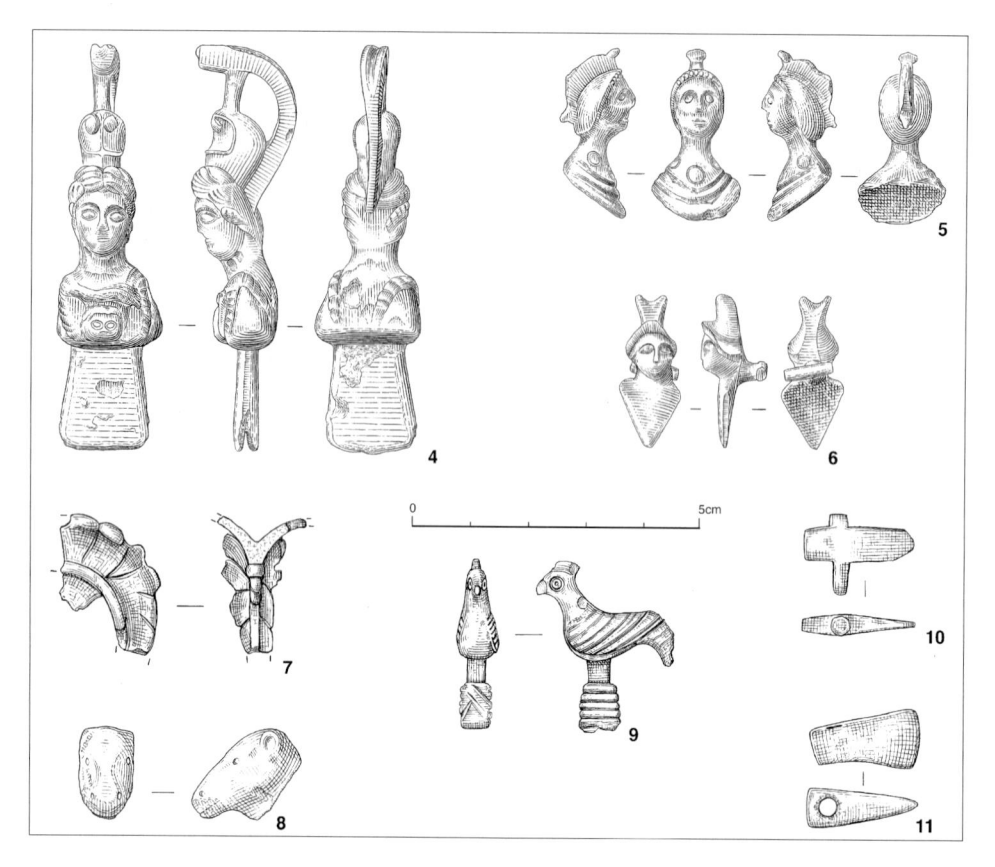

52 Artefacts attributed to the temple. © *The Trustees of the British Museum*

(*colour plate 14*) and five busts of Minerva; the rich assemblage found deposited in a pit contained window and vessel glass, a large group of complete later second-century Samian vessels, a pipe-clay figurine of a horse, *amphorae* and flagons, oyster and mussel shells, animal bone, floor tiles and *tesserae*, perhaps indicating that a mosaic once adorned the floor of the temple.

Beneath the gravel platform evidence was found for a timber predecessor to the later temple, perhaps of Flavian date, but with Middle and Late Iron Age pottery also present, suggesting the accumulation of several centuries. The main temple appears to have been in use from the mid-second to the early third century, and was probably decommissioned and possibly demolished at the same time as the administrative tower. Some Iron Age artefacts from Stonea strongly support the evidence for a much earlier temple already in the vicinity, and the location that was excavated by The British Museum should be regarded as containing evidence for continuity between both periods. Although there

THE ROMAN TOWN AND CENTRE FOR AN IMPERIAL ESTATE

are some characteristics of the design that are very typical of Romano-Celtic temples (see *51* inset), the circular *temenos* is unusual.

The majority of buildings at Stonea were timber built with wattle and daub walls (*Table 4*), and one of the most complete plans comes from Block 9 (*53*). In total there were at least 13 Roman buildings excavated in addition to the administrative block and the temple, and although some of these were single-phase, others were repaired a number of times, suggesting longevity of use. Ten of these buildings have been phased as contemporary with the administration complex, and thus dated from *c.* mid-second century to early third century; three were added after the administrative 'tower' building was abandoned and further buildings were built in Anglo-Saxon times.

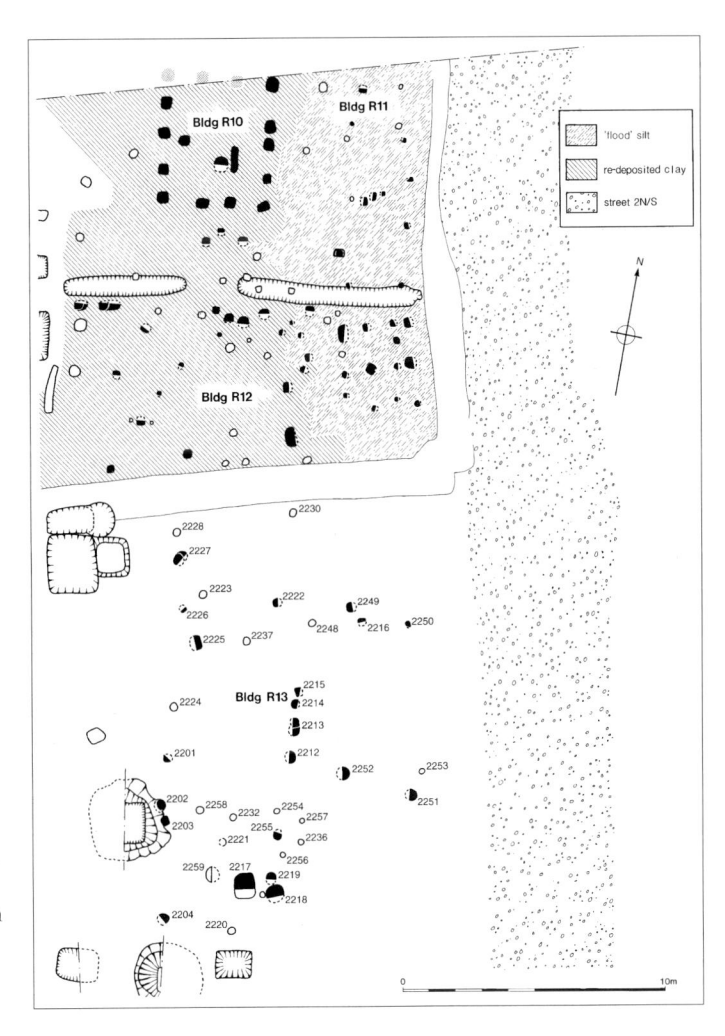

53 Example of Roman house plans at Stonea, Block 9. © The Trustees of the British Museum

STONEA AND THE ROMAN FENS

The buildings consist of houses and ancillary structures, all built with earth-fast timber posts or uprights supported on timber beams, and often defined by eavesdrip gullies which helped to identify the buildings on one plot from the next. Daub would have been used as the main form of walling, which would have been applied to a wattle frame attached to the upright timbers. Some houses were single aisled, but others appear to have had more than one substantial room. The orientation varied, with some buildings appearing to have gable ends on to the street, but others that ran parallel to it, with an eavesdrip gully separating the house from the roadway. They were mostly rectangular structures ranging from 3 x 5m to 6 x 13m in size, with load-bearing timber uprights along the walls to support the roof (see *Table 4* and *54*).

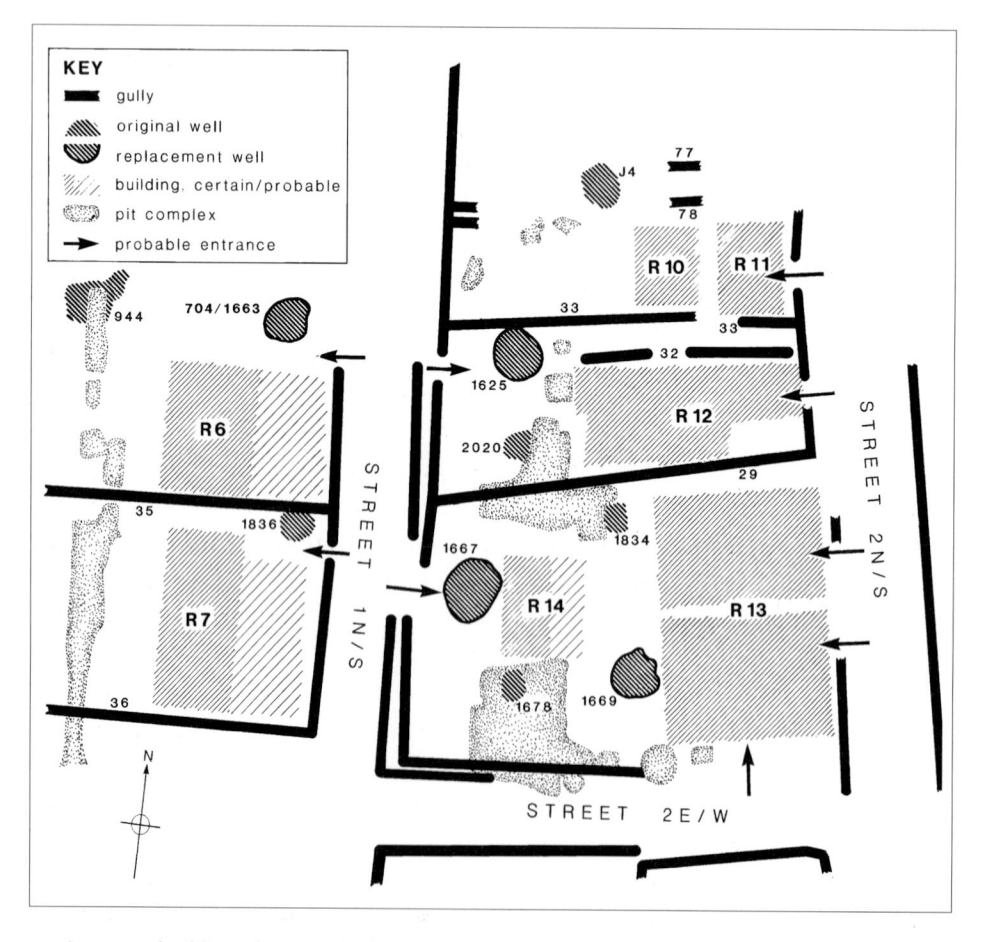

54 Access to buildings from roads. © *The Trustees of the British Museum*

THE ROMAN TOWN AND CENTRE FOR AN IMPERIAL ESTATE

SERVICE FEATURES

Around the main buildings the compounds within individual plots contained service features such as wells, ovens, rubbish pits, yards and outhouses. The yards and pits were often found on the inside part of the plot, away from the roadside and presumably at the backs of properties.

Pits were generally cut to about 1m in depth and were used for discarding waste. Groups of pits were found at the corners and aligned along the edges of properties, providing evidence for boundaries and showing that rubbish disposal occurred in a well-managed fashion (*56*). Pits from early periods of use were seldom cut by later features. In some cases it was possible to track a chronological progression from one end of a boundary to the other, and then a second parallel line located inside of the first as the longevity of occupation necessitated the taking of new land for dumping waste. This linear arrangement became more apparent with those pits that could be dated to the later part of the second century and early third centuries, whereas the distribution of the earlier pits appears to have been more random. Other pits were found in disused or undeveloped plots of land, including one group which consisted of a row of four vertical-sided examples which were most probably latrines.

Wells were identified in association with many of the properties, with dimensions *c*.2m in diameter and depth and therefore generally larger and deeper than the pits. One example was found to have had steps leading down into it with a possible handrail and decking. Another had post-holes indicating a well-house structure or lifting mechanism above it. Stone-lining survived in one example and others showed that they had been timber- or wicker-lined. Periodically these wells seem to have been decommissioned and used for rubbish disposal, with new wells being dug nearby if the property continued to be occupied.

Drainage was provided by gullies and ditches, discontinuous stretches laid out in the early life of the settlement on a gridded arrangement to manage low-capacity localised drainage. This was followed by an organic growth over time, the short sections slowly becoming joined up along property boundaries, which also helped to differentiate the edge of the streets. This was accompanied by a growth in size suggesting increased water consumption and waste generation as the town developed. Around the *insula* (Block 1) containing the administrative building, however, the drains defined the property plot from the foundation of the town, and were continuously redefined during later periods.

A large sump was discovered south of the administrative building, into which the eastern drain of Block 1 flowed. This sump comprised two rectangular trenches which together measured 27m x10m, and were over 3m deep. They had steeply sloping sides and were waterlogged so that a rich assemblage of organic

STONEA AND THE ROMAN FENS

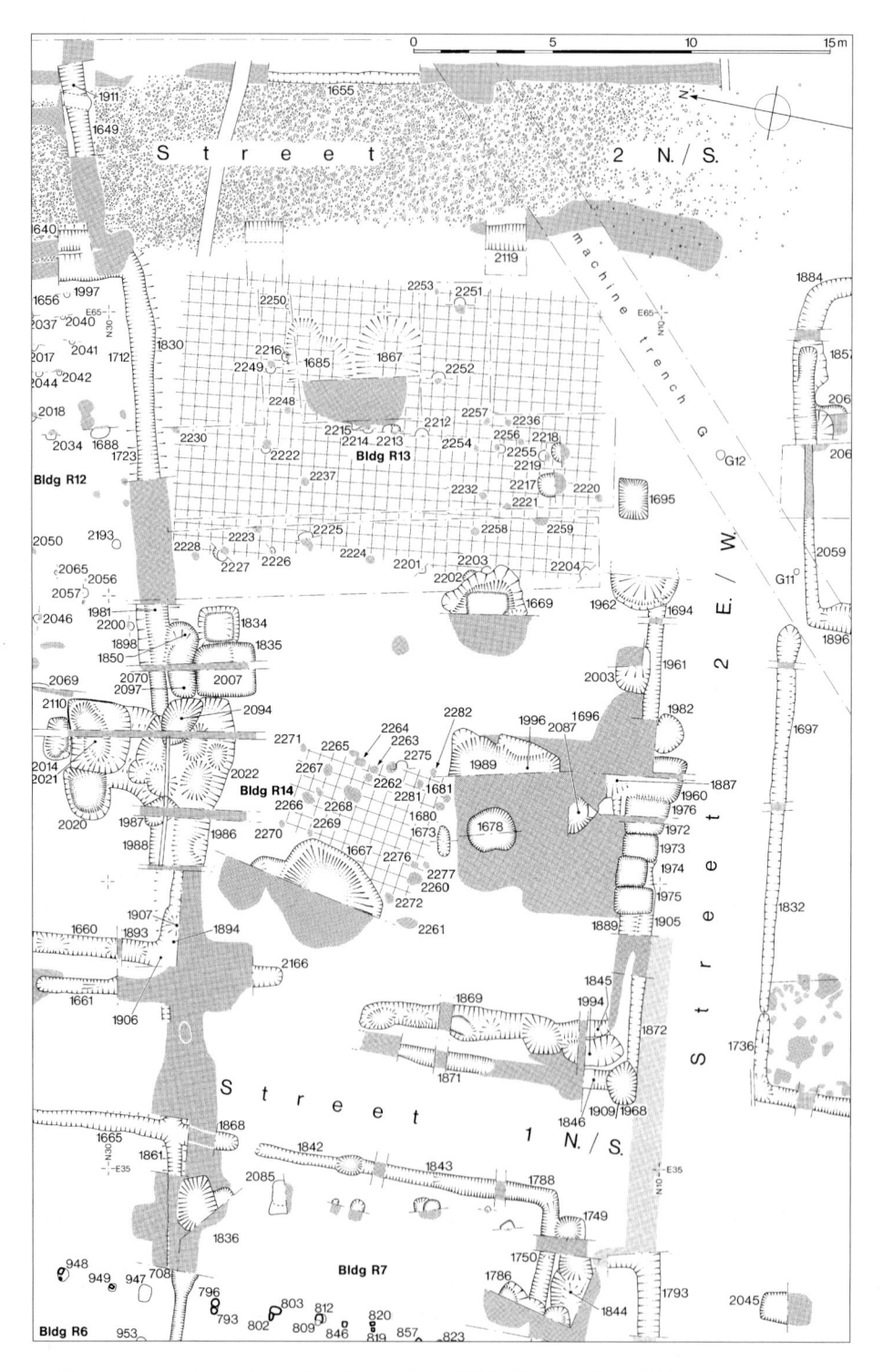

55 Property boundaries defined by lines of pits. © *The Trustees of the British Museum*

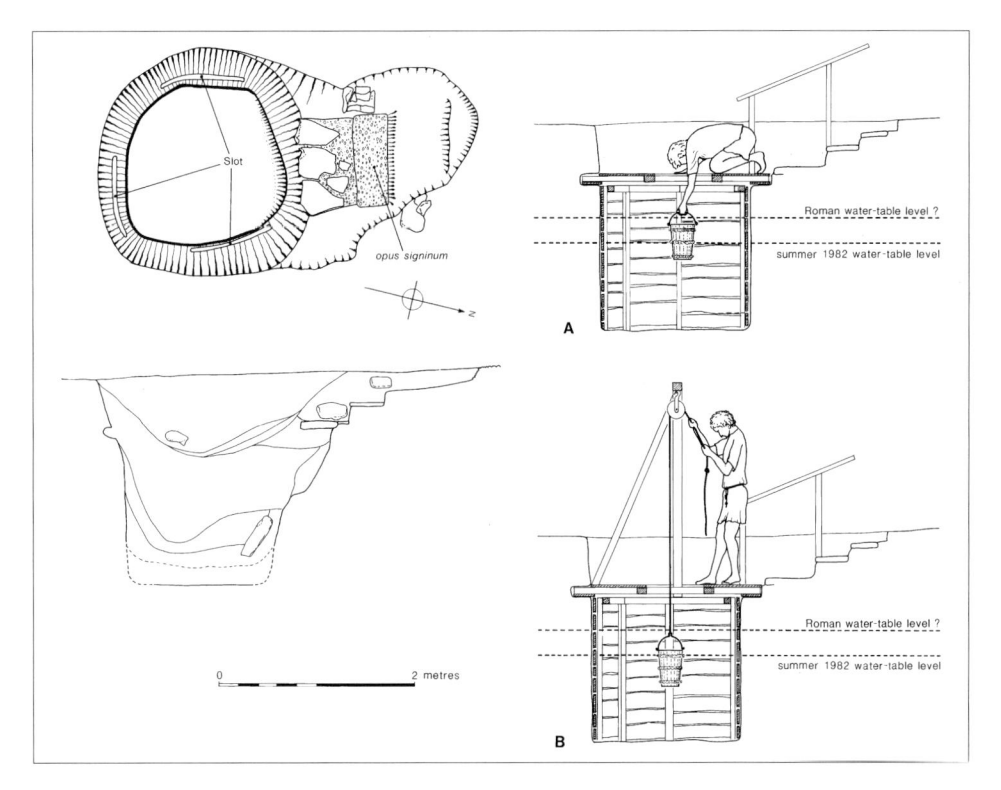

THE ROMAN TOWN AND CENTRE FOR AN IMPERIAL ESTATE

56 Reconstruction of a well from the town.© The Trustees of the British Museum

artefacts and other evidence was preserved. The sump appears to have been fenced off and slowly filled up during the second century, so that the later drains defining the eastern edge of Block 1 were seen to cut through the infill layers of the sump.

ECONOMY AND ACTIVITIES

Artefactual evidence from the excavations at Stonea provided a wealth of information about the lifestyles and prosperity of the population. Not only were there large amounts of domestic pottery, both fine and coarsewares (57), but the circumstances of disposal and the nature of the wet ground into which some objects found themselves has allowed a very high level of preservation (58), including wooden and leather artefacts, as well as items of food waste such as seeds and pips.

The building materials used in the initial construction of the town imply considerable expenditure, with limestone imported from some 25 miles away,

STONEA AND THE ROMAN FENS

57 Selection of pottery from Stonea: Nene Valley wares (mostly third-century date) and Samian, from the boundary ditch to the precinct of the administrative complex. © Ralph Jackson and The Trustees of the British Museum

probably from the area around Durobrivae on the western edge of the fens. Barnack stone was known to have been quarried during Roman times, and it would have been perfectly feasible to transport it to Stonea via existing watercourses and canals (*61*). In addition, tiles were found which would have been produced in a local kiln, for roofs, floors and hypocausts. *Tesserae* bear witness to mosaics and *opus signinum* shows that concrete was being made which would have necessitated the import of considerable quantities of lime or, alternatively, local burning of stone to produce it. Even the poorer structures would have required a quantity of timber which may also have been imported from the upland. The palaeoenvironmental evidence from the Camp, however, shows that the island was wooded in the preceding centuries and that woodland continued to exist within the general vicinity throughout the Roman period. Window and vessel glass, and Egyptian blue pellets have been found, presumably evidence of import of luxury goods. Although some painted wall plaster occurred in timber-frame houses, the majority of this came from the stone 'tower' administrative building, which included red and white panelling, speckled and marble effects, geometric designs and scenes of landscapes and figures. Thus, from the evidence about the buildings themselves much can be deduced about the prosperity of the settlement in its early years.

Trades such as tilers, builders, painters and carpenters are all represented by the evidence from the buildings, as well as many more. The craftsmen may have been itinerant, but the scale of construction would have meant they would probably have lived at the town for some years, all helping to contribute to a locally booming economy. From a variety of sources it has been possible to establish that a single man could produce up to 220 tiles a day, and those recovered at Stonea

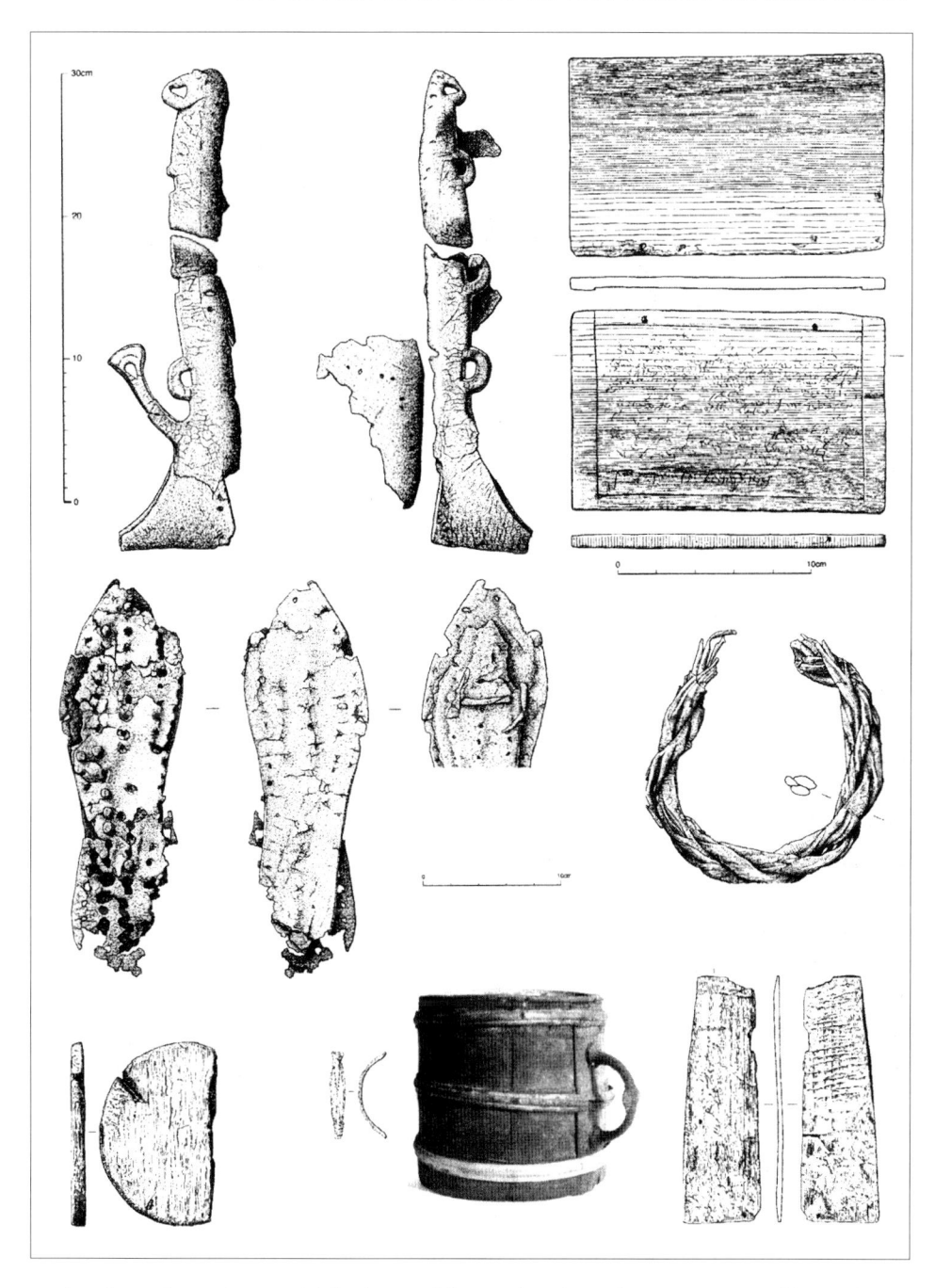

THE ROMAN TOWN AND CENTRE FOR AN IMPERIAL ESTATE

58 Artefacts of organic material: leather sandals, wooden frame for wax writing-tablet, withy handle (for bucket?), parts of a stave-built tankard and an example of a complete tankard from Pentuan. *Drawings © The Trustees of the British Museum, figure compiled by Gill Reaney*

show that they were manufactured through a moulding process. A total of 17,842 tile fragments were examined from the excavation, which allowed identification of 10 fabric groups with quartz-rich sand inclusions, and a hypothesis that three kilns produced the vast majority of tiles from local sources of Ampthill and boulder clay. Three types of mortar were also identified, a strong, durable lime mortar with crushed tile inclusions, a lime mortar without the inclusions which would have formed a weaker bond, and a mortar that was composed merely of an aggregation of clay and gravel.

The deep, sump-like feature to the south of the administrative building was infilled with large quantities of organic refuse including worked wood chips, pieces of timber, wooden artefacts, basketry and withy bundles, coppiced wood and roundwood. Because of the high water table at the site this organic evidence has survived for 2,000 years and it has provided a wealth of information on the importance of wood and timber to the economy, as well as on the skills of carpenters and types of wood exploited for different functions. In total 98,000 pieces of wood were analysed, of which 6,500 were of a size that gave useful results. Because each blow of an axe produces three to four chips, and any item will need a variety of processes such as splitting, shaping, dressing, shaving, honing and carving to produce a finished article, the rest of the assemblage were small chips from woodworking. The majority of the timber fragments would probably have derived from construction of the administrative building and identifiable items included planks, pegs, posts, stakes, slats, shingles, boards and linings, and woodworking debitage, although a range of tools and other artefacts were also found. The main type of timber chosen for construction purposes and for the production of artefacts was ash, but a significant proportion was also of oak and to a lesser degree of hazel. The predominance of ash probably relates to its qualities as a durable and heavy wood, and one which also makes a good fuel. Ash and oak were brought to site as raw materials and worked close to the point of use. The tree trunks were split axially following the lines of rays to produce an even grain. Evidence for axe cuts abounds, but sawing is not apparent even with roundwood. Ash predominates the roundwood assemblage, mostly of 20mm diameter but ranging up to 60mm in some instances. Blackthorn was important and generally found to be c.15mm diameter; a variety of other species were also utilised. The uses for this roundwood would have included fencing, hedging, hurdling, wattles, traps, basketry, screens, wickerwork and withies.

The wooden artefacts included four ash writing tablets, a complete spade (or becket) of ash with iron sheaf, parts of a hayrake and a pitchfork of ash, an ash tankard stave, an oak tankard or bucket base or barrel head, a twisted willow withy binding or handle for a bucket, bungs, stoppers, wedges, slotted frames and possibly a partly worked piece of furniture (*58* and *59*).

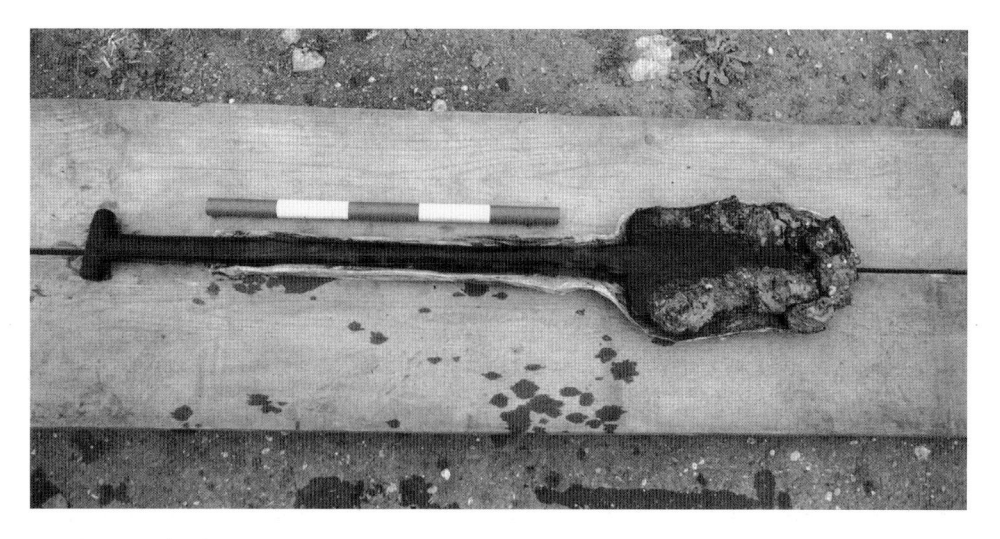

THE ROMAN TOWN AND CENTRE FOR AN IMPERIAL ESTATE

59 Photograph of Roman spade found in sump. © *Ralph Jackson and The Trustees of the British Museum*

Timber was therefore of considerable economic importance, and the proper management of this resource and clear ownership through land division would have been essential for the sustainability and maintenance of trade in this commodity. Evidence for such woodland management can be seen at Stonea through such items as a coppice stool found in the sump and the roundwood which probably derived from a regime of thinning out of top wood, as well as spring and autumn felling. The palaeoenvironmental evidence from the site shows that woodland was sustained throughout the Roman period and that all the timber could have come from local sources, although the scale of use at Stonea would argue for a more distant trade to supplement this local resource. In addition to the ash and oak woodland located on the island, other sources of timber would have come from fen carr (the alder-willow-birch woodland) which has been confirmed by pollen evidence as existing locally in the Roman period near Stonea Camp and Grange.

AGRICULTURE AND HORTICULTURE

The main basis of the economy throughout the Roman occupation (the second- or third-century town and its successor settlement of the third to fifth centuries and later) was that of sheep farming. During the course of The British Museum's programme of investigation, 19,000 animal bones were recorded from all types of context, including ditches, pits and wells, although the best preservation was seen to have occurred on those bones retrieved from the sump; only bones from wetland species of wild birds and fresh water fish were found in this deposit. The animal bone collection was dominated by cattle and sheep, which represented almost 90 per cent of all the bone recovered over both phases of occupation, with sheep accounting for the majority of the animals; a few goats and pigs, horse and various sizes of dog were found also, as well as domestic cats, chickens, geese, ducks and hare.

Sheep were the mainstay of the economy, with 60 per cent killed before they were two years old. A high proportion of head and feet parts suggest that the sheep were slaughtered and butchered at Stonea and then their carcasses were exported. Peaks in the age of death occur at three stages: for neonates; for animals in their first year during summer and autumn; and in spring and winter for the second-year animals. Such a kill pattern implies that the sheep were not being kept for their wool but principally for meat as lamb and mutton, and possibly for other commodities such as skins for parchment and sheepskins for household purposes. Bone measurements have demonstrated a high degree of standardisation, suggesting that a single flock or population of sheep was sustained at Stonea over several hundred years, throughout the Roman and Anglo-Saxon periods. Pathological indicators show that the livestock was extremely healthy, in spite of the rather wet conditions in much of the landscape round about, with little sign of liver fluke or other disease.

In contrast, the cattle, of Celtic short-horn variety, showed variable ages at death and all body parts were evenly distributed. The conclusion drawn from this evidence is that cattle were probably used for a variety of functions such as traction, dairying and occasional provision of meat and leather. The relative size of cattle compared to sheep, however, suggests that they would in fact have supplied approximately 75 per cent of the meat eaten by the local community at Stonea. Pigs displayed no obvious kill pattern and all parts of their bodies are represented in the assemblage. No old animals were found and there appears to have been a relatively high proportion of loss as neonates.

In summary, the animal husbandry at Stonea can be seen to have been well managed and, in spite of the emergence of a town and probable Roman administrative function, the basic rural economy followed a very traditional British Iron Age pattern with a heavy preponderance on sheep.

Evidence for arable farming generally came from carbonised seeds, pollen, and plant material preserved in waterlogged conditions, especially from the sump. In addition mineralised seeds were recovered from latrine deposits which demonstrated the importance of wheat within the diet. The main species identified include wheat and barley, with spelt wheat slowly giving way to more free-threshing varieties during the Roman period, and six-rowed hulled barley predominant throughout.

THE ROMAN TOWN AND CENTRE FOR AN IMPERIAL ESTATE

Straw fragments and chaff show some indication for activities such as threshing, raking, winnowing and sieving and weed species of arable crops show strongly throughout the Roman period. In contrast to this evidence for the production and processing of arable crops, there is very little evidence for grain storage.

Other crops identified by small numbers of seeds include oats and rye, flax, Celtic bean and pea. In addition to these a number of species were found of other medical, culinary, edible or functional use such as box leaf (as a purgative), hazelnuts, elderberry, blackberry, sloes, sweet gale (perhaps for brewing and preserving beer), as well as sedge and reeds (for thatching).

Only a few agricultural tools were found, but this is not surprising, as many of these would have been made out of wood and on the dry parts of the site such organic remains would have decayed. It is perhaps more surprising to note, however, that no iron plough-shares were found. Water conditions in the sump produced several wooden items of interest, including a hayrake dated to the third or fourth century, of a design typically used by farmers until recent times. It was made out of ash with a handle set into the clog by a mortice joint, and nailed in place. Wooden tines were evenly spaced along the clog, and this composite design was probably a Roman introduction to Britain. In addition to this a pitchfork, made from naturally formed ash roundwood, was found which probably would have had iron heads to the forks originally. A spade was recovered which was over 1m in length and made out of a single piece of ash with a T-shaped handle and a slender blade, shod with iron (*59*). On the right side of the spadehead wear from pushing down with the right foot had eroded the wood, giving the top of the blade an asymmetrical appearance. This was dated between the late second and early third centuries. Eight parts of grinding stones made from millstone grit were found, as well as 15 fragments of Niedermendic lava; both these imported types of stone would have been used for grinding grain to make flour. Other trade items included ten rubbing and grinding stones of micaceous sandstone, and 11 whetstones, mostly of Kentish ragstone. All of these finds point to some importance for agricultural and horticultural activities such as gathering hay and straw, and processing cereals. In addition to this there were a higher number of bone textile-working tools than would normally be expected on such a reasonably high-status site, dated to the first phase of Roman settlement. This indicates that Stonea was not only an administrative centre, but also that the community engaged in more typical rural activities as well.

Leather-working is indicated by the finds of four sandals in the sump (*58*). Perhaps these were made from leather produced at Stonea. They were all made of cattle hide, and included the nailed sole of a woman's or child's shoe, a man's shoe with similarities to the military *calceus* type found usually in the north of England (*58 bottom*) but providing good protection in wet and cold conditions, and a pair of men's one-piece shoes of a more traditional 'native' style (*58 top*).

Pollen, soil chemistry and molluscan analysis provide a good indication of the surrounding landscape during both phases of Roman occupation at Stonea. Fairly open country, with hedged fields of pasture and cereal cultivation, probable hedgerows, and patches of scrub and woodland existed throughout the Roman period. Within the settlement itself some trees and shrubs were growing (indeed, the only known paved area was around the tower building) and during the final phase of occupation blackberry and elder can be seen to have invaded the areas around wells, indicating disuse. The local groundwater would have been high, with wet marshy land and meadow in the general vicinity, and fresh water slum conditions in features such as ditches and gullies. Brackish conditions occurred at times in some features. A high nitrogen content to many of the soil samples suggests that manuring on the drier land of the island would have been undertaken. Fungi were also found, especially large numbers of puffballs, suggestive of deliberate collection, but their function is uncertain; perhaps for use as tinder or as a haemostatic for cauterisation, or even for hallucinogenic purposes.

LUXURY ITEMS AND IMPORTS

Amongst the carbonised seeds there were some rare finds such as lentils and fig pips, clear evidence for imports of luxury commodities from warmer climates. Usually such finds are made only in urban contexts or on military sites, so they are significant contributors to interpreting Stonea as an administrative centre with a wealthy elite who could afford luxuries. Oyster, cockle and mussel shells were found in reasonably large quantities at Stonea, perhaps unsurprisingly given its location fairly close to the Roman coastline. Such finds are common on Roman sites, but they indicate a vibrant market and efficient system of supply to keep such items fresh for sale and consumption after harvesting and transportation. The presence of a canal connecting Stonea with March and the Fenland waterways would have helped in such a trade.

Large quantities of vessel glass and a wooden tankard stave were also found, showing that the consumption of alcoholic beverages was important. The glass vessels included both tablewares and household/storage wares, and the glass was mostly in a colourless condition or used in blue and green, with just two examples in yellow-brown. Drinking cups were most common, with jugs, bowls and various types of bottle also present in the assemblage. They can be dated fairly closely as having been in use from the second quarter of the second century to the first quarter of the third century, coincident with occupation of the administrative complex and town phase of Stonea. The sweet gale plant remains might indicate local beer brewing, whilst *amphorae* fragments point to

THE ROMAN TOWN AND CENTRE FOR AN IMPERIAL ESTATE

the import of Mediterranean products such as olive oil and probably also of wine. Six types of *amphora* have been identified, of which one is an entirely new type, and few are characteristic of those used for transporting fish sauce. As a group they seem to date from the second century, although individual items could range from 50 BC to the third century AD. They originated from southern Spain and southern France, as well as Italy, and one substantially complete vessel, of a previously unknown type, was found with graffiti on it which said 'weight 11lb, weight full 33lb' (*60*), measurements that would seem to fit with the weights calculated for the vessel during analysis. The demise of *amphorae* imports seems to have occurred in the early third century, probably coinciding with the demolition of the 'tower' building and administrative complex.

Fineware ceramics from the site include flagons, beakers, pie dishes and bowls dated to the second century (*57*) and, in contrast to the earlier occupation, the third and fourth centuries had much less fineware. Three hundred decorated sherds and 3,000 plain sherds of Samian were recovered and this assemblage has, in general, been dated to the second half of the second century. Most originated from central Gaul, but east Gaulish decorated bowls and Antonine Lezoux ware predominates. In contrast to this there was a complete absence of Trajanic central Gaulish wares and a virtual absence of any Samian items from south Gaul. Rhenish and central

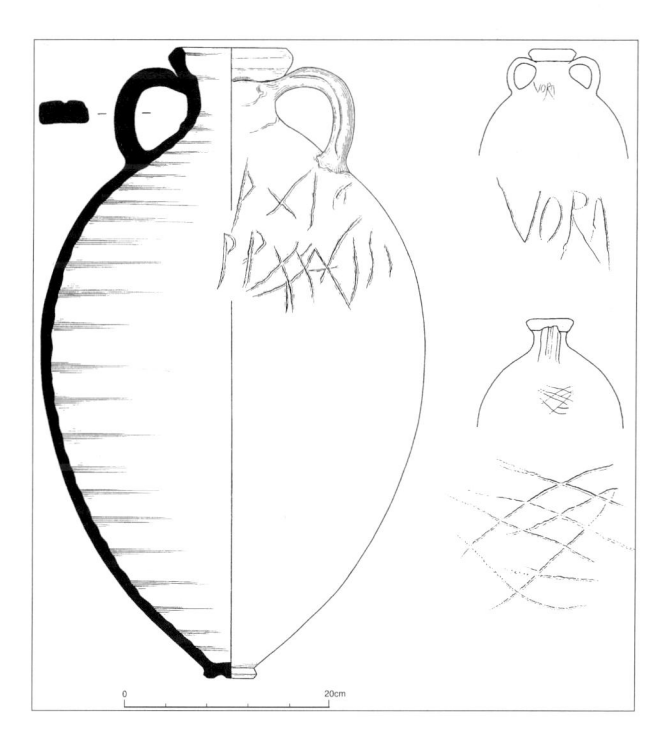

60 Amphora and graffiti. © The Trustees of the British Museum

Gaulish colour-coated wares were also present, as well as London and Colchester types from some of the earlier deposits. Stonea stands out amongst other Fenland Roman sites in the character and quantity of the imported wares found on the site; flagons and *amphorae* are largely absent from Fenland sites. There was no real pattern to the spatial distribution of the pottery, except for Barbotine decorated colour-coated pots which seem to have been concentrated in Blocks 8, 9 and 10. In common with other Fenland sites coarsewares were identified as having come from local sources such as the Nene valley potteries and Horningsea, on the Cam north of Cambridge. The dates of the pottery assemblage from different types of feature show that the pits and wells contained mostly third- or fourth-century pottery, whereas ditches and gullies included an element of earlier date as well as third- or fourth-century vessel fragments. Destruction deposits associated with the 'tower' building, however, were dated to the early third century.

A number of pellets of Egyptian Blue, an artifical glassy pigment for painting plaster or for use in cosmetics, were found in Blocks 3, 8 and 9. Egyptian Blue was a high-status commodity although the parts of the town that it was found in do not readily lend themselves to an interpretation of wealthy housing. Block 9, however, was also one in which painted wall plaster was found and Blocks 8 and 9 also contained a concentration of specially decorated Barbotine pottery.

A range of rather unexceptional jewellery has been found as a result of metal-detecting and excavation. The dating of the 95 bronze brooches is of interest because the great majority fall within the period AD 43-99, prior to the building of the town during the Hadrianic period. Some other examples of Romano-British brooches conform with other evidence to show that the site was occupied into the third century whilst continental examples show continuation into the fourth century. Apart from the brooches, 27 rings and 14 bracelet fragments (mostly of snake type) were recovered, in addition to some gold links from a necklace.

COINS

The coin assemblage has been particularly useful in refining the chronological development and periods of activity at Stonea. In total, 961 coins were recovered by excavation and surface collection (mostly through metal-detecting), and three coin hoards are known from previous discoveries. The earliest Roman coins found on the site date from the middle of the first century, but there is a significant absence of coins dating to the second half of the first century. Coinage studies show that the mid-Hadrianic period was the beginning of a major period of activity at Stonea but that the comparatively low occurrence of *denarii* suggests that there was no significant input by the military into construction of the town. The majority of

THE ROMAN TOWN AND CENTRE FOR AN IMPERIAL ESTATE

coins from the excavation belong to the period AD 117-161, with a second peak found in topsoil collection for the period AD 259-275 (including Gallic empire issues perhaps of local manufacture) and AD 330-378. The latest coins were from after AD 388, but significant patterns of wear on some coins suggest that losses continued into the fifth century. The evidence from the distribution of coin loss also shows that there was a spatial shift in the settlement during the fourth century, away from the excavated area and administrative complex at the west end of the town.

INDUSTRY

The excavations at Stonea produced some evidence from bronze-working in the form of crucible fragments containing very small amounts of copper, zinc, tin and lead identified through X-ray flourence analysis. Some iron-working evidence for smithying was also found, and a range of iron objects were found including keys, locks, tools, door furniture, structural fittings and personal items. Similarly a small number of lead objects were found including cams for window glazing, a vessel rim and a 1lb weight. This general corpus of material helps to suggest that Stonea was not a major centre of industry, but that instead its importance and main function lay elsewhere.

One of the slightly more notable iron artefacts recovered was a *stylus*. In combination with the four ash writing tablets the *stylus* provides slender but useful corroborative evidence in suggesting that the site enjoyed a major administrative role, and that some of the population during the first phase of occupation were primarily consumers rather than producers. This pattern in the make-up of the settlement and community seems to have altered during the first half of the third century, when the major buildings were demolished and the town gave way instead to a settlement dominated by farming but, during the fourth century, a number of pieces of evidence show that its importance as an administrative centre was restored or had remained intact, in spite of losing visibility in the archaeological record.

IMPERIAL ESTATE CENTRE AND URBAN STATUS

A hypothesis that the fens, or at least a major part of it, belonged to the emperor and was administered for the state by government officials has long been in vogue and much discussed in academic debate. There is a large body of evidence to demonstrate that widespread settlement or colonisation occurred in the fens during the second century, largely coincident with Hadrian's rule and visit to Britan in c.AD 122. Certain characteristics of the Roman development of the fens point strongly to a military, and therefore state-sponsored, origin: the roads and canals, and secondary land divisions and drainage schemes that relate to them, required specialist skills such as surveying and engineering, together with a substantial work force for construction. The Fen Causeway is one of the most impressive, and probably earliest, routes through the fens, with its Roman construction generally assigned to the first century, probably in the immediate years following the first Icenian revolt of AD 47. It runs eastwards from the fen edge at Peterborough, island-hopping through Whittlesey and March to eventually meet the Norfolk upland at Denver. Several canals were built to replicate much of this route, and roads and canals ran together and superseded one another during subsequent years (*61*).

Stonea fits into this pattern of state intervention as the nature of its principal building and gridded layout of streets reflect official direction rather than private enterprise. Stonea island appears to have been connected to the much larger island of March by two canals (*22, colour plate 10*), one running south from the settlement of Flaggrass located on the eastern edge of the larger island and astride the Fen Causeway and a second canal running east from Wimblington to Stonea. It would have been along these waterways and canals that the stone used in the construction of the Stonea administrative 'tower' building would have been brought, from areas such as Barnack near Peterborough, and the method by which salted meat was exported from Stonea. The *via decumanus* of Stonea has been traced a considerable distance westwards towards Hook on March island, showing that a terrestrial link also existed.

The finds at Stonea have lent credence to an interpretation of its function as an administrative centre, with the evidence of the luxuriously appointed principal building supplemented by writing tablets and a stylus, luxury imports of foodstuffs and pottery, a community which employed the use of coinage, unlike many other settlements in the fens at this time, and hints of military presence in the form of various metal items of personal equipment (*62*). Supervision of imperial estates and tax collection were jobs often undertaken by military personnel. Its administrative importance is further demonstrated during the fourth century when this official presence is reflected not only in new stone buildings with hypocaust and similar luxurious elements, but also in the discovery of eight crossbow-type brooches, some in silver and gilt, which represent a significant concentration of a relatively rare type generally associated with officials or soldiers (see *96*). Military belt fittings of this period also exist at Stonea and 40 per cent of the coins recovered from the site date from the fourth century, with some of very late issue demonstrating a continued use of coinage into the fifth century.

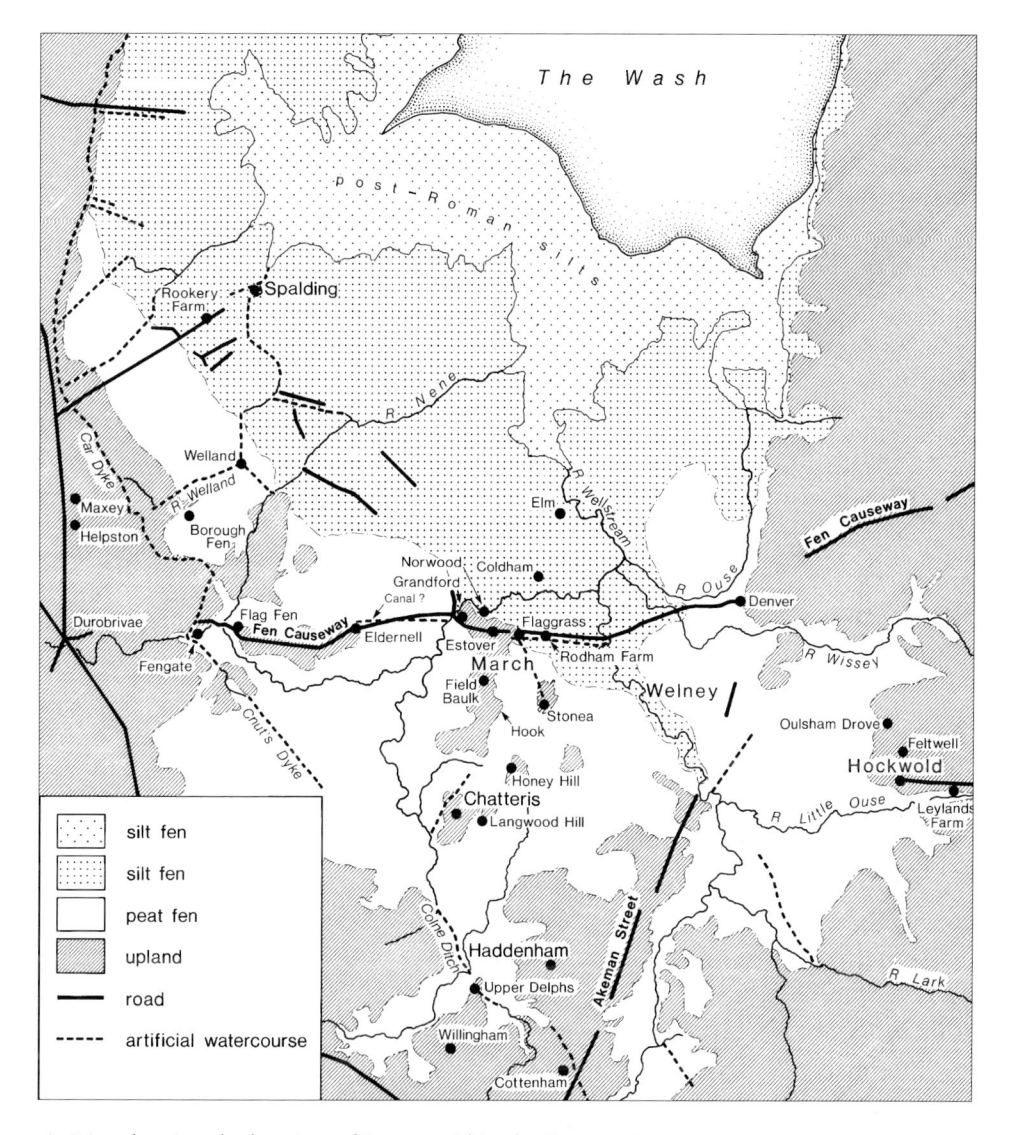

THE ROMAN TOWN AND CENTRE FOR AN IMPERIAL ESTATE

61 Map showing the location of Stonea within the Roman Fens.
© *The Trustees of the British Museum*

Stonea cannot be seen in isolation, and to interpret the site an understanding of its surrounding context and contemporary economy is needed. The evidence from many fen and fen-edge sites has demonstrated the importance of sheep-rearing for wool, dairy products and for meat. The rapid expansion of Roman settlement during the second century, and growth of occupation on the silt fen to exploit the salt from the sea water of the creeks, led to a large market for products from the upland, particularly from the Nene valley to the west of Peterborough;

62 Military metalwork from Stonea. *Ralph Jackson*

this led in part to the growth of Durobrivae as a large, wealthy town situated on Ermine Street. The canals and roads through the fens allowed ready passage and growth of commerce between the different regions surrounding the fens and the Fenland communities themselves, as well as access to the North Sea.

Salt-making was often a state monopoly, and the hypothesis for a Fenland imperial estate has been driven in part by the chronological connection with Hadrian, his wall and the need for sufficent supplies for the garrisons stationed there. The fens could have acted as a provider of meat, which was butchered and salted, before being transported via the canals and waterways, and sea-routes to the Imperial army. Grain from East Anglia could likewise have been moved easily through this region to supply military needs, both in Britain and further afield, perhaps for the garrisons along the *Limes*. Such strategic concepts help to substantiate the claims for a Fenland imperial estate, but the limits of this estate do not necessarily correspond with the whole of Fenland; much of the Lincolnshire fens and the south-eastern part of the Cambridgeshire fens were probably not included. At least two inscriptions would seem to indicate the existence of such an estate, or estates: a limestone block inscribed with 'PVBLIC' from Tort Field, Sawtry on the western edge of the fens which Professor Salway says 'leaves little doubt that this was imperial domain', and a boundary stone from Titchmarsh in Northamptonshire with the letters 'PP' which has been translated as '*(terminus) p(ublice) p(ositus)*'. This latter was found at the junction of two important roads near to the River Nene and in association with stone-built structures and artefacts that covered all centuries of Roman rule. Late Iron Age pottery suggests that this was an important place before the Roman occupation occurred, a situation which was certainly also true of Stonea. The wealth of Icenian coinage and other finds in the environs of Stonea Camp and the later town clearly demonstrate two things: firstly that both Stonea and March islands were well populated in the Late Iron Age and secondly that the land belonged to the Iceni. Prasutagus, the last king of the Iceni, was a client king of the Romans, but foresaw problems for his kingdom after his death and therefore tried to avert this by making the Emperor Nero a co-heir along with his daughters. The revolt and its subsequent suppression undoubtedly led to a great impoverishment of the region, and Tacitus relates how the Icenian aristocracy were deprived of their hereditary estates. In the light of such strong circumstantial evidence it would seem highly likely that at least the Icenian part of the fens were given over to the emperor in the wake of the Boudican revolt, but that it was not perhaps until the reign and visit of Hadrian that the economic potential of this land was fully appreciated and exploited, and that the plans laid at that time perhaps did not reach full maturity until the reign of Antoninus Pius.

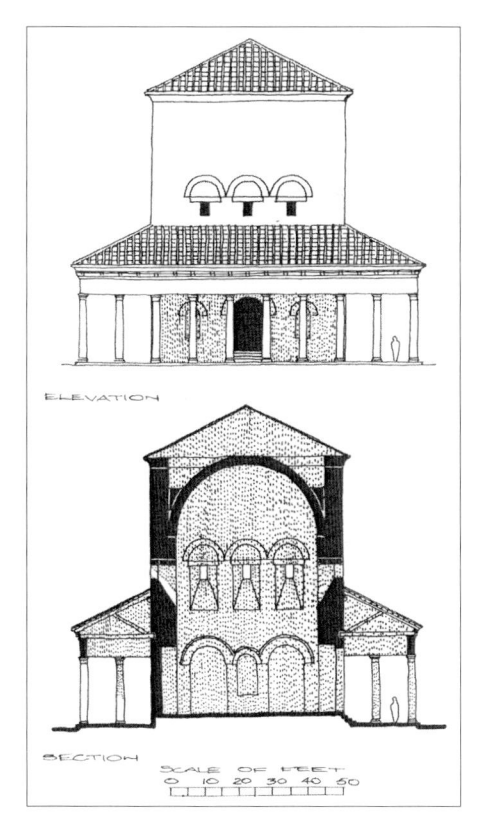

63 Autun temple reconstruction. *Drawn by Michael Green*

STONEA: A TEMPLE SANCTUARY?

An alternative interpretation of The British Museum's excavations is given here by Michael Green. He has examined the evidence for the tower reconstruction and compared this with Roman buildings of similar scale and design, applying an architect's analysis of the data.

Building R1, the central feature at Stonea comprised a rectangular area 16-16.25m x 16.8-16.9m which was dug in the Hadrianic period 1m down into boulder clay from the old ground surface (*49*). The slightly longer axis lay east–west with a later entrance portico lying on the east side fronting the street.

The masonry footings built around the perimeter of the excavation were, where surviving, 1.15-1.2m wide (i.e. about 4 Roman feet), but at floor level had been reduced by offsets on both sides of the wall to about 3 Roman feet. Over the base of the Roman foundation area a substantial platform of hardcore was spread in 3 layers, each layer sealed by a spread of lime mortar. The two upper levels of hardcore were integrated with the masonry walls, which were built directly off the lowest hardcore and mortar layer. The walls were free built with Barnack- and Blisworth-coursed, squared-rubble facing with a puddled rubble core. The structural hardcore platform was 0.8m (2.5 Roman feet) thick – from above it to the top of the concrete floor (with *opus signinum* finish) was about the same depth. This too would have had a hardcore substructure laid over the platform. For additional stability the concrete flooring slab would have been carried on the inner ledge of the wall. This massive substructure was no doubt felt necessary due to the instability of the clay subsoil.

The date of construction had a *terminus post quem* of AD 125. The Hadrianic Bath House at Godmanchester was of comparable date and erected exactly in the same principles. Indeed they may even have had the same architect and public works contractors. Any interior walls of this building would have been erected off the hardcore platform, but as most of this had been robbed out no evidence for internal structures was found during excavation.

What should be realised are the severe structural limitations of this building with its relatively slight walling round the perimeter. Rubble walls of this calibre and thickness could carry at most two storeys with safety. There is also the problem of spanning such a width with timber to support the upper floors. The distance is about 14m (46ft). Most traditional timber scantlings can only safely span about half this distance at the most. One of the hypothetical reconstructions

THE ROMAN TOWN AND CENTRE FOR AN IMPERIAL ESTATE

proposed in the publication of Stonea unfortunately appears to have overlooked some rather basic structural principles, and shows a four-storey tower block, which is simply not viable. The Autun (Saône-et-Loire) temple of this height required *cella* walls of a thickness of 2.5m or 8ft (*63*).

It was also suggested that the main room of the tower building was heated by a hypocaust system, but in fact no trace of *pillae* were found *in situ* on the surviving patches of substructure flooring, and the rationale for its existence is based in part on the discovery of flue tiles in the destruction debris over the structures. There was an extension to the building on the south side which has been interpreted as a *praefurnium*. As part of the second phase of construction a separate room with hypocaust, served by its own *praefurnium*, was discovered and this, no doubt, was part of the priest's quarters that wrapped itself round the back of the temple in a later phase.

I have been suspicious of the interpretation of this structure as an administrative centre from the outset. My architectural thesis many years ago was on Romano-Celtic temples and I recognised that this was a badly damaged example of this class of building.

Most are smaller and slighter than this one, but there are a number of cantonal temples on this scale. Indeed, if the surviving fragments of walls are treated as the foundations of an external portico, with the *cella* walls removed in the demolition process, we have a standard Romano-Celtic temple plan for a medium-sized shrine.

Although there may indeed have been an official presence at the site for administrating the collection of the *annona*, I would interpret the evidence primarily as suggesting a sacred centre, with one major Romano-Celtic temple (previously described as a tower and administrative centre) and at least one other temple building (R.15). This entirely changes the concept and interpretation of the Stonea site, which now emerges as the sort of market/fair site centred on a sacred complex, thoroughly familiar from other sanctuaries in Gaul and Britain.

Votive material has been found in the immediate locality, including a bronze of Minerva (*52*). My guess is that this deity was a tactful *interpreto Romani* for the dread Andraste, Goddess of Victory, propitiated by Boudica with human sacrifices. The sacred grove of Andraste is mentioned by Tacitus. Perhaps this was a diplomatic move by Hadrian who, in supporting the construction of the main temple, was conveying a sense of Romanitas to a former tribal focus of trouble under the Iceni. It may be significant that the small temple at Stonea (R.15) had a tree-pit in the centre of the *cella*, 1m wide and deep. A contemporary fresco shows how such 'sacred' trees were accommodated in shrines when they became old (*51*).

The temple appeared to have been abandoned *c.*AD 225 and the structure demolished and levelled in the late third century. I think we can see the interplay of market forces in these events rather than provincial politics. The onset of serious flooding in the earlier third century would have led to the abandonment of the summer pastures and the collapse of the pastoral economy in the southern Fenland. The priesthood of the temple would probably have been reliant on the market tolls from this trade. The closure of the market/fair would have effectively marked the end of the temple as a viable commercial concern. Abandonment of the building and possibly the site would have followed, especially since there is evidence for flooding. The focus of commercial agriculture in the region moved to the higher ground round the fens – places like Earith for example.

7

COMMUNICATIONS, FORTIFICATIONS, TOWNS AND DRAINAGE

Roman rule in the Fenlands brought with it the characteristic features associated with the Romans everywhere else, namely large engineering works such as roads, canals, planned towns and water management. In the immediate years after the Claudian invasion, East Anglia and the fens were largely bypassed by the main campaigning army, partly because the Iceni, based in Norfolk, northern Suffolk and the eastern fens, were regarded as a client kingdom of the Romans under their king Antedios, and later Prasutagus. The main road north between London, Lincoln and York – Ermine Street – would have been founded in this period. This road ran through Godmanchester where an early fort was located, before skirting the western fens to cross the Nene and Welland at Chesterton and Stamford respectively (*colour plate 15*).

This political alliance with the Romans probably arose out of Icenian tribal enmity with the Catuvellauni, the tribe who led the resistance to the invasion. The fact that the Iceni did not seem to have participated in any great measure in the pre-Conquest continental trade that helped the south-eastern tribes prosper, however, may have contributed to culture shock and a deterioration in relations when they were suddenly exposed to the new imperial power. When the governor tried to impose Roman law on them in AD 47, which included the removal of personal weapons, parts of the Iceni rose in rebellion. As a consequence of this a Roman military presence ensued including construction of a number of forts at places such as Saham Toney in Norfolk, Grandford on March island, possibly at Eldernell on Whittlesey island, and Longthorpe in Peterborough (*colour plate 14*); evidence from Stonea shows that military personnel were based at the Camp during this period and indeed it has been suggested that Tacitus' description of the battle between the Iceni and the Romans during this campaign could accord with the Iron Age fort at Stonea Camp. Whether this theory is true or not, it appears that the army decided to build a major route running west–east across the fens, to connect the upland at Peterborough with the Norfolk upland at Denver, making use of the fen islands of Whittlesey and March and creating a series of military outposts along it. This route has become known as the Fen Causeway and was built with both canal and road, crossing wet Fenland, rivers, saltwater creeks, as well as dry land, and was very probably based on a pre-existing Bronze Age routeway for much of its length (*12*).

The later Boudican revolt of AD 61 and its aftermath has already been discussed as a pivotal point in the development of the Roman Fenland, because it would seem that the lands of the Iceni passed to the emperor by means of a will drawn up by Prasutagus and as a punishment for their rebellion. The full potential of this land was not realised until some 60 years later when Hadrian's visit to Britain must have been the catalyst for a grand plan to develop the fens into a major resource for the state. It is in the Hadrianic and Antonine periods (AD 120-140s) that much of the Roman Fenland infrastructure was established in the form of new roads, canals, widespread settlement and reinvigorated salt production, field-systems and related drainage, and a probable administrative centre created at Stonea (*colour plate 15*).

COMMUNICATIONS

Roads

An east–west running routeway which linked the western upland at Peterborough with the Norfolk upland at Denver crossed the fens by means of island-hopping, with canals and embanked roads constructed over the wet peat fen and salt marsh. This road has been known for several centuries and has been investigated on many occasions ever since it was first identified as a possible Roman construction by Dugdale in 1772 who noted an 18m wide, 1m deep gravel road of 38km in extent; over the years it came to be called the Fen Causeway. In fact, its origin is probably much earlier, as a remarkable collection of Bronze Age artefacts and sites have been discovered along its route and, similarly to other roads in the country, it seems that the Romans chose to adapt a pre-existing routeway for their own purposes.

The Fen Causeway can be traced from the Peterborough fen edge at Fengate where it was excavated in 1989 and seen to have consisted of as a gravel-topped *agger* 1.3m thick (*colour plate 16*). At Northey it was found in excavations at Kings

COMMUNICATIONS, FORTIFICATIONS, TOWNS AND DRAINAGE

Major Roman Roads	Length (Km)	Width Agger (M)	Width Between Ditches (M)	Road Make-up And Height Of Construction	Resur- facings	Main Period Of Construction And Use
Akeman Street (Mere Way)	45	10	14	Gravel on clay		2nd C – ?
King Street	50	6-8	12	Gravel on cornbrash		Late 1st C – 6th C
Fen Causeway	38	18-20		1m deep gravel		Mid 1st C – 5th C
Fen Causeway; Fengate				1.3m deep gravel		
Fen Causeway; Eldenell				1.5m deep gravel on foundation of clay above wooden sticks		1st C
Fen Causeway; Estover		5-7		0.5m deep gravel capping		
Fen Causeway; Flaggrass		10				
Fen Causeway; Nordelph (London Lode Farm)		5-7	11-12	Briquetage on silts	Several	1st – 4th C
Fen Causeway; Downham West		5.2		0.1m deep briquetage on peat		
Fen Causeway; Downham West (2)		5.7		0.1m deep gravel on clay (1m deep)	2nd phase and 1-3 more fragmentary phases.	
Fen Causeway; Denver		9				

Table 5: Details of major Roman roads

Dyke in 1999-2000 (*13*) and from there it crossed Whittlesey and Eastrea islands before launching itself across a 7km wide stretch of peat fen on which it can be seen as a bank with a 20m wide gravel spread in association with a canal running from Eldernell to Grandford in March. The road then traversed the dry land at the north end of March island, excavated at Estover in 1960 and 1985 and found to be a gravel spread 5-7m wide and 0.5m deep. From Flaggrass (where the Fen Causeway was 10m wide) it crossed another long stretch of wet Fenland (6km), in one phase located on the bank of a parallel canal, to Christchurch, with timber supports for a bridge evident at its crossing point of the Old Croft River. From Christchurch it ran 10km slightly north-eastwards across salt marsh through Nordelph, where a gravel spread 6-7m wide is recorded, and, via a wooden bridge at Straw Hall Farm, Downham West, eventually it reached the fen edge at Denver (where excavations have shown it to be *c.*9m wide). The Fenland Management Project excavations in the 1990s at London Lode Farm, Nordelph revealed a steeply cambered, gravel-topped *agger* that had undergone many episodes of re-metalling, and had been inundated with flooding on at least two occasions (*64*).

STONEA AND THE ROMAN FENS

64 Section through the Fen Causeway at Nordelph, 1992. © *Mark Leah, with permission of Norfolk Archaeological Unit*

This section was cut through the more southerly (and later) of two roadways that formed the Fen Causeway in this area, and was located along the bank of a roddon. It had an *agger* 5-6m wide formed of silts and briquetage, with roadside ditches on either side 11-12m apart. The northern (earlier) route had been built on peat, an unstable foundation and a route that became inundated by marine-derived silts from Roman-period flooding. The later southern route was built on a more solid foundation – the banked-up levée of a roddon – and was refurbished on a number of occasions over a duration of perhaps 300 years. Further east the two routes merge into a single road, and at Downham West a second Fenland Management Project excavation showed that the first phase of road construction was founded on peat and consisted of a 5.2m wide, 0.1m deep spread of briquetage, some of which had slipped into two shallow wayside ditches. Flooding had covered this with laminated silts over which a second phase of road construction (*colour plate 17*) had included mounding up the *agger* by a further 0.9m, giving a total height of 1.2m, which was capped by a layer of gravel 5.7m wide and 0.1m thick. Further episodes of dumping indicate repairs and maintenance with at least one further phase of gravel capping surviving along the *agger*, although indications from erosion suggest that possibly three re-surfacings had originally occurred. A canal was cut contemporary with the second phase of the road.

COMMUNICATIONS, FORTIFICATIONS, TOWNS AND DRAINAGE

The date of the Fen Causeway as a Roman construction appears to have been early: a worn coin of Vespasian (AD 69-79) was found in 1938 when the 1.5m deep gravel road surface at Eldernell was quarried away, exposing wooden sticks as a foundation, or probably an earlier trackway beneath it. This is similar to the evidence for its construction revealed by the reclamation of the gravel metalling between Eldernell and March at the beginning of the twentieth century when the steeply cambered road was shown to have been founded on clay and wood, perhaps even a timber corduroy design. A spread of first-century AD sites have been identified along the route of the Fen Causeway, significantly earlier than most others in the Roman Fenland, with Neronian coins (AD 54-68) for example, and pre-Flavian Samian recovered at Grandford. Various scholars have suggested that it may even relate to the subjugation of the fens after the Icenian rebellion of AD 47, probably the same time that Stonea Camp was garrisoned, and that a fort was built at Grandford and possibly Eldernell. At Longthorpe in Peterborough a vexillation fort of the period c.AD 48-61/2 has been excavated by Professors Shepherd Frere and St Joseph and this may well support the hypothesis for a military origin and use of the road. It would also, of course, have connected with the Car Dyke once this was built, and would have run on westwards to Durobrivae and the junction of King Street and Ermine Street on the western side of the fens. On the eastern side the second-century Akeman Street would have met with it at Denver before joining with two routes east across Norfolk to the later cantonal capital at Caistor St Edmund (Venta Icenorum) and the Roman settlement and later fort at Caister-on-Sea; these roads would also have crossed the Peddars Way heading north to the north Norfolk coast and south to the Icknield Way with its long-distance connections to the Thames valley and west country.

Akeman Street Roman road runs north-eastwards from Cambridge along a peninsula of dry land towards the Isle of Ely (*65*), and from the north-east of the Isle at Littleport it crosses wet fen west of Southery and Hilgay to landfall at Denver, meeting with the Fen Causeway and various other routes. Excavations at Impington and Landbeach in 1991 and 1996 revealed it to have had a 10m wide gravelled *agger* set between small ditches 14m apart, and that its construction probably dated to Hadrianic or later times.

Its exact route through the Isle of Ely, Littleport and beyond is unclear, but it seems likely to have passed close to Stretham (the Anglo-Saxon name meaning a settlement on a Roman road) and Bedwell Hey Farm, where fifth-century Anglo-Saxon burials have been found. At Camel Road, Littleport, excavations in 1998 produced high-status pottery of Antonine date (*66*), and roof, floor and box-flue tiles as well as painted wall plaster indicating the proximity of a wealthy building. This has been interpreted as a possible *mansio* (it is *c.*18 miles [29km] north of the previous one at Cambridge and therefore approximately the

65 Akeman Street Roman road at Landbeach, viewed from the south heading to cross the Car Dyke at its junction with the present course of the A10 to Ely. © *Archaeological Field Unit Cambridgeshire County Council*

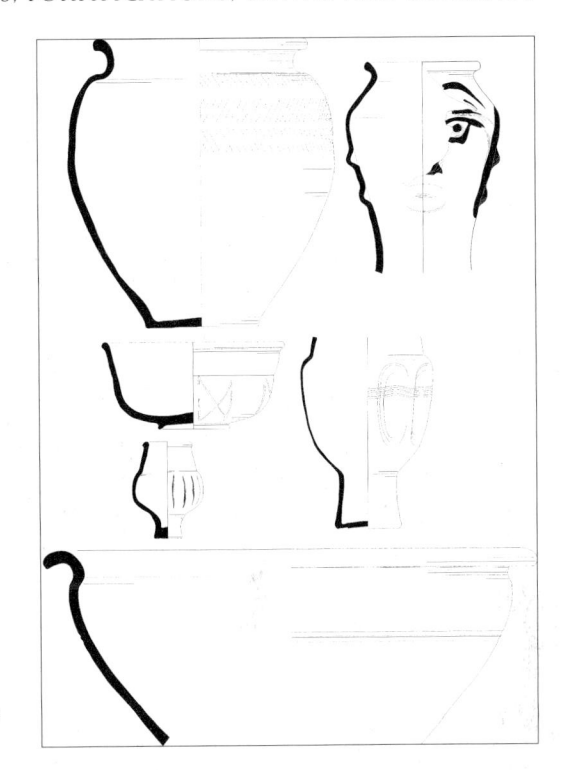

COMMUNICATIONS, FORTIFICATIONS, TOWNS AND DRAINAGE

66 A selection of pottery including face-jars from the mansio *at Littleport. © Archaeological Field Unit Cambridgeshire County Council*

correct interval for such an administrative rest house), suggesting the road would have passed through this area. Its passage over the wet Fenland north of here has left no definite clue and, although the roddon of the Old Croft River is full of Roman sites running up to Christchurch and the Fen Causeway, the straight cut of the Ten Mile River from Littleport has also produced Roman pottery during dredging operations; its orientation towards Southery, and the Norfolk fen edge beyond, would fit well with a continuation of the general line from Akeman Street further south (*colour plate 15*). Across the border in Norfolk the final section of road metalling at Cold Harbour Farm in Hilgay fen was reputedly destroyed in the 1940s (according to A.K. Astbury), but other than this report, no further evidence for its course has been left. The work of the Fenland Survey, however, might suggest an alternative route because the artefacts recovered by Bob Silvester in the 1980s on the Southery–Hilgay island include a north–south linear arrangement of sites which contain some tile and possible brick, in addition to substantial amounts of pottery. These all lie very close to the present A10 trunk road and it is quite possible, therefore, that Akeman Street lies beneath the modern road, a situation also the case for sections of the road further south, for example at Waterbeach. Such a design would have taken maximum advantage of the local topography including the tongue of land joining Southery with Hilgay, seems consistent with Roman road engineering as witnessed elsewhere in the fens.

Fen-edge roads include the first-century AD King Street, which diverged from Ermine Street at the crossing of the Nene at Durobrivae and ran north along the fen edge (67) through the small town at Bourne. From there two routes were available, one via Long Hollow to rejoin Ermine Street at Ancaster, and a second one that continued along the fen edge via Mareham Lane to Old Sleaford. The Roman road of King Street has been considered pre-Flavian in origin, and generally seems to have followed a more ancient prehistoric routeway. It was excavated in 1998 and shown to be 12-13m wide between broad and shallow roadside ditches. The road surface had been robbed in the area of the excavation, but elsewhere King Street can be seen surviving as an earthwork with an extant *agger* some 6-8m wide.

67 King Street at Ailsworth, viewed from the south. © Ben Robinson 2/8/02

COMMUNICATIONS, FORTIFICATIONS, TOWNS AND DRAINAGE

The Baston Outgang branches off King Street and takes the shortest crossing north-eastwards from Baston over the wet peat of Deeping Fen to the drier fen silts. It consists of a gravel spread which presumably originally capped a wooden causeway. From the western edge of the silts it continued north-eastwards, with a slight deviation to make best use of the higher land of a wide roddon, to Spalding, crossing the River Glen by a probable wooden bridge, and its total length before disappearing seawards was *c.*10 miles (16km). An Anglo-Saxon cemetery is known from the Baston end, and the early settlement of the *Spaldingas* probably collected around the river crossing. A scattering of Roman settlements is known to follow the route of this road, with droveways and field systems leading off from it. Its date of construction is uncertain, but some of the sites found in association with it are early, so that it is probable that it was second-century in origin. A possible continuation of this road exists to the north-east of Spalding along Halmer Gate.

Another possible road heads eastwards into the fen from King Street (Mareham Lane), which it crosses at Threekingham. This road is known appropriately as Salter's Way and is prehistoric in origin, running from Saltersford (Grantham) on the Witham to Horbling Fen where it partly follows the bank of a canal or drain, before terminating in Shoff Drove, Donington.

A number of lesser roads consisting of ungravelled, double-ditched lines seen as cropmarks on air photographs appear to have been laid out in the southern Lincolnshire fens, and continue into north Cambridgeshire; these have been described as 'limiting droves'. Some of these drove roads seem to have been prone to flooding and went out of use fairly quickly, and their construction was probably part of the ambitious planning of the main period of second-century colonisation. In effect they limit the area of siltland occupation, separating this from the wet peat fen to the west (e.g. in Thorney, Crowland, and the Deepings) which would have been susceptible to winter flooding. From Inkerson Fen on the border of Thorney and Wisbech St Mary, a 7km long straight drove can be seen to have run north-west through Wryde Croft and Gothic House Farm to the Old South Eau at Dowsdale Bar, and then continued for 1.6km north-eastwards along Dowsdale Bank. From here it progressed via a zigzag pattern north-westwards for 4km to meet with a drove that ran parallel to Asen Dyke; following this westwards it eventually met with another drove running along Welland Bank. It then followed a final north-west orientation of straight stretches to meet at right-angles with Baston Outgang. From here a further continuation heading north-west can be seen to be offset from the main road about a kilometre to the south. This then followed a series of turns and straight stretches for *c.*3km to Guthrum Gowt on the River Glen west of Spalding. From further cropmark evidence long distance internal siltland communications can be seen to have run through Gedney Hill from the north and west to places such as Throckenholt in the south-east and presumably on through a string of settlements to the Coldham area, perhaps meeting with the Fen Causeway and a route further south at the Old Croft River. At Coldham it would seem likely that a road ran north-eastwards to service the string of settlements skirting Marshland to Tilney. Another road that might have connected with this trans-siltland route has been identified at Grandford on March island heading north through Guyhirn, following the roddon of an old course of the River Nene. A further road appears to have met with, or run through, Whaplode Drove from the south-west, where a peninsula of upland extended into the fen and provided a route along the Shepea and Dowsdale Bank, running north-eastwards towards the sea. A brief look at colour plate 15 will reveal a fairly regular pattern of south-west/north-east running roads crossing from the upland to the silt fen and the Wash beyond, suggestive of a planned layout in keeping with the theories of an imperial intervention to develop Fenland.

In the south-eastern fens use of the ancient routes would have continued during Roman times, such as the one that ran along the spine of the upland at Soham and Wicken where they jut into the fens. A timber causeway of Bronze Age date is known to have crossed from Fordey–Little Thetford on the Isle of Ely, and others must have run across at Stuntney and Quanea to Ely. It is also possible that there was a crossing point from Dimmocks Cote, Wicken, to Stretham on the Isle of Ely, where a Roman villa was located on the fen edge. All these routes would have connected with the main road of Akeman Street, allowing access to the south-west or north-east along this major artery, and a branch road from Littleport might have run along the bank of the Old Croft River giving access to the north-west and the siltlands. Fen-edge roads would undoubtedly have joined the wealthy villas and settlements ringing the fens to the east and south in Norfolk, Suffolk and Cambridgeshire, and it is likely that a further route made use of the bank of Reach Lode to connect the southern fen edge with the tip of the Wicken peninsula, and then on by one of the crossing points to the Isle of Ely.

Canals and drainage schemes

Several parts of the Fen Causeway were originally canalised or constructed as combined canals and roads. Between the eastern island of Whittlesey, from Eldernell, to the north-western end of March island at Grandford the route has two canals which appear to cross one another. The first is 20m wide and runs for 7km, directly connecting the two islands. The second is 5km in length and connects Eldernell with the Roman course of the River Nene, which was canalised by the Romans to follow a curving route from Grandford north around the island towards Elm. On the eastern side of March island from Flaggrass a

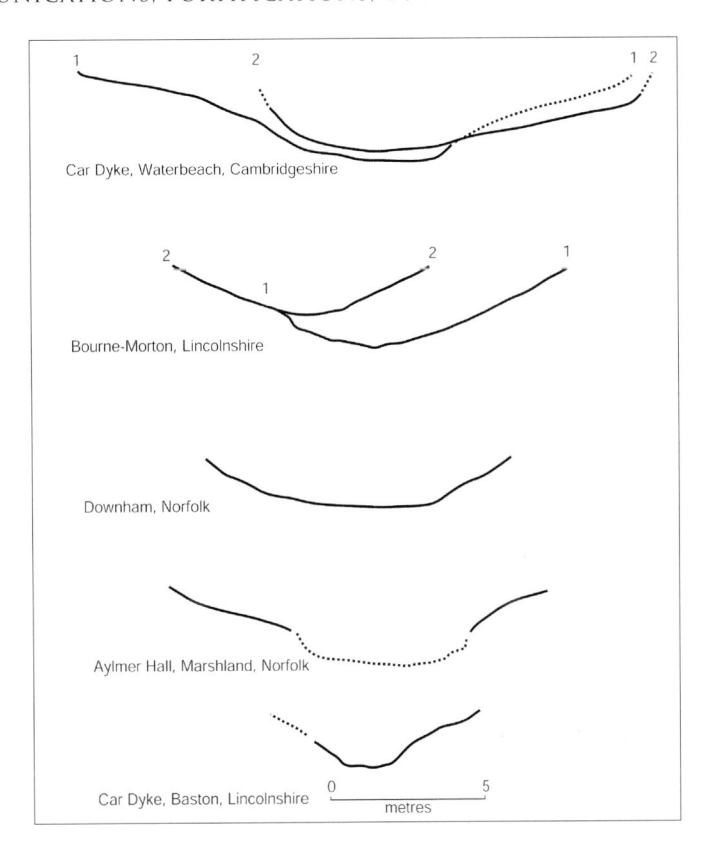

68 Comparative profiles of Roman canals. Author's collection

15-20m wide canal ran 6km eastwards through Rodham Farm to Christchurch, Upwell, where it joined the Old Croft River (the Wellstream). Another section began 0.5km north of this junction at Primrose Hall, Nordelph, with a 10km length of canal running beside the roddon of a natural watercourse, making a total length of 16km between March island and the upland at Denver. This latter length was excavated in the 1990s to the west of Downham Market as part of the Fenland Mangement Project and revealed a 9.5m wide canal, 1.8m deep, that had been cut originally into the south side of the roddon in the early second century AD (*68*). The early deposits in this canal showed they were of high-energy, tidal-derived origin, demonstrating direct contact with a tidal river, but that the later deposits indicate low-energy mud-flats or lagoon, conditions probably caused by the outfall of the canal having become blocked. This sedimentation seems to have occurred in the later second and early third centuries.

The Car Dyke canal was a massive feat of engineering originally identified as Roman in the eighteenth century by the antiquarian William Stukeley, who also came up with the idea that its purpose was to supply the northern garrisons with grain from East Anglia. It appears to have been built in a number of sections (*colour plate 15*) and to have linked with other features such as contemporary watercourses, but the discovery of causeways and sharp bends in parts of the monument have led to alternative interpretations: the first sees this as a large but conventional canal (*69*), whilst the second instead sees the Car Dyke as a catchwater drain for the western Fenland. It is comprised in fact of two distinctly separate parts: a series of straight cuts linking the River Cam at Waterbeach, near Cambridge, to a tributary of the Great Ouse 8km to the north-west at Cottenham, and a second part which runs for 65km from the Nene at Peterborough to the Witham at Lincoln largely following the 25ft (7.6m) contour along the fen edge, but dropping to 12ft (3.6m) above sea level through the predominantly gravel geology of the Witham Valley. From the Witham a further canal, Foss Dyke, connected to the Trent, and thus to the Humber estuary and rivers to York and further north.

The southern section was excavated in 1947 by Professor J.G.D. Clark, and more recently in 1993 and 1997 by Stephen Macaulay and Tim Reynolds (*70*). These investigations demonstrated that the original Roman cut was over 20m wide and 4m deep with a shallow profile and 5m-wide flat base (*68*), and a Roman recut 16m wide. Originally banks probably ran along both sides and snail species recovered from the basal silts show that the canal contained free-flowing,

69 Car Dyke at Waterbeach. © *Archaeological Field Unit Cambridgeshire County Council*

70 Excavation of the Car Dyke at Waterbeach in 1993, north-facing section. © *Archaeological Field Unit Cambridgeshire County Council*

well-oxygenated water. A dump of Antonine pottery (AD 140-180) containing wares from the Nene valley as well as local Horningsea products, shows that the canal was finished by this period and therefore construction could have begun in the Hadrianic period. At its junction with the Cam the canal opens out and deepens, perhaps for a docking area, and sluice gates must have been positioned here. A large timber building was found adjacent to it with beetles (*oryzaephilus surinamensis*) that indicate the probability of grain storage, strongly suggesting the presence of a granary or warehouse (*colour plate 18*). Dating evidence shows activity on the site from the mid-second to fourth centuries AD. Horningsea ware kilns were found to have been dug into one of the banks of the canal. Lock gates must have been used along its length because it rises towards Landbeach and Cottenham before falling again to its outfall at the tributary to the Ouse. The excavations in 1947 at Cottenham found that a causeway had been constructed across it during the fourth century (*c*.AD 375) and that this was associated with a well-preserved Romano-British settlement and field system at Bullocks Haste (*71*).

The northern part of the Car Dyke, on the other hand, has revealed a different pattern through investigations undertaken between 1974 and 79 (Brian Simmons).

71 Car Dyke as a cropmark, and associated field system at Bullocks Haste, Cottenham. © *Ben Robinson 27/6/92*

COMMUNICATIONS, FORTIFICATIONS, TOWNS AND DRAINAGE

CANALS	LENGTH (km)	WIDTH (m)	DEPTH (m)	BASAL WIDTH (m)	ROMAN RECUT	REDUNDANT BY
Car Dyke North	65					
Car Dyke North Thurlby		12	2.3	4.8 (channel)		
Car Dyke North Baston		13	3.6	2	None	c.3rd/4th C
Car Dyke South	8					
Car Dyke South Waterbeach		20-24	4	5	16m wide, 3.5m deep, 5m basal width	3rd C
Car Dyke South Cottenham		c.20	2.1	8.5		375AD
Fen Causeway; Eldernell - Grandford	7	20				Became road
Fen Causeway; Eldernell - River Nene	5	15-20				
Fen Causeway; Flaggrass - Rodham Farm, Christchurch	6	15.2				3rd C
Fen Causeway; Nordelph - Denver (Downham West 1-3)	10	9.5	1.7	5		3rd C
Bourne - Morton (Mor 70)	6.5	11-12	2.6	6	6.5m wide/1.5m deep	
Rippingale	2					
Deeping St James	1	30				
Aylmer Hall Tilney St Lawrence	5	12	3			3rd C
Murrow - Tholomas Drove, Wisbech St Mary	2	50				
Stonea E-W	1.3					
Stonea N	3					3rd C
Flaggrass N	0.4					
Colne Ditch	4					
Reach	4					
Southery	0.9					

Table 6: Roman canal dimensions

Along this stretch of the monument a total width of 52m (including both banks, berms and channel) has been recorded, with the canal itself some 12m wide and 2-3m deep at Thurlby. At Helpringham a well-preserved section survives, and on a number of transects across the Car Dyke in parts of Lincolnshire a reasonably consistent measurement of 13.7m (45ft) for each bank, 4.8m (15ft) for each berm and 4.8m for the channel has been recorded. A 27m wide gravel causeway was excavated at Billingborough which appears to have been an original feature of the monument, and thus would have necessitated the transport of goods overland or dragging of barges between two lengths of the canal. In 1989 further excavation at Baston by Reuben Thorpe and Torven Zeffertt revealed a Roman cut 13m wide and 3.6m deep with a flat base *c.*2m wide and evidence for fast-flowing water; a Roman flagon of second-century date was found near the base (*68*). In this area of south Lincolnshire the channel is composed of a number of short, straight stretches, whereas further north a more sinuous route is adopted as the Car Dyke drops towards the Witham, a mechanism presumably to maintain more of a level and probably involving the exploitation of a pre-existing natural watercourse.

STONEA AND THE ROMAN FENS

72 Car Dyke at Peakirk, viewed from the south. © *Ben Robinson 2/8/02*

Arnold Pryor carried out a survey of the Car Dyke between the rivers Nene and Welland in 1978 and concluded that it followed the 7.6m (25ft) contour, although it also included a surprising cut through the higher land of the ridge at Eye, effectively crossing the watershed to take run-off from the upland towards the Welland in the north, and the Nene towards the south. At Peakirk, a sharp-angled dogleg in the route of Car Dyke can be seen (72) and it is difficult to imagine why it was constructed like this if intended for the free movement of barges.

Simmons' and later interpretation has therefore seen the Lincolnshire Car Dyke as nothing more than a catchwater drain along the fen edge, but Donald Mackreth has pointed out that it cannot have functioned as a catchwater between the Nene and Welland as it runs against the natural drainage of the area. Further north the marshy area south of Bourne could have more effectively taken the upland waters away eastwards through improvement of the natural watercourses there, rather than having to make a new cut for the Car Dyke running northwards along the fen edge. Alternative theories can also account for apparent inconsistencies in an interpretation of its original function as a canal. During the great epoch of canal

COMMUNICATIONS, FORTIFICATIONS, TOWNS AND DRAINAGE

building in the period of the industrial revolution many stretches began life as non-continuous, with overland connections until a time when tunnels were added. Perhaps the original causeways in the Car Dyke are of similar origin, or perhaps they are later infill such as was found at Cottenham after the canal went into disuse. The strange kink in the line of Car Dyke at Peakirk is in fact not that dissimilar to the way in which Roman roads were constructed, with the road surveyed in sections, and straight lines between two points sometimes requiring slight adjustment such as abrupt kinks to join up two separately surveyed and constructed sections. The kind of barges employed by the Romans (*73*) can be found depicted in various contemporary scenes and these show short, stubby vessels with towing masts, which could have negotiated sharp bends with relative ease.

In summary, the Car Dyke probably acted as both a canal and a drain, but could also have had a third, and perhaps more significant function. Donald Mackreth has made a strong case that its design and siting could have been intended to act as a territorial boundary marker between the presumed Imperial lands of the fens and the well-populated upland of mixed ownership at their edge.

73 Reconstruction of a Roman barge. © *Jon Cane*

Other canals of more localised importance are found in several parts of the fens. In Lincolnshire the Bourne–Morton canal, 6.5km long and linking the Roman town at Bourne with a natural watercourse in Pinchbeck North Fen and access to the sea, also provided communication with local salt-making communities located on the silt fen. Excavation through this in the 1990s showed it to be 10-11m wide and 2.6m deep, with a *c*.6m-wide base which originally contained a sequence consisting of lagoonal conditions, followed by high energy estuarine waters, before returning to lagoonal conditions again (*68*). At this point it must have been almost silted up and was therefore recut to 29m width, and only 1.2m depth; foraminfera evidence shows that this second phase of the canal was initially open to estuarine influence, but that this changed to a marsh-creek type of environment as the canal silted up. At its eastern end soak drains seem to have been cut through the levees, and the Roman field ditches drained into these soak drains, which were presumably emptied at low tide.

A short stretch of canal (cut across a large roddon) at Rippingale runs for 2km heading for Car Dyke, and may have been designed to connect salt-working sites on the silt fens with the Car Dyke. Another possible canal linking Car Dyke with the silt fen could have existed further north running eastwards through Horbling Fen. At Deeping St James a 30m-wide canal runs for just 1km to allow access for the settlement complex at Priors Meadow to a large roddon which then connects with more salt-working communities and the sea. Some of the Lincolnshire rivers may also have been partly canalised, such as the Slea, the Bourne Eau, the Glen and possibly parts of the Welland and Witham. It is clear that successive episodes of silting occurred in some of the soak drains and canals, with refurbishment and recutting in an attempt to keep the system functional. A third-century date has been suggested for a re-routing of the River Glen for example, as scatters of Roman pottery indicating a string of small settlements follow the earlier course of the outfall. Peter Salway, however, makes a convincing argument from the political situation that, following some early third-century flooding and refurbishment, the remainder of the third century had a severe absence of centralised control and any serious attempt to reinstate Fenland drainage could not have occurred until stability was restored when Constantius Chlorus recovered Britain from the Gallic empire in AD 296.

A canal with a single offshoot has also been identified crossing the siltlands of the Norfolk Marshland. It is over 5km long running south-eastwards between Aylmer Hall at Tilney St Lawrence to the present course of the Great Ouse and cutting through the roddon of 'The Great Marshland River'; the subsidary channel, some 25m wide, joins it from 'Spice Hills' located to the south-west. The Aylmer Hall canal near Tilney was excavated in the 1990s and was recorded as 12m wide and up to 3m deep (*68*). It became silted up over a considerable period whilst maintaining

COMMUNICATIONS, FORTIFICATIONS, TOWNS AND DRAINAGE

an open connection with the sea throughout its use. The function of this canal was clearly to provide access to the communities that had established themselves on the silts of Marshland, with the Aylmer Hall canal constructed at the eastward extent of such settlement to run through a wet area and connect up with the natural waterways which provided a link to the Norfolk upland and the Wash. In effect this canal can be seen as a further element in the complex network of Roman Fenland communications and, although no specific date for its construction has been determined, it appears to have been cut into the peat underlying later flood silts. The scatters of pottery recovered by Bob Silvester during the Fenland Survey of Marshland cover the second to fourth centuries, and a second-century origin would therefore be in keeping; the considerable marine-derived silting-up deposits and flooding that occurred later in the history of the canal could be contemporary with the third-century fresh water inundation seen in the peat fens.

In north Cambridgeshire a similar short length of canal is found in Wisbech St Mary, where a straight length of roddon surviving to 50m width runs for 2km connecting the original course of the combined Ouse and Nene River with a slightly later outfall. Canals are also found connecting Stonea with March island, an east–west one running towards Wimblington and a north–south stretch connecting Stonea with the Fen Causeway at Flaggrass. A canal also heads north-westwards from the settlement at Flaggrass, perhaps to connect with the Nene and Great Ouse on its original course around the north of March island towards Elm (*colour plate 10*).

Colne Ditch (or Cranbrook Drain), which ran for *c*.4km along the south-western fen edge and has had Roman pottery dredged from it, may have been part of the Car Dyke network. It seems to have acted as a short-cut across a big loop in the course of the old Ouse avoiding Hammonds Eau (*colour plate 15*) and also to have acted as a route connecting the many Roman fen-edge settlements in this area including the market centre or 'town' at Earith (*78-80*). On the south-eastern fen edge several canals or lodes have been suspected of having Roman origin based upon their proximity to a swathe of intense and wealthy Roman settlement (including a number of villas) running through places such as Burwell, Reach, Swaffham Prior and Bulbeck, Bottisham, Great Wilbraham and Fulbourn. The most convincing example is the 4km length from Reach to Upware on the River Cam, along which many Roman finds have been made, and Cyril Fox suggested that a road followed its course along one of the banks. The fact that the Anglo-Saxon Devils Dyke was built to end at Reach strongly suggests that the canal there pre-existed this (*colour plate 24*) and thus must be Roman in origin. Large quarries for clunch exist at Reach and this, as well as grain, might have been one economic reason for the canal's construction. Apart from Reach Lode others at Burwell, Swaffham and Bottisham may also have their origin in Roman times, as the concentration of villa estates and other signs of wealth in this area would have at least benefited from, and perhaps owed their substantial success to, the creation of an efficient long-distance transportation network for their goods and produce.

A series of straight channels in the eastern fens effectively acted as drainage to bring water from the Cam–Granta waterway and divert it to flow via the Little Ouse into the Wash at the Lynn estuary. These include an artificial stretch of the River Lark from Isleham–Prickwillow east of Ely, a cut from Littleport–Brandon Creek (Ten Mile Bank River) and along the Little Ouse from Decoy Fen–Brandon Creek (*colour plate 15*). Although these have not been definitely attributed a Roman origin, substantial amounts of Roman pot have been found from dredging activities in these channels, with Samian and Castor ware demonstrating second-century activity. It is also possible that a short stretch of canal 900m in length, identified by Bob Silvester during the Fenland Survey as medieval, running west from Southery to the River Ouse could equally be Roman in date; its eastern terminus comes very close to two Roman sites and the possible route of Akemen Street.

SEA AND FEN BANKS

There are many earthwork banks which have been given the label Roman because of their size and length. In fact, there is no evidence to suggest that the Romans built any sea defences, but that instead these are all of late Saxon or medieval date because of the direct relationship of contemporary settlement that can be demonstrated for them. The same is probably true of fen banks, although Peter Hayes and Tom Lane have suggested that the 'limiting droves' for Roman settlement on the silts, which have been identified as parallel ditches from cropmark evidence, might be better interpreted as linear quarries for construction of low fen banks to protect the western siltlands from fresh water flooding via the peat fen.

FORTIFICATIONS

A vexillation fortress of 12ha was built at Longthorpe, Peterborough, around the middle of the first century. It was for $c.2,500$ men and may have been constructed soon after the Conquest or as a consequence of the first Icenian rebellion in AD 47. It protected access inland along the Nene valley and would have allowed deployment of troops rapidly eastwards along the newly constructed, or newly Romanised, Fen Causeway. A crossing point to the south bank of the Nene at

COMMUNICATIONS, FORTIFICATIONS, TOWNS AND DRAINAGE

Botolph Bridge was also controlled by this fort, and if the alignment of Ermine Street further south was followed in a northerly direction then it could originally have crossed the Nene at this point, giving greater strategic sense to the location of Longthorpe; the existing course of Ermine Street, however, heads north-west from Norman Cross to cross the Nene at Durobrivae, near modern Water Newton (*colour plate 15*).

A small fort was also located on the southern side of the Nene at this crossing point in Water Newton. It is 2ha in size and 4.5km from Longthorpe. As it has not been excavated its date is uncertain, and has been argued variously as pre-Flavian (i.e. middle of the first century) or possibly fourth-century in origin. Air photographs suggest that up to three forts had been constructed in this location or that it had multiple ditches. A rectangular, single-ditched enclosure located north of the Nene on the east side of King Street at Upton has been suggested as a Roman marching camp, but excavation by Adrian Challands in the 1990s showed that this was in fact of Neolithic date (see *14*).

Two early forts were also located at the strategic crossing point for Ermine Street on the Great Ouse at Godmanchester (*76*): a marching camp of the Conquest period to mid-first-century date and a vexillation fort assigned to the second half of the first century, and possibly built in the aftermath of the Boudican revolt. This second fort has a different orientation from the earlier one, and was presumably dictated by the course of Ermine Street running north-west/south-east.

Two forts have been identified at Grandford on the north-western part of March island straddling the Fen Causeway and located within the bend of an extinct river (*colour plate 7*). The larger and later one measured some 140 x 100m, at 1.4ha a size suitable for an auxiliary unit of 500 men, and items of first-century Roman armour have been found by metal-detectorists on the site. Tim Potter assigned a date for the first fort to *c*.AD 47 because of the possible historical connection with an Icenian insurrection, and dated the later fort to the immediate post-Boudican period during Suetonius' suppression of the Iceni, *c*.AD 61-2.

Another fort has been identified from air photographs by Rog Palmer at Eldernell, on the eastern 'promontory' of the eastern island of Whittlesey, 7km from Grandford west along the Fen Causeway. Only the southern ditch and short lengths of the returns on the western and eastern sides have been plotted to date, but this reveals a classic 'playing card' shape with a central entrance to the south, and a width of *c*.85m between western and eastern sides. The Fen Causeway was identified as approaching from the east, and then abruptly changing course to run around the eastern and northern sides of the camp. This provides us with a probable north–south length of *c*.120m for the camp, and therefore dimensions broadly similar to those at Grandford.

TOWNS AND CIVIL ADMINISTRATION

Durobrivae and the palace at Castor

The Roman town of Durobrivae (Chesterton) lies some 10km to the west of the Peterborough fen edge, sitting astride Ermine Street, located strategically near its junction with several other important Roman roads and the crossing point of the Billing Brook and the River Nene. Unlike most other Roman towns Durobrivae has never been built over in later times, which means that its state of preservation and completeness is probably very good. Although partly investigated in the nineteenth century by Edmund Artis, Durobrivae has not had the benefit of scientific excavation and publication. The information available is therefore limited, but Don Mackreth, as director of the Nene valley Rescue Committee, has made a very useful study of it, and of the exceptional palatial building at Castor which overlooks the town. By plotting over 1,000 air photographs he has recovered a remarkable plan of the town enclosed within an irregular-shaped wall (*74*), and of the wider suburbs that included extensive industrial production of pottery and metals, as well as several roadside cemeteries. The area of the walled town is 17.6ha, although the more extensive area including all the suburbs and industrial complexes amounts to *c.*110ha. Ermine Street bisects it from south-east/north-west and an irregular pattern of streets is laid off from this. The most complete coverage of cropmarks is concentrated towards the northern end near the river, and it is in this area that two large buildings dominate the plan of the town. The outline of one of these is clear enough to identify it as a possible *mansio,* and Don Mackreth has suggested that the other, lying adjacent to a temple complex, may either have been a large structure associated with the temple or possibly a building with an administrative function. The legal status of the early Durobrivae was that of a *vicus*, the lowest level of local government, as recorded by a stamp on a *mortarium* (CUNOARDA FECIT/VICO DUROBRIVIS), but it has been argued that by the end of the Roman period the town had grown significantly in importance, perhaps even achieving the status of a *civitas* or regional capital by the fourth century.

The development in the size, wealth and importance of Durobrivae appears to have been intricately connected with the colonisation and exploitation of the fens. Centred on major communication networks, Ermine Street to London, Lincoln and York, and roads to Leicester and the East Midlands, Durobrivae was also located on the western edge of the fens from where access via the Fen Causeway and the River Nene would have been very easy (*75*). The massive Nene valley pottery industries developed during the second century, and settlements throughout the fens show a large predominance of products from the Nene valley kilns. There was a symbiotic relationship between the fens and this western

COMMUNICATIONS, FORTIFICATIONS, TOWNS AND DRAINAGE

74 Right: Plan and air photograph of Durobrivae. *Courtesy Don Mackreth and Nene Valley Research Committee and Peterborough Museum and Art Gallery*

75 Below: The environs of Durobrivae. *Courtesy Don Mackreth and Nene Valley Research Committee*

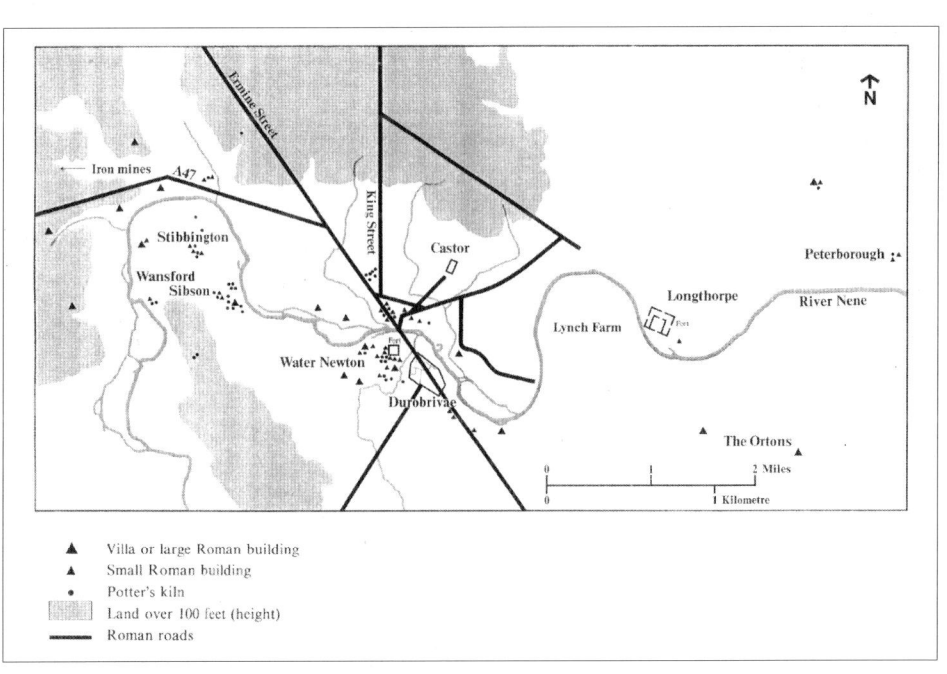

155

hinterland, rich in resources of clay and limestone, woodland and iron ore. The fens provided a major market for the goods that were produced in the industrial heartland of Durobrivae and the Nene valley and also produced valuable agricultural produce and salt, as well as a variety of other natural resources. If the model for an Imperially inspired venture to develop the fens is accepted, then control of the hinterland, or at least some aspects of it, would make sense and there is no reason to draw a firm line along the fen edge separating private from public ownership; the marker stone at Titchmarsh, some 15km west of the other marker of public land at Sawtry, would imply, for example, that some of the imperial estate extended beyond the confines of the fens.

If the large 'tower' building at Stonea was designed to act as an administrative centre for the imperial estate, surrounded by a new town in the middle of the fens, what then became of the administration when it was dismantled in the early third century? Don Mackreth has suggested that one of the major buildings in Durobrivae could have had an official function, such as that of managing the Fenland estate. Following the upheavals of the third century, however, a massive building project was under way just north of Durobrivae at Castor by *c.*AD 300, where a palace was constructed on three terraces built into the hillside (*100*). This single building covers 3.75ha, the Great Hall alone measuring 30 x 20m, and the edifice would have stood perhaps some 19m in height above the first terrace. Don Mackreth has argued that such a lavishly wealthy and imposing building must have been a residence and administrative centre for an Imperial appointment, and suggests that of the Count of the Saxon Shore. Perhaps part of the function of this establishment could have replaced Stonea as an effective focus for administration of the Fenland imperial estate, and included a tight control on Durobrivae and the Nene valley at the same time.

Godmanchester

The locally important town at Godmanchester (Durovigutum) is *c.*8ha in area and located *c.*10km from the fens westwards along the Great Ouse. It is situated on Ermine Street immediately south-east of Huntingdon, adjacent to the crossing of the Great Ouse. During the second half of the twentieth century Michael Green has conducted a long campaign of investigation to study Roman Godmanchester. The town appears to have grown up in a ditched enclosure south of the first-century forts (*76*), and at the junction of the Sandy and Cambridge roads with Ermine Street. The late first and second centuries show a town of timber-framed thatched buildings with cob and wattle walls and a busy industrial and market function, including pottery production and processing of agricultural produce. Evidence for metalworking, bone-working, baking, dairy processing and

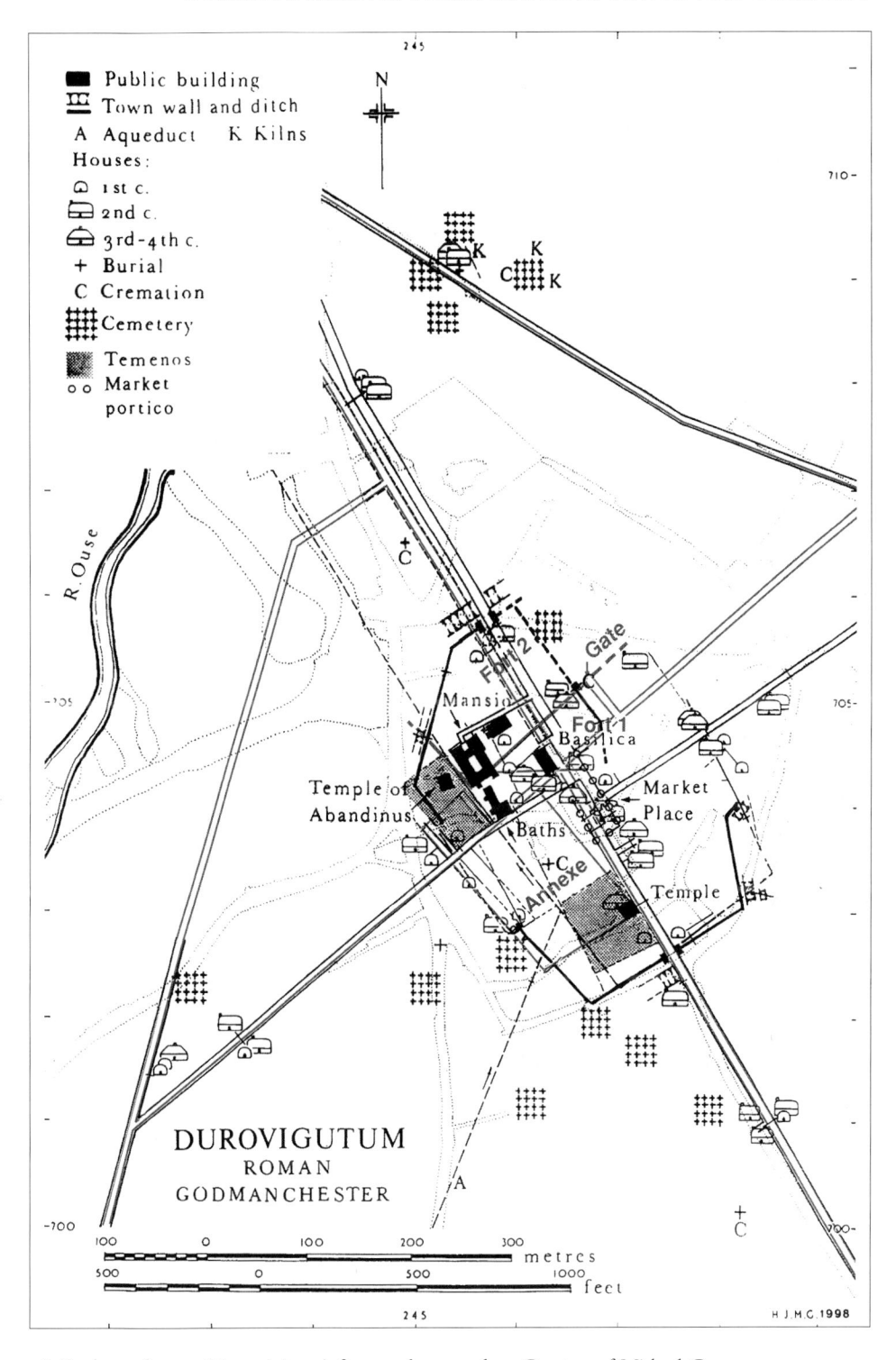

COMMUNICATIONS, FORTIFICATIONS, TOWNS AND DRAINAGE

76 Godmanchester (Durovigutum) forts and town plan. *Courtesy of Michael Green*

beer-making has been recovered by excavation, as well as *amphorae* containing mackerel or fish-paste, and shops selling glass and Samian ware. A masonry *mansio*, or official rest house, was constructed in the early second century complete with bath house, stabling, tavern and granaries; a temple to the local river god Abandinus was built close by, and 12 extramural cememteries have been identified. Developments in the third century included the establishment of an extensive pottery industry and construction of a masonry *basilica* and market place, requiring a realignment of the road pattern in the first quarter of the century, and the erection of substantial town defences in the later third century. These formed an irregular enclosure with a 10m wide ditch and 3m wide wall and rampart, with a 9m wide monumental gateway on the south side, but the defences appear to have been unfinished when a fire destroyed the town in *c*.AD 296. The town recovered and its use continued throughout the fourth century, but it appears to have contracted in size, centred on reconstruction of the *mansio* and construction of a second defensive circuit in the north-western part of the town, to protect the municipal and official buildings. Granaries and a mill were included within these defences, and the last resurfacing of Ermine Street occurred in the early part of the fourth century, after which a thick layer of rubbish accumulated. Saxon pottery has been found in the town and evidence for fifth-century occupation has been preserved in some parts, showing that in spite of its contraction use of the settlement continued in use for some time after withdrawal of the army in AD 410.

POSSIBLE TOWNS

Cambridge

The *c*.10-15ha Roman town at Cambridge (Duroliponte) is less than 5km from the southern fen edge and is located on a hill overlooking the River Cam, occupying and surrounding the area of a Late Iron Age (Belgic) defended settlement. From the 1940s to the 1980s John Alexander and a band of volunteers undertook a great number of excavations and rescue recording in advance, or during, demolition and reconstruction of the modern town around Castle Hill. The origin of the town seems to lie in the establishment of a small fort, probably post-Boudican, which was demolished to make way for the laying out of a town with gravelled streets during the second century (*77*). Simple rectangular buildings of wattle and daub were set in their own yards, although painted wall plaster and roof tiles suggest some were more luxurious than others. A stone-built *mansio* with hypocaust was built beside Akeman Street as it left by the north-east gate and another stone building, interpreted as a possible inn, was located

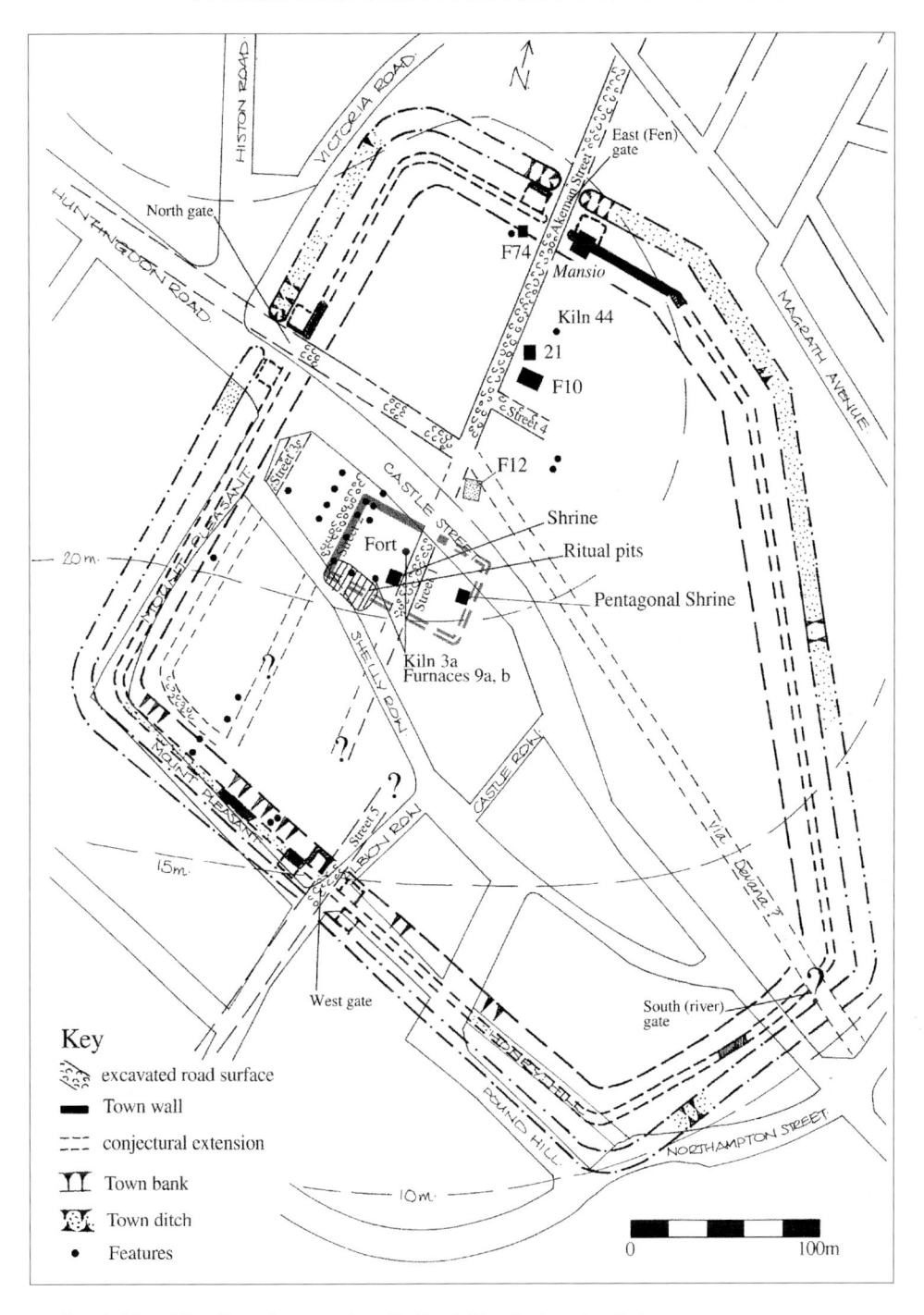

77 Cambridge (*Duroliponte*) town plan. © *Cambridge Antiquarian Society*

next to the central crossroads. Shrines and shafts with evidence for feasting were found in the south-western part of the town. Very little industrial evidence was discovered, although bone-pin making and some pottery manufacture occurred as extra-mural activities. During the second and third centuries the richer inhabitants were to be found in the suburbs, distributed along the major roads where buildings with tessellated pavements and window glass have been found. In the surrounding country a number of rich villas can be found set back from the major arterial routes. Industries such as pottery production, during the first century at Fen Ditton (Greenhouse Farm) and in the second to third century at Horningsea, can be seen to have developed as an important part of the economy. The defences which encircled the town in the fourth century were built of Barnack stone 2m thick, together with an earthen rampart and ditch. The town is surrounded by important fifth- and sixth-century Anglo-Saxon cemeteries and a Middle Saxon royal estate was established at Chesterton. This strongly suggests that in spite of its apparent lack of importance as a Roman town, Cambridge and the crossing point of the Cam was a strategically important place to control.

Earith

Another fen-edge settlement which could qualify as a town is that at Earith in the south-western fens of Cambridgeshire. Important finds have been recorded since the nineteenth century, and piecemeal rescue excavation has been undertaken by various people responding to threats of gravel extraction during the twentieth century. Michael Green has pulled together all this disparate evidence to present a coherent account of the site and I am grateful to him for making his unpublished material available to me (*78* and *79*). Metalled roads, ditched enclosures and at least 12 round and rectangular timber buildings have been dated in origin to the second century and continued on in to the fourth century. Aisled barns and possible granaries, wells, kilns and ovens (corn-dryers), a third- or fourth-century pottery kiln and slag from metalworking was all found in association with these buildings. A large number of quern stones have been found, as well as metalled mounds within ring-ditches which were probably threshing floors, large quantities of pottery and an unusually high percentage of horse bone, as well as cattle and other species. A temple complex clearly existed on the site, as revealed by several finds including a bronze figurine, a *genius*, as well as a large number of coins. The abundance of these finds in the absence of evidence for a villa allows interpretation of this settlement as a possible temple complex and market centre, or town. Other examples of similar size and nature are known from elsewhere in and around the fens and have been classified as large nucleated villages, places such as Hockwold and Denver in Norfolk, or Flaggrass and Coldham on March island

COMMUNICATIONS, FORTIFICATIONS, TOWNS AND DRAINAGE

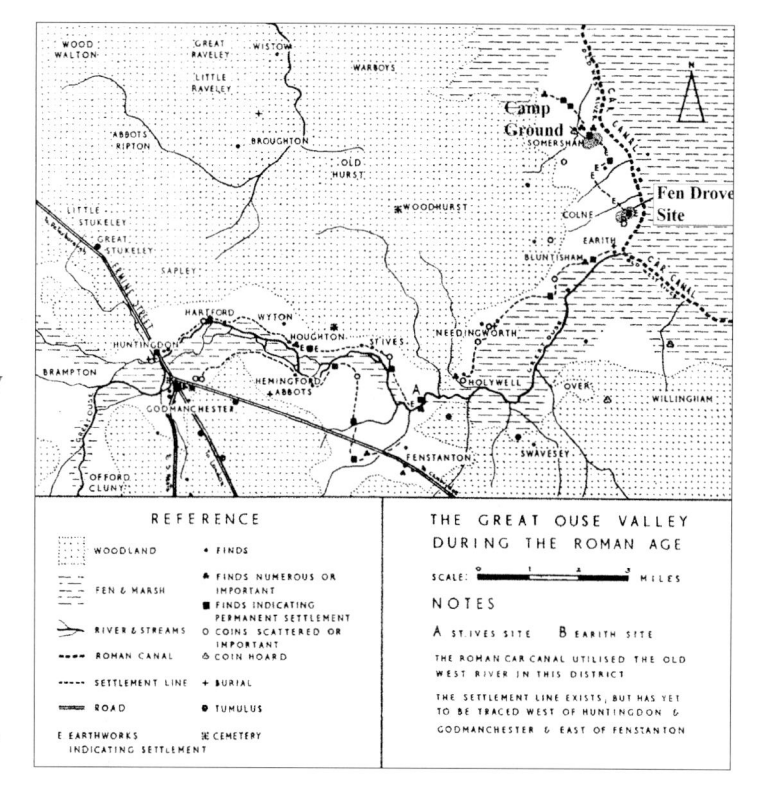

78 Right: Ouse Valley and area around Earith (with Camp Ground and Fen Drove sites marked). *Courtesy of Michael Green, adapted from* The Archaeological Newsletter 5, *1954*

79 Below: Plan of Roman settlement at Fen Drove, Earith. © *Michael Green*

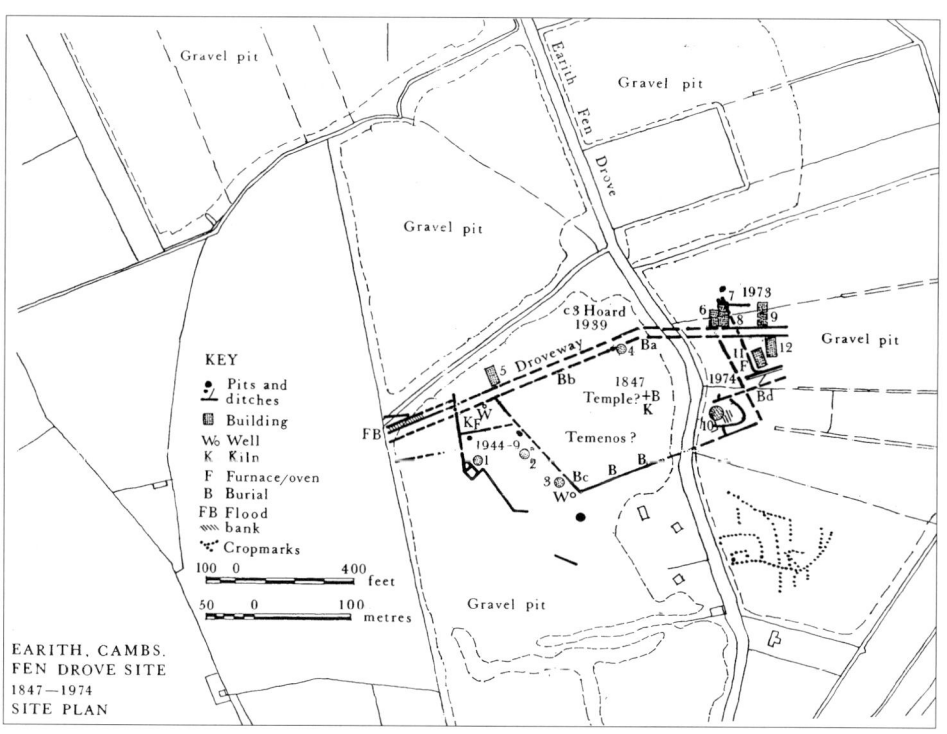

STONEA AND THE ROMAN FENS

and the silt fen, and Whaplode Drove and possibly Spalding in the Lincolnshire silt fen. In recent years Roddie Regan has conducted large-scale excavations on the remaining parts of it, uncovering a complex pattern of settlement spreading over a wide area of *c*.20ha (see special feature in this chapter and *80*).

Bourne

The probable fen-edge town at Bourne has never been excavated, but a number of finds indicate its importance and the extensiveness of the settlement there. Its location on a bifurcation of King Street, as well as Car Dyke, with canalised river (the Bourne Eau) and the Bourne–Morton canal originating from it, shows that it was a nodal point in the system of communications, connecting the fens with the upland and beyond. A number of different locations within the parish have produced evidence for tessellated pavements, tiles, hypocausts and limestone building material,

80 Plan of the Roman settlement at Camp Ground, Earith; top plan shows location of Camp Ground to Cranbrook Drain (possible part of Car Dyke) and other settlement clusters in vicinity (note: the grid squares are 1km); bottom plan is a detail of Camp Ground showing complex pattern of ditched features including three of the Iron Age enclosures, the trackway and defences to the Roman settlement, and the findspot for the bust of Jupiter. © *Cambridge Archaeological Unit*

COMMUNICATIONS, FORTIFICATIONS, TOWNS AND DRAINAGE

demonstrating that wealthy buildings existed, and there have been many finds of pottery and coins recorded from the modern town. The spring at St Peter's pond which is the source for the Bourne Eau could have been seen as a sacred site, and at least one bronze figurine (of a horse) has been found, although it is unprovenanced. Pottery production in the third and fourth centuries occurred at Bourne and a kiln has been found in close proximity to the Bourne–Morton canal.

Sleaford

Sleaford was an important tribal centre for the Corieltauvi during the Late Iron Age, strategically located to control the crossing of the Slea and access to the northern Fenlands. It was probably the site of a mint based on the evidence from the biggest collection of coin pellet moulds known from northern Europe, and could be regarded as a proto-town which was naturally adopted during the early Roman period. The settlement covered approximately 24ha and would thus have been the second largest fen-edge town after Durobrivae. Its floruit was in the second century and included stone buildings with painted wall plaster and window glass, corn-drying kilns and aisled barns. To the east on the fen edge at Heckington tile kilns have shown the existence of an important tile-manufacturing industry in the locality. Sleaford does not appear to have been walled in the later Roman period and may therefore already have lost such importance as it once had by this time, although excavations in 1984 close to the Roman road of Mareham Lane produced 260 coins of the late third to early fourth centuries.

Horncastle

Horncastle (possibly Bannovalium) is located c.10km north of the Lincolnshire fen edge, on the River Bain which drains into the fens, joining with the Witham at Tattershall. A second river, the Waring, helps to protect the town from the north. Finds from the area show it was occupied from the first to fourth centuries and was founded on an Iron Age predecessor. Buildings included painted wall plaster, mortar floors and masonry walls. The walls that surround the town were 5.5m wide and at least 3m high, with bastions of unusually square design, and staggered gateways to the west and east. It is thought that construction of the walls date to the fourth century and that the site might have acted as a centre and depot for parts of a mobile field army engaged in defence of the Saxon Shore. Although the defended part is small at c.0.2ha, buildings and other finds including cemeteries show that the core of the town itself extended over at least 2.5ha and that the spread of Roman settlement material indicates an area of perhaps as much as 54ha in total.

THE ROMAN CAMP GROUND, COLNE FEN, EARITH

Christopher Evans and Roddy Regan

Having seen piecemeal investigations during the 1970s, the Earith fen edge has long been renowned for its Roman findings (*78* and *79*), and in 1997 the University's Cambridge Archaeological Unit began a series of systematic excavations in the Hanson quarry across the north of this swathe of Roman occupation, in Colne Fen. To date four of the terrace's Iron Age compounds have been excavated (*80*). The archaeology of ensuing Roman occupation is framed by its proximity to the Roman canal of Car Dyke just to the east and its probable continuation along the Cranbrook Drain to the north; Turkington Hill Villa, Somersham, lies to the north.

In 1999 a major Roman 'official state' farm complex at Langdale Hale at the southern end of the Colne Fen terrace was excavated, and in 2001 the Late Roman Camp Ground complex on its north side was dug.[1] Extending in total over more than 7ha, the nine-month-long excavation of the latter's central swathe involved open-area excavation across 5ha. The settlement proved extraordinarily dense in both its features and finds, with more than 70,000 pottery sherds and 2,000 coins recovered.

In the main Late Roman phases, bisected by a central road/trackway, the core of the settlement had a polygonal perimeter. Its eastern side was defined by a double-ditch flanked embankment, whereas to the west a ditched trackway deflected around the compounds and its sides were also probably embanked (*80*). Certainly 'heavily' enclosed, if its banks were capped with hedges then this might amount to a rudimentary defence.

The measure of the Roman settlement, albeit largely in contrast, is obviously with Stonea. Whilst having its origins in the first to early second centuries (the locale also having two Middle/Late Iron Age compounds sited there beforehand), the Camp Ground saw its floruit in the third and fourth centuries (and continued until the early decades of the fifth, but without subsequent Saxon settlement): in other words, after Stonea's demise as a major civic and administrative centre. Though not having any building of the quality of Stonea's stone tower, the series of more formally laid out compounds north-east of the central road have been tentatively identified as its civic quarter and, apart from a major granary, included

COMMUNICATIONS, FORTIFICATIONS, TOWNS AND DRAINAGE

an imposing building range (16.5 x 39m) that may well have been comparable to the stone-footed aisled building at Langwood Farm (97).[2]

In total, 52 structures were present within the Roman Camp Ground. Many were of ancillary status and included a number of raised-floor granaries. Its residential buildings – of which a maximum of 12 seem contemporary in any one phase – were both of 'standard' post-built type and also used 'mass-' or bulk-timber foundations. Evidently drawing upon granary-style construction techniques, the latter had their walls carried on what can only have been rough-trimmed tree trunks (up to 10m in length) set into building trenches.

The settlement's compounds were tightly bunched. It is estimated that it would have had a resident population of between 50 and 120 individuals, and have been village-sized. Whilst farming was practised, this may have been limited as many of its compounds were too small to house stock and, within the core of the settlement, there were no obvious 'internal' trackways to facilitate the movement of animals. It may, in fact, be the case that only the more 'open', paddocks west of the polygonal core were actually farmsteads, with the remainder being something else. Given this, while there is no evidence that any specialist craft production was practised, the quantity of its coins would attest to trade. The most likely explanation surely lies in the settlement's relationship to the canal system and it may well have been a transhipment centre, sending out grain and, in return, receiving goods such as Nene valley wares for trade into its hinterland. Some of the settlement's larger buildings may well have belonged to successful traders and otherwise bargemen (and their families) may also have been in residence.

One rather surprising facet of the settlement's record is the high representation of Fenland species, an aspect that is similar to evidence from the Roman Shrine excavation at the Upper Delphs, Haddenham[3] (Evans & Hodder in press), which produced a wide variety of wetland birds, including pelican. Equally noteworthy is the occurrence of otter; present in all of the Roman phases, they account for 2 per cent of the total bone assemblage. While their remains may attest to trade in pelts, no characteristic butchery or skinning cuts have been identified. Another, and perhaps more likely possibility is that they were taken in an effort to curtail competition for fish resources, as quantities of fresh water fish bone are present in the site's floatation residues and many line-/net-weights were also recovered.

One truly remarkable finding from the excavation was a finely sculpted relief panel bust of Jupiter. The quality of its stonework is unparalleled in the region and clearly it derived from a much larger sculptural frieze. The bust was recovered from the uppermost fill of the large, sub-rectangular compound around which the western polygonal perimeter deflects. Near it human remains were found and it was probably reset in the locale as a grave-marker. Despite intensive excavation in the vicinity, both there and elsewhere across the site, no other dressed, let alone sculpted, stonework was recovered and the settlement's structures seem otherwise without architectural/sculptural pretensions. It must, therefore, be concluded that the source of the bust panel lay off-site, perhaps originally from the villa known across the Cranbrook Drain.

The excavation of the Camp Ground complex (and shortly its publication) provides an important counterpoint to Roman Fenland studies. As an alternative type of 'centre', and with evidence of 'official' participation/regulation throughout Late Roman times, its sequence (and story) markedly differs to that of Stonea.

Notes

1 Regan, R. 2003 *An Archaeological Excavation at Colne Fen, Earith: Langdale Hale (Sites V & VI)*. CAU Report 537
   Regan, R., C. Evans and L. Webley 2004 *The Camp Ground Excavations, Colne Fen, Earith*. CAU Report 654
2 Evans, C. 2003 Britons and Romans at Chatteris: Investigations at Langwood Farm, Chatteris. *Britannia* 34: 175-264
3 Evans C. and I. Hodder (in press) *Marshland Communities and Cultural Landscape: The Haddenham Project 1981-87* (II). Cambridge: McDonald Institute Research Series

8

THE ECONOMIC BASE AND RURAL SETTLEMENT OF THE ROMAN FENS

The mainstay of the Roman Fenland economy appears to have been in stock husbandry, principally sheep, and in the production of salt from evaporation of sea water (*colour plate 15*). These two industries went hand-in-hand and together account for the majority of settlement activity and land management for which we have archaeological evidence. As demonstrated by excavations at Stonea, the slaughter of sheep for export as carcasses during the second and third centuries is the most archaeologically visible agricultural activity at the site, and this can be seen also at many of the other contemporary Fenland sites that have been investigated. The manufacture of salt allowed the meat to be preserved and therefore allowed its long-distance transportation, presumably to supply a major consumer such as the Roman military, especially the garrisons on Hadrian's Wall. Around these two core parts of the economy a whole plethora of other activities occurred, some as service industries such as peat-cutting for fuel for the fires to evaporate brackish water and make salt, or the barge and ship transportation of the meat to take it to its distant markets. Supplies for the Fenland settlers were also required, such as pottery which led to the development of major industries around Durobrivae and many lesser production centres along the fen margins in the south and west.

Meat was not, however, the only requirement of the army and this was not the only product of Fenland stock husbandry. For example, gut was essential for providing strong and flexible bindings and was used to produce the springing to power the army's artillery; leather and hides were necessary for shoes, personal protective clothing and shields, for horse harness and general strapping, for tents and for commonplace items (such as buckets) that required ease of transportation as the army marched. Wool and textile manufacture would have been another by-product, although the archaeological evidence for this is less complete. Tim Potter, however, has drawn attention to the unusual frequency of loom-weights within the fens and its margins, and the production of cloth may have been a significant industry of the region, an activity often located on large estates. Dairy products, on the other hand, have left a trace through the relative frequency of cheese presses found in the Fenland and its margins, and the finer grades of salt produced in the Fenland industries would have been used in cheese-making. The predominance of sheep bones from Fenland sites suggests that it would have been milk from ewes that probably formed the staple for the dairy industry, and this industry could have been of greater local importance than that of meat production, which would most likely have been aimed at a specifically military market. At Godmanchester, for example, Michael Green has traced the whole sequence of dairy processing through a variety of different second-century pottery vessels found at one particular location, presumably a dairy within close proximity to its market in the town. He has stressed how this pastoralist economy would have included a large element of transhumance, making full use of the summer grazing provided by the fens during the driest part of the year, a tradition that can be traced back into prehistory, and one that emphasises the continued economic importance of the rich peat pastureland within the Roman period.

Settlement evidence shows that a large-scale colonisation occurred in the second century, but that severe problems developed during the third century, leading to retraction of settlement and piecemeal abandonment, especially in the southern (peat) fens. In the silt fen this hiatus in the third century appears to be less marked, and around the fen edge the pattern is perhaps more erratic. Evidence of widespread fresh water flooding has been found spreading out along the major river valleys into the fens, which choked drainage channels and inundated low-lying settlement. By later Roman times two different patterns of settlement are detectable, and Peter Salway argues for the development of *vicani* on the fen islands and especially on the silt fen, and *coloni* in association with villa estates along the fen edge. Both of these are forms of nucleated settlement akin to later villages. Michael Green believes that these large nucleated villages are also a product of the particular topography of Fenland, acting as winter homes for the summer pastoralists during their retreat from the peat fen to the slightly higher silts and fen edge in winter. Collection of taxes and control of movement, as well as surveillance of the population by the authorities, was better served in Fenland by the existence of these market and administrative centres where animals and products would have been brought in for sale, rather than trying to exert control through a chain of forts.

AGRICULTURE

Animal husbandry was of prime importance to the Roman Fenland economy. Statistics of different species of animal bones recovered from a variety of excavations in the fens has shown that 40-70 per cent were from sheep, 25-40 per cent were from cattle, and that horse and pig were represented by between 3 and 12 per cent, and 3 and 6 per cent respectively. The ages of sheep revealed by analysis of the bones show that a majority of animals were kept into their second or third years, which would be consistent with wool production. At Stonea, however, there seems to be good evidence to suggest at least 60 per cent of the sheep followed a kill pattern during their first or second years; a large percentage of feet and skull bones were also found which, together with the age of death, strongly suggests that Stonea was exporting carcasses and trading in meat rather than wool. Domestic consumption of meat on the site, however, shows that beef would have provided the greater part of the local meat diet. In contrast to the kill pattern for sheep the cattle bones show that all ages are represented, and probably these included animals used for traction and dairy production as well.

A comparison of faunal assemblages from several fen margin sites near Peterborough over the first four centuries AD has been undertaken by Ian Baxter and Mark Hinman, and this has shown that a mixed agriculture based on small farms was the norm in the Late Iron Age (*colour plate 19*), with small-scale pottery production, but that towards the end of the first century there was a general shift to larger field systems and abandonment of small domestic units within them. The field systems are visible in the form of droves and stockyards reflecting a specialism in stock management, especially cattle for dairy and meat production, managed perhaps on a ranch-type system (*colour plate 20*). The indication is that the animals were taken off site for consumption elsewhere, probably initially for a military market and later for the nascent town at Durobrivae. This evidence for a reorganised and more specialised agricultural environment is supported by Steve Kemp's excavations at Glinton in 1996, which produced large quantities of secondary grain processing dated to the later half of the second century AD. Such a concentration of cereal processing is unlike the evidence from adjacent sites such as Maxey or Werrington, and suggests that harvested crops were brought to specific specialist locations for processing, and later storage and distribution. Part of this fen-edge reorganisation might have come about during the second century in response to construction of the Car Dyke, which would have formed a barrier for access to traditional areas of grazing. This would have provided instead an improved transportation system in the form of canal barges, and thus an economic stimulus for adapting farming practices to new opportunities presented by the canal.

Baxter's and Hinman's survey of sites and faunal assemblages shows consolidation of new, larger farms over the next century which included stone buildings at places such as Longthorpe, whilst increased prosperity is evident at Orton Hall Farm and Tort Hill East at Sawtry, and eventually reoccupation of smaller units occurred once more at Lynch Farm, Maxey and Werrington during the third century. A shift back to more mixed agriculture becomes evident during the third and fourth centuries (*colour plate 21*), with malting kilns discovered at sites such as Haddon showing production of beer from the locally grown cereals, and pathologies of cattle demonstrating their use in this period for traction. The percentage of horses in the assemblage increased slightly on most sites during the later Roman period, perhaps also for traction, but at Tort Hill East, immediately adjacent to Ermine Street, the numbers were consistently higher and may reflect its use as a *mansio* and horse relay station for the administration. During the fourth century a shift back to a generally pastoral economy appears to have occurred.

Cheese presses, a distinctive type of ceramic pot with sieve arrangement, have been found at a range of sites in the fens and around the margins such as at Godmanchester, Haddon and Longthorpe. At the latter site excavation of a pottery kiln revealed great numbers of cheese presses, and three distinct types were categorised: a disc shape, conical shape and bowl shape. These numbers and diversity help to indicate the importance of this staple product of the Fenland economy; a product that would have been preserved by the inclusion of locally manufactured salt, and have been available for long-distance transport as well as local consumption. A fuller discussion of this 'white meat' industry is presented in the special feature on dairy production at Godmanchester, an example that probably illustrates what was happening all around the fens but has been largely ignored by the reports of most excavations which instead have focused on describing the physical remains such as pottery and animal bones, rather than interpreting their function and the economy that these remains imply.

TEXTILES

Textile production in Roman Britain has been suggested by J.P. Wild to have been its leading industry by at least the late third century. Although archaeological evidence is scant in comparison to such better attested industries as pottery manufacture, nonetheless a limited selection of artefacts (of woollen, flax and other garments surviving in waterlogged deposits and sometimes preserved in minerally replaced form) of animal bone and figurines, and of written records gives an indication of its distribution and importance. He points

THE ECONOMIC BASE AND RURAL SETTLEMENT OF THE ROMAN FENS

to the Diocletian price edicts of AD 301 as demonstrating the high esteem with which British clothing was held, with the *birrus* (a woollen hooded cape) and the *tapete* (woollen rug) amongst the first- and second-class grades of such textiles. The expertise and quality of the raw product already existed within the Iron Age community, but the infrastructure to manufacture textiles on the scale needed by the empire was developed through Roman administrators and the army. The presence of a large military presence, especially during the second century, would have required a correspondingly large output in high-quality textiles to clothe soldiers and keep them warm. J.P. Wild has calculated that this might have amounted on average to some three weeks' work for each household, seasonally undertaken, and probably developed from a basic domestic activity into a more centrally organised industry based upon villa estates and possibly imperial/military landholdings such as the Fenland imperial estate. Weaving mills and production centres were established during the third century, with one imperial mill being recorded in the *Notitia Dignitatum* at *Venta*: perhaps Venta Icenorum (Caistor by Norwich).

From the Fenlands a significant number of loom-weights have been recovered in comparison to their general rarity overall within Romano-British sites, from sites such as Lakenheath, Denver, Welney, Wimblington, Grandford, Flaggrass and Coldham, as well as Stonea, and Spalding New Cut in Lincolnshire. From the excavations at Orton Hall Farm Don Mackreth has suggested the presence of a mill close to Durobrivae, on the margins of the fens and presumably part of an imperial estate.

RAW MATERIALS

The fens were a rich environment, full of resources that could be exploited by man, as had been the situation for thousands of years before the Roman colonisation of the area. The fen islands and fen edge had provided locations for settlement which were safe from flooding, but around which fields could be cultivated and advantage could be taken of the fens for summer grazing and for the variety of raw materials the fen had to offer. Although faunal remains from Roman Fenland sites show few examples of wild animals, decorated pottery from the Nene valley shows clearly how fond Romans were of hunting, certainly an occupation followed by those wealthy enough to pursue it. In addition wildfowl, fish, eels, and shellfish abounded, and all must have been exploited during Roman times, even though the evidence has been rarely found. Oyster, mussel and winkle shells, however, are an ubiquitous component of nearly every Roman site which has any pretensions of importance, and locally collected varieties would most likely account for the shells found at places like Godmanchester and Cambridge, other Roman towns, and many other contemporary sites in the region. During the medieval period fishing rights and mussel beds had great commercial importance and were jealously guarded by their owners, such as the monasteries and bishops, and by analogy we can presume the same to have been true during Roman times.

Fen carr woodland and more substantial trees on the islands or fen edge would have provided a plentiful stock of timber for many needs from the manufacture of composite tools to the construction of boats and houses. Wickerwork and basketry would have been used for containers, fish-traps, hurdles, and other items, whilst reeds and sedges would have been harvested for thatching, flooring and bedding material.

PEAT FUEL

Peat was extracted on an extensive scale during the second and third centuries, and the remains of Roman peat cuttings or turbaries can be seen at a number of locations (Wimblington and Christchurch in Cambridgeshire, and Upwell, Nordelph, and Downham West in Norfolk on either side of the Fen Causeway – see *colour plate 10*). Peat can be used as a fuel and it seems likely that much of it would undoubtedly have been used to supply the salterns and thus provide a relatively cheap and easy means to heat the hearths and furnaces needed to evaporate the salt from the sea water. Rowena Gale's analysis of charcoal from the flues and hearths of Iron Age and Roman salterns at Cowbit Wash, Morton Fen, and Middleton, however, has shown widely different results, perhaps indicating that whatever was locally available was utilised. Small roundwood appears to have been favoured, mostly of alder and willow, but also including thorn, fruit, and hazel, as well as cereal-threshing waste and many seeds and small-stemmed herbaceous plants which were found at one site, and gorse and heather at another.

Peat would have required intensive manual labour to cut it and bulk transportation of the product to its place of use, most probably by barge along the many Fenland waterways. At Stonea a narrow wooden spade with iron edge to it was found preserved within a waterlogged sump. The shape and size of this article is similar to the more modern becket, or peat-cutter's spade (*59*).

THE ECONOMIC BASE AND RURAL SETTLEMENT OF THE ROMAN FENS

SALT INDUSTRY

Salt-making was one of the most important activities on the silt fen and along the roddons backing up into the peat fens during the second and early third centuries. The nature of the industry was different from that found in some other areas of Roman Britain such as production from brine springs at Droitwich and the Cheshire *-wich* towns, but was more similar to that from coastal sites such as the Red Hills in Essex and those along the south coast. Fenland salt was extracted during the Roman period by allowing tidal waters to flow into channels and settling tanks at high tide, and then the brackish water was removed into coarse, baked-clay troughs supported on clay bars above hearths (salterns) which evaporated the water to leave salt. The baked-clay equipment used in this process often broke up, so that great spreads and mounds of this material, known as briquetage, have been found to have accumulated in many locations. The Lincolnshire siltlands formed the centre of production, and in Cambridgeshire most of this activity occurred in a concentrated zone along the southern edge of the silt fen especially in Elm and Upwell, and along roddons such as the Old Croft River. Accompanying this industrial activity was the collateral impact necessitated by a demand for fuel, which the fens could supply in large volume through the existence of fen carr woodland and peat.

The origins for salt-making can be found in the Early Iron Age, perhaps even as early as the Late Bronze Age, reaching a peak in the early-middle Roman period, but with much of the Fenland salt production appearing to have ceased by the fourth century. This decline has been attributed to factors such as changing environments, which involved reduction in tidal velocity and salinity, and encroachment of the peat fen. Iron Age exploitation appears to have originated as speculative, seasonal enterprises devoid of domestic evidence, moving into a more intense phase of production within the Late Iron Age when evidence for permanent settlement has been found in close association with salterns. Analysis of the design, size, and fabric composition of the briquetage has allowed a typological progression and technical development of the industry to be proposed by Elaine Morris and Sarah Percival consisting of four broad phases, which can be assigned periods based on associated ceramics: the Late Bronze Age/earlier Iron Age characterised by shelly, limestone-gritted, clay, round-bottomed evaporation troughs set on pedestals directly over hearths; later Iron Age characterised by organic, tempered fabric and more refined trough supports, and the development of ovens; early Roman characterised by sub-rectangular, flat-bottomed pans together with bricks, bars, rods, wedges and clips, and placed within ovens; and late Roman, which saw metal pans replace ceramic ones, massive pedestals and long-chambered ovens (*81*).

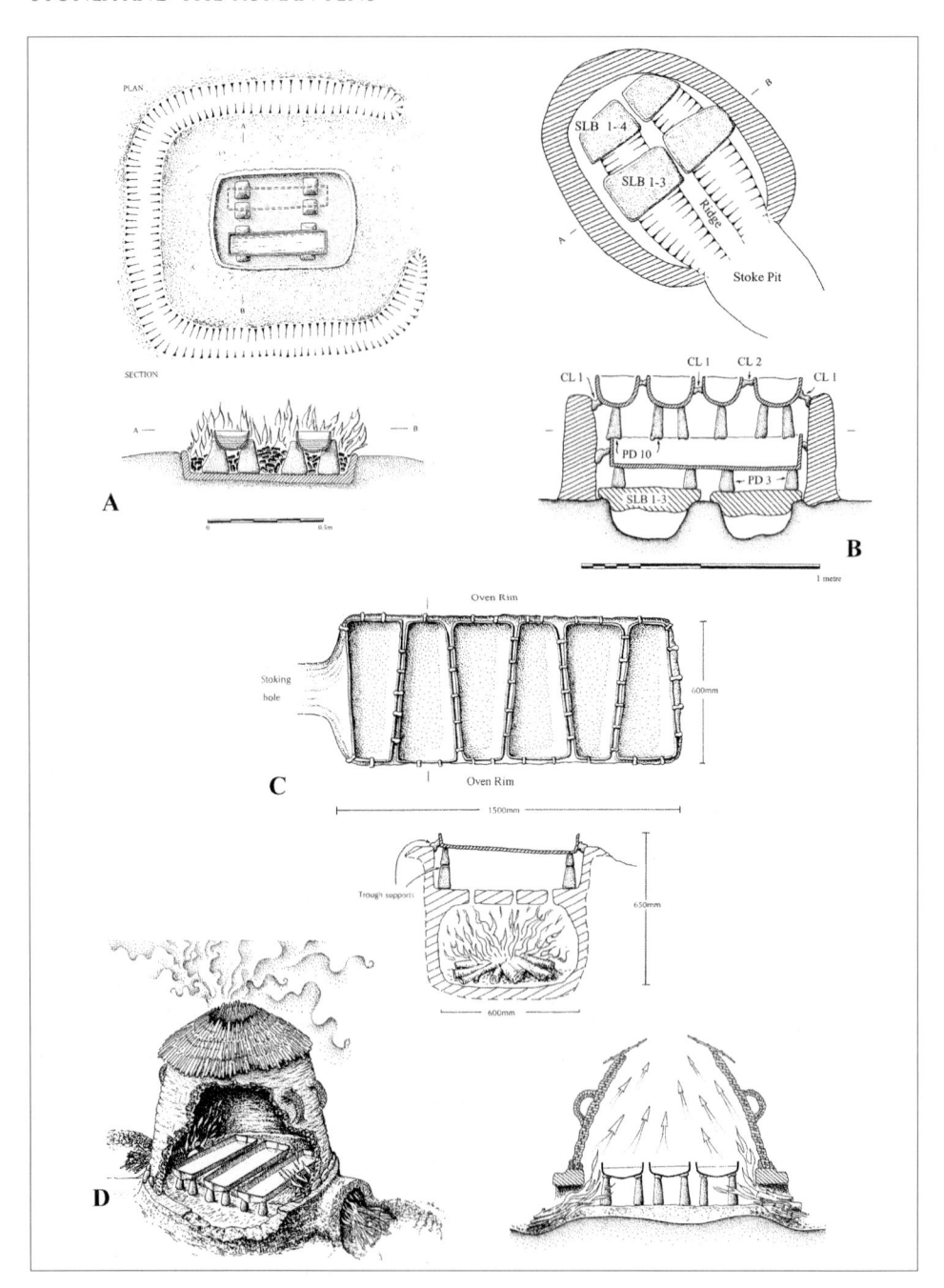

81 Reconstruction of salterns, A & B Middle Iron Age. A) possible reconstruction of hearth system; B) second-first century BC oven reconstruction based on evidence from Cowbit (top plan without containers shown); C) schematic arrangement of clay pans and supports based on evidence from Ingoldmells Beach; D) Late Roman reconstruction based on evidence from Middleton, with lead pans. *With kind permission of Tom Lane and Elaine Morris, from* Lincolnshire Archaeology and History Report Series 4

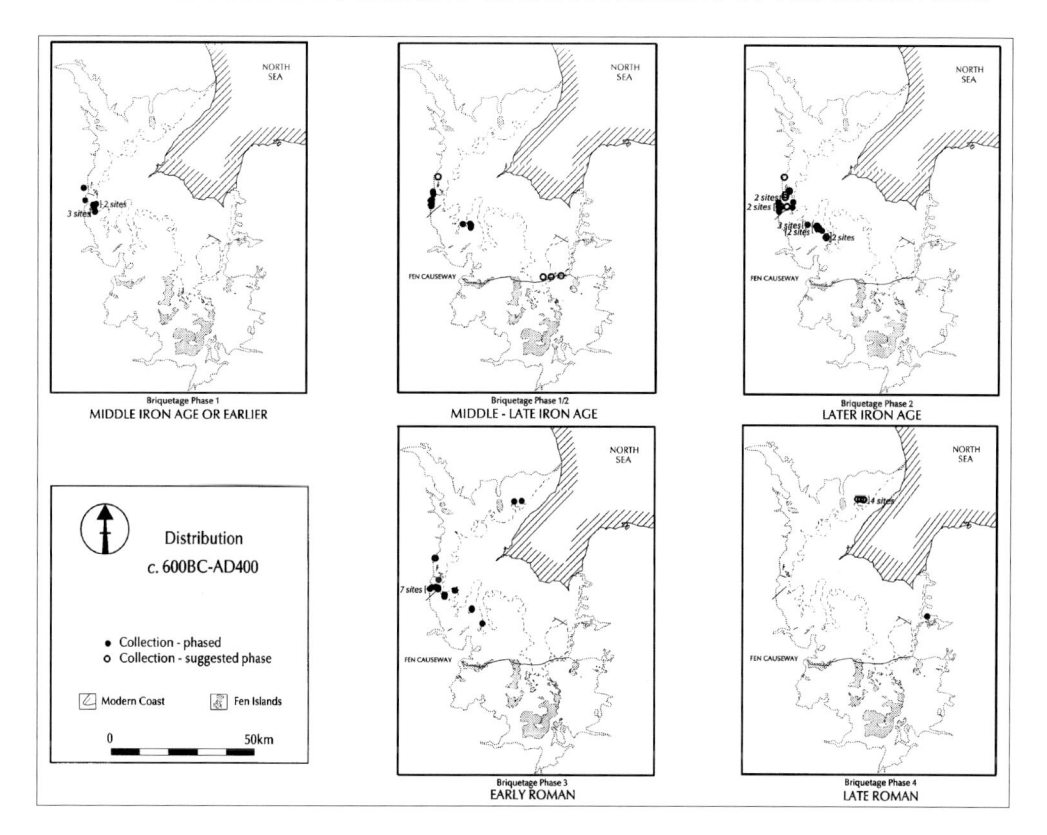

THE ECONOMIC BASE AND RURAL SETTLEMENT OF THE ROMAN FENS

82 Chronological development and distribution of salterns across Fenland. With kind permission of Tom Lane and Elaine Morris, from Lincolnshire Archaeology and History Report Series 4

The distribution of these sites is concentrated in Lincolnshire (*82, colour plate 15*), Phase 1 being around the south-western margins of the Lincolnshire fens, and with intensification and expansion during Phase 2 northwards along the fen edge and spreading to some isolated sites on the western side of the silt fens (so that the fuel for heating the saltern hearths could be most effectively extracted from the peat). There is also, however, a possible linear group of this period found along the Fen Causeway in Norfolk, at West Walton, Downham West and Nordelph. During Phase 3, the Roman period, it is this silt-fen based industry which saw rapid expansion especially in Lincolnshire and northern Cambridgeshire, with a spread south-eastwards into Norfolk (the most important site being at Middleton in the Nar valley, which came to prominence in Phase 4).

There is chronological evidence to show that saltern sites slowly retreated a little way into the interior of the silts as the period progressed, presumably to avoid rising waters in the peat fen, and by the fourth century the industry as a series of small-scale enterprises appears to have largely collapsed. One or two sites displaying highly organised and more intense production, however, carried on into Late Roman times. These included some sites in Wrangle, along the Lincolnshire coast in the northern fens, Norwood in Cambridgeshire, and the exceptionally large and geographically isolated site of Middleton in Norfolk (*colour plate 26*). This recent evidence for continuation of successful salt production on an industrial scale contradicts previous arguments which had believed that the Fenland industry, and coastal salt-making in general, had reached its zenith during the second century and thereafter went into decline, and the belief that inland production areas such as Droitwich and the Cheshire -*wich* towns monopolised trade in this commodity during later Roman times.

Excavations at Middleton as part of the Fenland Management Project have demonstrated that the salterns at Middleton were conducted as an industrial unit with several phases of production and reorganisation evident. Although the local resources would have allowed other salterns to operate in the Nar valley, this did not occur; iron and pottery manufacture have been found in the vicinity. The careful layout of the capture and processing arrangements at Middleton and the sophistication of the techniques for salt production witnessed there show that the site was capable of making large quantities of refined salt. No evidence for domestic occupation exists on site and the animal bones that were found were principally horse, interpreted as the remains of transport animals rather than food waste. The layout of the site and the organisation of the surrounding landscape strongly suggest a planned and centralised control, perhaps part of a reinvigorated imperial estate which is discussed in the next chapter. Nar valley pottery has been found at some of the Saxon Shore forts (such as Caister-on-Sea) (*colour plate 28*), at which there has also been evidence for considerable animal butchery. This may indicate a specific military use and organisation for the salt. The third- to fourth-century date established for Middleton is not unique within eastern Britain, as recent fieldwork has started to discover other sites that can be tentatively given similar dates, such as Tilney St Lawrence in Norfolk, Gosberton and Pinchbeck in Lincolnshire, Norwood in Cambridgeshire, and at least two of the Red Hills along the Crouch in Essex.

CERAMIC INDUSTRIES: POTTERY, TILES, MOSAICS

Major pottery production centres are known from various areas around the fens, some of which functioned for most of the Roman period, and others of which flourished for relatively short periods. The largest and most productive was the industry based around Durobrivae, the Nene valley potteries, extensively investigated by the Nene Valley Research Committee and most thoroughly

THE ECONOMIC BASE AND RURAL SETTLEMENT OF THE ROMAN FENS

83 Nene Valley hunt cup.
© *Peterborough Museum and Art Gallery*

published by Rob Perrin (*83*). Products from this manufacturing centre dominated pottery assemblages throughout the fens during the second century, and remained the most significant component in the later period as well. The origins lie within the earliest phase of Roman occupation, with kilns dated to the first century (*colour plate 19*) found at Water Newton and in association with the fort at Longthorpe. Further east along the Nene at Stanground numerous fen edge-kilns have been identified and excavated, constructed of limestone and tile, and continuing into at least the first quarter of the third century. Distribution of Nene valley wares, however, goes far further afield than just the fens and fen margins and the industry continued to prosper throughout the fourth century. It specialised in household and tableware, and a great variety of form and decoration was employed in its production. The river and road networks radiating out from Durobrivae in all directions would have provided an easy means of distribution (*75*), and the local source of clay and fuel for the kilns from the wooded hills of Huntingdonshire and Northamptonshire were readily exploited. The Fenland and its rapid colonisation during the Hadrianic and Antonine period provided a rapidly expanding market place for the early potters, but their continued success depended on a wider appeal than just within the fens.

Both Godmanchester and Cambridge had their own industries, which could perhaps be better referred to as the Ouse and Cam valley potteries. Excavations by Michael Green have discovered kilns and products dating from the second to fourth centuries consisting of buff-wares and greywares, which in form and type are distinct from neighbouring areas. The second-century highly fired greywares he has associated, at least in part, with the needs of dairy production, whereas the buff-wares were designed for a domestic market. Recent excavations have revealed kilns of first-century date downriver at Swavesey, and fieldwalking by David Hall discovered other first- and second-century kilns at Over. To the east of Cambridge an early centre of production has long been known from War Ditches, Cherry Hinton, but a concentrated group of 11 first-century kilns at Fen Ditton was excavated in the 1990s by David Gibson and Gavin Lucas, and dated to the Claudio-Neronian period. To the north along the Cam are the well-known Horningsea kilns, which can be found on either side of the river and produced coarseware storage jars during the second and third centuries. Local sources of clay and probable wooded areas just north of Cambridge provided the raw materials, and exportation was via the rivers and the Car Dyke canal. Horningsea ware is found in the fens but it is also found on a much more widespread basis than this, with sherds being excavated at forts along Hadrian's Wall, strongly supporting the notion of the fens in part being an imperial estate, the products from which were used for supplying the garrisons along the northern frontier. It is generally assumed that Horningsea ware was used for containing and transporting grain, and during excavations at the junction of Car Dyke and the River Cam in 1997 Stephen Macaulay found not only kilns dug into the bank of the canal, but also a probable timber grain warehouse (*colour plate 18*). The amount of grain that could be transported in this manner, however, would seem to be limited and this method was not very practicable as the containers would be heavy and liable to break; grain can be transported in organic containers much more simply, by sack, barrel or wooden bin, and could be poured into carts, canal barges, or sea-going boats with ease if there was a need to move grain in bulk.

Elsewhere in Fenland pottery manufacture does not seem to have had the same industrial scale of production as in the areas described above, although along the eastern fen-edge kilns have been found at Lakenheath in Suffolk of first-century date, and later ones at Shouldham and the Nar valley in Norfolk. These latter ones are dated to the third and fourth centuries. In Lincolnshire pottery manufacturing is known from Thurlby and Bourne on the fen edge, and from the towns of Great Casterton and Ancaster further inland. Glazed pottery from Spalding New Cut might indicate a kiln on the silt fen.

Tile kilns have been discovered at a number of places, although tile manufacture

THE ECONOMIC BASE AND RURAL SETTLEMENT OF THE ROMAN FENS

would probably have followed any large building project. It is therefore to be expected that tile kilns will be found at places such as outside small towns, or at major centres such as Stonea and Castor. The major villas and smaller stone-built residences would have had tiles produced locally, and fieldwalking on one such site at Fordham, for example, has produced evidence for the suggestion of two phases of roofing to a small rural 'villa'. More intensive production and more permanent kilns have been identified through recent excavations at places such as Hacconby on the fen edge in Lincolnshire, at Wittering near Durobrivae (*84, colour plate 22*) and at Little Thetford on the Isle of Ely.

Although tessellated pavements are a feature of many villas around the fen edge, full-blown coloured mosaics are less common. Around the Nene Valley, however, and northwards along the Lincolnshire fen margin, a school of mosaic manufacture flourished in the third quarter of the fourth century with its base at Durobrivae. This specialised in geometric patterns (*colour plate 23*) consisting of eight-lozenged stars and interlaced octagons and circles, designs that were distinct from the figured mosaics characteristic of the other parts of Britain of this period. Secondary workshops were probably established in Leicester and Lincoln. Yet it seems probable that the origins of this school lay earlier, perhaps in the latter part of the third century, and that is was perhaps to service the massive building programme at Castor.

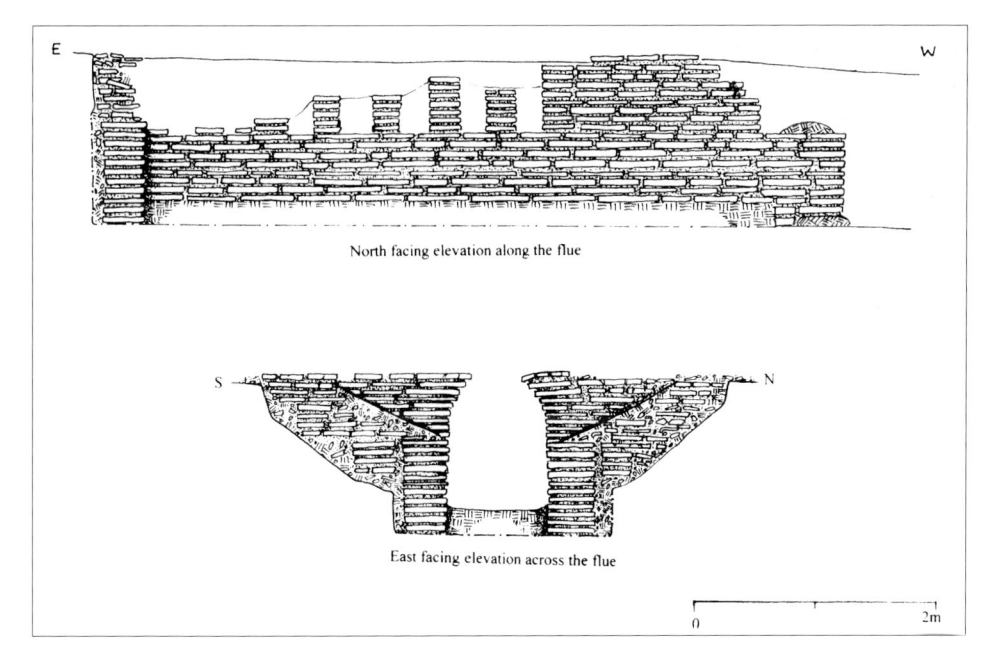

84 Elevation of Wittering tile kiln 1993. © Ron McKenna

SERVICE INDUSTRIES AND ANCILLARY TRADES: STORAGE, TRANSPORTATION, BUILDING SERVICES, METALWORK

A wide range of service industries would have existed, although evidence for them can be indirect and slim. Storage of manufactured goods and agricultural produce would have required specialist structures such as warehouses, aisled barns and granaries, examples of which are frequently found in the archaeological record, but their precise role and function is less often examined in detail. The custodianship and management of such business would have required responsible individuals to devote themselves to it, and to the organisation of transport and shipping. The finds of *amphorae* fragments from important places such as Stonea, as well as one still containing mackerel paste excavated from Godmanchester, demonstrate the widespread trading networks that were in operation, and how the Fenland waterways would have helped in facilitating such trade (*colour plates 15 and 26*).

There are several locations where inland ports and harbours have been suggested, but few that have any material evidence to help substantiate such suggestions. Within the Guyhirn Washes earthworks located on a rodden of one of the old courses of the Nene and Ouse rivers have been tentatively interpreted as a harbour by Bob Davis (*85*). He has identified a series of platforms from his survey, which he has interpreted in part as a set of wharves, bordered by a 1km-long bank which was built to keep the level of the river high enough to be used for boats in the harbour, rather than allowing it to spread over the flood plain. Pottery of second- and third-century date and some briquetage has been recovered from the site, and its location appears to form a nodal point in communications on the edge of the silt fen. A similar port would have existed at Reach (*colour plate 24*), but it is difficult to date the surviving inlets and wharves to the Roman, medieval or post-medieval periods. The timber-frame granary excavated at the south end of the Cambridgeshire Car Dyke would argue for a port at the junction of the canal where it widens out to meet with the Cam. A great many other such places, large and small (such as the Earith area discussed in the previous chapter), must have dotted the fens and acted as centres for storage and distribution. Other evidence for water transport includes a number of finds from the fens of possible cargoes, lost when barges might have sunk in old watercourses, such as a group of 20 querns from the Roman Welland in Crowland Common, a large number of terracotta lamps from the old course of the Nene in Whittlesey, pottery and stone from the Cambridgeshire Car Dyke and a palaeochannel of the Cam at Swaffham Bulbeck, and 'hoards' of pewter from Whittlesey Mere and the River Lark in Suffolk.

The use of building stone in areas devoid of such natural resources (such as the fens) required an industry for extraction and distribution of good-quality stone. The best locally available was limestone or ragstone, which was to be

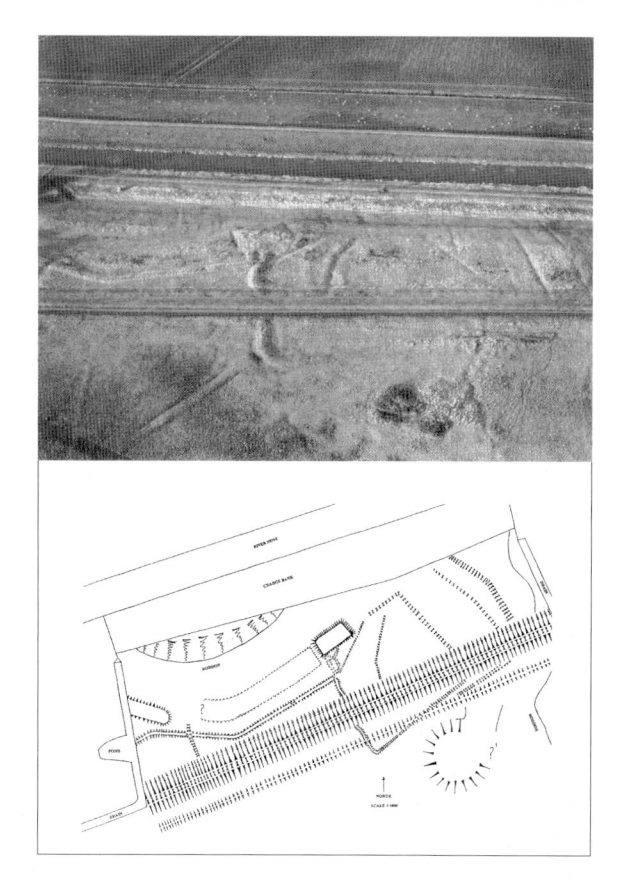

THE ECONOMIC BASE AND RURAL SETTLEMENT OF THE ROMAN FENS

85 Guyhirn Roman earthworks in the Washes: a possible harbour. Survey and plan © Rob Davis and Charlie Kitchen 1992-3; air photograph © Ben Robinson 4/1/02

found in large quantities along the western fen edge, particularly from the Huntingdonshire/Northamptonshire area. The most important quarry was that at Hills and Holes, Barnack. This fine-quality building stone was extensively mined and transported all over the Fenland region to construct villas and official buildings, and would have constituted an important industry throughout Roman times. Clunch or Totternhoe stone, from the southern fen edge, would have been an important secondary source and the location of quarries at Reach, near to the probable Roman canal of Reach Lode and close to an important villa, suggest large-scale exploitation from this source.

Carpenters would have been in great demand for construction of carts and boats, buildings and barrels, tools and containers and many more items as well. In spite of the potential for organic preservation within Fenland waterlogged soils, however, only a very few special sites such as Stonea Grange have actually produced surviving examples from this industry. Nevertheless, epigraphical sources record that the Emperor Julian in 379 brought large numbers of ships and grain over from Britain to resupply his Rhineland garrisons after barbarian invaders had been driven back from Gaul, and a likely source for this grain, and the route by which it would have been exported, was East Anglia and the Fenland basin.

Metalworkers are better represented in the archaeological record in the form of smelting or smithing slag, and iron or bronze artefacts are more likely to survive through the centuries. Iron-working was particularly important within the Nene valley area, but slag deposits have also been found on the fen edge, for example at Morton in Lincolnshire and at Pentney in Norfolk. Michael Green has excavated an iron and bronze metalworker's shop at Godmanchester which produced crucibles and tuyeres as well as slag.

Skilled tradesmen such as builders, thatchers and tilers would have been in demand, with those involved probably acting as itinerant craftsmen, being employed around towns and large estates. The construction of even small-scale 'villas' or Romanised well-to-do farmhouses would have necessitated the setting up of local tile kilns, as transportation of large quantities of heavy and easily breakable products such as brick and tile would not have been very sensible.

The maintenance of the economic infrastructure such as drainage and road repairs would have been planned and managed by officials, supported by specialists such as military surveyors, and presumably would have required the periodic large-scale employment of troops or peasants. Many more activities can be imagined, some from an official need and others as part of private venture, but all accumulating into a complex set of economic relationships which helped support the prosperity of the region.

FIELD SYSTEMS AND THE CHARACTER OF RURAL SETTLEMENT

Roman land division and field systems within the fens include a variety of different arrangements. Some show elements of a planned landscape, while others would appear to be more organic in origin. The latter, however, may be more a product of following the natural topography, and the imposition of a more regularised pattern of fields would have been inappropriate. The nature of the land use would also have influenced the kind of field pattern we would expect to see.

The most regular layout is a rectilinear gridded pattern of fields observable at Christchurch, Upwell, although smaller clusters of enclosures laid out in the form of a grid occur frequently elsewhere throughout the silt fens. The Christchurch field system (86) lies a few kilometres to the east of Stonea and has been described as the closest example to centuriation known from the fens, indicative of strong central authority following through a planned division of the landscape for colonists. This would be understandable within the context of an imperial estate,

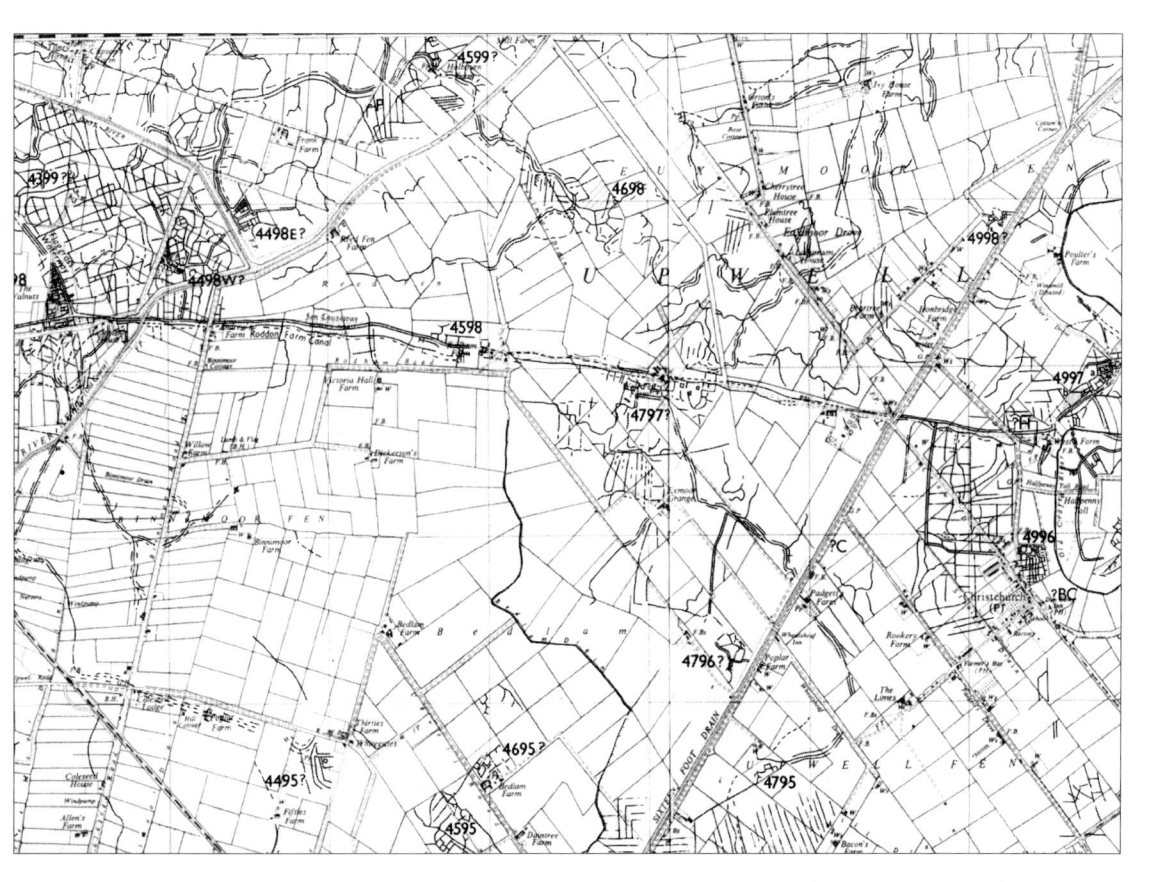

THE ECONOMIC BASE AND RURAL SETTLEMENT OF THE ROMAN FENS

86 Centuriation: Roman field systems at Christchurch and cropmark evidence along the Fen Causeway March–Upwell. From The Fenland in Roman Times 1970 *with kind permission of the Royal Geographical Society*

but the question has been raised as to why, if the land was part of the *res privata*, more of it does not accord with such planned allotment. The rectangular fields at Christchurch cover 85ha and are aligned on north–south and east–west axes, apparently offset from the Fen Causeway in the north, and the Old Croft River in the east. The system measures 34 *actus* north–south and 20 *actus* east–west (1,200 x 700m), which is significant in that the *actus* was the measurement used to lay out centuriation, commonly on a grid of 20 *actus*. Further south and west of this block other examples of gridded fields are apparent, although these are not always on the same alignment. Seven kilometres further east along the Fen Causeway in Norfolk another similar block of fields exists at Straw Hall Farm, Downham West (*87*), measuring *c*.800 x 800m. Traces of other fields offset to the north of the Fen Causeway are visible between the Christchurch and Straw Hall

183

STONEA AND THE ROMAN FENS

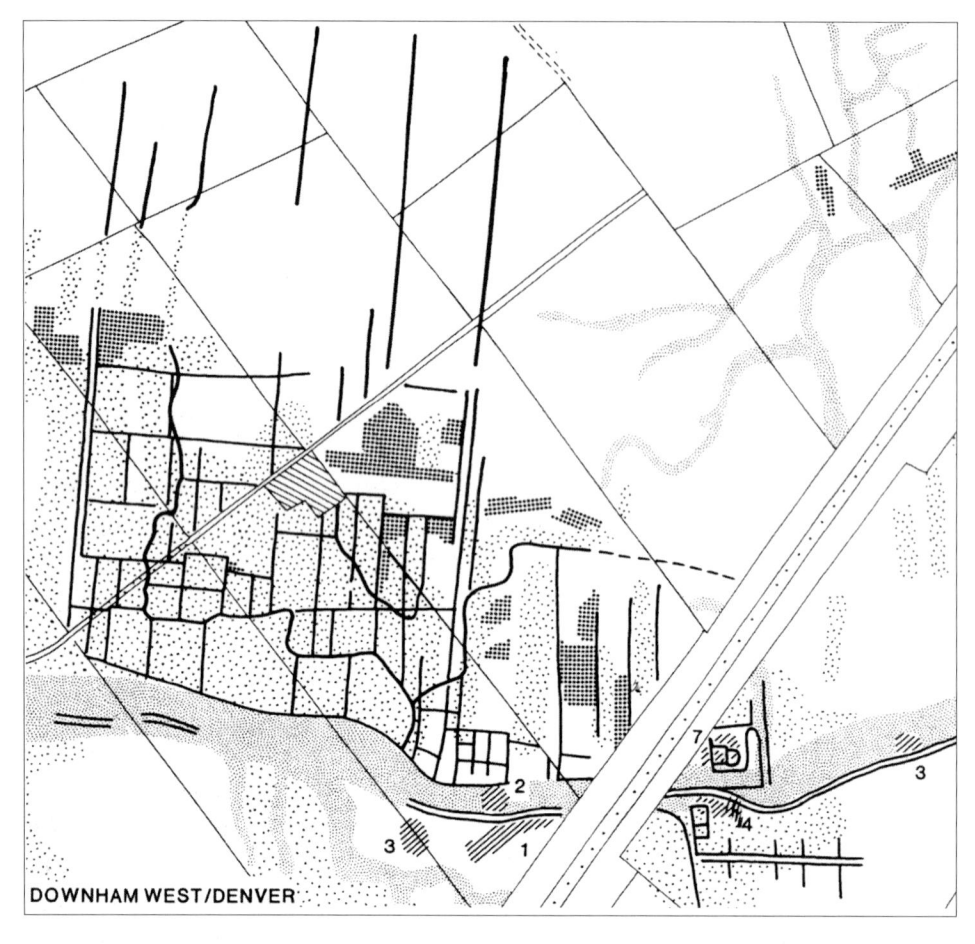

87 Centuriation at Downham laid off from the Fen Causeway. Courtesy of Rob Silvester and English Heritage, from East Anglian Archaeology *52*

blocks; a tentative date of early third century has been given to a field ditch in this system when it was excavated in 1993 as part of the Fenland Management Project investigation into the Fen Causeway at Downham West. The full picture of this system has been much obscured by later flooding and deposition of silts, and also by the extensive extraction of peat during Roman times. These turbaries – regular strips excavated through the peat – became filled with silt during the third century or later. They also occur west of Christchurch and their orientation is broadly the same as the regular field systems, suggesting that the layout of the turbaries was following the same planned pattern.

On Stonea and the neighbouring islands of March, Manea and Chatteris large settlements spread over the landscape with extensive enclosures and droves.

THE ECONOMIC BASE AND RURAL SETTLEMENT OF THE ROMAN FENS

The Fen Causeway provided an axis off which these systems were laid at places such as Flaggrass, Estover and Grandford (*86, colour plate 15*). The Flaggrass system consists of a grid pattern of enclosures on the northern side of the Fen Causeway and Rodham Farm Canal, orientated north-west/south-east 1,200 x 1,000m in extent; though not as regular as the system at Christchurch it is nonetheless a well-defined block of land that has been subdivided into many large paddocks. By contrast the cropmark evidence from Stonea shows clusters of small enclosures with some longer ditches and droves (*colour plate 10*). In the fens such concentrated areas of dense cropmarks with small subdivided plots is generally interpreted as settlement because fieldwalking over such patterns of cropmarks has usually produced abundant artefactual evidence implying domestic occupation.

North of March these settlements include extensive areas such as Coldham, Gedney Hill and Whaplode Drove (*6 and 22*), as well as smaller settlements such as Norwood, Waldersea and Stags Holt, all of which were intermingled with industrial activity, small creeks, droveways and paddocks. The proximity of Norwood to the zone of the Fen Causeway probably argues for an early foundation and pottery recovered through Tim Potter's excavations has been given a Flavian date. The possible town at Grandford and large village at Flaggrass had pre-Flavian origins, whereas Coldham seems to have originated in Hadrianic times, i.e. during the early second century. They all continued into the late Roman period. The buildings at Coldham were of wattle and daub with clay floors and tiled roofs, set in ditched enclosures, associated with abundant pottery, and with salterns interspersed within the settlement. Although early Roman coins were not frequent, and sites such as these were probably not part of the monetary economy, generally the fens appear to have a significant number of coins from the late Antonine period indicating the relative prosperity that the region enjoyed during this particular period of the mid-second century. In the third century coin hoards were hidden at both Coldham and Flaggrass.

Further south on Chatteris island two complexes at Honey Hill and Langwood Farm were linked by a small road, sharing a ridge with a number of other settlements that seem to have originated during the Bronze and Early Iron Age. Langwood Farm was investigated in 1993 as part of the Fenland Management Project and this produced artefactual evidence over 10ha for occupation, dated by ceramics and metalwork from the Late Iron Age (with a possible hiatus at the end of the first and early second centuries) until the middle of the third century AD, when the lower lying areas of the field system were liable to flooding and the settlement seems to have been abandoned.

At another central Fenland site, Throckenholt, an arrangement of roughly parallel droves on a north-west/south-east axis with paddocks offset from them and dispersed settlement nuclei distributed through the system, can be seen on air photographs. Ceramic evidence has demonstrated that the field system was laid out in the middle to late second century and was abandoned in the early third century. Silts derived from flooding infilled all the field ditches and led to abandonment of the site, after which brushwood accumulated in the un-maintained ditches and finally peat growth in more recent times. During investigations in 1993 as part of the Cambridgeshire County Farms Evaluation Programme directed by the author, a rather modest assemblage of second-century Samian and some high-status pottery, as well as bone needles and nails, was found. The date and affluence of this assemblage is broadly in common with the results from David Hall's fieldwalking of the Cambridgeshire fens and from other excavation of similar sites. During the Antonine period and late second century the Fenland communities appear to have been reasonably affluent, with good contacts further afield allowing the importation of pottery and millstones from distant sources.

Elsewhere in the fens and fen edge general alignments can be seen of long individual ditches or droveways which perhaps acted as ranch boundaries, and off which groups of smaller fields were laid out. Along the roddons within the peat fen the narrow expanse of slightly higher land afforded by the silt levees of the rivers led to ribbon exploitation along them. Droveways followed the line of the roddon, and small paddocks for domestic occupation, yards and stock-holding ran off from the droves. Salterns were frequently dispersed amidst these small enclosures. Don Mackreth has drawn attention to this same phenomenon occurring along the Nene and Welland valleys and gives an example of one such route showing as a ditch line joining strings of settlements together through Helpston, Glinton and Etton.

On the silt fen small, square fields predominated, a shape and size inconsistent with arable agriculture (see 6); these can be interpreted as grass paddocks for stock, plots for kitchen gardens and perhaps orchards, as well as yards and settlement enclosures. 'Fen circles' are a particular type of feature in the silt fen which can be seen from the air, and are on very rare occasions found on the ground as earthworks as for example in Hilgay. Rog Palmer has plotted hundreds of these features and analysed these in conjunction with earlier work by Derek Riley. The circles are between 7 and 17m in diameter but lack any associated artefactual evidence, and have therefore been interpreted as stack-stands for drying hay.

Detailed analysis of the cropmark and artefactual evidence from the Lincolnshire siltlands was undertaken by Sylvia Hallam in the 1960s, from which she derived 10 categories of settlement-related field systems and attributed a broad chronological development to them. During the first century *small* irregular settlements made up of 2-3 farms, and loose agglomerations of these, were found concentrated around watercourses and industrial sites. During the second century large irregular settlements built up along these watercourses and new regular farmsteads were founded, some of which appear to have been very short-lived, and there was a gradual development of rectilinear patterns with older settlements to create compound groups. In contrast to these, open settlements can also be found dating to the second century located on expanses of silt fen, as well as compact settlements that had developed from discrete blocks (for example around crossroads or T-junctions) and which flourished in the second century. During the third century tight clusters of enclosures developed and large dense nuclei appear which by the fourth century can be seen to have had some reduction in size, and it is generally this type, and those that developed into important trading centres located on nodal points of the communication network and often associated with sites of religious significance, that survive beyond AD 350.

Work by the Fenland Survey in the 1980s did not try to address the question of the form of settlement and field systems, but instead concentrated on discovery of new sites and an accurate mapping of the changing Fenland environment. The survey confirmed the relatively dense spread of settlement along the western fen edge (*colour plate 14*), and the relative wealth and extent of settlement and related activity stretching across the marshes from Billingborough and Pointon to Bicker Haven. This area includes the well-preserved and extensive Roman earthworks at Horbling. Around the northern fen edge, however, settlement was poorer and more scarce. On the salt marshes and silt fen the survey verified the ubiquitous nature of Roman settlement and salt-working and demonstrated that this constituted a major expansion of human habitat from the area previously settled during the Iron Age. Chronologically, the survey also showed that there was a rapid flourishing of Roman sites in the south-western Lincolnshire fens, but that south of Morton much of this settlement went into decline during the third and fourth centuries.

In Norfolk clusters of settlements have been found by the Fenland Survey in Marshland which continue the distribution pattern set by these on the Cambridgeshire and Lincolnshire silt fen. Late Roman flooding has covered many of the marshland sites and so a true picture of their nature lies hidden, but there is no reason to suspect that they did not follow a similar pattern of small paddocks. Many of the marshland sites have been found as pottery scatters situated on roddons, which emphasises the similarity with sites further west. Further south the peat fen prevented much settlement, which instead is concentrated along the fen edge and on Hilgay and Southery islands, as well as occurring as a linear spread along the Fen Causeway.

In the southern fens the field system at Bullocks Haste, Cottenham, has often been used to illustrate Roman agricultural practice, and the coincidence of these fields with a settlement and the line of Car Dyke has contributed significantly to their importance as a group worthy of investigation. A series of rectangular ditched enclosures are arranged off a doglegged holloway or droveway (*11* and *71*). Within one of the enclosures narrow ridges 20 x 4m have been found and identified as lazybeds, a type of spade cultivation probably for horticulture or specialist crops. At Rectory Farm, Godmanchester, and in the Roman town, similar lazybeds have been found by Michael Green and less certain examples are also suggested from cropmarks near to Denny Abbey and from excavated evidence at Milton, as well as at Stonea Grange. It has also been suggested that some of these features could indicate Roman vineyards, as recently discovered at Caldecote in the claylands of South Cambridgeshire by Scott Kenney, and at Wollaston in Northamptonshire by Ian Meadows.

LATER ROMAN LANDSCAPE REORGANISATION AND NUCLEATED SETTLEMENT

Many Fenland settlements provide evidence for major flooding events during the third century, the cause of which was probably due more to socio-economic factors than to any climatic or environmental origin. Although this did not seem to affect settlement on the silt fen, within the peat fen and its margins, where efficient drainage was of the utmost importance, the consequences of this flooding appear to have been severe. Reoccupation of settlements, however, began during the third quarter of the third century, and this resurgence included a number of fresh foundations. These often took the form of nucleated villages rather than small clusters of farms, and the extent of some of these settlements is often impressively large. Settlements can be divided up into large conglomerations of 12-16ha such as Grandford at 12ha and Coldham at 16ha, and smaller order settlements of less than 4ha such as Norwood at *c.*3ha. In addition, other later Roman Fenland settlements appear to continue a more traditional theme, consisting of groups of small enclosures, paddocks and homesteads, connected by double-ditched droveways. Domestic and industrial debris is often encountered in close proximity.

Later Roman sites are also associated with an increased visibility of wealth evidenced by the use of imported stone from the east Midlands for house-building, a number of coin hoards of late third- and fourth-century date including eight particularly large ones, and finds of pewter and bronze vessels. Coldham for example, demonstrates this pattern through a rich assemblage of late Roman metalwork attributed to the area. Stonea Grange also recovered some of its former prosperity during the fourth century where evidence can be seen for the rubble infilling of the depression left after demolition of the 'tower' building c.75 years earlier, and construction of a stone-built house with the trappings of luxury such as hypocaust and window glass. In addition the coins from Stonea reflect this new-found vigour, with 40 per cent of the assemblage from the site being attributable to the fourth century, some of this being from the very last part of it. In addition to both of these indicators of wealth (pretentious stone buildings and coins) eight relatively rare brooches have been found of third- and fourth-century date, of which one was of silver and two were gilt bronze: these probably belonged to officials, or soldiers performing civil functions. Some military belt fittings of the period were also found at Stonea.

At the abandoned settlement of Langwood Farm, Chatteris, this resurgence in Fenland prosperity is also evident through construction of a three-roomed stone-built structure, or 'aisled barn' (13.5m wide by 25.7m long, the main room being over 20m long) with a tiled roof supported on pillars and side walls (97). This building sat within a ditched compound c.100m square and was associated with a group of ditched paddocks which lacked later reorganisation (and therefore suggest a very limited period of use). Although the pottery found around was predominantly coarseware, a significant collection of fineware was used by Chris Evans to suggest that the stone building was not abandoned until the mid-fourth century. In an area devoid of building stone the construction of this building elevates the importance of its occupants and its function. Its location straddles a probable route between Stonea and the fen-edge temple, industrial and settlement complex of Earith, Colne and Somersham to the south-west. Unlike Stonea, however, the surrounding settlement at Langwood Farm was abandoned by the middle of the fourth century and there was no indication found for an Anglo-Saxon presence.

On the western fen edge there is clear indication for several phases of landscape reorganisation and changes to agricultural regimes which can be traced throughout the Roman period, but there are specific changes which can perhaps be linked to the effects of the third-century deterioration of Fenland. At Glinton, for example, excavations by Steve Kemp in 1996 revealed a series of ditched enclosures which formed part of an agricultural unit for stock management, but which changed to crop processing, principally spelt wheat, in the later second century. This seems to have been part of a system of specialisation and sending surplus production to supply centres away from the site itself: places such as Durobrivae and Stonea would have been prime recipients as they were major consuming centres at this time. During the third century, however, Glinton shows that a weedy grassland landscape returned, with much oak and elder charcoal present in paleaoenvironmental samples, possibly a direct result of the effect of flooding and a breakdown of established patterns of supply and demand

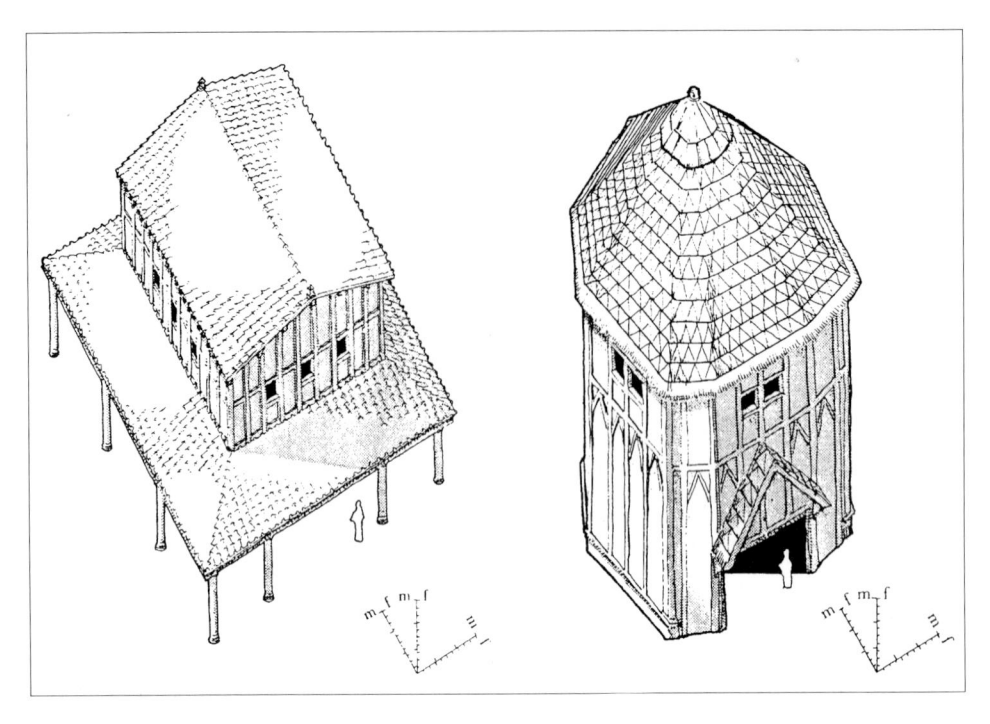

88 Reconstructions of the Godmanchester temples 2 and 3 (early fourth century) from the shrine of Abandinus. © *Michael Green*

coincident with political upheaval. A large midden deposit was developed on the site in this period, a stone-lined well was dug (perhaps associated with a timber structure around it) similar to other examples discovered at sites such as Maxey and Botolph Bridge in Peterborough, and an exceptional discovery was spruce pollen in considerable quantities. Spruce has been detected also from the sump at Stonea, and from a possible ornamental pond at the Rectory Farm villa, Godmanchester. Traditionally it has not been thought to have been introduced to England at such an early date, and its occurrence at Stonea and Godmanchester has been taken to suggest a high-status garden feature. The large quantities recovered at Glinton, however, do not fit well with this hypothesis as Glinton was not a high-status site, but the possible connection with Stonea, which has been suggested as a market for its cereal production, is possibly supported by the coincidence of this rare find of spruce. Glinton was abandoned during the mid-third century and shows little sign of having been reused when other sites were revitalised in the fourth century.

THE ECONOMIC BASE AND RURAL SETTLEMENT OF THE ROMAN FENS

VILLAS

It is often stated that the fens do not contain villa estates, and this has been used as one piece of evidence to suggest that much of Fenland was the *res privata* of the Emperor. Even so, villas are found along many of the fen margins and it is possible that their lands extended into it. Even if an imperial estate dominated the fens, during the later Roman period there may well have been a change in the way that the estate was run and it is possible that it was divided up between a number of private individuals and officials to farm in exchange for rents. The lasting legacy from this may be reflected in stone buildings to all intents and purposes resembling the remains of villas.

The evidence from the Nene northwards along the Lincolnshire fen edge, and from the villas clustered around the south-eastern edge of the fens, reveals considerable wealth and a flourishing of construction activity in later Roman times (*25, colour plates 15* and *26*). Many examples from the Durobrivae school of mosaics are found within the Lincolnshire villas of the landowning elite, and the concentration of rich late Roman hoards from the region provides a further indication of their affluence. The villa estates derived much of their income from animal husbandry, utilising rich and extensive pastureland along the river valleys and chalk downlands, with summer grazing on the fens. Arable farming would also have been important, and the transport system provided by the Fenland waterways, as well as the availability of a good road network, would have allowed the export of bulk commodities such as grain. South-eastern Britain and East Anglia in particular were known in the Roman period as being important sources for bread wheat.

In the south-eastern part of Fenland, villas are found at a number of places on the upland immediately overlooking the fen edge (places such as Methwold, Feltwell, Brandon, Mildenhall, Isleham, Soham, Fordham, Burwell and Reach), as well as several heading north from Cambridge at *c.*1-2km intervals along Akeman Street: Arbury, Kings Hedges and quite probably one at Milton, as well as Stretham on the south-eastern tip of the Isle of Ely. On the south-western fens the only known villas on the fenward side of Godmanchester are found along the Ouse at Rectory Farm and Somersham. Another is known from Huntingdon at Mill Common, next to Ermine Street, and recent excavation by Mark Hinman probably indicates a third on the top of the hill at Hinchingbrooke. Progressing north along the fen edge, a concentration of villas is encountered along the Nene and around Durobrivae, and in Lincolnshire several more are offset from King Street at places such as Helpston, Barnack, Barholm, Wilsthorpe, Bourne, Billingborough and perhaps Heckington. The apparent absence of villas between Cambridge and Godmanchester might be accounted for by the presence of several temple complexes, and the extensive land ownership they would have enjoyed. The absence of villas between the Ouse and the Nene is perhaps due the the nature of the local environment, which has heavy clay hills and and was therefore generally unattractive for farming.

HOSTELRIES

Mansiones, the rest houses for Roman officials, livery stables and hostelries for travellers, were distributed along major roads at intervals of approximately 15 miles. Within the Fenland area they have been identified at towns such as Cambridge, Godmanchester and Durobrivae, but they have also been tentatively identified elsewhere along Ermine Street at Sawtry, and at Littleport (or possibly Stretham) along Akeman Street as it passed through the Isle of Ely. Others must also have existed along the Fen Causeway as it crossed the fens, presumably at somewhere such as Grandford and possibly Denver.

The most intensively investigated one is the *mansio* at Godmanchester, which was a large courtyard building, reconstructed at least once in its lifetime. Associated with the residential function of the main block were a number of structures such as a bath-house, a tavern (represented by the recovery of *amphorae* and many drinking vessels), a temple, an aisled barn, two granaries, stables, and a small brewery attached to the bath-house with granaries and water-mill.

Other examples include a grand building adjacent to a possible temple complex which can be seen in the ground plan of Durobrivae as mapped from air photographs, and at Cambridge a stone structure which was found beside Akeman Street as it left the town by the north-east gate. At Littleport excavations at Camel Road in 1997-8 (at a site adjacent to Akeman Street and the Old Croft River) recovered box-flue tiles, fragments of painted wall plaster and lime-plastered daub and an assemblage of pottery, the majority of which dates from the Antonine period through to the mid-third century, although Hadrianic and early fourth-century sherds extend the lifespan of occupation to either side of its floruit. The bulk of the pottery was composed of high-status vessels such as East Gaulish Samian and *amphorae*, which pre-date the import of third-century Nene valley finewares, and consist of wine flagons, plates and beakers. Glass vessels were also present,; the significance of such a group of finds strongly supports the theory that the site is that of a *mansio* beside the Roman road.

On Ermine Street at Sawtry, approximately midway between Godmanchester and Durobrivae, excavations have revealed extensive Roman period and earlier occupation, and some reasonably high-status finds such as painted wall plaster, in addition to an unusually high percentage of horse bone. A possible signal station stood close by on Tort Hill, and an inscription defining the boundary of public land (the imperial estate) was found in close proximity to this. This is undoubtedly the location of an important *mansio* as a staging post between two towns.

CORN TAX

The collection of taxes constituted an important element of the later Roman empire. Demands had grown for defence in an economic environment that was no longer as buoyant as that in the earlier period when the empire had been expanding and developing new markets. One of the main forms of taxation was the *annona* or corn tax levied on landowners and tenant farmers alike. Towns seem to have formed a central role in the gathering of this tax, in its storage in purpose-built granaries, and in controlling the milling of grain for flour. Alison Taylor, for example, argues that the small area enclosed by the fourth-century walls at Cambridge took no regard for protection of the wealthier parts of the Roman occupation, but instead were driven through existing buildings without regard for the plan of the settlement that had developed over the centuries. She interprets this, together with similar small walled towns at places such as Great Chesterford, as evidence for defended tax collection points where the grain gathered for the *annona* was stored in large granaries, before being distributed to the Roman armies on the frontiers of the Rhine and Hadrian's Wall. Defence was needed not only against marauding Anglo-Saxon raiders, but also against the local population, whose poverty and resentment against heavy taxation for an army that did not seem to provide an effective protection was a threat to the imperial administration itself.

Although the towns might have acted as central points of storage and distribution for the grain tax, the initial collection would have been undertaken by more local agents – bailiffs – in the countryside. Stone-built houses at a number of Fenland sites, such as that recently investigated by Chris Evans at Langwood Farm, Chatteris (97), might indicate higher-status accommodation for *Conductores*, rent collectors and bailiffs for an imperial estate.

TEMPLES AND RELIGIOUS BELIEFS

Temples and shrines are known from many parts of the fens and fen edge (*colour plates 15 and 26*). The association with water and liminal places were important characteristics of Roman and prehistoric sacred sites. These shrines and temples would have formed focal points for the local community, and places of pilgrimage for people from further afield. They would have had a significant economic impact on the surrounding communities who serviced and supplied them, as the people who stayed at these temples would have needed housing, food and other services. Over time the temples acquired great wealth and possibly large landholdings which probably extended into the fens.

STONEA AND THE ROMAN FENS

Stonea has been shown to have had a relatively important temple during the second and early third centuries (*51*), and others are known from islands such as Manea and Chatteris, as well as the fen edge and surrounding towns. Hockwold on the Norfolk fen edge is a good example, as is the newly discovered temple at Gallows Hill overlooking Reach villa and the fens at Swaffham Prior. A concentration of such sites is found in the south-western fens, either side of the Great Ouse at Earith, Willingham, Cottenham and on a small island at Haddenham.

In plan the temples are generally square, with corners orientated to the cardinal points. A veranda or ambulatory surrounded an internal room or *cella*, and the whole was contained within a larger compound (*temenos*). In the towns, however, the plans varied, with a pentagonal temple at Cambridge and a polygonal temple in Godmanchester, possibly a tower (*88*), in addition to earlier temples of more conventional plan. The principal deity associated with these temples has occasionally been identified through the type of offering, figurines or other dedication found at them. At Stonea the dedication seems to have been to Minerva; at Godmanchester (on the Great Ouse) to the local Celtic river god, Abandinus, as recorded on a plaque; at Cambridge a subterranean chamber containing many broken items of tableware and animal sacrifices also produced an intaglio of Bacchus. Cult worship of the reigning emperor also occurred, with a bust of Commodus having been found at Cottenham for example, and possibly one of Antonius Pius at Willingham. Four temples were found here, and with one of them a very rare array of metalwork including the regalia to adorn priests and many bronze figurines (*89*), and another temple was present across the Great Ouse at Earith from which the statue of a *genius* was recovered in 1979 (*90*).

At Hockwold-cum-Wilton, on the Norfolk fen edge where the Little Ouse river emerges, a priest's spiked headpiece decorated with Celtic-type bearded figures, together with five other diadems, indicate the presence of an important temple. At Deeping St James in the south-western Lincolnshire fens three ritual crowns or priest's headpieces have also been found, as well as third-century coin hoards, indicating the presence of another important temple between Prior's Meadow and Frognall. The discovery of a bronze horse figurine near the spring at Bourne could suggest that another temple lies in this vicinity and it seems reasonable that a town like Sleaford would have required a temple too.

Although the Roman foundations for these temple sites often date to the second century, many of them seem to represent a continuation of earlier traditions. At Haddenham for example, the octagonal Roman shrine surrounded by a rectangular ditch was located on top of a Bronze Age barrow. Sacrifices of complete sheep were found here, as well as mandibles and hooves from many more sheep. It was remodelled in the third century as a square timber shrine more akin to other examples along the Ouse and to some Iron Age designs.

THE ECONOMIC BASE AND RURAL SETTLEMENT OF THE ROMAN FENS

89 Above: Seventeen bronze artefacts from Willingham temple including a bust of Antoninus Pius. © *Cambridge University Museum of Archaeology and Anthropology (accession numbers 1918.160.1-8, Z15185-9)*

90 Right: Statue of the genius from Earith. *Courtesy of Michael Green*

Michael Green has explored in some detail the iconography and symbolism of Fenland cults, using folklore memories and traditions in many cases to illuminate ancient practices, and seeing the impact of Romanisation on the previous religious beliefs of the native British populations. In essence he argues for a division between the more ancient Earth Gods which continued to be worshipped by the more conservative Fenland communities (belonging to the Iceni and Corieltauvi tribes during the Late Iron Age) and the Sky Gods of the Catuvellauni found within the Upland of Cambridgeshire and Huntingdonshire. The gods represented at the shrines along the Great Ouse for example, he sees as boundary gods protecting each tribal group from the other along their shared frontier. The gods were warring with one another, in the same way as the communities themselves engaged in inter-communal warfare, and many of the deities identified as Roman gods and goddesses were also Celtic, possessing specific attributes and dual personalities in the same way as Hindu gods have male and female, and light and dark sides to their characters or atavars. Such a belief system is very much in the tradition of Indo-European culture, but with increased Romanisation the need to have tribal gods to protect particular territories reduced and this could have helped the success of the socially organised, and later state-sponsored, introduction of Christianity.

At Gallows Hill, Swaffham Prior, investigations at a complex cropmark site located on a hilltop close to Devils Dyke (*colour plate 25*) were undertaken in the 1990s as part of a long-term programme of archaeological work on Cambridgeshire County Council's Farm Estate. During this investigation we found a substantial *temenos* 80 x 90m laid out with three internal enclosures (one double-ditched) containing at least two masonry structures, perhaps a *cella* for a shrine and a mausoleum (*91*), as one of these was found to contain a skeleton; a double-ditched trackway led directly downhill from the *temenos* to the large villa at Reach. The orientation of all the enclosures place the corners at the cardinal points. Within the inner part of the double-ditched enclosure air photographs have revealed faint traces of what might be a circular structure, possibly an earlier Iron Age temple, and the ceramic evidence from the site points strongly to its pre-Conquest origins and first to second century heyday (*92*). The site has commanding views over the fens to the north and over Newmarket Heath to the south and conversely it would have dominated the skyline from either direction. Its design and location is closely paralleled by Harlow and other temple sites. Little artefactual evidence for third- or fourth-century use has been found suggesting an attrition of the religious beliefs associated with this site, although during the early Anglo-Saxon period it was reused for pagan burial during the sixth century. The apparent abandonment of the temple during the later Roman period could be seen in association with the adjacent evidence for

THE ECONOMIC BASE AND RURAL SETTLEMENT OF THE ROMAN FENS

91 Excavation of the cella or mausoleum at the Roman temple, and an Anglo-Saxon burial (in background) at Swaffham Prior, 1993. © Archaeological Field Unit Cambridgeshire County Council

Christianisation at Burwell and Wilbraham, both with their respective villas, as a consequence of changing patterns of belief and identity amongst the Fenland and fen-edge communities.

The extent of temple ownership of land and rents is unclear but in recent years there has been growing discussion over the importance of such institutions. Places such as Earith and Willingham and Hockwold could indicate the importance of temples for economic stimulation as market centres. The Thetford treasure, for example, reveals the wealth that such temples could have accumulated, even at the end of the Roman period. The pattern of ownership within the fens, especially within Late Roman times, was therefore one that was more complex than can be summarised within a simple statement that part of the fens was imperial estate and the rest villa-owned land; significant areas could have been temple property, and the organisation of such estates might not have conformed with either the villa estate or imperial estate models.

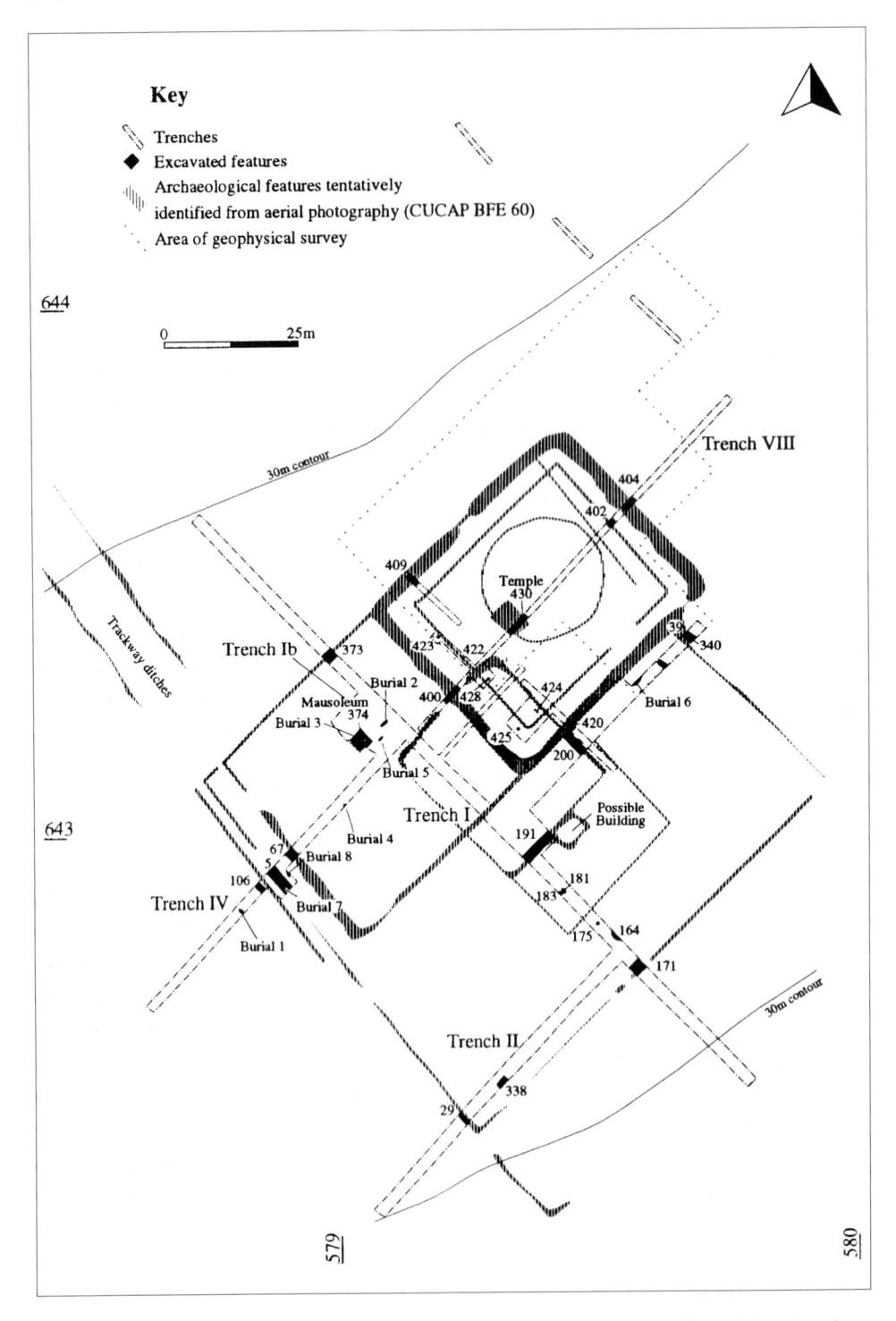

92 Plan of the Romano-Celtic temple and Anglo-Saxon cemetery at Swaffham Prior (see also colour plate 25). © *Archaeological Field Unit Cambridgeshire County Council*

DAIRY PRODUCTION AT GODMANCHESTER

During his extensive campaigns of excavation at Durovigutum, Michael Green discovered evidence for dairy processing in the form of various pottery vessels used in the preparation of hard and soft cheeses, milking coggs or buckets and a series of highly fired greyware bowls in three distinct sizes. Using classical texts and pictorial evidence, contemporary knowledge of dairying, and the wider implications of a landscape well known for its lush water meadows and grazing, as well as the evidence from faunal remains, he has been able to reconstruct some of the main elements in this major industry of the Roman Fenland.

One particular dump of pottery found to the south of the Roman town appears to have derived from a clearing out of a Flavian/Hadrianic period farmstead during the early second century AD. Shallow bowls, a milking cogg, storage jars and a cheese press were found as part of this assemblage. Roman pottery was rarely glazed and so, in order to enhance sterile conditions and reduce bacterial infection of dairy produce, non-porous pottery which had been fired at temperatures in excess of 1,000°C was employed in dairy processing.

Sheep were particularly productive and these were the preferred animals for the Fenland dairy industry as indicated by the archaeological evidence of large numbers of sheep bones on Roman sites in the region. Classical authors such as Columella and Varo speak of ewes' milk as being a staple of the common diet, the most nourishing of dairy foods and as satiating the needs of the peasants. Michael Green has researched information on modern dairy production and notes that 'Ewes produce 20 per cent milk solids, cows 11 per cent and goats 10 per cent'; sheep's milk also contains a higher percentage of protein than either cows' or goats' milk. Milk and cheese are the main products, as the naturally homogenised nature of ewes' milk prevents its use for the production of butter. Two distinct types of cheese were produced: soft or 'green' cheese (curd or cottage cheese), which would have been traded the next day, in the early morning market and consumed very quickly, and a hard cheese which could have been traded over long distances because of its qualities of preservation and salt content. This second commodity required a more complicated preparation process, and the conditions and duration of storage allowed cheeses to mature in highly individual ways, which accounts for some of the distinct flavours that different varieties of hard cheese have developed over time.

STONEA AND THE ROMAN FENS

In essence, the production of cheese is achieved by adding rennet to coagulate full-cream milk, but many local variations and unique starter cultures give cheeses their individual characteristics. These starter cultures are essential as, through the addition of carefully cultured strains of bacteria, the sugars in the milk are broken down to form lactic acid. Although cheese only needs milk, starter, coagulant and salt (and perhaps colour) as ingredients, its treatment can involve up to 15 stages. The cheese making process is well described by Columella for both soft and hard cheese. The first part of the process involved the straining of milk to remove unwanted items such as hair. Archaeological finds have been made of perforated ceramic bowls probably used for this purpose in conjunction with a fabric strainer. After the curd had been weighted and pressed to separate out the whey, soft cheeses were then moulded by hand. To make hard cheese the milk would be curdled with rennet derived from plants such as butterwort or from the stomach linings of calves, lambs or kids and then heated to help separate the whey during pressing. Fine-quality salt was added before a second pressing, probably using bowls with many holes bored in their lower sides, and a cheese press which consisted of a perforated and ridged ceramic disk on which the cheese was placed within the bowl, before a heavy stone was placed on top (93). Once pressing was complete the cheese could be drained, wrapped and exported over long distances. One particular type of vessel found at Godmanchester, dating from Flavian times until the fourth century, was a small bowl with flared rims and cordoned shoulders, which would have made a good storage jar for butter

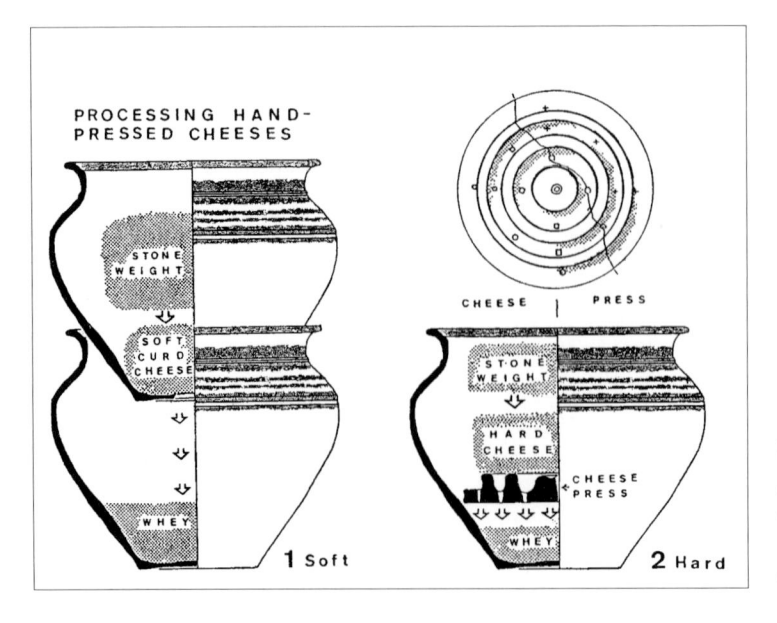

93 Cheesemaking: based on excavated ceramic vessels from Godmanchester. © Michael Green

and dairy products in general, as fabric covers could be easily fastened around the rim to protect the contents during storage or transportation. The ceramic vessels and cheese presses would have been easy to clean thoroughly and then reused for the next production. In contrast, *mortaria*, which were also used in the process as an ideal vessel for hand-pressing soft cheeses and pouring off the whey through the spout, would have retained bacteria around their gritted surfaces and this would have helped curd formation without the need for additional rennet.

9

THE DEVOLUTION OF THE ROMAN FENS

POLITICAL AND ADMINISTRATIVE CHANGES DURING THE THIRD TO FIFTH CENTURIES

The third century was a period of political turmoil for the Roman empire and for a period of some 50 years the situation was generally chaotic. The end of the second century had seen rapid changes in emperor, due to rival claims and civil war. In 193 Septimius Severus seized power and established the Severan dynasty which lasted until AD 235. Septimius was an energetic leader renowned for ruthlessness and his main challenge came from Clodius Albinus, declared emperor 196-7, whose main support and base was in Britain. In the later years of his reign, after he had defeated Albinus, Septimius Severus was in Britain, and he remianed there until his death in 211. Not only did he, as emperor, divide Britannia from a single province into two, but he is also credited with reorganising the imperial estates by introducing the *res privata* and a new department of state to administer it more effectively; these crown lands had become vastly increased by Septimius' policy of confiscating the property of those who had opposed him, and in Britain it is probable that many of Albinus' supporters suffered this fate. Peter Salway argues that it was at this time that the imperial estate in the fens was enlarged by the absorption of southern and eastern fen-edge villa estates. After the murder of the last of the Severan line, Severus Alexander, the empire was plunged once again into civil war for 50 years, during which period a breakaway state with separate 'emperors' was established in the north-west provinces from 259-273, the *Imperium Galliarum*.

The ascendancy of Diocletian in 284 led to fundamental reforms in many aspects of the empire, amongst which was the establishment of the Tetrarchy, a shared system of rule that was designed to help prevent rivals and coup d'états. Diocletian made Maximian emperor in the west – the two emperors now having the title Augustus – and created two secondary rulers to assist them, Constantius Chlorus and Galerius, as a western and an eastern Caesar. By these means Diocletion intended that responsibility and decision making could be more effectively undertaken, whilst progression to emperor would come about in turn for the Caesars. Unfortunately this did not prevent a usurper, Carausius, seizing power in Britain between 286-296.

Roman Britain after the defeat of Carausius in 296 was brought back into the fold of the western empire, and for some periods of time during the early fourth century was visited by the emperor or Caesar. In fact, Constantius Chlorus died at York in AD 306, and his son not only took over as Caesar in the west, but also then proclaimed himself Augustus, which led to a further 20 years of civil war until by 324 Constantine I (Britannicus) had mastery of the empire. He radically reorganised the army and built upon Diocletian's reforms in civil administration. These changes affected Britain in several ways, and these consequences gave context for developments within the fens and on the fen margins in the same way as they would have influenced other parts of Britain.

Britain became a single administrative unit called a diocese, and its previous division into two provinces (*Britannia Inferior* and *Britannia Superior*) was now changed to four provinces: *Britannia I* (western Britain), *Britannia II* (northern Britain), *Maxima Caesariensis* (southern Britain) and *Flavia Caesariensis* (eastern Britain). Beneath this level of government the *civitates*, largely the tribal divisions of pre-Roman Britain, administered territories from their *civitas* capitals, and below this a form of local government would have existed for towns and rural communities. Both the *civitates* and local government depended on obligation from the landowning class (*curiales*) to service them and allow the administration to function.

The diocese came under the governorship of a *Vicarius* based in London, and each province had its own civil administrator, a *praeses*. Beneath these top officials a bureaucracy of lesser officials saw to the civil and financial administration of the country and of the imperial estates. The command of the military was divided between the *comes* or *dux Britanniorum* who had responsibility for the frontier zone of Hadrian's Wall, and the *comes maritimi tractus* or *comes litoris Saxonici* (count of the Saxon Shore) who commanded the defences against sea-borne raiders from the North Sea. The army itself was a different organisation from the legions and auxiliaries that had provided the military might for conquest during the early empire. Pressure from barbarian tribes north of the *Limes* and the weakness of the empire through civil war during the third century had shown that once the frontier defences had been breached there was nothing to prevent invaders penetrating deeply into the empire, and thus a fresh strategy and new type of military machine was needed to act as an effective defence. In brief this can be divided into two parts, the *limitanei,* which were permanent troops stationed at the frontiers to defend Hadrian's Wall and the *Limes*, and the *comitatensis,* which were mobile field armies and higher-grade regiments that could be rapidly deployed wherever they were most needed. In addition, Roman towns were walled, and defended by bastions which gave enfilading fire for artillery. The size of military units was smaller than those of the legions, and it was no longer necessary for them to be drawn from Roman citizens. Barbarians were encouraged to serve the empire, either as *laeti,* groups who had surrendered and were allowed to settle if they supplied men to be trained as Roman soldiers, or *foederati* who were brought into the army through treaties with external tribes and fought under their own leaders in their own traditional ways.

The economy of late Roman Britain was essentially rural, and towns generally went into decline. Taxes were ever more necessary for the empire to defend itself and for the emperor to provide bread for Rome and placate potential discontent. It has been calculated that between a quarter and a third of all produce was given in taxation, the *annona* or bread tax being the most ubiquitous one. It was the landowning class who were the easiest to collect taxes from, and in turn this put pressure on the peasantry, the *coloni*. Despite episodes of civil war and raiding, the fourth century was in fact a period of renewed economic prosperity for the Romano-British, especially evident by the construction of rich villas in parts of southern Britain and an accumulation of wealth revealed by hoards of Late Roman treasure. The Fenland region was a prominent area of wealth, having more silver and pewter hoards than any other region in the country.

In spite of the comparative security of the four provinces during the fourth century, often referred to as the 'Golden Age' of Roman Britain, Britain was not isolated from the effects of barbarian attacks along the continental imperial frontier, episodes of political instability and military opportunism, as well as raiders on its own coasts. In AD 350 Magnentius, an army commander in Britain, declared himself western Augustus on the death of Constans. He was defeated by the eastern Augustus Constantius in 353, who became sole emperor as Constantius II until his death in 361, and severe reprisals were taken against Magnentius' supporters in Britain. In 367 a massive wave of attacks, called the '*barbarica conspiratio*', breached the continental frontier along the Limes and made large-scale incursions into Britain, killing the count of the Saxon Shore in the process. The whole of the diocese of Britannia was on the verge of collapse, and so the Augustus Valentinian I appointed Count Theodosius to restore order in Britain with four *comitatensian* regiments.

In AD 383 another commander in Britain, Magnus Maximus, rebelled and took troops over to the continent to defeat and kill the western Augustus

STONEA AND THE ROMAN FENS

Gratian, after which Magnus controlled the north-western provinces from Trier, until he was killed in 388 by Theodosius I. Effectively the bulk of the army had left the shores of Britain in support of Magnus, and the civil adminstration had to look largely to its own defence. By the early years of the fifth century before final withdrawal of the last parts of the army in AD 410, Britain was becoming more remote from imperial interests and priorities, although taxes were still being exacted. Peter Salway suggests that between AD 407 and 410 Britain threw out the imperial officials, reducing the administration of the four provinces to the level of *civitas* and below.

By providing this thumbnail sketch of 200 years of Roman history we now have a context for events which can be used to help interpret the archaeological evidence from the Fenland. What late Roman evidence has been gathered from the fens, what were the major challenges that had to be addressed in the third and fourth centuries, and what changes can we see between later Roman times and the earlier period?

STONEA AND THE WIDER FENLAND LANDSCAPE IN THE LATER ROMAN PERIOD; THIRD CENTURY FLOODING (*colour plate 25*)

As briefly outlined at the end of Chapter 6, Stonea continued to be occupied throughout the Roman period, in contrast to many other sites within the peat fen which saw extensive abandonment during the third century. This abandonment was due to two factors, one of a physical nature and the other political, and both were closely interrelated. Many sites such as Upwell, Welney, Hockwold, Earith, Fengate, Grandford and Flaggrass have shown flood episodes with thick deposition of silts covering earlier features. These deposits probably derive from more intensive clearance and ploughing of the surrounding upland, with silts washed down into the Fenland rivers, and a breakdown in the system of drainage which thereby prevented escape of these silt-laden waters into the Wash, leaving any site below *c*.3m above sea level vulnerable to inundation. The maintenance which ensured effective drainage of the low-lying areas bordering the peat fens had been in operation for some 50-75 years, and could well have required a complete overhaul and re-design. Peter Salway attributes this breakdown in maintenance and therefore vulnerability to widespread flooding as being a direct consequence of internal strife as emperors came and went during a series of rebellions and civil wars, leading to an inevitable lack of interest in the management of imperial estates. Without the centralised authority to direct operations in the fens the systems that had been built up during the second century decayed and sites such as Hockwold were abandoned. Three attempts

THE DEVOLUTION OF THE ROMAN FENS

to recover the situation have been identified by Professor Salway, which he has equated with the intercession of Septimius Severus at the beginning of the third century, with Diocletian from 284-287, and then from AD 296 once Britain had been regained by Constantius Chlorus. He also argues that the Fenland imperial estate was enlarged by appropriation of villa estates along the Suffolk and Cambridgeshire fen edge as a punishment to supporters of his rival, Clodius Albinus, and the presence of Septimius Severus in Britain at the beginning of the third century would have led naturally to his interest in overcoming the effects of flooding and reinvesting in the estate in order to make it more profitable for the imperial coffers.

The town at Stonea seems to have escaped the worst of this flooding, although silting deposits within the street-side drainage ditches and increasing size and complexity of drainage features throughout the third century show that there were some problems encountered here too. On the eastern edge of the island Tim Potter's excavations at the Golden Lion Inn (*19*) showed that this settlement lying at just 2.5m above sea level was abandoned in the third century due to flooding, whilst the town itself, located on a slightly higher part of the island, presumably remained comparatively drier. The general political climate which led to a disinvestment in the fens as an imperial estate, could be part of the reason for the abandonment and demolition of the administrative tower building *c.*AD 220, but Stonea's location on the junction of the peat and silt fens probably contributed to its continued viability as a settlement, in line with the rest of the silt fens which seem generally to have been less affected by the problem of third-century flooding. Some of the settlements on the silt fen even seem to have prospered during this period but, although a handful of saltern sites has been found which date from the fourth century, as a major Fenland industry salt-working slowly died out during this period so the relative prosperity of the silt fen must be attributed to some other activity (*colour plate 26*).

The evidence from Stonea shows that the population continued to occupy much of the town, although the grid plan of streets began to become encroached upon, and not all the residential blocks continued to be inhabited (*94*). There was a marked reduction in affluence as recorded by items such as imported *amphorae*, east Gaulish Samian or glass objects. Coins, on the other hand, were found dating from the third and fourth centuries including three hoards from the island of AD 250-275 date. A silver vessel was also recovered with one of these hoards.

The economy remained based upon lamb and salt meat, although during the third and fourth centuries cultivation of spelt wheat and barley seems to have taken on a more important role for local consumption, and ovens or kilns became a feature of many domestic enclosures, structures separated from the living quarters presumably to prevent fire hazard. Ten of these clay ovens were excavated

STONEA AND THE ROMAN FENS

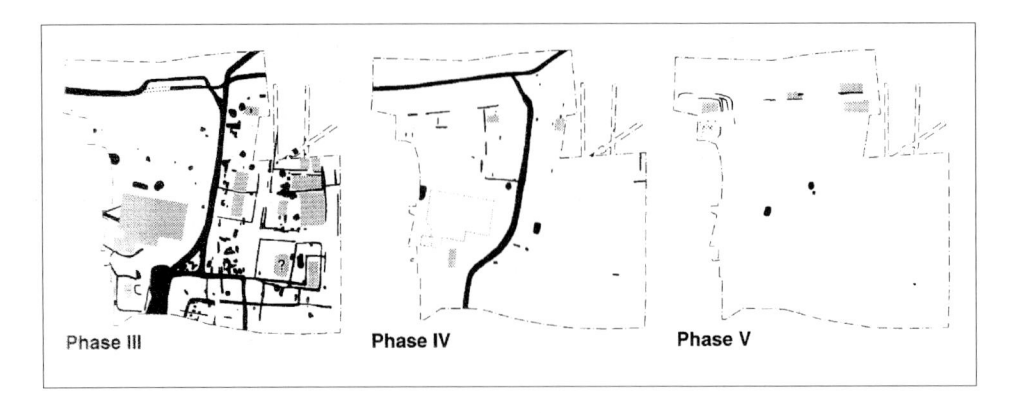

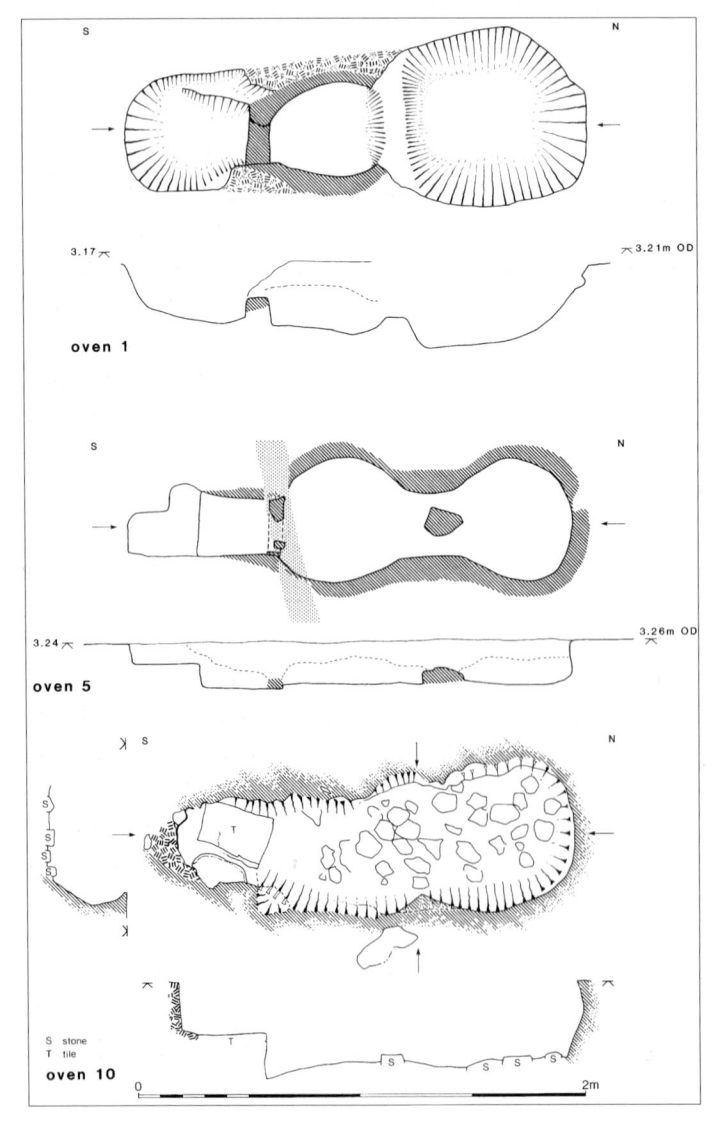

94 Above: Comparative plans of settlement at Stonea 'town' for the second century (Phase III), late Roman (Phase IV) and early Anglo-Saxon (Phase V) periods. © *The Trustees of the British Museum*

95 Left: Ovens from late Roman Stonea. © *The Trustees of the British Museum*

during the 1980s and consisted of two designs: a bottle shape and a figure-of-eight (*95*). They had been subject to a low operating temperature and were mostly orientated north–south; all were located in the northern part of the site. Although there was no palaeoenvironmental evidence to support an interpretation for their use, it is highly probable that they were domestic bread ovens, perhaps a necessity during the later Roman occupation because of the removal of a more centralised system of bread production and distribution which might have been a part of the administrative nature of the second-century town.

Seven of the 11 *insulae* or residential blocks show evidence for rebuilding and continued domestic use during the third and fourth centuries, and a group of latrines were established during the third century in an unused block; a number of pits at corners of properties might also have been used for this purpose, located so as to be as far away from the habitation area as possible whilst still remaining within each domestic precinct. Wells were also evident during this later period, at least one of which was wicker-lined. Towards the end of the Roman period these wells became increasingly used for rubbish disposal, which suggests that this part of the town was becoming peripheral to the main occupied areas further east or poses the question: from where were the inhabitants taking their fresh water?

Following demolition of the tower building a large hole would have been left on the site for much of the third century, but other parts of the precinct were used for new buildings. To the south a north–south-orientated, rectangular, clay and mortar-floored structure 11.5 x 9.5m was constructed out of timber, daub and stone. It also seems to have had window glass and a hypocaust, and was situated on the highest point of the site, suggesting that in spite of the demolition of the main second-century building, the block in which it was located continued to maintain its importance and was a residence for a person of significance. This structure may have overlain an earlier one, but there were at least two phases which can be dated to the late third and early fourth centuries. In the north-eastern corner of the precinct a rectangular timber post-built structure 5 x 3m was constructed with daub walls and a tiled roof. This was found in association with metalwork, an oven and a midden deposit and surounded by an enclosure 33 x 18m, suggesting that it was a separate entity from the southern building although both were located within the same main second-century precinct.

In the early fourth century a new major phase of building occurred in the main precinct. The hole left after demolition of the tower building was infilled and a stone-built structure with hypocaust and window glass was constructed over the top. Because of plough damage little detail of this building was found in excavation, and this ploughing could also account for the limited amount of evidence for fourth-century buildings in the area excavated generally. Such a phenomenon has been recognised at many Fenland sites, with large quantities of third- and fourth-century pottery found in plough soil after the first ploughing of earthwork sites, such as Grandford and Flaggrass during the 1950s and 1960s. Stone buildings of this date were found by Tim Potter during his excavations at Grandford prior to ploughing and they were just 35cm below the field surface.

The indication of high-status buildings of this period at Stonea fits well with the pattern over other parts of the fens where such structures have been identified. At Stonea a small but significant assemblage of high-status metalwork has also been found, together with large quantities of fourth-century coins (40 per cent of all coins found on the site date from this period), demonstrating that it was a place of importance once again, and occupied by officials, some perhaps military. Eight brooches of divided bow and crossbow type were found, including gilt and silver-plated examples, together with some military belt fittings, and this represents a significant group of a relatively rare type, a type generally worn by state officials (96).

Elsewhere in the peat fen settlements were not so fortunate, and the third century appears to have been a difficult time for the Romano-British population. Settlements as far afield as Catswater at Peterborough, Denver in Norfolk, Hockwold in Suffolk and Coldham in the central fens for example, were all abandoned during the third century. In contrast to this, Durobrivae and the Nene valley flourished and expanded rapidly. Evidence from a number of investigations in the surrounding landscape, at places such as Haddon, Maxey, Werrington and the Ortons (75, *colour plate 26*), have shown that reorganisation of the landscape occurred during the third century, with changes to the pattern of field ditches, and less emphasis on stock. Perhaps there was an enlargement of landholdings as witnessed, for example, by the relationship between the farm sites of Monument 97 and its successor (although spatially separated) at Orton Hall Farm. The excavations Don Mackreth has undertaken at Orton Hall Farm, Peterborough, have led him to suggest this was part of a state-controlled enterprise, if not part of the imperial estate itself. During the first half of the third century the farming complex was rearranged and he suggests this could in part have been to accommodate displaced people and animals from the Fenland.

During the third century the form in which the Fenland imperial estate was managed probably changed in line with other state land from that controlled by a central administration to one of short-term leases for a number of tenants. There was a distinction between the main estate, the *saltus*, and a series of farms on the skirtland, called *fundus*. A level of bureaucrats developed whose job it was to gather the rents, gaining income for themselves and passing on revenue to the emperor; these *conductores* may be responsible for the construction of a series of small villas along the south-eastern fen edge.

THE DEVOLUTION OF THE ROMAN FENS

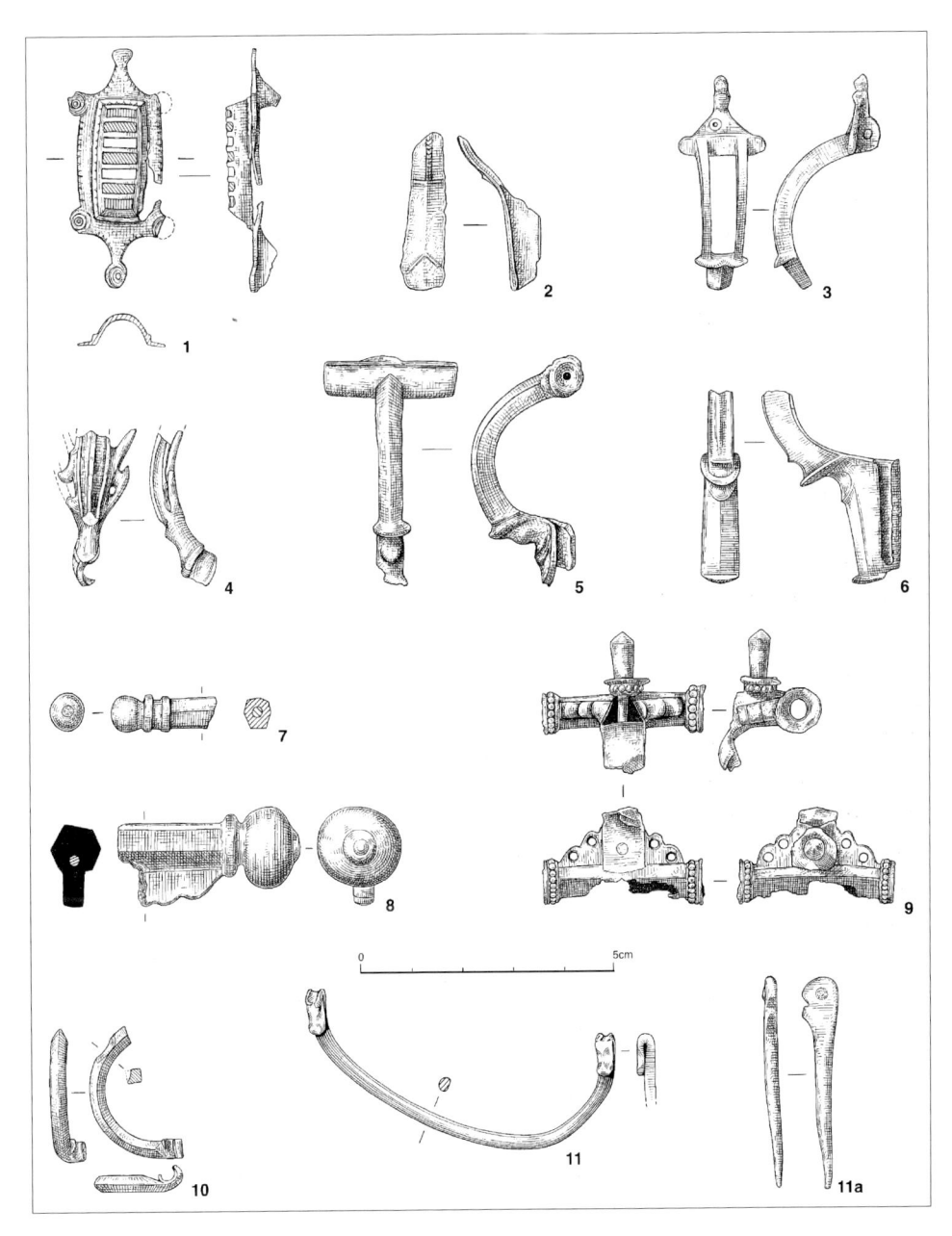

96 Brooches from Stonea (mostly late Roman). © The Trustees of the British Museum

STONEA AND THE ROMAN FENS

THE REINVESTMENT

Further changes to the management of all imperial estates appear to have been introduced in the early fourth century in response to the need to repopulate and reinvigorate their productivity after long periods of neglect and abandonment, and this scenario would seem to be relevant within the context of the Fenland. To attract new tenants a system of perpetual leases subject to fixed ground rents was developed to replace the previous administratively costly system of short-term leases. In addition, for a number of years new tenants were exempt from normal charges exacted on imperial tenants, and they were free from various taxes. Later in the fourth century the system changed further, to one of freehold subject to a perpetual rent charge; in effect the imperial estate became largely a series of franchises. In the fens it is possible that these changes are reflected in stone-built houses of this period which have been identified in the towns of Grandford and Stonea, presumed to be for state officials and tax collectors. But it is also possible that the lessees of the *res privata* or their bailiffs lived in the stone-built houses found in the fens and on its margins, such as that recently identified by the Fenland Survey and Management Project at Langwood Farm, Chatteris. The design of such aisled buildings contained domestic arrangements at one end, and a great barn in the remaining area (97).

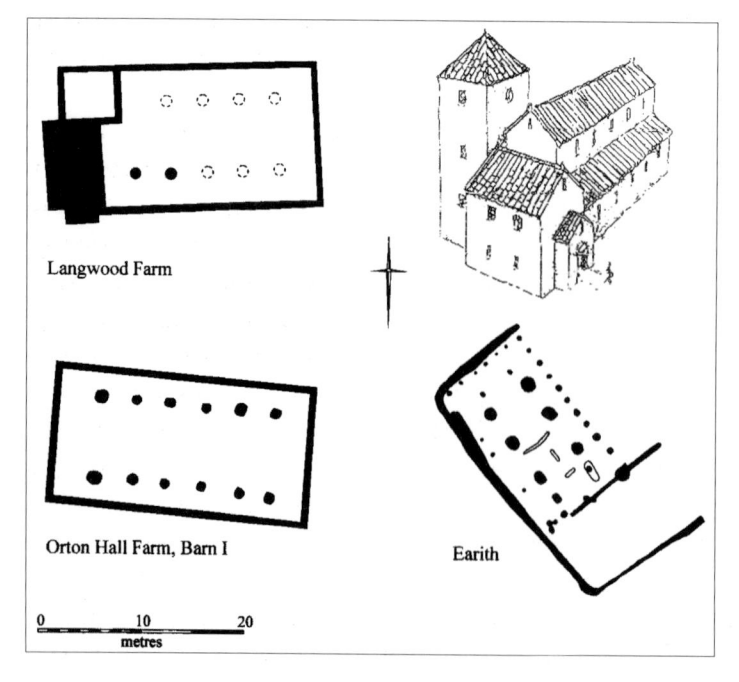

97 Reconstruction of the late Roman stone building from Langwood Farm, Chatteris. With kind permission Chris Evans © Cambridge Archaeological Unit

THE DEVOLUTION OF THE ROMAN FENS

Adjacent to many of the small villas found skirting the southern fens were *coloni*, or small settlements of peasants beholden to the villa. The villa and settlement at Hockwold provide a good example of this arrangement, and Professor Salway's excavations revealed a lack of coinage suggesting that a system of exchange based on obligation existed between the villa and its *coloni*; the people appear to have been effectively serfs. In the central and northern fens, however, larger villages existed, *vicani*, implying that the communities were registered by district rather than by landowner, indicating a freer arrangement of non-tied peasants. At the central Fenland sites of Grandford, Coldham, Norwood, and Flaggrass (*22, colour plate 26*), for example, there is excavated evidence for reoccupation during the fourth century, with final abandonment occurring in the last decades or possibly not until the fifth century. The stone buildings constructed and in use during this period display prosperity by the very fact that the building stone had to be imported from the East Midlands. This indicates not only that sufficient wealth was being generated in the rejuvenated Fenland to purchase and transport the stone, but also that there was the infrastructure to organise and distribute the stone on this industrial scale. Window glass and tiles, including flue tile indicating that a heating system had probably been installed, and fragments of daub decorated with lozenge-shapes and whitewash, all point to the high status of the stone buildings at Grandford, but during the second half of the fourth century the undefended 'town' appears slowly to have been abandoned. The large village at Coldham, however, has evidence which could suggest that it continued as a successful settlement well into the fifth century, similar to the pattern at Stonea, with late Roman pewter and bronze vessels being found, as well as early Anglo-Saxon urns.

At Langwood Farm and Honey Hill, on the eastern spur of Chatteris island, a large area of cropmarks interpreted as an Iron Age and Romano-British settlement and field system was investigated as part of the Fenland Management Project in 1993. This consisted of a system of ditched paddocks laid off from a droveway running along the Langwood ridge (*c*.4m above sea level) connecting the two settlements. The most impressive discovery was that of a stone building measuring almost 26m in length and 13m across, set within a ditched enclosure 100m across, both of which were aligned at 45 degrees from the droveway suggesting that this construction was a later imposition on the pre-existing field system. At its north-western end a small room with a rammed masonry floor and a tower suggest domestic accommodation, and the remaining area to the south-east was divided into a central part with two side aisles by means of large timber posts to support the roof (*97*). The pottery evidence from the excavation would suggest that this building was abandoned around the middle of the fourth century, whereas the bulk of the pottery from fieldwalking the surrounding field system and settlement was dated from the second to mid-third century AD. This site would seem to illustrate the initial Fenland colonisation followed by an episode of abandonment during the third-century crisis (the lower parts of the site fall to 2.1m AOD and would have been liable to flooding), before reinvestment occurred at the turn of the third and fourth centuries, clearly demonstrated by the impressive building which would have stood on the highest point.

On the western and northern fen margins, however, villas seem to have continued to develop and be occupied right through the fourth century (*colour plate 26*), with evidence from Great Casterton of construction for a grain-drying oven in the early fifth century. The style of mosaic at Great Casterton has been recognised in several other villas, showing that the workshop that produced it had a flourishing trade in the fourth century. Denton villa's mosaic, for example, can be dated to *c*.AD 370. Tile kilns at Heckington and Heighington show production in the late third and fourth centuries, presumably for the local market and villas at places such as Heckington, Osbournby and Ashby de la Launde. The important villa at Haceby slightly further inland has, however, been given an end date in the 360s, similar to that at Barnack given as AD 370. Mill Hill, Durobrivae and Helpston villas also continued into the fourth centuries. On the Ouse the large complex at Rectory Farm, Godmanchester, included two large-aisled barns, four other large buildings with wide stone wall foundations and 32 ovens, all attributed to the third and fourth centuries, and a formal garden which included a pond containing evidence for luxury imports such as fig and grapes, as well as rare evidence for the early introduction of spruce.

CIVIL AND MILITARY ADMINISTRATIVE REFORMS: CIVITAS, SAXON SHORE, DUROBRIVAE AND CASTOR

The town of Durobrivae at Water Newton and the palatial complex just to the north of it across the Nene at Castor are essential elements of the late Roman Fenland and the revival of its economic importance. The growth of Durobrivae during the second and third centuries to become one of the largest towns of Roman Britain can be attributed to its strategic location as a focal point for the communication network and its ability to exploit a wide range of natural resources to fuel its booming manufacturing industry (*75*). Its wealth came from the Nene valley potteries (which reached their zenith during the third and fourth centuries), iron-working and stone quarrying, and it was home to specialist industries such as a mosaics workshop. Dense extramural settlement can be seen to have existed, with wealthy potters' houses spreading along Ermine Street and beside the Nene; these do not display a decline until *c*.AD 350.

Although originally a *vicus*, by the fourth century Durobrivae's status might well have been raised to that equivalent of a *civitas*, a level of civil importance which would have been in accord with its size, type of internal buildings, and impressive defences. The *civitates* were territorial units of local government based on tribal groupings, but even in the early period of Roman rule there had been some conflation to create more administratively sensible territories, and by the late Roman period some further such reorganisation was clearly advisable. Durobrivae not only enjoyed a considerable advantage due to its strategic location and commercial success, but it was also situated on the frontier between the Catuvellauni and Corieltauvi (Coritani) with their capitals at Verulamium (St Albans) and Ratae Coritanorum (Leicester) respectively (*colour plate 7*). To the east, Venta Icenorum (Caistor by Norwich/Caistor St Edmund) was the capital of the Iceni *civitas*, and Durobrivae filled a geographical space between these different *civitas* capitals. An informal inscription on a roofing tile found at Tripontium which refers to *civitas Corielsolilorum* can, with good reason therefore, be attributed as referring to Durobrivae. In support of its elevated status is a milestone found one mile outside the town which shows that distances were being measured from it, and two further milestones made in the same manner out of Barnack Freestone have been found at Girton, next to Cambridge, which John Whitwell takes as possible evidence for Duroliponte to have been included within the administrative area attached to Durobrivae. The fact that a large part of the area of this new *civitas,* which would have included parts of both Catuvellauni and Corieltauvi territory, would have extended into the fens and therefore an area that would have included the imperial estate, might also have been a significant factor in any civil reorganisation. Don Mackreth has identified a large building within Durobrivae as a possible administrative centre which he tentatively associates with the running of the imperial estate, and the historic relationship between the economic development of the Nene valley and the fens might have been considered as an important element in any attempt to revive the financial productivity of the *res privata*.

In line with other late contenders identified as *civitates,* such as Carlisle and Ilchester, Durobrivae's layout displays little regard for a rigid street plan and its walls seem to have consisted of a single phase of defence which enclosed 17.6ha (*74*). Bastions were positioned at regular intervals along the walls and the gateways for Ermine Street were staggered to strengthen defence of these main points of entry. The date of construction for this wall remains uncertain, but it is most likely to have been in the late third or early fourth century.

One kilometre to the north lies the small village of Castor (*colour plate 2*), so named because of the impressive Roman ruins that were visible here. During the late third century a massive design was executed which included creation of two terraces into the hillside facing Durobrivae, and erection of a single building on three levels, a single complex of palatial proportions 270 x 140m in area. Some of this complex was excavated by E.T. Artis in the early nineteenth century (*98* and *99*), and further investigations were undertaken by J.P. Wild and others in the twentieth century. The foundations were built with stone laid in herringbone fashion, and of a size capable of supporting the vast rooms towering above (*100*). Hypocausts show that heating was provided in main rooms, and that a bath-house was attached. Extensive use of mosaic pavements and painted wall plaster was employed to decorate the building. The scale of this enterprise can be none other than state sponsored, and Don Mackreth convincingly suggests that the most likely officer for whom this complex would have acted as official residence and headquarters was the count of the Saxon Shore. Located on a hub of land communications, Castor is also on the navigable Nene which would have given rapid and easy access to the fens and, via the Fenland waterways, to the Wash and the North Sea (*colour plates 26* and *28*). A great military leader situated at Castor would also have been able to control and call upon the resources of imperially owned land to help provision troops and naval forces. The site at Orton Hall Farm, together with its mill and evidence for brewing, would have been of primary importance in this, but so too would the Fenland

98 A view of excavations at Castor by E.T. Artis (from *Durobrivae* 1828) showing the foundations of a bathhouse with St Kyneburgha's in the background. *Courtesy Peterborough Museum and Art Gallery*

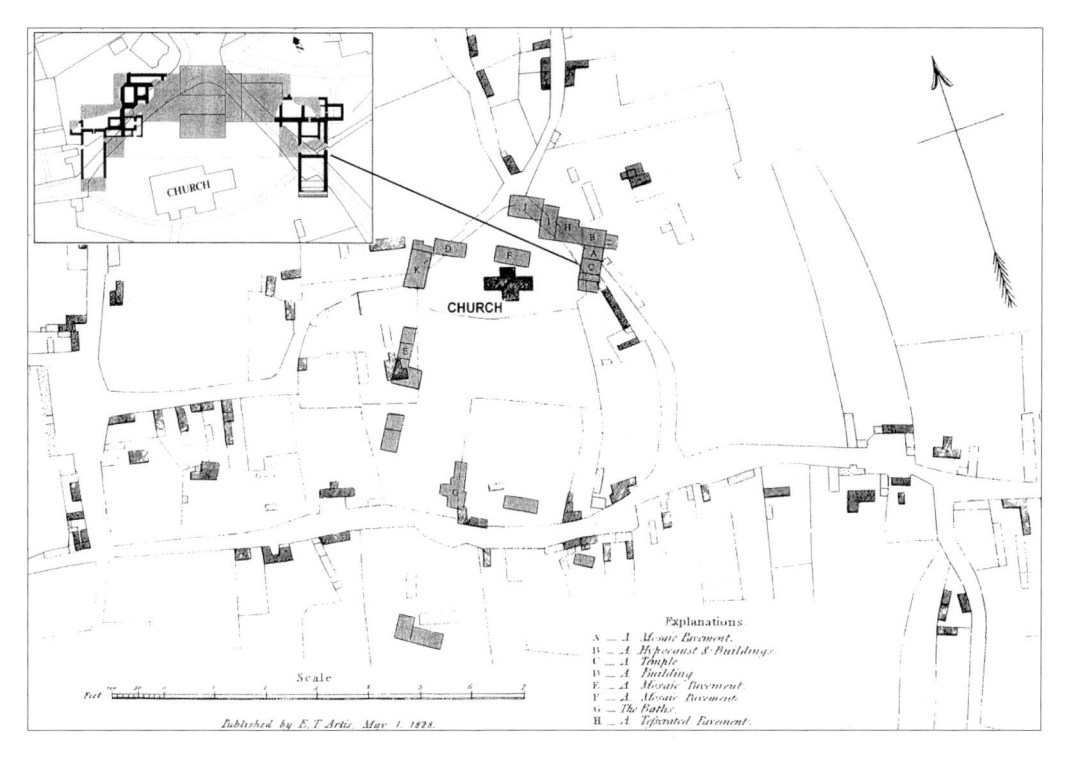

99 Plan of Castor in the 1820s with the areas excavated by E.T. Artis (from Durobrivae 1828) and Don Mackreth's plan of the palace superimposed. Courtesy Nene Valley Research Committee

estate. Don Mackreth has equated the fortunes of Orton Hall Farm with the fortunes of the army and has argued for the billeting of troops on local householders during the third century, in line with the Roman custom of *hospitalis*, the granting of one-third of house or land by a house-holder to their 'guests'. He places the end of Roman occupation at Orton Hall around AD 375, probably contemporary with Magnus Maximus' rebellion. Thereafter he suggests that the farm was given over to accommodate Anglo-Saxon *foederati* and their families, an interpretation that helps explain the archaeological evidence for continuance of occupation with Anglo-Saxon cultural attributes into the fifth century. It is also understandable in the context that Orton Hall Farm, having been part of the *res privata* or state-controlled land, would have been seen as public land which could be used for buying the services of Anglo-Saxon mercenaries to defend the area after departure of the military for the continent in support of Magnus Maximus; there may have been few officials at the end of the third century who would have objected on behalf of the emperor to this arrangement. The territory of the farm at this period may still have been extensive, with some of the Anglo-Saxon pottery having been manufactured from clay provenanced from up to 60km

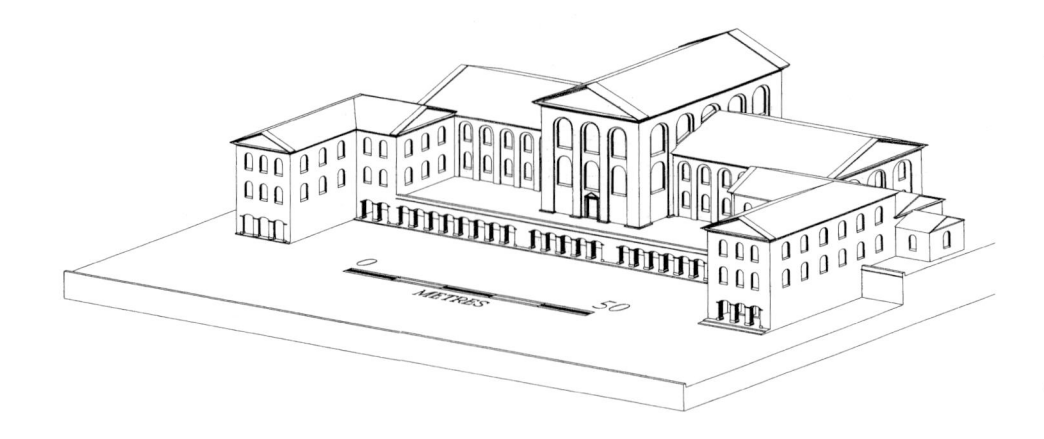

100 Reconstruction drawing of the Roman palace at Castor. With kind permission Don Mackreth and Nene Valley Research Committee

away, but its general deterioration is probably due to lack of maintenance once the farm had been handed over to the federate troops.

The later Roman system of defence relied on the creation of coastal forts and strongpoints to look out for sea-borne raiders and give early warning of attack, and also small strongpoints and stations at key inland locations to control the communication network and act as military depots for supplies. Defence in depth was provided by walled towns with detachments of troops, backed up by mobile field armies which could move rapidly to wherever they were required. This system of defence stretched from the south coast and around the eastern seaboard, including such prominent forts as Portchester, Dover and Richborough, and four Saxon Shore forts along the East Anglian coast at Bradwell, and Walton Castle in Essex, Burgh Castle, Suffolk, and Brancaster on the north Norfolk coast (*colour plate 29*). In Lincolnshire the defences were set back further inland with Burgh-le-Marsh as the most easterly at the northern end of the fens, and Horncastle *c.*20km to the west. It has also been suggested that there may originally have been one or two coastal signal stations in Lincolnshire similar to those known from the Yorkshire evidence, but that these have since been washed away by the sea. The main part of the fens, however, would have been very vulnerable from attack via the Wash and the great rivers that had their outfall there, such as the Nene and Great and Little Ouse for access to Cambridgeshire, Norfolk and Suffolk, or via the Welland and Witham further north in the Lincolnshire silt fen. A powerful force based around Durobrivae and able to deploy quickly eastwards from their central point of command would, therefore, make strategic sense.

THE EVIDENCE FOR EARLY CHRISTIANITY IN FENLAND
(colour plate 26)

In 313 Christianity was legitimised within the empire at the edict of Milan, and the organisation that was established for it tended to mirror the organisation of the empire itself based upon dioceses and parochiae. Indeed, there is debate over the extent to which church leadership took over from Roman civil administration in Britain once the imperial system began to collapse at the beginning of the fourth century. There are a number of examples of early Anglo-Saxon churches having been sited in the remains of Roman centres, sometimes reusing buildings such as *basilicas* as at Wroxeter, which were probably related to the continuance of the traditional significance of these locations.

At Icklingham, Burwell and Great Wilbraham for instance, important Roman Christian artefacts have been recovered – lead baptismal vats – presumably associated with the villas located there (*101*). Two more examples came from Willingham (the location of important Romano-Celtic temples) and from the Great Ouse near Huntingdon, near the great villa at Rectory Farm outside Durovigutum. A further lead baptismal vat was found along the Nene upriver from Durobrivae at Ashton, Northamptonshire (*102*). Pewter vessels with chi-rhos of the fourth century come from various locations in the fens. A square pewter plate with a chi-rho from Earith Road, Willingham (*104*), was found by a metal-detectorist, buried with two plain pewter plates. Another pewter plate with a cross

101 Lead vat from Burwell. *Author's collection*

STONEA AND THE ROMAN FENS

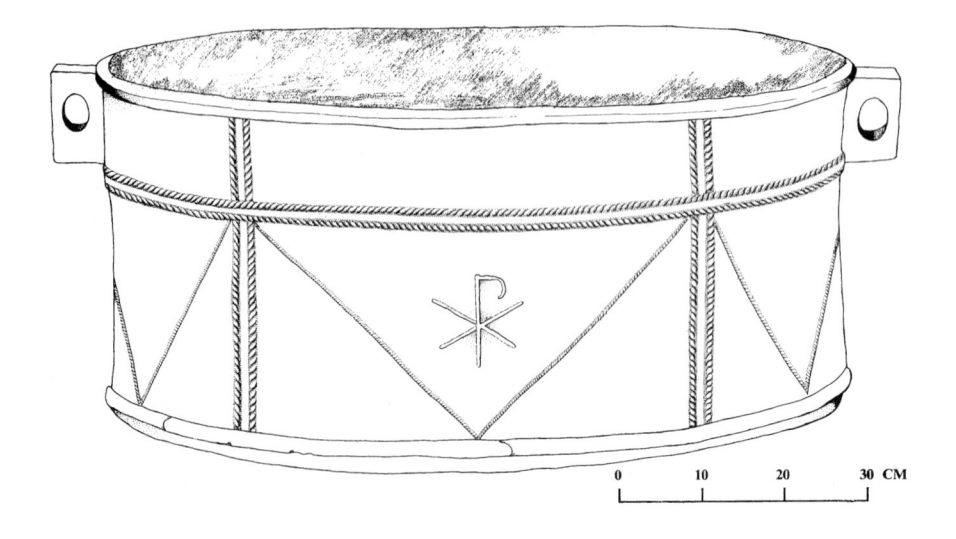

102 Lead vat with Chi-rho from Ashton, Northamptonshire. *Nene Valley Research Committee*

103 Lead tazza with chi-rho from Sutton, Isle of Ely. *Courtesy of Alison Taylor*

THE DEVOLUTION OF THE ROMAN FENS

inscribed on the base was found at Bottisham, a pewter bowl with a chi-rho was found near Ely and another at Welney with a chi-rho and an alpha and omega. At Sutton in the Isle of Ely, a lead tazza (*103*) found with six large platters and a bowl was decorated with a chi-rho between an alpha and omega, an owl, peacocks and Nereids. On the underside an inscription could indicate that these items belonged to a bishop (SUP...T...EPICL Q '*Supectili epi(scopi) clerique*'). A silver ring was found at Woodhurst (an area with seemingly sparse Roman activity) on which was inscribed URS ACIVIVAS ('D. Ursacius may you live') and a chi-rho. Pewter vessels were also found in locations as diverse as Whittlesey Mere, at Coldham, and on the silt fen north of March; a silver jug has been reported as coming from Stonea, and a pewter jug from Quanea, near Ely, as well as third-century pewter vessels from the River Lark in Suffolk, and from Landwade just across the border in Cambridgeshire, and a hoard of metal vessels from Burwell; at least some of

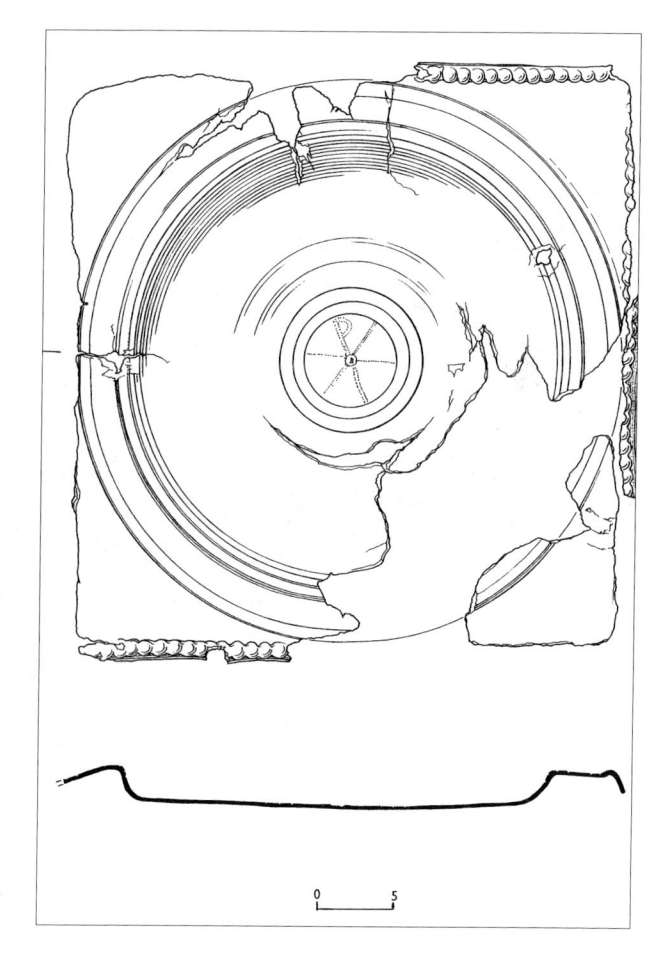

104 Lead platter with chi-rho from Earith Road, Willingham. *Drawn by Joanna Richards*

STONEA AND THE ROMAN FENS

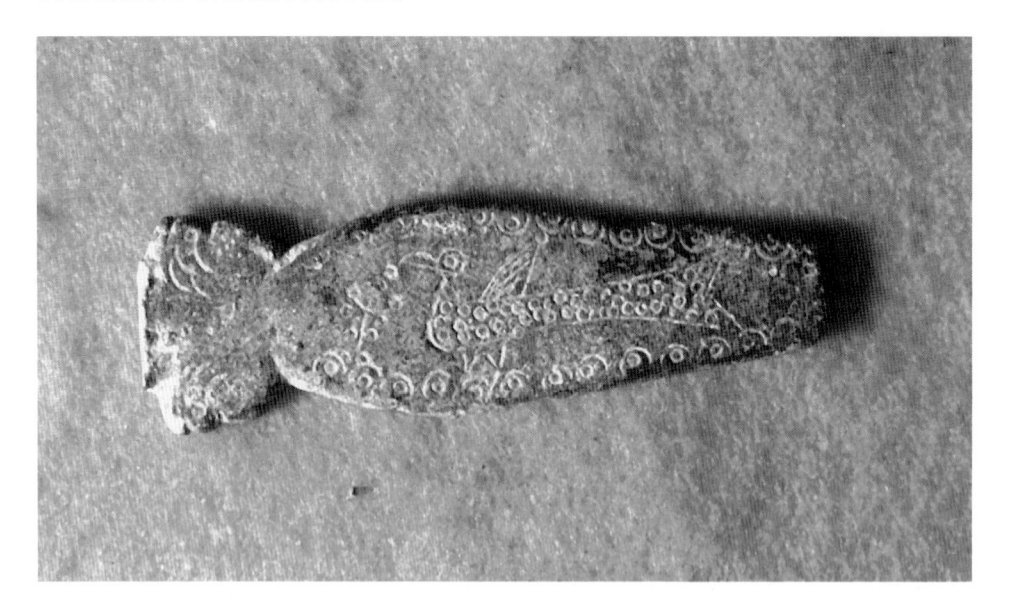

105 Bronze artefact from Grandford with Christian symbol of peacock. Courtesy of Alison Taylor

these seem to be closely associated with Christian sites and symbols. Lode, Great Wilbraham, Grandford and Orton Longueville have all produced artefacts in lead and bronze with peacocks and other Christian symbols (*105*). In addition, well-known hoards of Christian silver come from Water Newton (the earliest known set of church plate) and Mildenhall (*106* and *colour plate 27*).

Although we cannot reconstruct the diocesan structure of Roman Christianity in the fens we can suggest where centres of Christian faith may have been located, based upon the finds of valuable artefacts and Christian symbols. To the north lies Lincoln which, with London and York, has claim for the earliest bishoprics, and a bishop from here may have attended the Council of Arles in AD 314. Excavations in the 1980s at St Paul in the Bail near the cathedral discovered the foundations of an early apse-ended timber church in the Roman *forum* (and at least two later Anglo-Saxon ones), confirming Lincoln's significance for early Christianity in Britain. The Water Newton treasure (*colour plate 27*) was found very close indeed to Durobrivae, and the importance of this town in Late Roman times would surely have attracted a church and associated ecclesiastical organisation. Adjacent to Durobrivae is Castor with its palace, a centre of great civil and military power. Castor became an early Anglo-Saxon monastery, and this choice of location could have been brought about by its historic connotations as a late Roman centre of Christianity.

On the River Great Ouse the town of Godmanchester, a place of local importance on major communication routes, would also have been a likely

THE DEVOLUTION OF THE ROMAN FENS

candidate as a centre for Christian worship, and the lead vat found in the river helps support this suggestion. The lead vat at Willingham and pewter plates there strongly suggest that the tradition of religious significance for this area continued through from Romano-Celtic origins into Christian worship. East of Cambridge the lead vats at Burwell and Great Wilbraham suggest another such centre on the southern fen edge and possibly a further one to the east at Mildenhall.

FENLAND AT THE END OF ROMAN RULE

The Roman settlement and organisation of the fens during the fourth century was considerably different from that of its foundation in the second century. It is probable that private enterprise had largely replaced imperial initiative in developing a viable economic environment in which the local communities could prosper. The vast lands of the *res privata* had been franchised and wealthy landowners held villas on the fen margins, and quite probably Fenland as well. Some of these were clearly of considerable importance and people who could amassed hoards of pewter, silver and gold which have been recovered from their hiding places some 1,600 years later. They could have been aristocrats who held land in many parts of the empire, but brought part of their accumulated wealth to Britain, presumably because of its comparative stability. It also appears that many of them had become Christian.

Further division of crown lands might have occurred as a result of the military needs of the province, with grants of land to *foederati*, Anglo-Saxon warriors and their families who were helping in the defence of the province. Temples and the church might also have acquired land through endowments from wealthy patrons, and the status of the *vicani* in the silt Fenland is unclear: were these in fact freemen, making a living from smallholdings as peasant farmers? The result of all this was fragmentation in what had been a massive corporate enterprise, and towards the end of imperial rule in Britain, the civil administration likewise changed and became more locally focused.

By the beginning of the fifth century the effectiveness of central civil and military authority had largely dissipated, and Professor Salway suggests that the Romano-British actually expelled the last of the imperial officials during the period 407-410. Peter Salway makes the point that on the continent large areas of *res privata* were taken over by invading barbarian leaders to form the basis of royal estates in their own right, but that this did not happen in Fenland because the officials had left and therefore the imperial estate had ceased to function. The evidence from Stonea would contradict this, as there is now a clear indication for continuity, and a number of other sites also display this direct connection

STONEA AND THE ROMAN FENS

106 The Mildenhall hoard of Christian treasure. © The Trustees of the British Museum

between fourth-century Roman occupation and fifth- to sixth-century Anglo-Saxon presence, as well as considerably more circumstantial evidence to suggest a greater degree of overlap between the two periods than previously demonstrated. The Anglo-Saxon halls at Stonea, in the same quarter of the town that had traditionally been associated with power and prestige (*94*, *107* and *108*), surely indicates the transferral of status from Rome (and the Romano-British) to control and ownership by the Anglo-Saxon newcomers – the English.

10

FENLAND AND THE BIRTH OF ENGLAND

The end of Roman Britain and the change to Anglo-Saxon England is a period that has attracted much debate and speculation. What happened to the cities, economy and institutions of Roman Britain, and to the Romano-British people, in the years following AD 410 when the Roman military was formally withdrawn? There are two principal schools of thought: one that argues for a major break, linked with famine and possibly plague destroying large numbers of the Romano-British population, leading to wholesale takeover of the land by the new Anglo-Saxon migrants; and an alternative argument that presumes comparatively small numbers of Anglo-Saxons came over to Britain, but that they subdued the local population and ruled them in the place of Roman administrators, villa owners and local leaders.

The truth probably lies somewhere in between these two viewpoints, with a gradual deterioration in the economy and prosperity of Roman Britain and related decay in administrative organisation over the duration of the fifth century, whilst Anglo-Saxon migration and colonisation grew in intensity as the century developed. Warfare between the newcomers and the resident population was part and parcel of the period, as was the seizure of power by local British leaders, tyrants, who fought amongst themselves as well as against the Anglo-Saxons. Vortigern is the name or title of one of these British rulers, and he is attributed with inviting Saxon federates (*foederati*) to settle in Britain in the AD 430s in return for providing military defence to the British population. These Saxon federates later rebelled against British rule, and the Gallic Chronicle gives *c.*442 as the date when authority in Britain passed to the Anglo-Saxons. Bede suggests a slightly later date, of 449 for the *Adventus Saxonum*. Archaeology is now providing evidence to show that there was perhaps more continuity and symbiotic development between the two peoples than could have been demonstrated a generation ago, perhaps through an exchange of ideas and by implication a gradual acculturation of the British by the Anglo-Saxons rather than widespread replacement of the population. In addition to the historical sources, place names are important in tracing the areas of colonisation, whilst archaeological evidence for the physical presence of the Anglo-Saxons comes mostly from settlement and cemetery remains. The excavations undertaken by The British Museum at Stonea Grange have provided important evidence in the question of continuity between the two periods.

TRIBAL GROUPINGS AND ANGLO-SAXON SETTLEMENT WITHIN THE FENLAND REGION (*colour plates 26 and 28*)

Four earth-fast timber buildings dated to the period AD 400-650 were found at Stonea Grange. Three of these were located on the slightly raised area of the main east–west Roman road, and the fourth slightly to the south. The post-holes did not provide unambiguous patterns for the buildings but they can be reconstructed as rectangular, double-squared, modular buildings typical of Anglo-Saxon halls, orientated east–west and with dimensions in the range of 3-4.5m wide and 7-10.5m long (*107*). Compounds appear to have surrounded each building, and a possible *Grubenhaus* (sunken hut) was found placed over the mound where the tower building had once stood.

One of the halls has a particularly complex pattern of post-holes and series of fencelines, demonstrating that it was renewed at least once, and had some possible additional features such as an arc of post-holes (an apse?) at the west end, and an annex to the south (*108*). Although Anglo-Saxon pottery on site was scarce, the majority of it was found around this building and, together with the evidence for renewal, it suggests that this probably belonged to an important family. The basic plan appears to show a building 7 x 4m within a sub-rectangular compound *c.*25 x 20m delineated by shallow gullies. An eastern entranceway, perhaps once cobbled, was detected and much of the southern area of the compound was covered by an occupation deposit 0.2m thick. In addition to the pottery, an antler comb, bone pins and some Roman coins and bronze work were found. Animal bones and bone artefacts such as pin beaters suggest that sheep continued to play a dominant part in the economy of the settlement, as they had done during the Roman period, and there is such similarity between the size and morphology of the bones from both periods that it seems likely that the same flock continued into the Anglo-Saxon period. The use of pig for meat increased during this period to rival that from sheep; seeds from spelt wheat and barley attest to some arable cultivation.

FENLAND AND THE BIRTH OF ENGLAND

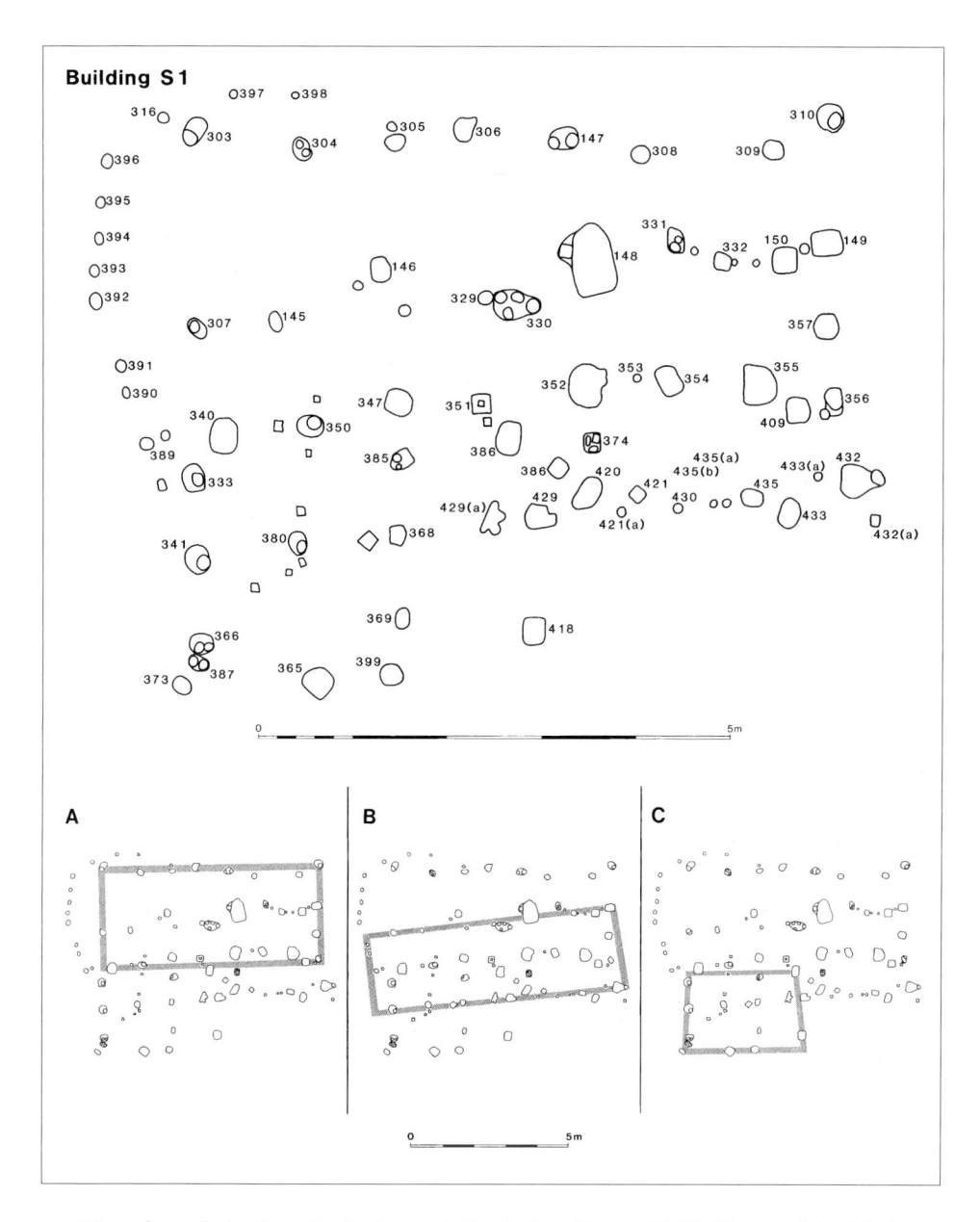

107 Plan of post-holes from Anglo-Saxon timber halls at Stonea. © *The Trustees of the British Museum*

108 Excavation of an Anglo-Saxon hall at Stonea Grange. © Ralph Jackson

During the Roman period there had been a regional fall in sea level and the environment became increasingly drier into the fifth and sixth centuries, obviating the necessity seen during previous centuries for continued maintenance and renewal of drainage features at Stonea. Some of these earlier ditches and gullies were, however, reused during the Anglo-Saxon period, as were one or two pits and a well, and four pits were newly dug. The articulated skeletons of a pig and a dog were found in two of these features, clearly not resulting from domestic rubbish, presumably evidence for customs which were alien to earlier phases on the site.

All of the evidence above suggests that a different population occupied these buildings from the Romano-British community – people who followed a different building tradition, had different cultural artefacts and different customs. The location of the buildings is, however, interesting in that they occupy the higher elevation of the road, if not already defunct by this time then immediately made so by the deliberate positioning of the buildings and compounds over it (*94*). As the environment was dry during this period this location would not have been determined to escape lower and wetter land. Instead it suggests two possibilities, that the location was chosen because of its historic importance within the earlier town (i.e. the new Anglo-Saxon elite deliberately connecting their control with the previous centre of Roman power), and also that perhaps ownership and property rights elsewhere were being respected (a case that is also made in support of continuity at Orton Hall Farm near Peterborough). The late Roman settlement seems to have moved eastwards, apart from a single high-status building located over the original tower building, and therefore by positioning their new buildings over the *agger* of the road at the west end of the former town, and adjacent to the previous seat of power, the Anglo-Saxon community were stating their own importance, without taking over the parts of the settlement that might still have contained a Romano-British community. Although no precise dating for the buildings can be ascertained, it is clear by the recutting of some late Roman features that their construction was not so much later that these earlier features had lost their significance, and therefore a strong suggestion for continuity can be put forward at Stonea between one period and the next, between late Roman and Anglo-Saxon occupation. Martin Welch has given a sound argument to suggest that these newcomers were part of an Anglo-Saxon group called the *Gyrwe* (the 'fen dwellers') in the *Tribal Hidage*, and referred to by Bede's *Historia Ecclesiastica* as the *South Gyrwa* (*colour plate 28*).

Early Anglo-Saxon domestic evidence such as that discovered at Stonea is rare, but a number of sites around the margins of the fens have produced early finds that help to construct a picture and distribution of Anglo-Saxon settlement

109 Roman artefacts and Anglo-Saxon comb (probably fifth century) from Orton Hall Farm. *Courtesy Peterborough Museum and Art Gallery*

during the fifth and sixth centuries AD (*colour plate 25*). The best evidence for continuity of occupation at a single site is that provided by Don Mackreth's excavation at Orton Hall Farm, Peterborough, where he argues that a working Roman farm passed directly into the hands of an Anglo-Saxon group. Early Anglo-Saxon pottery was found here, including a bi-conical urn and a hand-made *mortarium* which is a very rare copy in form and function of a typical Roman artefact. A Barred Zoomorphic decorated comb was found in the same deposit (*109*), dateable to the fifth century, and argued by Don Mackreth as belonging to the first quarter of the century. Three halls and a *Grubenhaus* (sunken hut) were built during the fifth century, respecting the earlier Roman layout of the farm, but by the sixth century the site was abandoned. A number of early Anglo-Saxon finds have been made in this general area, such as a brooch found at North Bretton also dated to the first half of the fifth century, whilst *c.*7km to the south-west an Anglo-Saxon timber post structure and early pottery was found within the bath-house of the villa at Haddon. In addition, the excavation of a Middle Anglo-Saxon settlement at Maxey in the 1960s, close to the line of King Street and in quite close proximity to a number of early Anglo-Saxon burial locations, suggests that earlier occupation during the period would also have occurred here. This hypothesis was subsequently substantiated through evidence gathered by the Nene Valley Research Committee in fieldwalking next to King Street, and from excavations by Judith Roberts at Lyndon Farm in 1997 which produced fifth- to sixth-century Anglo-Saxon pottery, loom-weights, a bone needle and red deer antler, from pits within a Roman settlement complex of second- to fourth-century date.

At Castor a rich and abundant assemblage of artefacts, coins, pottery and stone-carving bear testament to the significance of its importance during the Middle and Late Saxon (Christian) period, with *Grubenhauser* and other features demonstrating reuse of domestic occupation within the great Roman palatial complex, and it is quite possible that this more visible later Saxon presence hides the evidence for less obvious sub-Roman or pagan Saxon occupation during the sixth and seventh centuries. It would seem very likely that a place of such importance as Castor would have continued its connotations with power and control beyond the Late Roman period. Its adoption by a wealthy part of the Middle Saxon community, and therefore in all probability its position as the centre of a Mercian royal estate, is evident from the foundation of a monastery at Castor, large quantities of Ipswich ware and metalwork, an ornate Late Saxon seax (a single-bladed short sword) scabbard chape and a Late Saxon and Norse hoard of 500 coins. The concentration of such wealth from the eighth to eleventh centuries could indicate that there was, in fact, continuity at Castor from the end of Roman rule (when the existence of a palace provides clear evidence for its importance) through the Early Anglo-Saxon

FENLAND AND THE BIRTH OF ENGLAND

period, but a continued importance that only became visible in the archaeological record during Middle and Late Saxon times.

In the south-western Lincolnshire fens Early Anglo-Saxon settlement was found often in association with Middle Saxon material, and these sites were plotted by Peter Hayes and Tom Lane during the Fenland Survey in the 1980s. Their work has shown that two groups emerged, one that settled on the dipslope inland from the fen edge and a second group, which settled on the silt fen (*colour plate 28*). The first group consisted of a dispersed pattern of settlement on the upland, away from the clusters of Roman sites along the fen edge, suggesting a change in economy to one based largely on subsistence farming. Early sites have been found in Thurlby next to where King Street crossed the River Glen (at Kate's Bridge), as well as at Bourne, Morton and Billingborough. A focal point and potential market centre is represented by a concentration of sites around Hoe Hills at Pointon and Dowsby (*colour plate 25*). Continuity from Roman occupation appears highly likely in at least four cases, one on the north side of the fens at Stickford located in a strategic position to command access to and from the fens for what was to become the kingdom of Lindsey, and others at Billingborough and Hacconby, and around the Roman town at Bourne. These are also on major routeways and reflect the pattern seen in Cambridgeshire for early colonisation of strategic locations. The pattern shown by the second group on the silt fen was also dispersed and located along the landward (peat fen) side, although situated back from the Roman fen edge to avoid the seaward expansion of the peat fen at this time. Some of these settlements, in Gosberton and Pinchbeck for example, were found by excavations undertaken as part of the Fenland Management Project to have reoccupied Roman sites, although whether this could represent a continuity in population is impossible to say on present evidence. There must have been some trade and contact between these two Anglo-Saxon communities in spite of the fresh water fen between them, and the Fenland waterways would have provided easy access for both local and sea-going Anglo-Saxon boats; in addition the Roman lines of communication would have remained open. This dichotomy in occupation between two distinct geographical zones has prompted Hayes and Lane to extrapolate back from Middle Saxon documentary sources (the *Tribal Hidage*) and equate the siltland settlement with a tribal group known as the Spalda, and the western fen edge settlements with the Bilmiga. Evidence of an Anglo-Saxon presence around modern Spalding has been demonstrated also, and control of the crossing point of the Glen and Welland there, and of access along the river to the North Sea, would have given the area an important strategic role within the northern fens.

In Norfolk the attribution of the Wisbech area and the River Wissey as the area settled by a people called the Wixna (or Wissa) recorded in the *Tribal Hidage* seems likely and, although very few early Anglo-Saxon sites have been identified, a band of Middle Saxon settlement was discovered by the Fenland Survey looping around the northern part of Marshland. The flooding that effected the earlier Roman settlement in this zone might have prevented its exploitation by Anglo-Saxon pioneers, or the evidence may be hidden beneath silts, but drier conditions during the Middle Saxon period might have led to seasonal grazing followed by permanent settlement on higher ground such as roddons. With marine flooding becoming a serious problem in later Saxon times a sea bank around the edge of the Wash was built in this area, such as can still be seen at Leverington. These sea defences were originally attributed to the Romans by antiquarians, because of the size of such an enterprise, but Middle Saxon sites have been found in relation to the sea bank that show they pre-date it, and Late Saxon sites on the landward side of it have revealed no evidence for flooding within pits and ditches, thus showing that by this time the settlements were well-protected. Crop evidence from excavated sites in Norfolk and Lincolnshire show that barley and oats, horsebean and peas, together with some flax and linseed, were the dominant cultivated plants. The weed species found with these demonstrated that they had been grown locally on the silt fen as part of the economy of permanent settlement rather than imported by seasonal pastoralists. Once sea banks had been created, removing the frequent inundation of saltwater, the silts would have been able to support crops within a period of three years.

Along the fen margins of Norfolk, Suffolk and Cambridgeshire Anglo-Saxon settlements grew up, exploiting both upland and fen. These strongly suggest a continuity in concept if not in population between the previous Romano-British communities living along the fen edge and utilising both the upland and Fenland resources. Much of this area had been controlled by villa estates, and it is possible that the Anglo-Saxon pattern derives from this, either as direct takeover of existing landownership, or through a gradual melding between the Roman organisation of the landscape with their new settlements, and inter-marriage between the new migrants with the native population. At the Little Oulsham villa, Feltwell, for example, a fifth-century Anglo-Saxon sword has been found, whilst Early Saxon pottery found at another Feltwell site and one in Southery, as well as on the site of a large Roman complex along the Nar valley at Pentney, tentatively demonstrate such continuity. Sites such as Eriswell (Lakenheath), West Stow near Icklingham, Snailwell, Waterbeach and Willingham have produced evidence for *Grubenhauser* and earth-fast timber halls, as well as pottery and other artefacts of Early Anglo-Saxon date (*colour plate 26*). In addition, a Roman site on the Isle of Ely was found by the Fenland Survey also to have Early Anglo-Saxon pottery, and another settlement is known to have stood on the hill at Bedwell Hey Farm, Little Thetford.

FENLAND AND THE BIRTH OF ENGLAND

The Roman town of Godmanchester also has evidence for Early Anglo-Saxon occupation with pottery and a possible *Grubenhaus* found in the town centre, overlying the southern defences of the town. This evidence was preserved through its slumping into the backfill of the town ditch. Dispersed settlement is also found along the gravel terrace around the town to the north-east including a timber-lined well at the site of the Rectory Farm villa, and settlement consisting of *Grubenhauser* and timber post-built halls have been found to the east, at Cardinal Way. A possible *Grubenhaus* has been identified further east along the Ouse along with Early Anglo-Saxon artefacts at St Ives. All of this evidence is strongly suggestive of some continuity or at least co-habitation with existing British communities.

EARLY ANGLO-SAXON CEMETERIES AND THEIR STRATEGIC LOCATIONS

Apart from the evidence provided by settlement there is another even more important source of information about the early Anglo-Saxons: their burials and cemeteries. Two principal burial customs were followed by the immigrants: cremation and inhumation, and in both of these gravegoods were placed with the burials. The quality of information given to us about the Anglo-Saxons from this data is remarkably good, especially from the less acidic soils of Cambridgeshire and Lincolnshire, where the fine preservation of bone allows detailed study of the skeletons to be undertaken. From this we can reconstruct much about the lives of individuals and characterise the population in general, as well as many aspects of their social organisation and beliefs. The artefacts buried as gravegoods tell us about technology, trade, craftsmanship and aesthetics, ethnic origins and social status, and provide a reasonable chronological framework in which to place the burials. Although recent advances have helped to refine dating techniques for the period, most artefacts can at best give a date range that is no finer than 50 years, so it is difficult to tie down those that were early fifth century and therefore within the period of transition with the demise of Roman Britain. There are a few items (such as a particular type of military belt fitting first introduced with Count Theodosius's campaigns in AD 367) which are attributed to Anglo-Saxons employed as soldiers (*foederati*) by the Roman administrators and are therefore seen as being of late fourth- and mid-fifth-century date. In addition, there are some artefacts commonly found amongst late Roman burials which appear to have become adopted by the early Anglo-Saxon migrants, such as specific types of beads and bangles, and the rite of cremation seems to occur most frequently (although not exclusively) within the early period of migration,

110 Excavation of sixth-century Anglo-Saxon burials at the Three Kings, Haddenham, 1990. *Author's collection*

during the fifth and sixth centuries. From this corpus of material it has been possible to suggest cemeteries and groups of burials which are of fifth-century date (at least in origin), as opposed to others which date predominantly from the sixth or seventh centuries, and thus a pattern of colonisation can be sketched out within the Fenland region.

Many of the early cemeteries, with origins attributed to the fifth century, can be found around Roman towns, such as several significant burial grounds in Cambridge (St John's College cricket ground and Girton amongst others). They are also found in close association with villas (such as Little Wilbraham [*111*], and at the Romano-Celtic temple of Gallows Hill, Swaffham Prior [*92*], in close proximity to Reach villa). These clusters may in fact disguise something else, that the cemeteries are actually located near to major rivers and routes through the area, and this pattern may reflect the positioning of *foederati* or Anglo-Saxon

FENLAND AND THE BIRTH OF ENGLAND

settlers to control these routes (*colour plate 25*). An example of this is the cemetery discovered during construction of an airfield at Bedwell Hey (Ely Fields) Farm on the Isle of Ely during the Second World War. This 'hilltop' location controlled access to the Isle along Akeman Street from the south and possibly also eastwards from the Barway–Little Thetford causeway which gave access to the Isle from the mainland at Wicken. A similar location at the Three Kings, Haddenham, revealed burials excavated by Ben Robinson in 1990 (*110*), and this Anglo-Saxon presence probably fulfilled the same purpose by defending the Isle from access along Aldreth Causeway. Cemeteries around Soham reflect the importance of another route from the upland by causeway at Stuntney and Quanea to Ely. The cemetery at Little Wilbraham sits astride the Roman route known as Street Way, which runs parallel to the Icknield Way, and other early Anglo-Saxon finds further south-west suggest a similar arrangement on Street Way at Shardelowes Well, Fulbourn, where the Fleam Dyke terminated. At Cambridge a number of roads ran through the town, and these would have been important to control, which helps to account for such a concentration of Anglo-Saxon cemeteries around the town.

Along the Nene valley a small group of burials, perhaps part of a larger cemetery, were found within the defences of Longthorpe Fort. These were mainly cremations, dated by a fourth-century coin and decorated Anglo-Saxon pottery to the fifth century. Although the first-century fort had been long abandoned, its defences might still have been evident and occupation of the fort would have given control to the Nene crossing point at Botolph Bridge. A fifth- to sixth-century barrow containing a bossed urn, cremations and two horse burials was also recovered on the west side of Peterborough at Orton Waterville during the 1970s; the presence of a barrow and horse burials indicates a wealthy and important primary burial. The circumstances of the discovery, however, as part of pipe-laying operations, precluded a more widespread excavation. Further west along the Nene Anglo-Saxon burials have been found at Nassington and Water Newton, well located to control Ermine Street at its crossing point of the Nene, and Ben Whitwell believes these cemeteries probably represent an Anglo-Saxon community that was directly connected with Durobrivae. East towards the fens, other early cemeteries are known from nineteenth- and early twentieth-century finds such as those from Fletton and Woodston in Peterborough, at Helpston, or beside King Street. A sixth-century group of 32 inhumations, one cremation and a Roman sarcophagus was found in 1987 at Gunthorpe on the fen edge, with another group found during construction of the Market Deeping bypass in the late 1990s in Maxey. Further burials were found on King Street in 1998 when three sixth-century graves were found to have been cut through the road surface at Ailsworth, close to the discovery of a sixth- or seventh-century hanging bowl and rich belt fitting (*112*) made during construction of the Castor bypass in 1990. This strongly suggests the existence of a significantly wealthy 'princely burial'.

In Lincolnshire Anglo-Saxon cemeteries have been found almost exclusively just inland from the fen, on the upland of the fen margin (*colour plate 26*). Two small groups of fifth- and sixth-century burials have been found at strategically important locations along King Street, firstly at Tallington in 1965 and 1997 (which would have been close to the road's crossing point of the Welland) and at Baston where King Street runs beside Car Dyke and joins with the Baston Outgang. Further inland at Great Casterton, Stamford, Anglo-Saxon and Roman burials have been found set into the counter-scarp bank of the town defences, and further west along the Rivers Glen and Welland there are early cemeteries at Empingham and North Luffenham. Conforming with the pattern of Anglo-Saxon burials around strategic Roman towns, a fifth- to seventh-century cemetery of Angles and Frisians was found at Lovedon Hill, Hough-on-the-Hill, with homemade pots copied from Roman wheel-made originals and a possible start date for the burials of *c.*AD 425. This cemetery was distinct and separate from the nearby late Roman Christian burial site on the west side of Ancaster. Burial urns, bossed and cordoned pottery and an iron spearhead from Anglo-Saxon graves have also been found inland from the fen margins at Threekingham. Other Anglo-Saxon burials have been found at Heckington, the Roman town of

111 The landscape around the Anglo-Saxon cemetery and Roman villa at the Wilbrahams (looking south), Cambridgeshire, 2001. *Author's collection*

Sleaford (including the find of a military belt fitting), Ruskington, and a sword burial at Horncastle, and a large, early-period cemetery just north of the fens is that at Hall Hill, West Keal, near Stickford. Further east, two burial mounds at Cock Hill, near the Roman settlement at Burgh-le-Marsh, and Partney contained a sixth-century belt buckle, and on the fen itself at Friskney nineteenth-century finds of a spear and comb suggest that there were further burials in this coastal location.

On the eastern side of the fens early cemeteries are known in Suffolk from Holywell Row and Eriswell, Lakenheath, and Mildenhall, as well as burials on Hilgay island in Norfolk (*colour plate 26*), near to the possible line of Akeman Street, and up the Nar valley at Tottenhill and Wormegay. On Fenland islands in Cambridgeshire isolated burials or small groups have been found of fifth- and sixth-century date, such as those at Chatteris, Manea, Whittlesey, and a significant group on the Isle of Ely at Haddenham, Sutton, Little Downham and Ely itself. This scatter of chance discovery probably represents only a small part of the cemetery evidence which indicates a much more intense occupation of the fens by the Anglo-Saxons than is immediately apparent from the scant settlement evidence and isolated burials.

PLACE NAMES, BRITISH AND SAXON POPULATIONS, AND EARLY CHRISTIANITY

During the sixth century the picture of widespread Anglo-Saxon Fenland colonisation can be corroborated by the pattern of settlement from East Anglia in general, but the possible continuation of a native Romano-British element within the Fenland community might be assumed from place-name evidence and some documentary sources. Around Wisbech, for example, there are a group of place names with the Old English *walh* in them (e.g. Walton, Walpole, and Walsoken), which could derive from the same word as Welsh, the Anglo-Saxon for foreigner, Briton or Welshman. Place names with Old English *Cumbre* in them are also seen as meaning Briton or Welsh, such as Comberton just to the west of Cambridge. In Felix's biography of the life of St Guthlac it is recounted that, whilst he lived as a hermit on the Fenland island of Crowland, St Guthlac was surrounded by British hosts and demons speaking with sibilant speech; it is possible that this could have some historical significance and is a reference to welsh speakers – in other words, a native British population around him. Most place names in the southern fens are of Anglo-Saxon origin, with names now ending in *-ea* or *-ey* (originally *-eg*) meaning an island, Stonea for example means stony island, and eu or eau means a river. Those parishes with the suffix

-*ham* are often associated with early Anglo-Saxon settlement (at least from the seventh century if not earlier), and there are a number of these within the fens and fen edge, in fact 25 per cent of parishes in south-east Cambridgeshire and the southern fens end in -*ham*. Others with the -*ton* ending (old English -*tun*) are also found, possibly suggesting expansion and consolidation of settlement a little later in the period, in the eighth century, and the majority of these are found in the upland west and south-west of the Fenland basin, seemingly coincident with Mercian supremacy in the region. Chesterton immediately east of Cambridge was, for example, a Mercian royal estate. These endings were prefixed by either personal names, such as Wilburga for Wilbraham, or by topographical features such as Ford-*ham* or Stret-*ham*. The earliest Anglo-Saxon place names are, however, topographical, and these could well be translations from the original Celtic and relate to parts of the large estates that passed from Romano-British ownership into that of the Anglo-Saxons, such as the villa estates on the southern and eastern fen edge at Feltwell, Hockwold, Snailwell, and Burwell, or Landbeach and Waterbeach. Within the central fens places such as Thorney, Wisbech, March, Upwell and Welney, for instance, owe their names to such topographic characteristics.

The evidence for Anglo-Saxon settlement provided by fifth- to sixth-century settlements and cemeteries reveals a distribution confined within Norfolk and Suffolk, the fens and south-east Cambridgeshire. In contrast it would appear that, outside of this core area of migration, much of west Cambridgeshire and Huntingdonshire together with Hertfordshire and west Essex remained

112 Gilt buckle and Hanging Bowl from Castor *c.*seventh century. *With kind permission of Ian Meadows and Peterborough Museum*

as predominantly British-controlled areas until at least the late sixth and early seventh centuries.

Castor had been an extremely important late Roman centre with its palatial buildings and commanding position. It is no surprise therefore to see it emerge within Anglo-Saxon times as an important place with a double monastery founded in the seventh century and attributed to two daughters of King Penda of Mercia, Kyneburgha and Kyneswytha. Archaeological evidence has revealed *Grubenhauser* and Anglo-Saxon artefacts within Roman buildings just north of St Kyneburgha's church, predominantly of Middle Saxon date although with some pottery and artefacts tentatively assigned to the earlier, pagan, period. North of the village close to King Street an exceptional find from the sixth to seventh centuries was the recovery in 1990 of an ornate belt buckle and parts of a hanging bowl from a pit that also contained an iron spearhead (*112*). This suggests the possibility of a very wealthy pagan Anglo-Saxon grave, perhaps a 'princely burial' which may have been beneath a barrow, although the nature of its discovery has only given an incomplete assemblage on which to base this suggestion. Significantly important graves of this type are often found associated with boundaries, and perhaps acted as markers to proclaim the territorial rights of a ruling family to other groups. It would seem more than mere coincidence that this location was chosen for such a display of prestige and it is therefore

113 Altar buried in pit at Wilbraham Villa, 1990. © *Archaeological Field Unit Cambridgeshire County Council*

probable that it was part of a direct attempt to identify a legitimacy to territorial ownership through 'hereditary' relationship to the Late Roman palace and centre of power at Castor itself. If this was the case, Castor could well have been an early royal estate, and the establishment of a monastery at Castor would be in keeping with Middle Saxon practice.

Other early Anglo-Saxon monastic foundations were made by the royal families of East Anglia and Mercia during the seventh century at Ely, Soham and Medeshamstede (Peterborough). These were also minsters, with some monks acting as priests over wide parishes (*parochiae*), and secondary minsters were founded at March, Burwell and Thorney respectively. Peterborough may have had another daughter minster at Botolph Bridge (Orton Longueville), south of Longthorpe Fort. Chatteris was probably another early minster, whereas those at Godmanchester, Cambridge and St Ives might be somewhat later, perhaps of eighth-century foundation. Although Ramsey Abbey established a priory at St Ives in the Late Saxon period when a stone coffin was discovered in 1001 (claimed to contain the bones of what was to become the town's patron saint), the Christian origins of the site are much earlier, in that St Ivo was a seventh-century Persian Christian missionary who came to Britain and died at Slepe, the old name for St Ives on the Huntingdonshire Ouse. By association, therefore, it it likely that Slepe was potentially an early Saxon Christian site either founded by St Ivo, or to which he had deliberately travelled. Hermitages are recorded of St Guthlac at Crowland, and another at Throckenholt.

Anglo-Saxon acquisition of Romano-British estate centres can be suggested by archaeological evidence for Haddon Villa and Orton Hall Farm, Peterborough, or from Great Wilbraham and Feltwell in the south-eastern fens, and these sites could also potentially help reveal a possible continuation of Roman Christianity within the Fenland region. House-churches or estate chapels have been discovered as part of large Late Roman villas in Dorset, and this tradition seems to have been generally followed (or possibly adopted) in the Middle Saxon period when it was the royal family and large estates who created churches on their land to provide for the religious needs of their communities. Many of the centres of early Anglo-Saxon monasticism are also places which have evidence for important late Roman Christianity, a situation which has been seen more clearly in south-western England where several Roman temples were adapted for Christian worship in the sub-Roman period, but its occurrence in eastern England has been less obvious. Despite dating from a period some 200 years after Rome left Britain to look after its own affairs therefore, this co-location of minsters with seats of royal or aristocratic power provides possible links between the emerging Anglo-Saxon elite with their Romano-British forebears, as such arrangements seem to indicate some continuity in the basic division of landholding which

FENLAND AND THE BIRTH OF ENGLAND

had presumably been carried through the sub-Roman period. For example, at Burwell and Great Wilbraham important Roman Christian artefacts have been recovered, including lead baptismal vats, which appear to be associated not only with proximity to springs but also to the location of important villas. In addition, a pagan Roman altar was found buried in a pit at the Great Wilbraham Villa (*113*), a custom which has been identified at sites such as Uley Temple, Gloucestershire, showing the metamorphosis of such temples into Christian centres during late Roman times. The fact that Early Anglo-Saxon cemeteries are found in close proximity to both these villas strongly suggests that they remained a focus, in all probability as continuation of centres for (villa) estates, during the fifth and sixth centuries. It is possible that Christian worship may also have survived as part of the estate package that transferred from Romano-British control to Anglo-Saxon overlordship. A study of other such evidence within the region shows a general pattern which tentatively supports a suggestion of continuity.

Icklingham, a site along the River Lark in Suffolk, for example, contains a late Roman church, a plastered baptismal tank, and a lead baptismal vat, as well as a concentration of early Anglo-Saxon cemetery and settlement evidence. Along the Norfolk and Suffolk fen-edge archaeological evidence has been used to suggest Middle Saxon ecclesiastical foundations at places such as Bawsey, West Dereham and Wormegay, closely associated with the spread of Roman fen-edge sites (*colour plate 26*), as well as at Staunch Meadow, Brandon, in Suffolk. Another example of a baptismal vat came from Willingham (the location of important Romano-Celtic temples) and two more from the Great Ouse near Huntingdon near the Rectory Farm villa and town of Godmanchester. Pewter vessels with chi-rhos have been found at Sutton in the Isle of Ely and Earith Road, Willingham (both places with evidence for Early Anglo-Saxon occupation), as well as Welney. Hoards of late Roman Christian silver come from Water Newton (*colour plate 27*, a complete altar set), and Mildenhall (*106*), and a further impressive hoard of gold jewellery, silver items and precious stones, probably a temple treasure, was found in 1979 at Gallows Hill, Thetford, which has been dated to the early fifth century; Thetford was later to develop as the site for an Anglo-Saxon cathedral. At Coldham, north of Stonea, pewter and bronze vessels of fourth-century date were found, suggesting wealth and continued importance at this site into the later Roman period. The discovery of Anglo-Saxon urns at Coldham by Tim Potter suggests that this site continued to be occupied into the early Anglo-Saxon period, perhaps in a similar way to the settlement at Stonea.

STONEA AND THE ROMAN FENS

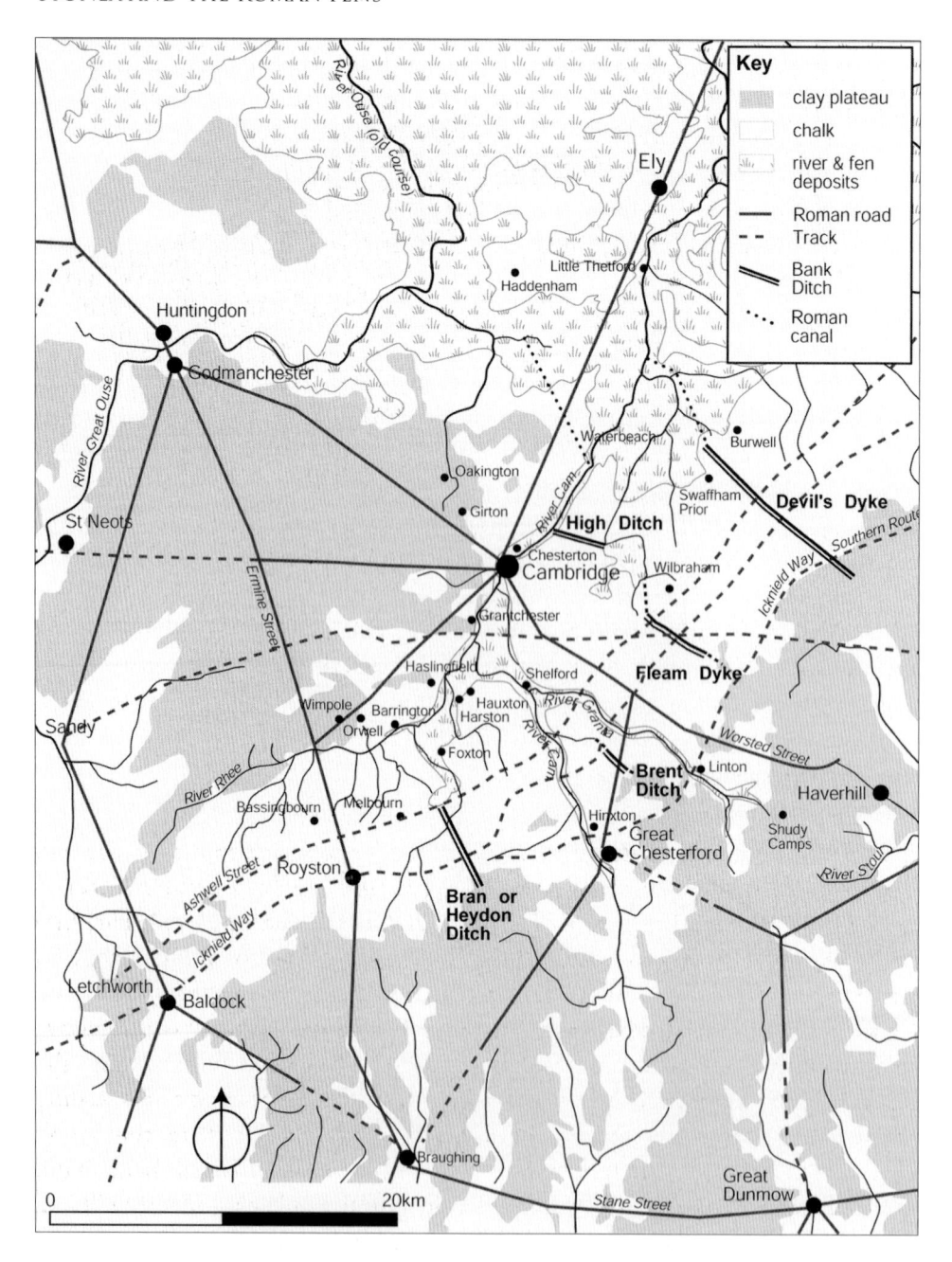

114 A map of the Cambridgeshire Dykes. Drawn by Sarah Wroot

FENLAND AND THE BIRTH OF ENGLAND

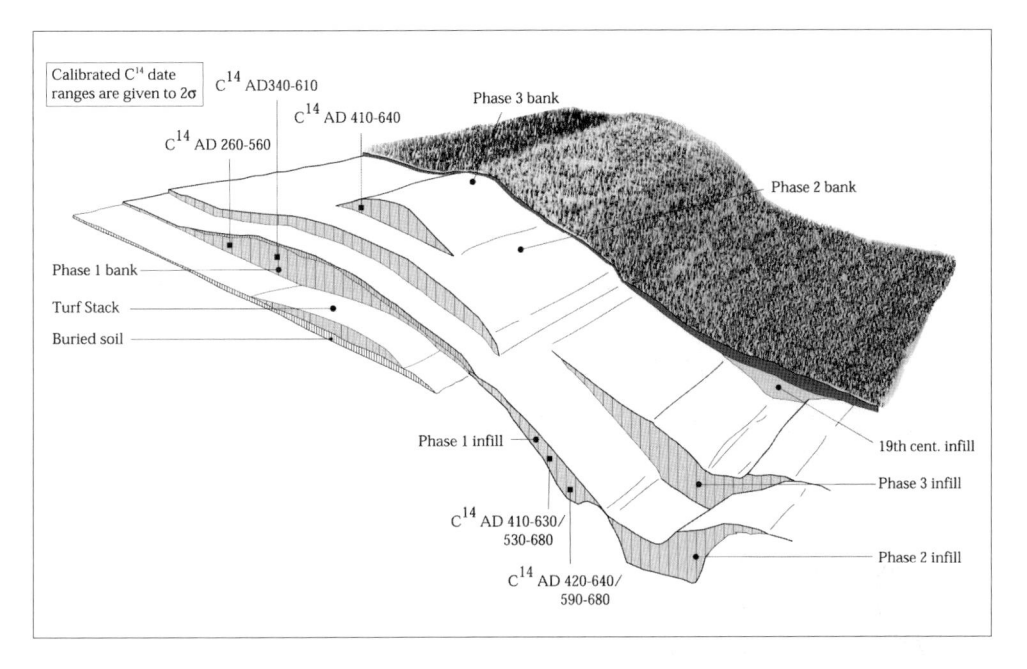

115 A 3D model of Fleam Dyke with results of radiocarbon dating. *Drawn by Jon Cane*

TERRITORIAL BOUNDARIES

One type of monument that survives from this period of sporadic warfare and gradual colonisation by the Anglo-Saxons is substantial linear ditched and banked earthworks. Four of the most impressive are found in south Cambridgeshire built across the chalk zone of the Icknield Way and thus controlling access to East Anglia (*114*). Their southern ends are located in the clay hills which separate Cambridgeshire from Essex, a geological area that would not have been attractive to early Anglo-Saxon farmers and was probably heavily wooded, whilst the northern ends terminated in wet areas such as springs, meres and rivers leading to the fens. The largest of these is Devils Dyke, which runs for 11km from Wood Ditton in the south, through Newmarket Heath, to join with Reach Lode in the north. It was over 10.5m high from base of ditch to top of bank, and was built in a single phase; the freshly excavated chalk that made up the bank would have stood out brightly across the East Anglian landscape, clearly marking out the boundary between the East Anglian heartland of Anglo-Saxon colonisation and areas further west which were disputed territory. Within this western frontier land three other dykes, Fleam Dyke, Brent Ditch and Bran Ditch, were constructed, all following the same design, and all with their ditches on the western side, showing they were defending the east against attack from the west. Excavations undertaken at

STONEA AND THE ROMAN FENS

Fleam Dyke in 1991 and 1992 have revealed a complex pattern of construction and remodelling over three or four main phases, and animal bone from key layers within the monument have shown that it was first built during the fourth or fifth centuries (cal AD 330-510) (*115*). Brent Ditch seems closely connected with Great Chesterford and might have had some relationship to this well fortified Late Roman town, mill, and major granary. The evidence from the Dykes and fifth- to seventh-century Anglo-Saxon cemeteries in south Cambridgeshire suggest that this was a frontier zone between an area with a strong British ruler and the Anglo-Saxon migrants, and that repeated campaigns led to the construction of a series of boundaries and linear defences; during the sixth and seventh centuries the Anglo-Saxons gained ascendancy, but during the fifth century it would seem likely that much of the Chiltern region including west Essex and Hertfordshire continued to be governed by the British. Further north, along the southern and western margins of the fens, this situation would also seem to hold true, with the middle Ouse valley and southern Huntingdonshire remaining remarkably empty of Anglo-Saxon evidence until at least the sixth century, and mostly even later. The Nene and Welland valleys, however, show far more evidence for early incursion and colonisation by the new immigrants.

Other examples of linear earthworks, boundaries or defences, occur in Suffolk and Norfolk (*colour plate 28*), although the dating of these to either the Iron Age or Anglo-Saxon periods is uncertain. The Black Ditch in Suffolk seems to continue the distribution pattern of the Cambridgeshire Dykes although its design as a V-shaped ditch is different from the Cambridgeshire ones (but similar to the first phase of Fleam Dyke). The Black Ditch occurs in close association with early Anglo-Saxon settlement at West Stow and Mill Heath, and an important late Roman Christian site at Icklingham (Camboritvm), and terminates at the River Lark along which many Anglo-Saxon sites have been found. Further north in Norfolk there are five similar monuments, four of which form a distinct group and are often referred to as Devils Dyke. They are more appropriately named Bircham, Foss, Laun and Panworth Ditches and they all cut Roman roads. They are situated in two pairs either side of the central Norfolk watershed along which the Peddars Way runs. Bicham and Foss Ditches effectively cut off promontories sticking out into the fens with Bicham Ditch terminating in marshland and the River Nar to the north, and River Wissey to the south, while the Foss Ditch terminates at the River Wissey to the north and the Little Ouse to the south. The ditches of these two face west while those to the east of the watershed, Laun and Panworth, have ditches to the east. The dating evidence strongly suggests these are post-Roman, and it is possible that the western ditches form the boundary between the Wissa in the fens to the west with another Anglo-Saxon group who occupied central Norfolk. These ditches would also appear to define the particularly rich late Roman fen-edge communities, such as Feltwell and Hockwold, from the newcomers to the east. The Laun Ditch, on the other hand, has been excavated on more than one occasion and has pre-Roman origins. The last Norfolk Dyke, Gaboldsham Ditch, runs between the River Thet in the north from West Harling, to the Little Ouse in the south, effectively sealing a stretch of land between the two rivers, which meet at Thetford and the Icknield Way. Given the occurrence of a late Roman hoard of great importance at Thetford (the product of a probable temple treasury and from an area also well known for the Late Iron Age temple at Fisons Way), this ditch could form another in the series of dykes built during the early post-Roman period to act as boundaries and perhaps defences between one community and another. Chris Scull draws attention to the correlation that some of these dykes have with the boundaries of the medieval bishopric of Norwich, which could have derived its diocese from a historic system of territorial division, an East Anglian *provincia*, the boundaries for which had become fossilised within the linear earthworks.

THE FOUNDING OF ENGLAND

There is much potential evidence within the Fenland region to help explore the period of transition from Late Roman times into the Middle Saxon period; the fens themselves must have acted as a frontier during this period, enabling a degree of independence to be retained by many small tribal groups who are named in Saxon documents, in contrast to other small groups within the heartlands of the emerging kingdoms of Mercia and East Anglia who were subsumed at an early date. As with the prehistoric period, the environment of the fens lent itself to being populated by a specialist people, semi-independent of their more powerful neighbours, and forming a natural barrier to political and military expansionism from the Midlands. The rivers that drained into the Wash via the fens provided easy access for the new Anglo-Saxon migrants, who would have maintained close contacts with their homelands across the North Sea. The islands would have provided fertile land on which to settle, and it would have been comparatively easy to control the few routes that crossed the fens, the Roman roads and earlier routeways. Thus, control of this region was essential in providing security to the development of settlement within Norfolk and Suffolk, one of the heartlands of Anglo-Saxon migration. From this safe base in East Anglia Anglo-Saxon colonisation was able to expand westwards and northwards during the fifth and sixth centuries to meet with similar groups in what were to become the kingdoms of Mercia and Lindsey, and therefore we can see that the fens played a significant role in the creation of England as we know it today.

BIBLIOGRAPHY

CHAPTER 1

Artis E.T. 1828 *The Durobrivae of Antoninus*
Clark J.G.D. 1949 'Report on excavations of the Cambridgeshire Car Dyke 1947' *Antiquaries Journal Vol. XXIX*, 145-163
Fox C. 1923 *The Archaeology of the Cambridge Region* Cambridge University Press
Hall D. and Coles J. 1994 *Fenland Survey: An essay in landscape and persistence* English Heritage
Hutchinson J.N. 1980 'The Record of Peat Wastage in the East Anglian Fenlands at Holme Post, 1848-1978 A.D.' *Journal of Ecology 68* 229-249
Mason H.J. 1973 *An Introduction to the Black Fens* Avocet Ltd
Phillips C.W. (ed.) 1970 *The Fenland in Roman Times* Royal Geographical Society Research Series No. 5
Tomlinson S.R. 1974 'Edmund Artis, Antiquary' *Durobrivae 2*
Tomlinson S.R. 1978 'The Antiquary and the poet: Edmund Artis and John Clare' *Durobrivae 5*

CHAPTER 2

Godwin H. 1978 *Fenland: Its Ancient Past and Uncertain Future* Cambridge University Press
Waller M. 1994 'The Fenland Project, Number 9: Flandrian Environmental Change in Fenland' *East Anglian Archaeology 70*

CHAPTER 3

Ashwin T. 1996 'Neolithic and Bronze Age Norfolk' *Proceedings of the Prehistoric Society Vol. 62*
Davies J. 1996 'Where Eagles Dare: the Iron Age of Norfolk' *Proceedings of the Prehistoric Society Vol. 62*
French C.A.I. '1994 Excavation of the Deeping St Nicholas Barrow Complex, South Lincolnshire' *Lincolnshire Archaeology and Heritage Report Series No. 1*
French C.A.I. 2000 'Development of Fenland in Prehsitoric Times' in Kirby T. and Oosthuizen S. (eds) *An Atlas of Cambridgeshire and Huntingdonshire History* Centre for Regional Studies Anglia Polytechnic University
Evans C. & Knight M. 2001 'The "community of builders": the Barleycroft post alignments' in Bruck J. (ed.) *Bronze Age Landscapes Tradition and Transformation* Oxbow
Healy F. & Housley R. 1992 'Nancy was not alone: human skeletons of the Early Bronze Age from the Norfolk peat fen' *Antiquity 66*
Hill J.D., Evans C. & Alexander M. 1999 'The Hinxton Rings – a Late Iron Age Cemetery at Hinxton, Cambridgeshire, with a Reconsideration of Norther Aylesford-Swarling Distributions' *Proceedings of the Prehistoric Society Vol. 65*
Hill J.D. 2000 'The Iron Age' in Kirby T. and Oosthuizen S. (eds) *An Atlas of Cambridgeshire and Huntingdonshire History* Centre for Regional Studies Anglia Polytechnic University
Hinman M. 2001 'Ritual Activity at the foot of the Gog Magog Hills, Cambridge' in Bruck J. (ed) *Bronze Age*

BIBLIOGRAPHY

Landscapes Tradition and Transformation Oxbow
Last J. 2000 'The Bronze Age' in Kirby T. and Oosthuizen S. (eds) *An Atlas of Cambridgeshire and Huntingdonshire History* Centre for Regional Studies Anglia Polytechnic University
Malim T. 2000 'Neolithic Enclosures' in Kirby T. and Oosthuizen S. (eds) *An Atlas of Cambridgeshire and Huntingdonshire History* Centre for Regional Studies Anglia Polytechnic University
Malim T. 2000 'The Ritual Landscape of the Neolithic and Bronze Age along the middle and lower Ouse Valley' in Dawson. M. *Prehistoric, Roman, and Post-Roman Landscapes of the Great Ouse Valley* Council for British Archaeology Research Report 119
Malim T. 2000 'Prehistoric Trackways' in Kirby T. and Oosthuizen S. (eds) *An Atlas of Cambridgeshire and Huntingdonshire History* Centre for Regional Studies Anglia Polytechnic University
Malim T. 2001 'Place and Space in the Cambridgeshire Bronze Age' in Bruck J. (ed) *Bronze Age Landscapes Tradition and Transformation* Oxbow
May J. 1976 *Prehistoric Lincolnshire* The History of Lincolnshire Committee
Pendleton C. 2001 'Firstly, let's get rid of ritual' in Bruck J. (ed) *Bronze Age Landscapes Tradition and Transformation* Oxbow
Pollard J. 2000 'The Neolithic' in Kirby T. and Oosthuizen S. (eds) *An Atlas of Cambridgeshire and Huntingdonshire History* Centre for Regional Studies Anglia Polytechnic University
Potter T.W. and Robinson B. 2000 'New Roman and prehistoric aerial discoveries at Grandford, Cambridgeshire' *Antiquity, 74 No 283*
Pryor F. et al. 1985 'The Fenland Project No. 1: Archaeology and Environment in the Lower Welland Valley' *East Anglian Archaeology 27* (2 volumes)
Pryor F. 1999 *Farmers in Prehistoric Britain* Tempus
Waller M. 1994 'The Fenland Project, Number 9: Flandrian Environmental Change in Fenland' *East Anglian Archaeology 70*
Yates D. forthcoming 'Bronze Age Fields; East Anglia and the Fenland Region'

CHAPTER 4

Green M. 1995 *Celtic Goddesses: Warriors, Virgins and Mothers* British Museum Publications
Haigh D. 1988 *The Religious Houses of Cambridgeshire* Cambridgeshire County Council
Hall D. 1992 'The Fenland Project, No. 6: The South-Western Cambridgeshire Fenlands' *East Anglian Archaeology 56*
Jackson R.P.J. and Potter T.W. 1996 *Excavations at Stonea, Cambridgeshire 1980-85* British Museum Press
Malim T. 1991 'The Sconce, March Civil War Fortifications' *Cambridgeshire County Council Archaeological Report No 34*
Malim T. 1992 'Stonea Camp: An Iron Age Fort in the Fens' *Cambridgeshire County Council Archaeological Report No 71*

CHAPTER 5

Evans C. & Knight M. 2002 'A Great Circle: investigations at Arbury Camp' *Proceedings of the Cambridge Antiquarian Society Vol. XCI*
French C. 2004 'Evaluation survey and excavation at Wandlebury ringwork, Cambridgeshire 1994-7' *Proceedings of the Cambridge Antiquarian Society Vo.l XCIII*
Jackson R.P.J. & Potter T.W. 1996 *Excavations at Stonea, Cambridgeshire 1980-85* British Museum Press
Malim T. 1992 'Stonea Camp: An Iron Age Fort in the Fens' *Cambridgeshire County Council Archaeological Report No 71*
Malim T. & McKenna R. 1994 'Borough Fen Ringwork: Iron Age Fort' *Fenland Research No. 8*
Sealey P.R. 2000 'The Boudican Revolt against Rome' *Shire Archaeology No.74*
Tacitus *Annals* xxii 31
Webster G. 1978 *Boudica: The British Revolt against Rome AD 60* Batsford
Webster G. 1993 *Rome against Caratacus* Batsford

CHAPTER 5 SPECIAL FEATURE RADIOCARBON DATING

Bronk Ramsey C. 1995 'Radiocarbon calibration and analysis of stratigraphy' *Radiocarbon 36*, 425-30

Bronk Ramsey C. & Hedges R.E.M. 1997 'Hybrid ion sources: radiocarbon measurements from microgram to milligram' *Nuclear Instruments and Methods in Physics Research B, 123,* 539-45

Buck C.E., Christen J.A., Kenworthy J.B. & Litton C.D. 1994 'Estimating the duration of archaeological activity using 14C determinations' *Oxford Journal of Archaeology 13,* 229-40

Buck C.E., Kenworthy J.B., Litton C.D. & Smith A.F.M. 1991 'Combining archaeological and radiocarbon information: a Bayesian approach to calibration' *Antiquity 65* 808-21

Buck C.E., Litton C.D. & Scott E M 1994 'Making the most of radiocarbon dating: some statistical considerations' *Antiquity 68,* 252–63

Buck C.E., Litton C.D. & Smith A.F.M. 1992 'Calibration of radiocarbon results pertaining to related archaeological events' *J Archaeol Sci 19* 497-512

Gelfand A.E. & Smith A.F.M. 1990 'Sampling approaches to calculating marginal densities' *J Amer. Stat. Assoc. 85* 398-409

Gulliksen S. & Scott M. 1995 'Report of the TIRI workshop, Saturday 13 August 1994' *Radiocarbon 37* 820-1

Hedges R.E.M., Bronk C.R. & Housley R.1989 'The Oxford Accelerator Mass Spectrometry facility: technical developments in routine dating' *Archaeometry 31* 99-113

Mook W.G. 1986 'Business meeting: Recommendations/Resolutions adopted by the Twelfth International Radiocarbon Conference' *Radiocarbon 28* 799

Noakes J.E., Kim S.M. & Stipp J.J. 1965 'Chemical and counting advances in liquid scintillation age dating, in Proceedings of the 6th international conference on radiocarbon and tritium dating' (eds E.A. Olsson and R.M. Chatters) 68-92

Rozanski K., Stichler W., Gonfiantini R., Scott E.M., Beukens R.P., Kromer B. & van der Plicht J. 1992 'The IAEA 14C intercomparison exercise 1990' *Radiocarbon 34* 506-19

Stenhouse M.J. & Baxter M.S. 1983 '14C dating reproducibility: evidence from routine dating of archaeological samples' *PACT 8* 147-61

Stuiver M. & Kra R.S. 1986 'Editorial comment' *Radiocarbon, 28* (2B), ii

Stuiver M. & Polach H.A. 1977 'Reporting of 14C data' *Radiocarbon 19* 355-63

Stuiver M. & Reimer P.J. 1986 'A computer program for radiocarbon age calculation' *Radiocarbon 28* 1022-30

Stuiver. M., Reimer P.J., Bard E., Beck J.W., Burr G.S., Hughen K.A., Kromer B., McCormac F.G., van der Plicht J. & Spurk M. 1998 'INTCAL98 radiocarbon age calibration, 24,000-0 cal BP' *Radiocarbon 40* 1041-84

CHAPTER 6

Jackson R.P.J. & Potter T.W. 1996 *Excavations at Stonea, Cambridgeshire 1980-85* British Museum Press

Millett M. 1990 *The Romanisation of Britain* Cambridge University Press

Taylor J. 2000 'Stonea in its Fenland context: moving beyond an imperial estate' *Journal of Roman Archaeology Vol. 13*

CHAPTER 7

Alexander J. & Pullinger J. 1999 'Roman Cambridge: Excavations on Castle Hill 1956-1988' *Proceedings of the Cambridge Antiquarian Society LXXXVIII*

Burnham B. & Wacher J. 1990 *The 'Small Towns' of Roman Britain* Batsford

Crowson A. Lane T. and Reeve J. 2000 'Fenland Management Project Excavations 1991-1995' *Lincolnshire Archaeology and Heritage Report Series No 3*

Davies J. 1996 'Iron Age and Roman' in Margeson S., Ayers B., Heywood S., (eds) *A Festival of Norfolk Archaeology* Norfolk & Norwich Archaeological Society

Fincham G. 2004 *Durobrivae: A Roman Town Between Fen and Upland* Tempus

Fox C. 1923 *Archaeology of the Cambridge Region* Cambridge University Press

Green M. 2000 'Roman Godmanchester' in Kirby T. and Oosthuizen S. (eds) *An Atlas of Cambridgeshire and Huntingdonshire History* Centre for Regional Studies Anglia Polytechnic University

Hall D. 1987 'The Fenland Project, No. 2: Cambridgeshire Survey, Peterborough to March' *East Anglian Archaeology 35*

Hall D. 1996 'The Fenland Project, No. 10: Cambridgeshire Survey, Isle of Ely and Wisbech' *East Anglian*

BIBLIOGRAPHY

Archaeology 79
Hall D. & Coles J. 1994 *Fenland Survey: An essay in landscape and persistence* English Heritage
Hayes P.P. & Lane T.W. 1992 'The Fenland Project, No. 5: Lincolnshire Survey, the South-West Fens' *East Anglian Archaeology No. 55*
Lane T. 1993 'Fenland Project, No. 8: Lincolnshire Survey, the Northern Fen-edge' *East Anglian Archaeology No. 66*
Macaulay S. and Reynolds T. 1996 (revised) 'Car Dyke: A Roman Canal at Waterbeach' *Cambridgeshire County Council Archaeological Report No. 98*
Macaulay S. 1997 'Akeman Street Roman Road and Romano-British Settlement at Landbeach, Car Dyke Farm' *Cambridgeshire County Council Archaeological Report No. 141*
Macaulay S. 2002 'Romano-British Settlement at Camel Road, Littleport, Cambridgeshire' *Cambridgeshire County Council Archaeological Report No. 205*
Mackreth D. 1980 'Durobrivae' in *Durobrivae: A Review of Nene Valley Archaeology: 7*
Mackreth D. 1984 'Castor' in *Durobrivae: A Review of Nene Valley Archaeology: 9*
Mackreth D. 1996 'Orton Hall Farm: A Roman and Early Anglo-Saxon Farmstead' *East Anglian Archaeology 76*
Phillips C.W. (ed) 1970 *The Fenland in Roman Times* Royal Geographical Society Research Series No. 5
Potter T.W. & Potter C.F. 1981 'A Romano-British Village at Grandford, March' *Proceedings of the Cambridge Antiquarian Society Vol. LXX (for 1980)*
Potter T.W. 1981 'The Roman Occupation of the Central Fenland' *Britannia Vol. XII*
Potter T.W. and Robinson B. 2000 'New Roman and prehistoric aerial discoveries at Grandford, Cambridgeshire' *Antiquity 74 No. 283*
Pryor A. 1978 'The Car Dyke' in *Durobrivae: A Review of Nene Valley Archaeology: 6*
Salway P. 1981 *Roman Britain* The Oxford History of Britain OUP
Sealey P.R. 2000 'The Boudican Revolt against Rome' *Shire Archaeology No. 74*
Silvester R. 1988 'Fenland Project, No. 3: Norfolk Survey, Marshland and the Nar Valley' *East Anglian Archaeology 45*
Silvester R. 1988 'Fenland Project, No. 4: Norfolk Survey, the Wissey Embayment & the Fen Causeway' *East Anglian Archaeology 52*
Taylor A. 2000 'Roman Cambridge' in Kirby T. and Oosthuizen S. (eds) *An Atlas of Cambridgeshire and Huntingdonshire History* Centre for Regional Studies Anglia Polytechnic University
Taylor A. 2002 'Supplying the frontier zones: the role of the East Anglian Fens' *British Archaeological Reports International Series 1084 (II)*
Taylor C. 1973 *The Cambridgeshire Landscape* Hodder and Stoughton
Thorpe R. & Zeffertt T. 1989 'Excavation of the Lincolnshire Car Dyke, Baston' *Fenland Research No. 6*
Wallis H. 2002 'Roman Routeways across the Fens: Excavations at Morton, Tilney St Lawrence, Nordelph and Downham' West *East Anglian Archaeology Occasional paper 10*
Whitwell J.B. 1970 'Roman Lincolnshire' *History of Lincolnshire Vol II* Lincolnshire Local History Society
Whitwell J.B. 1982 'The Coritani: Some Aspects of the Iron Age Tribe and the Roman Civitas' *British Archaeological Report British series 99*
Wilkes J.J. & Elrington C.L. 1978 *The Victoria County History of the County of Cambridge and the Isle of Ely Vol. VII: Roman Cambridgeshire* Oxford University Press

CHAPTERS 8, 9 AND 10

Bliss K. 1988 *Practical Cheesemaking* Crowoood Press
Bray S. and Malim T. 'A Romano-British Temple and Anglo-Saxon Cemetery at Gallows Hill, Swaffingham Prior' *Cambridgeshire County Council Archaeological Report No. 100*
Dallas C. G. 1973 'The Nunnery of St Kyneburgha at Castor' *Durobrivae 3*
Ellis P., Hughes G., Leach P., Mould C. & Sterenberg J. 1998 'Excavations alongside Roman Ermine Street, Cambridgeshire, 1996' *Birmingham University Field Archaeology Unit Monograph Series 1 BAR Series 276*
Esmonde Cleary A.S. 1989 *The Ending of Roman Britain* Batsford
Evans C. 2003 'Britons and Romans at Chatteris: investigations at Langwood Farm, Cambridgeshire' *Britannia XXXIV, 175-264*
Frend W.H.C. 2000 'Roman Christianity' in Kirby T. and Oosthuizen S. (eds) *An Atlas of Cambridgeshire and Huntingdonshire History* Centre for Regional Studies Anglia Polytechnic University
Gibson D. and Lucas G. 2002 'Pre-Flavian kilns at Greenhouse Farm and the social context of early Roman

pottery production in Cambridgeshire' *Britannia XXXIII, 95-128*
Green H.J.M. 1954 'The Basis of Roman Economy in the Great Ouse Valley' *The Archaeological Newsletter Vol. 5. No. 2*
Green H.J.M. 1986 'Religious cults at Roman Godmanchester' in Henig M. & King A. (eds) *Pagan Gods and Shrines of the Roman Empire* Oxford University Committee for Archaeology
Green H.J.M. and Henig M. *1988* 'A Roman Bronze Figurine from Earith' *Cambridgeshire Journal of the British Archaeological Association CXLI*
Heritage Lincolnshire *c.2000 The Roman Trail: Finding out about the Romans in North Kesteven* North Kesteven District Council
Hinman M. 2003 'A Late Iron Age Farmstead and Romano-British Site at Haddon, Peterborough' *Cambridgeshire County Council Archaeological Field Unit Monograph No 2 British Archaeological Report 358*
Jones A. 2003 'Settlement, Burial and Industry in Roman Godmanchester' *Birmingham University Field Archaeology Unit Monograph Series 6 BAR Series 346*
Jones M. 2002 *Roman Lincoln: Conquest, Colony and Capital* Tempus
Kemp S. 2003 'Romano-British Enclosures and Crop Processing: A15 Werrington to Glinton Bypass Archaeological Excavations 1996' *Cambridgeshire County Council Archaeological Report No. 128*
Lane T. & Morris E. 2001 *A Millennium of Salt making: Prehistoric and Romano-British Salt Production in the Fenland* Lincolnshire Archaeology and Heritage Reports Series No. 4 Heritage Lincolnshire
Mackreth D. 1988 'Excavation of an Iron Age and Roman enclosure at Werrington, Cambridgeshire' *Britannia XIX*
Malim T. 2000 'The Anglo-Saxon Dykes' in Kirby T. and Oosthuizen S. (eds) *An Atlas of Cambridgeshire and Huntingdonshire History* Centre for Regional Studies Anglia Polytechnic University
Malim T., Penn K., Robinson B., Wait G. & Welsh K. 1997 'New Evidence on the Cambridgeshire Dykes and Worsted Street Roman Road' *Proceedings of the Cambridge Antiquarian Society 85*
McIntosh J. & Wait G. 1992 *The Romans in Cambridgeshire* Cambridgeshire County Council
Mckenna R.F. 2001 'Excavations and Observations at Site 5a, Lidgate Close, Botolph Bridge, Orton Longueville, Peterborough 1997-1999' *Peterborough Archaeology Group*
Meaney A. 1964 *A Gazetteer of Early Anglo-Saxon Burial Sites* Allen and Unwin
Murphy P. 1994 'Anglo-Saxon arable farming on the silt fens – preliminary results' in *Fenland Research No 8 1993*
Network Archaeology Ltd *1999 Peterborough to Luton 1050mm Gas Pipeline* Report No. 135
Oosthuizen S. 2000 'Placenames 650-950 AD' in Kirby T. and Oosthuizen S. (eds) *An Atlas of Cambridgeshire and Huntingdonshire History* Centre for Regional Studies Anglia Polytechnic University
Oosthuizen S. 2000 'Anglo-Saxon Monasteries and Minsters' in Kirby T. and Oosthuizen S. (eds) *An Atlas of Cambridgeshire and Huntingdonshire History* Centre for Regional Studies Anglia Polytechnic University
Penn K. 1996 'The Early Church in Norfolk: some aspects' in Margeson S., Ayers B. and Heywood S. *A Festival of Norfolk Archaeology* Norfolk and Norwich Archaeological Society
Perrin J.R. 1999 'Roman Pottery from Excavations at and near to the Roman Small Town of Durobrivae, Water Newton, Cambridgeshire 1956-58' *Journal of Roman Pottery Studies 8*
Pryor F. et al. 1985 'The Fenland Project No. 1: Archaeology and Environment in the Lower Welland Valley' *East Anglian Archaeology 27* (2 volumes)
Roberts J. 2000 'Roman Occupation at Lyndon Farm, High Street, Maxey' *Cambridgeshire County Council Archaeological Report 181*
Scull C. 1992 'Before Sutton Hoo: Structures of Power and Society in early East Anglia in The Age of Sutton Hoo.' *The Seventh Century in North-West Europe* The Boydell Press, Woodbridge
Scull C. 1993 'Archaeology, Early Anglo-Saxon Society and the origins of Anglo-Sxaon Kingdoms' *Anglo-Saxon Studies in Archaeology and History 6*
Taylor A. 1999 *Cambridge: the Hidden History* Tempus
Taylor A. 2002 'Supplying the frontier zones: the role of the East Anglian Fens' *British Archaeological Reports International Series 1084 (II)*
Upex S.G. 1992 'Excavations at a Roman and Saxon site at Haddon, Cambridgeshire 1991'
Upex S.G. 1993 'Excavations at a Roman and Saxon site at Haddon, Cambridgeshire 1992-3'
Welch M. 1996 'The Archaeological and Historical Setting of the Anglo-Saxon Settlement' in Jackson R.P.J. & Potter T.W. 1996 *Excavations at Stonea, Cambridgeshire 1980-85* British Museum Press
Whitwell J.B. 1970 'Roman Lincolnshire' *History of Lincolnshire Vol II* Lincolnshire Local History Society
Whitwell J.B. 1982 'The Coritani: Some Aspects of the Iron Age Tribe and the Roman Civitas' *British Archaeological Reports 99*
Woodward A. 1992 *Shrines and Sacrifice* Batsford/English Heritage

INDEX

Figures in brackets refer to illustrations.

Abandinus 158 (88), 194
Actus 183
ADAS 43
Adventurers 54
Aescwen 52
Ailsworth (67) 235
Aisled
    barn 160, 163, 180, 189, 192 (97), 213, 214
    building 164-5
Akeman Street 137-140 (65) 143, 152, 158, 191, 192, 235, 237
Alder 73, 119, 172
Alderton, Ann 18
Aldreth 30, 34, 235
Alexander, John 16,158
Amphora 39, 110, 122 (60), 123-4, 158, 180, 192, 207
Ancaster 140, 178, 236
Andraste 86, 131
Anglo-Saxon 45, 92, 98, 111, 120, 151, 189, 193, 213, 217, 222, 223, 224, 225, 226 (107), (108), 229 (109), 230, 231, 232, 233 (110), 235 (111), 236, 237, 238, 239, 240, 241, 243, 244, 245, **colour plates 26 and 28**
    burial and cemetery 137, 141, 160 (91), 196 (92), 226, 230 (110), 234, 235, 236 (111), 237, 239, 241
    charter 52
    estate 51, 160, 240, 241
    place names 52, 137, 226, 237-8
    grange 52
    hall 10, 52, 53, 224, 226 (107) (108), 230
    settlement 10, 52, 98, 99, 101, 137, 141, 158, 164 (94), 226, 229, 230, 231, 234, 235, 237, 241, 244, 245
Anguillara 107
Animal husbandry see stock
Annona 131, 193, 205
Antedios 133
Antoninus Pius (Antonine) 129, 134, 137, 146, 177, 185, 186, 192, 194 (89)
Arable 53, 56, 58, 120-1, 186, 191
Arbury 191

Arbury Camp 37, 88, 89
Arles (Council of) 222
Armour 153
Artillery 167
Artis E.T. 11, 154, 216, 217
Asen Dyke 141
Ash 75, 118, 119, 121
Ashby de la Launde 214
Ashton 219 (102)
Astbury AK 139
Autun 107, 108 (63), 131
Aucissa (40) 83
Annals 58
Axe 48, 50, 109, 118
Aylesford-Swarling 37
Aylmer Hall 150
Babraham Road 37
Bacchus 194
Bain 163
Baldock 40
Bannovalium 163
Barge 147, 148 (73), 149, 167, 169, 172, 178, 180
Barholm 34, 191
Barley See Cereal
Barnack 35, 116, 126, 130, 160, 181, 191, 214, 215
Barrow (Roman) 40 (17) (18)
Barroway Drove Beds 30
Bartlow 37
Barway 235
Basilica 107, 158, 219
Basket(ry) 118, 172
Baston 141, 147, 236
    Outgang 141, 236
Bathhouse 130, 158, 192, 230
Battery Hills 54
Battle 58, 82
Bawsey 241
Baxter, Ian 169, 170
Bead 50
Bede 225, 229
Bedford (Duke of) 54
Bedwell Hey Farm 137, 232, 235
Beer (Celtic) and Brewery 40, 121, 122, 157, 170, 192, 216 (112)
Beetle 73, 146
Belt Fitting 126, 189, 210, 236, 237, 239

Benwick 53, 87
Berries 121, 122
Bicker Haven 187
Billing Brook 154
Billingborough 147, 187, 191, 231
Bilmiga 231
Birch 73, 82, 119
Bircham Ditch 42, 244
Birrus 171
Bishop (Roman) 222
Black Death 53
Black Ditch 42, 92, 244
Bluntisham 37
Bog Bodies 82
Bog Oaks 14, 24
Bone 68, 86, 89
    animal 71, 72, 81, 89, 110, 119-120, 160, 165, 168, 169, 170, 171, 176, 192, 197, 226, 244
    bird 120, 165
    fish 120, 165
    human 70 (33), 71, 72, 79, 80, 81, 82, 84, 94
Bone Working 156, 170
Borough Hill (43)
Borough Fen 35 (15), 40,88, 89
Boston 11, 29
Botolph Bridge 153, 190, 235, 240
Bottisham 151, 221
Boudica(n) 39, 88, 93, 129, 131, 134, 153, 158
Boundary (frontier incl. "Limes") 34, 37, 40, 42, 51, 84,88, 98, 99, 101, 102, 104, 113 (55) (57), 128, 149, 186, 196, 204, 205, 239, 243-245
Bourne 140, 148, 150, 162, 178, 191, 194, 231
    Eau 150, 162, 163
Bracelet 77, 83, 124
Bradwell 218
Braham Farm 54
Bramble (Blackberry) 73, 122
Bran Ditch 243
Brandon 191, 241
    Creek 152
Brent Ditch 243, 244
Bridge 135, 141
Briquetage 86, 135, 173, 180

251

British Geological Society 18, 25
British Museum 9, 11, 18, 45, 50, 52, 58 (27), 62, 66, 84, 110, 119, 130, 226
Briton 237
Bromwich J 15
Bronze Age 25, 30, 32, 33, 34, 36, 37, 44, 45, 49, 85, 134, 142, 173, 185
  barrow 36, 37, 39, 45, 49, 50, 58, 84, 86, 194
  burials 10 (13), 35, 37, 39, 49, 50
  flints 14, 37, 39, 50
  hoards 32
  metalwork 32, 37, 39, 50
  pottery 50, 85
  settlement 32, 37, 50
  weapons 34, 37, 50
Brooch 77 (40), 83, 124, 126, 189, 210 (96), 230
Buckett 118, 168, 199
Bullocks Haste (11) (71), 146, 187
Burgh Banks 89
Burgh Castle 218
Burgh-le-Marsh 218, 237
Burial (see also Bronze Age, Iron Age) 70, 75, 82, 84, 86, 165
  cremation (18)
  Roman (cemetery) 70, 154, 158, 160, 163, 235, 236
Burwell 151, 191, 197, 219 (101), 221, 223, 238, 240, 241
Butt Lane 40
Buttery Clay 24, 25
Caister-by-Norwich 97, 171, 215
Caister-on-Sea 137, 176
Caistor St Edmund 39, 137, 215
Caldecote 188
Cam 31, 37, 40, 88, 124, 144, 146, 151, 158, 160, 178, 180
Camboritum 244
Cambridge 16, 37, 82, 83, 89, 124, 137, 144, 156, 158-160 (77), 172, 178, 191, 192, 193, 215, 223, 234, 235, 237, 238, 240
Cambridge University 18, 24, 164
Cambridgeshire Archaeological Committee 18
Cambridgeshire County Council's (Archaeological Field Unit, Archaeological Service) 46, 58, 186, 196
Camel Road 137, 192
Camercon Fiona 76
Camp Ground 164-166
Camulodunum 88, 93
Canal 44, 54, 116, 122, 126, 128, 133, 134, 135, 136, 142-152, 162, 165, 169, 178, 181, 185, **colour plates 10, 15 and 24**
Cannonball 53
Canterbury 97
Car Dyke 11 (2), 16, 137 (65), 143-149, (69), (70), (71), (72), 150, 162, 169, 178, 180, 188, 236
Carausius 204
Cardinal Way 233
Careby 89
Carlisle 215
Casket 40
Castle Hill 158
Castor 12, 154, 156,179, 214, 215 (98) (99) (100), 216 (99) (100), 222, 230,

236 (112), 239, 240, **colour plate 2**
ware 152
Cat 120
Catswater 210
Cattle (Cows) 40, 53, 84, 93, 120, 121, 160, 69, 170, 199
Catuvellauni 34, 37, 40, 88, 89, 93, 133, 196, 215
Cavalry Barn 54
Cella 108, 131, 194 (91), 196
Centuriation (86), 182-5 (87)
Cereal (crops, grain, seed) 40, 42, 67, 73, 74, 75, 86, 120-2, 128, 143, 146, 151, 165, 169, 170, 172, 178, 181, 182, 186, 189, 190, 191, 192, 207, 214, 226
Challands Adran (14) 153
Chariot 85
Chattens 29, 30, 33, 34, 36, 37, 43, 44, 50, 54, 88, 184, 185, 189, 193, 194, 212, 213, 237, 240
Cheese (making, press, etc) 168, 170, 199-201(93)
Cherry Hinton 90, 178
Chesterton 54, 133, 154, 160, 238
Chi-rho 219 (102) (103), 221 (104), 241
Chicken 120
Chiltern 244
Chippenham 37
Chisel 50
Christchurch 135, 139, 143, 172, 182-4 (86)
Christian(ity) 196, 197, 219 (105), 222, 223 (106), 230, 236, 237, 240, 241 **colour plates 27**
Church 219, 222, 223, 240, 241
Cirencester 97
Civil War, the 53, 54
  Also Civil Wars, Roman 203-206
Clark Graham (JGD) 14 (5), 16, 24, 144
Claudius (Claudian) 79, 92, 133, 178
Clodius Albinus 203, 207
Clunch 181
Cock Hill 237
Coin(age) 41, 51, 77, 79, 84, 85, 86, 87 (42), 88, 93, 124-5, 126, 129, 160, 163, 164, 165, 185, 189m 207, 210, 213, 226, 230, 235
  Hoards 45, 188, 194, 207
Colchester 39, 40, 51 (40), 88, 93, 97, 98, 124
Cold Harbour Farm 139
Coldham 142, 160, 171, 185, 188, 210, 213, 221, 241
Coles J 9, 16
Colne 164, 189
  Ditch 151, (80)
Coloni 168, 205, 213
Columella 199, 200
Comberton 237
Commodis 194
Conington 24
Constans 205
Constantine I (Britannicus) 204
Constantius 205
Constantius Chlorus 150, 204, 207
Coppice 75, 118, 119
Coriebrolsilorum 215
Corieltauvi 34, 40, 79, 88, 89, 163, 196, 215
Cottenham 16 (11), 144 (71), 146, 149, 187, 194

Coveney 37, 88
Cowbit 172 (81)
Cranbrock Drain 151, 164, 166
Cromwell 54
Cross G W 54 (23) 79
Crouch 176
Crowland 53, 141, 180, 237, 240
Crucible (see mould)
Cumbre 237
Cunobelin 40, 79, 88
Dairy 120, 127, 156, 168, 169, 178, 199-201
Dalham 52
Danish 52
Davis Bob 180
Decoy Fen 152
Deepings 141
  fen 141
  market 235
  St James 150, 194
  St Nicholas 35
  West 35
Dendrochronology 75
Dennoy Abbey 54, 188
Denton 214
Denver 16, 30, 32, 33, 126, 134, 135, 137, 143, 160, 171, 192, 210
Devil's Dyke 151, 196, 243, 244, **colour plate 24**
Diatoms 44
Dimmocks Cote 37, 142
Dio Cassius 86
Diocletian 171, 203, 204, 207
Ditches 244
Doddington 52, 53, 87
Doddington Leam 54
Dogs (hunting) 40, 120, 228
Donington 32, 141
Dorset 240
Dover 218, 231
Downham Market 143
Downham West 135, 136, 172, 175, 183-4 (87), **colour plate 17**
Dowsby 231
Dowsdale 141, 142
Droitwich 173, 176
Duck 120
Dugdale 134
Durobrivae 12 (3), 116, 127, 137, 140, 153, 154-156 (74) (75), 163, 167, 169, 171, 176, 177, 179, 189, 191, 192, 210, 214, 215, 216 (98), 218, 219, 222, 235
Duroliponte (Durolipons) 158 (77), 215
Durovigitum 156 (76), 199, 219
Dux Britanniarum 204
Dyke 40, 44, 51, 53, 54, 56, 88, 92, 151 243, 244, 245 (114) (115), 243-245
Earith 16, 132, 151, 160-2 (78) (79) (80), 164-6, 180, 189, 194 (90), 197, 206 (97), 219 (220), 241
East Midlands 213
Eastrea 135
Egyptian Blue 116, 124
Elder 189
Eldernell 33, 133, 135, 137, 142, 153
Elm 142, 151, 173
Ely 34, 43, 52, 103, 142, 152, 221, 237, 240
  Abbot of 52
  Bishop of 53
  Isle of 22, 29, 30, 33, 34, 37, 54, 88,

252

INDEX

137, 142, 191, 192 (103), 221, 232, 235, 237, 241
Empingham 236
England 225
English (the) 224
English Heritage 9, 16, 56
Epona 109
Eriswell 232, 237
Ermine Street 128, 133, 137, 140, 153, 154, 156, 158, 170, 191, 192, 214, 215, 235
Estate (Iron Age, Roman, Imperial, Anglo-Saxon) 42, 51, 53, 56, 125-129, 149, 156, 160, 168, 171, 176, 178, 182, 191, 192, 197, 203, 204, 206, 207, 210, 212, 215, 217, 223, 230, 240, 241
Estover 33, 135, 185
Etton 34, 49, 186
Evans Chris 89, 164-6, 189, 193
Exeter 97
Eye 35, 148
Famine 42, 93, 225
Farcet 24
Fat Hen 73
Feast(ing) 84, 86, 158
Felix 237
Feltwell 191, 232, 238, 240, 245
Fen Causeway 32 (13), 33, 36, 54, 126, 134-137 (64), 139, 142-3, 151, 152, 153, 154, 172, 175, 183, 184, 185, 187, 192, **colour plates 16 and 17**
Fen Circles 186
Fen Clay 22, 23, 25, 30
Fen Ditton 160, 178
Fengate 10, 32, 35, 36, 134, 206, **colour plate 16**
Fenland Archaeological Trust 18
Fenland in Roman Times, The 9 (1) (6), 16, 18, colour plate 1
Fenland Project (Fenland Survey, Evaluation and Management Project) 9, 16, 18, 23, 28, 37, 45, 52, 135, 136, 139, 143, 152, 176, 184, 185, 187, 212, 213, 231, 232, **colour plate 1, colour plate 10**
Fenland Research Committee 9, 14, 24, 25
Fenland Stratigraphy 22 (8), 24, 25, 29-31
Field Baulk 87 (42), 93
Field Systems (enclosures, droves, paddocks, hedges) (6) 14, 34, 37, 40, 42, 45, 52, 122, 134, 141, 146, 150, 165, 169, 171, 182-190, 210, 213, **colour plate 10**
Fig 122, 214
Figurine 109-110, 160, 163, 170, 194
Fish (Fisheries) 53, 165, 171, 172
paste/sauce 123, 158
Fishbourne 105
Fiskerton 34
Fisons Way 86, 245
Flag Fen 32, 35, 36
Flaggrass 33, 37, 87, 126, 135, 142, 151, 160, 171, 185, 206, 210, 213
Flagon 110, 123-4, 147, 192
Flandrian 14, 64
Flavian (pre-flavian) 76, 110, 137, 140, 153, 185, 197, 200
Fleam Dyke 235 (115), 243, 244
Fletton 235

Flooding 15,22, 26, 43, 45, 50, 68, 69, 70, 74, 80, 81, 89, 135, 141, 151, 152, 171, 184
marine 26, 30, 44, 45, 136, 206, **colour plate 6**
third century 25, 26, 28, 131, 150, 151, 168, 185, 186, 187, 188, 189, 206, 207, 214
Foederati 205, 217, 223, 225, 233, 234
Foraminifera 25 (30), 68, 74, 150
Fordey 33, 34, 142
Fordham 37, 179, 191, 238
Fort (Roman) 133, 137, 152-153, 156 (76), 158, 168, 178, 218, 235, 240, **colour plates 7 and 15**
Forum 104,107, 222
Foss (Dyke) 42, 144, 244
Fowler Gordon 14, 16, 25
Fox Cyril 14, 56, 57, 151, **colour plate 3**
Frisians 236
Friskney 237
Frognall 194
Fuel 172, 173m 175, 177
Fulbourn 151, 235
Fungi 122
Funthams Lane (13)
Gaboldsham Ditch 92, 245
Gaius 79
Gale Rowena 172
Galerius 204
Gallic Chronicle 225
Gallic Empire (Imperium Galliarum) 150, 203
Gallows Hill 194, 196, 234, 241
Garton Station 85
Gedney Hill (6) 141, 185
Geese 120
Genius 160, 194 (90)
Geology 23-24, 43, 60, 67, 69, 83, 243
Gibson David 178
Girton 215, 234
Glass
vessel 105, 110, 116, 122, 158, 192, 207
window 99, 105, 106, 110, 116, 125, 160, 163, 189, 209, 213
Glen 141, 150, 231, 236
Glinton 169, 186, 189, 190
Goat 120
Godmanchester 16, 33, 36, 97, 130, 133, 153, 156-158 (76), 168, 170, 172, 178, 180, 182, 187, 190 (88), 191, 192, 194 (93), 199, 200, 214, 222, 233, 240, 241
Godwin Harry 14, 22, 24
Gog Magog 89
Gold 50, 79, 93, 124, 223, 241
Golden Lion Inn 45, 53, 54, 207
Gosberton 176, 231
Gothic House Farm 141
Graffiti 123 (60)
Grain (see Cereal)
Granary (grain and warehouse) 40, 146, 158, 160, 164, 165, 178, 180, 192, 193, 244, **colour plate 18**
Grandford 36, 70, 87, 133, 135, 137, 142, 153, 171, 185, 188, 192, 206, 210, 212,213 (105), 222, **colour plate 7**
Grange
Saxon 52
medieval monastic 53
Grange Stonea 43, 44, 45, 50, 52, 53

(24), 54, 56, 84, 85, 86, 181, 188, 226
Grantham 141
Gratian 206
Great Casterton 178, 214, 236
Great Chesterford 193, 244
Green Charles 16
Green Michael 16, 130, 156, 160, 168, 178, 182, 188, 196, 199
Green Miranda 86
Greenfield Ernest 16
Greenhouse Farm 160
Gregory Tony 86
Grubenhaus(er) 226, 230, 232, 233, 239
Gunthorpe 235
Gut 167
Guthrum Gowt 141
Guyhirn 142, 180
Gyrwe 229
Hacconby 179, 231
Haceby 214
Haddenham 36, 49, 165, 194 (110), 235, 237
Haddon 170, 210, 230, 240, **colour plates 19-21**
Hadrian ('s, 'ic) 79, 124, 125, 128, 129, 130, 131, 134, 137, 146, 177, 185, 192, 199
wall 11, 167, 178, 193, 204, 205
Hall David 18, 25, 45, 178, 186
Hall Hill 237
Hallam Syliva 15, 186
Halmer Gate 141
Halt, Stonea 45, 49
Hammon's Eau 151
Hanging Bowl 235 (112), 239
Harbour (see Port)
Hardings Drain 53 (24), 54
Hare 120
Harlow 196
Hay, rake 118, 121
Hayes Peter 18, 152, 231
Hazel 73,75, 118, 121, 172
Heckington 163, 191, 214, 236
Heighington 214
Helpringham 147
Helpston 12, 186, 191, 214, 235
Hemp 73
Henge (13) 39
Hides 167
Hilgay 137, 139, 140, 186, 187, 237
Hills and Holes 181
Hinchingbrooke 191
Hinman Mark 169, 170, 191
Hinxton 37
Historia Ecclesiastica 229
Hoard (see also Bronze Age, Iron Age) 180, 191, 205, 221, 222 (106), 223, 230, 241, 245
Hockwold 16, 25, 29, 37, 70, 160, 194, 197, 206, 210, 213, 238, 245
Hod Hill (40) 83
Hoe Hills 231
Holbeach 11
Holkham 89
Holme Posts 12 (4)
Holocene 22, 24, 26
Holywell Row 237
Honey Hill 44, 50, 185, 213
Horbling 32, 141, 150, 187
Horningsea 124, 146, 160, 178
Horncastle 163, 218, 237

253

Horse 89, 160, 163, 169, 170, 176, 192, 194
  harness 85, 167
Horseley Fen 36
Horsey 36
Horticulture 188
Hough on the Hill 236
Houghton 33
Humber 144
Huntingdon 33, 37, 53, 156, 191, 219, 241
Hypocaust (and box-flue tiles) 99, 104, 105, 107, 116, 126, 131, 137, 158, 162, 189, 192, 209, 213, 216
Iceni (Icenian) 39, 42, 51, 58, 79, 86, 87 (42), 88, 89, 93, 126, 129, 131, 133, 134, 153, 196, 215
Icklingham 42, 92, 219, 232, 241, 244
Icknield Way 34, 42, 92, 137, 235, 243, 245
Ilchester 215
Impington 137
Ingoldmells (81)
Inkerson Fen (141)
Insula(e) 99 (46), 101-103, 113, 209
Intercalated Peat 26
Ipswich Ware 230
Ireton 54
Iron Age 25, 30, 34, 37, 39, 40, 42, 44, 45, 49, 50, 52, 74, 80, 81, 86, 89, 92, 93, 96, 98, 110, 120, 128-9, 169, 171, 172, 173, 185, 187, 194, 196, 244, 245
  barrow 40
  burial 37, 40, 80, 81, 82, 89, 90, 95
  fort 10, 34, 35 (15), 37 (16), 39, 40, 42, 47, 51, 60, 62, 82, 88, 89, 90 (44), 92, 134, **colour plates 8, 9, 11, 12 and 13**
  hoard 39, 77, 79, 88
  metalwork 76, 77, 85
  settlement 10, 35, 37, 40, 41, 51, 52, 76, 83, 84, 85, 86, 87, 88, 89, 90, 158, 163, 164, 173
  shrine/temple 10, 36, 51, 82, 194, 196
  storage Pit 40
Iron Working 40
Isleham 191
  hoard 31
Ivy 73
Jackson Ralph 9, 107
Julian 181
Jupiter 165
Kate's Bridge 231
Kemp Steve 169, 189
Kenney Scott 188
Kiln 12, 116, 146, 154, 160, 163, 170, 177, 178 (84) 182, 207, 214, **colour plates 15, 19 and 23**
King Street (14) 137, 140 (67), 141, 153, 162, 191,230, 231, 235, 236, 239
Kings Dyke 134-5
Kings Hedges 191
Kings Lynn 53
Kirkburn 85
Kyneswytha 239
Lade Bank (9)
Lakenheath 171, 178, 232, 237
Lamp 180
Landwade 221
Landbeach 137 (65), 146, 238
Lane Tom 18, 152, 231

Langdale Hale 164
Langwood Farm 165, 185, 189, 193, 212 (97), 213
Langwood Ridge 213
Lark 31, 37, 152, 180, 221, 241, 244
Latrine 101, 113, 120, 209
Laun 244, 245
Laun Ditch 92
Lazybeds 188
Lea (or Lee) 40, 88
Lead (101) 219, 220 (102), 221 (104), 222, 223, 241
Leather 89, 115 (58), 120, 121, 167
Leicester 40, 97, 154, 179, 215
Lentil 122
Leverington 232
Lincoln 31, 97, 133, 144, 154, 179, 222
Lindow Man 82
Lindsey 231, 245
Little Downham 237
Little Oulsham 232
Littleport 137 (66), 139, 142, 152, 192
Lode 222
Log-boat 33, 34, 36
London 97, 133, 154, 222
London Lode Farm 135
Long Hollow 140
Longthorpe 83, 133, 137, 152, 153, 170, 177, 235, 240
Loom-weight 86, 168, 171, 230
Lords Bridge 37
Lovedon Hill 236
Lower Peat 22, 24, 25, 30
Lucas, Gavin 178
Lynch Farm 170
Lyndon Farm 230
Lynn 152
Macaulay, Stephen 144, 178
Mackerel 158, 180
Mackreth, Donald 148, 149, 154, 156, 171, 186, 210, 215, 216, 217, 230
Magnentius 205
Magnus Maximus 205, 206, 217
Maiden Castle 82
Malting 170
Manea 44, 88, 184, 194, 237
Mansio 137 (66), 154, 158, 170, 192
Mausoleum 196 (91)
March 9, 25, 29, 30, 33, 36 37, 43 (22), 53, 54, 87 (42), 93, 101, 122, 126, 129, 134, 135, 137, 142, 143, 151, 153, 160, 184-5, 221, 238, 240
Mareham Lane 32, 140, 141, 163
Market (centre, fair) 131-2, 151, 156, 158, 160, 163-5, 168, 197, 214, 231
Marshland 187, 232
Maxey 25, 34, 49, 169, 170, 210, 230, 235
Maximian 204
McKenna Ron 89
Meadows Ian 188
Meadow Lane 37
Meadowsweet 73
Medeshamstede 240
Medieval (Middle Ages) 28, 30, 45, 53, 54, 57, 103, 152, 172, 180, 245
Mercian 230, 238, 239, 240, 245
Mercury 109
Mesolithic 25, 48, 50
  occupation 14
Metal detecting 57, 77, 83, 85, 109, 124, 153, 219

Metalwork (Roman) 98, 125, 154, 156, 160, 176, 180, 182, 185, 188, 194, 209, 210, 214, 221, 226, 230
Methwold 37, 191
Middleton 172 (81), 175
Milan (Edict) 219
Mildenhall 191, 222, 223 (106), 237, 241
Mile Ditch 42
Mill Common 191
Mill Heath 244
Mill Hill 214
Mills
  water 158, 192, 216, 244
  weaving 171
  wind 53, 54
Milton 11, 40 (18), 187, 191
Minerva 109, 110, 131, 194
Minster 240
Mollusc (snail) 37, 68, 73, 74, 122, 144
Monastery (eries) 52, 63, 172, 222, 230, 239, 240
Morris Elaine 173
Morton 150, 162, 172, 182, 187, 231
Mosaic 12, 99, 110, 116, 176-9, 191, 214, 216, **colour plate 23**
Mould (+ crucible) 50, 125, 163, 182
Oak 73, 75, 80, 82, 118, 119, 189
Oat (See Cereal)
Old Croft 135, 137, 142, 143, 173, 183, 192
Old South Eau 141
Olive Oil 40, 123
Oppidum 39, 40, 42, 51, 88, 93
Opus signinum 103, 105, 116, 130
Ordnance Survey (OS) 45, 50 (28), 81, 83
Orton Hall Farm 170, 171, 210 (97), 216, 217, 229 (109), 230, 240
Orton Longueville 222, 240
Orton Waterville 235
Ortons 210
Osbournby 214
Otter 165
Ouse Great 16, 25, 31, 33, 34, 36, 40, 43, 54, 144, 146, 150, 151, 153, 156 (78), 178, 180, 191, 192, 194, 196, 214, 218, 219, 222, 233, 240, 241, 244
  little 31, 37, 152, 194, 218, 244, 245
Oven 99, 113, 160, 173 (81), 207-209 (95), 214
Over 178
Palace (palatial building) 105,154,156, 214, 216 (100), 222, 230, 239, 240
Palaeolithic 48
Palisade 62
Palmer Rog 153, 186
Panworth 92, 244
Parliamentary 10, 53
Partney 237
Pasture (grazed grassland, pastoral, meadows) 45, 53, 56, 74, 75, 81, 86, 89, 122, 132, 168, 170, 171, 191, 197
Peakirk (72) 148, 149
Peddars Way 137, 244
Pes Monatalis 102, 103
Pelican 165
Penda 239
Pentney 182, 232
Percival Sarah 173
Periglacial 24
Perimarine 26

INDEX

Perrin Rob 177
Peterborough 23, 25, 32, 83, 89, 126, 127, 133, 134, 137, 144, 152, 154, 169, 190, 210, 229, 230, 235, 240
Peterborough Museum 18
Soke of 25
Pewter 180, 188, 205, 219, 221, 223, 241
Pig 120, 169, 226, 228
Pinchbeck 150, 176, 231
Pit Alignment 37
Pitchfork 118, 121
Pits 82, 83, 84, 85, 89, 98, 99, 101, 102, 109-110, 113, 120, 209, 228, 230, 239, 241
Plaster (wall, painted) daub, whitewashed) 105, 116, 124, 137, 158, 163, 192, 213, 216
Pointon 187, 231
Pollen 25, 26 (9) (10), 29, 44, 45, 67, 73, 74, 119, 120, 122, 190
Port 180 (85), **colour plate 24**
Portchester 218
Post-medieval 53, 67, 101, 180
Potter Christopher 9, 45, 26
Potter Tim (1), 9, 25, 45, 51, 58, 76, 84, 107, 153, 168, 185, 207, 210, 241
Pottery (see also Neolithic, Bronze Age) 75, 76, 83, 85, 86, 87, 93, 98, 110, 115 (57), 123-4, 126, 129, 137 (66), 139, 146, 150, 151, 152, 154, 156, 158, 160, 163, 164, 167, 169, 170, 176-179, 180, 185, 186, 187, 189, 192, 196, 199-201(93), 210, 213, 214, 217, 226, 230, 235, 236, 239
Praefurnium 104, 131
Prasutagus 93, 129, 133, 134
Prickwillow 152
Primrose Hall 143
Princely Burial 40, 236, 239
Priors Meadow 150, 194
Pryor Arnold 148
Quanea 34, 142, 221, 235
Quarry 56, 151, 152, 164, 181, 214
Quaternary 23
Quern (grinding stone, millstone) 121, 160, 180, 186
Radiocarbon 23, 25, 26, 44. 52. 53. 68, 70, 71 (38), 79, 80, 89, 94-6
Ramsey 30, 34, 240
Ratae Coritanorum 215
Razor 50
Reach 142, 151, 180, 181, 191, 194, 196, 234, 243, **colour plate 24**
Rectory Farm 188, 190, 191, 214, 219, 233, 241
Red Hills 173, 176
Reed 121
Regan Roddie 162, 164-6
res privata 183, 191, 203, 212, 215, 217, 223
Revolt and Rebellion
Icenian (46 – 47 AD) 39, 93, 126, 133, 137, 152, 153
Icenian Boudican (60 – 61 AD) 39, 42, 79, 88, 93, 129, 134, 153
Reynolds Tim 144
Richborough 218
Riley Derek 186
Ring 50, 124, 221
Ring-ditches 48, 49 (21), 50, 83, 84, 160

Rippingale 150
Road (6) 42, 44, 50, 54, 98, 101, 126, 127, 133-142, 151, 177, 182, 185, 191, 228, 229, 235, 236, 244, 245, **colour plates 15, 16 and 17**
Roberts Judith 230
Robinson Ben 235
Roddon 14, 22, 25, 26, 44, 54, 68, 69, 82, 86, 88, 95, 135, 141, 142, 143, 150, 151, 173, 186, 187, **colour plate 10**
Rodham Farm 143, 185
Rollo Lindsay 76
Rome 88, 93, 107, 205, 224, 240
Round-house 85, 87, 88
Rounds Hill 89
Route (way, track) 33-34, 54, 126, 134, 136, 137, 140, 141, 142, 152, 189, 231, 234-5, 245
Royal Geographic Society 16 (6)
Royalist 53
Royston 42
Ruskington 237
Sacred (centre, glade, grove) 82, 86, 131, 163, 193
Sacrifice
animal 194
human 82, 131
Saham Toney 133
Saint Albans 40, 51, 88, 97
Saint Ives 16, 37
Saint Joseph (Prof.) 137
Saint Peters Pond 163
Salt (extraction, making, working, production, etc.) 40, 52, 86, 87, 128, 150, 167, 172, 173-176, (81) (82), 286, 207, **colour plate 15**
Salters Way 32, 141
Saltersford 32, 141
Salway P 9, 16, 128 ,150, 168, 203, 206, 207, 213, 223
Samian 76, 98, 110 (57), 123, 137, 152, 158, 186, 192, 207
Sanctuary 131
Sandal (shoe) (58) 121, 167
Sandy 156
Sawston 37, 90 (43)
Sawtry 128, 156, 170, 192
Saxon 28, 84, 152
Shore, County of 156, 204, 205, 216
defences/forts 163, 176, 218, **colour plate 28**
monastic grange 10
Sconce 54
Scored ware 40
Scull Chris 245
Seal 150
Seax 230
Sedge 73, 121, 172
Seed (pip – see also cereal) 115, 122
Septimus Severus 203, 207
Settlement Roman (Colonisation) (6) 42, 52, 98, 101, 122, 125, 126, 127, 137, 141, 142, 150, 151, 152, 154, 160, 163, 164, 165, 168, 182-190, 207 (94), 210, 213, 214, 223, **colour plates 10 and 15**
Severus Alexander 203
Shardelowes Well 235
Sheep 40, 99, 119, 120, 127, 167, 168,

169, 194, 197, 207, 226
Shellfish 110, 122, 171, 172
Shennan Ian 26
Shepea 142
Shepherd Frere 137
Shippea Hill 14 (5), 24, 25
Shoff Drove 141
Shouldham 178
Shrine (see temple)
Signal station 192, 218
Silchester 97, 98, 103
Silver 79, 88, 93, 126, 189, 205, 207, 210, 221, 223, 241
Silvester Bob 139, 151, 152
Simmons Brian 146, 148
Skeleton 52 (34), 69, 70, 74, 82, 84, 90, 196
Skertchly S B J 14, 24
Skull 71 (36), 74, 80, 89, 95
Slave 40
Slea 150
Sleaford 140, 163, 194, 237
Slepe 240
Sloe 73, 121
Snail (see Mollusc)
Snailwell 37, 232, 238
Soar 32
Soham 29, 37, 142, 191, 235, 240
Soil survey 18
Solifluxion 24, 43, 60, 67, 69
Somersham 29, 33, 164, 189, 191
South Cadbury 82
South Creake 88
South Lincolnshire Archaeological Unit 18
Southery 137, 139, 140, 152, 187, 232
Spade 118 (59), 121, 172
Spade cultivation 188
Spalding 11, 16, 141, 162, 171, 178, 231
Spaldingas 141
Spaldon 231
Spice Hills 150
Spruce 190, 214
St Albans 215
St Guthlac 237, 240
St Ives 233, 240
St Ivo 240
St John's College 234
St Kyneburghas 216, 239
St Paul in the Bail 222
Stags Holt 185
Stukeley William 11, 143
Stamford 11, 133, 236
Stanground 36, 177
Stanway 40
Staunch Meadow 241
Stickford 231, 237
Stickleback 73
Stickney 23, 30
Stitches, The (Farm) 10, 52, 53, 54, (23) (24), 56, 57
Stock 40, 54, 75, 120, 167, 169, 186, 189, 191, 210
Stort 40, 88
Strapend 53
Straw Hall Farm 135, 183
Street Way 235
Stretham 54, 137, 142, 191, 192, 238
Stukeleys (Great and Little) 40 (17)
Stuntney 34, 142, 235

255

Suetonius 153
Survey (Roman) 99-103, 126, 149, 182
Sutton 36 (220), 221, 237, 241
Swaffham (Prior and Bulbeck) 151, 180, 194 (91) (92) 196, 234, **colour plate 25**
Swavesey 178
Sweetgale 121, 122
Sword cut 52, 71 (36) (37), 74, 80, 81, 84, 93-4
Tacitus 38, 51, 58, 86, 129, 131, 134
Tallington 236
Tankard 77, 83, 88 (58) 118, 122
Tapete 171
Tattershall 163
Tavern (inn) 158, 192
Tax (see also annona) 168, 193, 205, 206, 212
Taylor Alison 193
Temenos 109, 111, 194, 196
Temple (Shrine) 84, 85, 86, 98, 107, 108-111 (51), 130-1, 154, 158, 160, 189 (88), 191, 192, 193-7, (91) (92), 223, 234, 240, 241, 245, **colour plates 14, 15, 25 and 26**
Ten Mile Bank 139, 152
Terret 85
Terrington Beds 30
Tessera(e) (tessellated pavement) 110, 116, 160, 162, 179
Textiles 40, 120, 121, 127, 168, 169, 170-1
Thames 31, 40, 88, 137
Theodosius 205, 206, 233
Thermokasts 24
Thet (River) 245
Thetford 39, 52, 86, 197, 235, 241, 245
    Little 33, 34, 142, 179, 232
    Castle 89
Thorn 73, 88, 118, 172
Thorney 141, 238, 240
Thorpe Reuben 147
Threekingham 32, 141, 236
Three Kings (110) 235
Throckenholt 142, 185, 240
Thurlby 147, 178, 231
Tile 116, 118, 131, 137, 139, 158, 162, 163, 176-179, 182, 185, 189, 209, 213, 214, 215, **colour plate 22**
Tilney 142
    St Lawrence 150, 176
Timber, timber-frame (see also Woodland) 62, 67, 73, 75, 76, 80, 89, 98, 103, 105, 111, 112, 113, 116, 118, 119, 130, 135, 137, 142, 146, 156, 160, 165, 172, 178, 180, 190, 194, 209, 213, 222, 226 (107), 230
Titchmarsh 128, 156
Torc 93
Tort Field 128
Tort Hill 170, 192
Tottenhill 237
Town 42, 43, 44, 47, 51, 52, 53, 79, 93, 97-129, 133, 140, 154-163, 160, 169, 182, 188, 193, 194, 197, 204, 205, 214, 218, 222, 224, 228, 229, 231, 234, 235, 236, 237, 241, 244, **colour plate 15**
Track (way) (see Route)
Trajan (ic) 123
Trent 31, 144
Tribal Hidage 229, 231
Trinovantes 37, 39, 40, 88, 93
Tripontium 215
Trumpington 37
Turbary 172, 183, **colour plate 10**
Turkington Hill 164
Uley 241
Upper Delphs 26, 36, 49, 165
Upper Peat 22, 25, 30
Upper Silt 22, 25, 30
Upton 34 (14), 153
Upware 151
Upwell 143, 172, 173, 182 (86), 206, 238
Ursacius 221
Valentinian 205
Varo 199
Vat (tank) 219 (101) (102), 223, 241
Vegetation zones (10) 26
Venta Icenorum 137, 171, 215
Verulamium 93, 98, 215
Vespasian 137
Vicani 168, 213, 223
Viking 52
Villa 97, 142, 151, 152, 160, 164, 166, 168, 171, 179, 181, 182, 188, 190, 191-192, 194, 196, 197, 203, 205, 207, 210, 213, 214, 219, 223, 225, 230, 234, (111). 238 (113), 240, 241, **colour plate 26**
Vortigern 225
Waldersea 185
Waller Martyn 18, 26
Walpole 237
Walsoken 237
Walton 237
Walton Castle 218
Wandlebury 37, 82, 88, 89, 90
War Ditches 37, 82, 83, 88, 90, 178
Warboys 34
Wardy Hill 37, 88
Warham Camp 88
Waring 163
Water Flea 73
Water Newton 97, 153, 177, 214, 222, 235, 241, **colour plate 27**
Wattle (and daub) 103, 111, 112, 118, 156, 158, 185, 209
Welch Martin 229
Well 50, 98, 99, 113 (56), 120, 122, 160, 190, 209, 228
Welland 31, 34, 40, 43, 88, 133, 148, 150, 180, 186, 218, 231, 236, 244
    bank 35, 141
Wellstream 143
Welney 171, 206, 238, 241
Welsh 237
Welshman 237
Welwyn 40
Werrington 169, 170, 210
West Dereham 241
West Harling 245
West Keal 237
West Richard 18
West Stowe 232, 244
West Water 33, 54
Westry 33
Westwalton 175
Whaplode Drove 142, 160, 185
Wheat (see cereal)
Whittlesey 30 (13), 33, 36, 126, 133, 134, 135, 142, 153, 180, 239
    Mere 12, 221
Whitwell B. 235
Whitwell J. 215
Wich 173, 176
Wicken 37, 142, 235
Wicker 113, 172, 209
Wilbraham (111), 238, (113)
    Great 37, 151, 197, 219, 222, 223, 240, 241
    Little 234, 235
Wilburga 238
Wilburton
    hoard 37
Wild J.P. 170, 171, 216
Willingham 26, 30, 34, 88, 194 (89), 197, 219 (104), 223, 232, 241
Willow 119, 172
Wilsthorpe 191
Wimblington 43, 53, 87, 126, 151, 171, 172
Wine 40, 92, 123, 192
Wisbech 43, 54, 231, 237, 238
Wisbech Museum 79
Wisbech St Mary 141, 151
Wissa 244
Wissey 31, 37, 231, 244
Witham 29, 31, 34, 141, 144, 147, 150, 163, 218
    shield 34
Wittering 179 (84), **colour plate 22**
Wixna 231
Wollaston 188
Wood Ditton 243
Wood Walton 34
Wooden Artefacts 115 (58), 118, 121
Woodhurst 33, 221
Woodland 44, 73, 74, 75, 82, 86, 116, 122, 156, 178, 243
    fen/alder carr 26, 30, 44, 45, 119, 172, 173
    management 36, 45, 75, 119
Woodston 235
Woody Nightshade 73
Wool, woollen (see Textiles)
Wormegay 237, 241
Wrangle 176
Writing Tablet 118, 126
Wroxeter 97, 98, 219
Wulston 52
Wyrde Croft 141
York 97, 133, 144, 154, 204, 222
Zeffertt Torven 147

256